*American Religions
and the Family*

American Religions and the Family

HOW FAITH TRADITIONS COPE WITH
MODERNIZATION AND DEMOCRACY

Edited by Don S. Browning and David A. Clairmont

COLUMBIA UNIVERSITY PRESS

NEW YORK

Columbia University Press
Publishers Since 1893
New York   Chichester, West Sussex
Copyright © 2007 Columbia University Press
All rights reserved

Library of Congress Cataloging-in-Publication Data
American religions and the family : how faith traditions cope with modernization
and democracy / edited by Don S. Browning and David A. Clairmont.
p.   cm.
Includes index.
ISBN 0–231–13800–8 (cloth : alk. paper)
1. United States—Religion. 2. Family—Religious life. 3. Religion and
culture—United States. I. Browning, Don S. II. Clairmont, David A.
BL2525.A543 2006
201′.7—dc22   2006018055

Printed in the United States of America
c 10 9 8 7 6 5 4 3 2 1

CONTENTS

PREFACE

This volume is a collection of papers prepared for a consultation of the contributing authors that was held at Emory University. The consultation was part of a larger conference entitled Sex, Marriage and Family in the Religions of the Book held at Emory in March 2003. The consultation was jointly sponsored by the Center for the Interdisciplinary Study of Religion at Emory under the direction of John Witte Jr. and the Religion, Culture, and Family Project at the University of Chicago Divinity School, directed by Don S. Browning.

The larger conference of which this consultation was a part focused on the traditions of Judaism, Islam, and Christianity in their worldwide expressions and called on scholars from several academic disciplines to address a variety of issues pertaining to marriage and family. These included the psychology and sociology of family structures, legal issues such as divorce and child custody, and theological and historical studies about the impact of religion on marriage and family in societies of the past and the present. The consultation entitled American Religions and the Family considered many of the same themes but included Hindu, Buddhist, Confucian, and Native American religious thought. The consultation also confined consideration of these religions to the context of North America and the various influences and expressions of religious traditions on family life.

Studies about the effect of religious thought and behavior on American society have never been more timely or more important. People around the world are discovering that recent global political and economic events cannot be understood in their fullness without comprehending something about religion, how it functions, and the many ways it can be used to the benefit and detriment of societies throughout the world. The current worldwide discussion about the future of families is one important part of contemporary discourse about religion. This volume brings together scholars from various academic specialties to begin exploring this topic.

We, the editors, see this book as initiating a discussion about American religions and the family. Future studies will take up each tradition in more detail, and important work on the connection between immigration and religious life continues to emerge and no doubt will supplement, and in some cases challenge, the preliminary work undertaken here. To take full advantage of these essays, as in the context of a classroom discussion, the reader should also consult primary sources that have played a formative role in the development of religious thought about marriage and family. This book's companion volume is *Sex, Marriage and Family in the World Religions*, edited by M. Christian Green, Don S. Browning, and John Witte Jr., and **it** provides a selection of such texts for study and discussion.

We wish to thank John Witte for his generous support of this project. We also thank the Division of Religion of the Lilly Endowment for its support through the Religion, Culture, and Family Project at the University of Chicago, and the Pew Charitable Trusts and Emory University for their support through the Center for the Interdisciplinary Study of Religion at Emory. We thank Christian Green, formerly of the Religion, Culture, and Family Project and now with the Harvard Divinity School, for giving us a helping hand. We also express our gratitude to Eliza Ellison, Anita Mann, April Bogle, and Janice Wiggins of the Center for the Interdisciplinary Study of Religion for their energetic help in organizing the consultation that produced this book. We want to thank Sarah Schuurman of the University of Chicago Divinity School for joining the team and helping us prepare the final manuscript.

After the manuscript for this book was completed, Lee Teitelbaum died. We would like to extend our sympathy to his family and acknowledge his outstanding contributions to American law pertaining to marriage, family, and children.

Don S. Browning
David A. Clairmont
CHICAGO

American Religions
and the Family

PART I

American Religions

THE QUESTION OF MODERNIZATION AND FAMILY LIFE

CHAPTER 1

Introduction

DAVID A. CLAIRMONT AND DON S. BROWNING

Over the last several decades Americans have been involved in a momentous debate about the well-being of families. While religion has played a significant part in this debate, most Americans still perceive it as a narrow dispute between the Christian religious right and the secular left. This national conversation is often acrimonious. We are familiar with the contentious topics such as abortion, homosexuality, and out-of-wedlock births, but many other topics also are being discussed and deserve closer attention. What is more important is that other religious voices, not just those of Protestant evangelicals and Roman Catholics, for instance, are entering the conversation, both directly and indirectly.

This debate is particularly complex because of a frequently overlooked variable: the impersonal forces of modernization. Broadly speaking, *modernization* has often been used to refer to the variety of modern forces unleashed in American society, and throughout the world, that are drastically changing the patterns and rhythms of contemporary social life. Life is faster, and forms of interpersonal dependencies are shifting. We work harder, have less time with our children, have less control over their lives, and worry about new influences on both our young people and ourselves as adults and parents. However, modernization also brings higher levels of education, more affluence, and less hierarchical patterns of interdependence that many people value.

As the editors of this book, we thought that society should begin to listen to a wider range of religious voices on the topic of families. Moreover, we felt that it was important to involve these voices in existing studies dealing with the effects of modernization on families and religions. To advance these goals we formulated the following question: *How have the major religions of the United States coped with the pressures of American-style modernization and American-style democracy, particularly with respect to their traditional teachings about marriage and family life?* The processes of modernization ripple through the social and cultural systems of most countries of the world, but they do so in different ways in different places. Because modernization and democracy display distinctive patterns as they unfold in the United States, the more long-standing American religions, as well as the more recently recognized traditions, face special challenges in understanding what these processes mean for their family traditions.

This book examines the responses to modernization of several different American religions. We look at Protestant Christianity (in its mainline and evangelical forms), Native American religions, Judaism, Roman Catholicism, Latter-day Saints, various expressions of black religions, Confucianism, Buddhism, Hinduism, and Islam. These religions made their appearance and gained visibility at different times in American history. Protestants interacted with Native Americans in the early centuries of the founding of the Republic. Judaism and Roman Catholicism became more visible in the late nineteenth century. Chinese immigrants brought Confucianism and elements of other native Chinese traditions during the late nineteenth and early twentieth centuries. Buddhism, Hinduism, and Islam (with the exception of African varieties of Islam among enslaved people) came even later.

All these religions at various times have undertaken self-assessments as new circumstances arose in the form of economic, political, legal, and cultural changes. These changes pushed these religions to consider critically how their teachings were expressed in the past and how they should be offered in new situations and to new audiences. This is not surprising because challenges arise for communities in response to external and internal pressures on their common life. These challenges may take the form of internal disputes about the meaning and scope of teachings, insufficient attention to the material and emotional needs of individual members, or ideological conflicts with neighboring communities.

This book considers a series of cultural and social changes that have begun to gain the attention of religious communities in the United States and have proved increasingly important in academic, legal, and policy debates about family life. These changes include the tenuous financial and political situations of many immigrant communities, the effects of new communication technologies on family behavior and religious identity, the influence of the academic study of religion on the self-interpretations of religious groups, and the consequences of state-imposed family laws for inherited family traditions. Modernization, as we define it, significantly affects the course of these social changes and raises questions about the meaning and propriety of older marriage and family customs. It also raises concerns about what constitutes a faithful response consistent with the identities of these traditions and how these identities are challenged and reconstituted over time.

Locating the family debate within the full range of interactions among family, religion, and modern social processes marks a significant departure from the usual perception of the debate as confined to a conflict between conservative Christian teachings and secular humanism that many people believe exhausts the religion-family issue. To guide the essays in this book we felt it was important to formulate a set of specific questions to prompt critical thinking about how religious traditions use their multiple oral, textual, and ritual resources to meet the new challenges of family life, and we gave those questions to the chapter authors. Their essays address these questions to varying degrees. Please note, however, that the religious traditions and the scholarly specialties of the different authors make some questions easier to answer than others. Thus the reader will learn something about how different religions perceive modernization and how different disciplines—history, theology, sociology, comparative religion, law, and anthropology—think about common questions:

1. Is it possible to identify a tradition's core ideas and practices about family, marriage, and children?
2. How do these traditions present justifications for their ideas and practices, if any?
3. What are some of the modifications of these ideas and practices that the traditions have developed in coping with modernization and democracy in the American context?
4. Are certain tensions or divisions in regard to family issues evident among different branches of a single tradition?
5. Can generalizations be developed, with appropriate qualifications, about how each tradition is interpreting, coping with, or critiquing the American-style democratic polity or American-style modernization?
6. Are there illustrative events, issues, or confrontations with the law and other sectors of society that give insight into a tradition's style of coping, adaptation, or reconstruction?
7. What are some key commonalities and differences among these traditions when viewed from the perspective of this coping process?

Not all contributors give these questions equal weight, and the reader will find different approaches to thinking about them throughout this book. Connections among family, religion, and the forces of modernization take on patterns specific to the historical experiences of religious communities. The various religious communities described in these chapters hold differing definitions of family, religion, and tradition. Despite the diversity in subject matter and scholarly perspective, the contributors are united in the conviction that far too little attention has been paid to how adherents to these traditions have shaped their reflections on family life, the social structures that support or hinder traditional religious and family practices, and the connection between family life and religious identity.

FAMILIES, RELIGIONS, AND THE PHENOMENON OF MODERNIZATION

Among the more frequently cited developments affecting both families and religions, the phenomenon called modernization may be the least understood. Modernization is often thought to refer to two developments that stem from the higher valuation of rationality that emerged with the Enlightenment. First, the kind of rationality valued was primarily technical rationality, the discernment and use of efficient means to achieve human satisfactions. Second, the main emphasis that developed with respect to this kind of rationality was the use of these efficient means to increase the productivity of modern market systems.

Modernization as the spread of technical rationality can go beyond the cost-benefit logic of the market and subtly affect other areas of life.[1] Not only can it be expressed in the form of national and global capitalism, it can also inform governmental bureaucratic patterns—patterns that sometimes make it more difficult for individuals and groups to initiate and exercise democratic deliberations. Both forms of technical rationality tend to spill over into the world of everyday face-to-face interactions, thereby colonizing, as Jürgen Habermas puts it, the life world of civil society.[2] Technical rationality, it is generally believed, does not address the moral propriety of the ends selected but rather the most direct and quickest means of bringing about whatever ends the individual or the group desires.

Modernization is related, but not equivalent, to the phenomenon of globalization.[3] The spread of market forces, technological innovation, and the increased speed of monetary and information flows are characteristics common to both. However, globalization also includes immigration, electronic communication, and the exchange of cultural artifacts, styles of life, and generation of new meanings. Many essays in this book focus as much on the forms of social change associated with the more abstract processes of modernization or even the wider phenomenon of globalization, but it is useful to view these changes in relation to the more general forces that may stimulate them.

Thus modernization poses new challenges *and* new opportunities both to long-standing religious institutions and to families. In short, modernization puts pressure on tradition, cultural memory, and connections with the past, be they religious, familial, or both. Modernization challenges certain traditional religious teachings and understandings of familial continuity, often bringing out the traditions' own capacities for critique, self-assessment, and reform. Religious and family traditions have developed various strategies of response to these challenges; these strategies of coping, adaptation, and response are precisely what the essays in this book investigate.

WHAT ARE THE "AMERICAN RELIGIONS" AND HOW WERE THEY SELECTED?

Multiple options exist for defining the "American religions." Our principle for selecting traditions to study centers on identifying communities in the United States that have a history of active engagement with visible cultural trends. Three specific concerns commend this strategy.

First, to be considered an "American religion," a tradition must have a sufficient historical record in the United States to provide scholars with a sizeable body of evidence for making a meaningful analysis. Second, a tradition must have explicitly engaged—through appropriation, adaptation, or rejection (and often a mixture of all these)—American-style modernization and democracy in its political or social forms. For example, a tradition with a sizeable immigrant population in the past or present often faces legal challenges to its establishment and expansion. Such religious or ethnic communities must navigate a path that their members accept as a balance between maintaining inherited values and adapting to new cultural situations. Third, a tradition must exhibit at least some interest in its family forms, practices, and kinship networks and show some concern for what new social contexts mean to existing customs.

Closely related to selecting which religions to compare is the question of why families should function as a central organizing category. At the outset we should recall that many people think that the current debate about the well-being of families has been provoked primarily by so-called evangelical Protestant Christians. This perception is not incidental to the role that Protestant Christianity played in forming American ideals about families when modernization was taking shape in nineteenth- and early twentieth-century America. While the public face of the debate about families has retained the facade of a simple liberal-conservative dichotomy, the actual historical interactions of religion, philosophy, and law in shaping our ideas about family reveal a far more subtle set of influences.

Recent studies suggest that the importance of family to Christian thought is neither simple nor consistent.[4] The centuries-old debates in Christian theology about family issues and the influence of these controversies on family law in Europe and the United States are just now being uncovered. The heritage of these debates continues to affect current thinking about the nature of marital contracts and the terms for their formation and dissolution. Families and kinship networks are often the first and sometimes the only communities upon which immigrants rely as they attempt to establish themselves in new contexts, even if these networks do not map neatly onto current legal definitions of family. For different reasons Native Americans have found in their families both a refuge and a bulwark against the tides of change that threaten their physical, economic, and social health. Furthermore, the changes and growth of American family law continue to create new legal environments for both immigrants and long-standing populations.

Finally, families are worthy of attention because debates about their importance have begun to spread around the world. While this is significantly attributable to the spread of modernization and the development of new communication technologies, the new global concern about families also draws heavily on the associated effects of war, disease, and the economic inequities affecting individual and family survival. The health of women and children in developing nations is often affected by family disruption occasioned by regional conflicts and crises such as the AIDS epidemic. A comparative consideration of families in the United States has potential to contribute to the emerging global, and increasingly interreligious, conversation about families.

FAMILIES, RELIGIONS, AND THE RESPONSES TO MODERNIZATION

To this point, we have offered a general picture of how modernization and related social changes affect religious traditions and the families that they support and guide. In this book we ask whether it is possible to distinguish different kinds of responses that religions, in their teachings about family, have made to modernization. We also consider whether the responses of actual families, drawing on their religious and cultural heritages, differ from the idealized norms of traditional teachings. Some essays describe how particular traditions expect family life to proceed in the American context (chapters 10, 12, and 13, on Confucianism, Hinduism, and Islam). Other essays (chapters 3, 6, and 13, on Protestantism, Catholicism, and Islam) emphasize as well the tension between what actual families do and what some leaders of these traditions want them to do.

The contributors make various suggestions about how the religious traditions that they study have responded to the challenges facing families in contemporary society. We find five responses to the effects of modernization on religions and families in these chapters, and we have developed these into the following typology: *evolution, accommodation, modulation of distinctiveness, transformation,* and *strategic limitation.* The essays that follow illustrate these responses either explicitly or implicitly.

This typology comes with a warning, however: it must be read and used with care. It should be used primarily to provoke discussion and should not be viewed as a definitive characterization of any of these traditions viewed as a whole. The typology is intended to offer ways of thinking about religious responses to modernization *with respect to considerations of family* and should not be taken as a statement about each tradition's response to all aspects of social change. Each tradition is complex, and subcommunities within them have responded to modernization and its various social changes in different ways. Each chapter tells the story of a prominent, but not the only, response to be found in a particular religious tradition. Any one of these strategies might be adopted by one branch of a tradition, while some other strand of that same tradition pursues another strategy. Furthermore, some religions reviewed in this book have not considered organized engagement with modern society as a goal worth pursuing. Neither does the category of modernization as described earlier elicit equally strong interest from all religious perspectives. Some cope with modernization by appearing to ignore it. Finally, this typology may characterize the approaches of the various authors as much as it characterizes the traditions themselves. Although the authors are all competent scholars of the traditions they describe (and were chosen for this reason), they represent different disciplines—anthropology, history, sociology, theology, and the critical study of religion. Part of what they see in the traditions they describe might be a product of their respective discipline. Part of what they observe might also reflect their own individual scholarly priorities. We think this disciplinary diversity actually adds to the interest of these chapters. It raises the question of what the various authors see and what difference their academic discipline might make in influencing what they see. We should also note that, although the authors discussed this typology and found it illuminating when they met and reviewed each other's chapters, the way we use it in this introduction most likely reflects our personal and academic values. Thus we offer this typology both to stimulate discussion and to illustrate the complexity of the interpretive process that goes into understanding the religions and their family traditions.

EVOLUTION

Because a central element of modernization is the spread of technical rationality throughout different areas of society with the hope of advancing human well-being, interpretive strands within a religious tradition often see modernization as actually advancing human life. An important corollary, however, to the ability of reason to expand material well-being through its technical deployment is also its ability to critically challenge traditional authority structures through its critical deployment. In other words, modernization may loosen the faithful from the authority of tradition. Some groups within a tradition may see this as threatening, while others see it as an important advance in a tradition's thinking.

This loosening process has been construed in different ways. As Julie Rubio points out in chapter 6, "Marriage, Family, and the Modern Catholic Mind," tensions exist about the role of reason in official Roman Catholic teachings on marriage and family. Most Catholics laud the power of human reason to grasp the basic goodness of marriage and family as proper ends of human life, but many Catholics are ambiguous about the proper means to achieve these ends. The Protestant reformers believed that reason guided by scripture was a useful tool for dismantling illegitimate expressions of church authority, namely, those that interfered with a person's relationship to God. At the same time Protestants remained skeptical about reason's power to know God apart from the revelation found in their religious texts. The Protestant Reformers believed scripture taught that God ordained marriage and family as parts of the civil order and as such they were necessary for a harmonious social existence but were not in themselves means or sources of grace and salvation.

The role of reason in the interpretation of scripture differed in Islamic communities. A complex relationship existed between small communities of authoritative interpreters and those who requested their guidance in practical matters. Interpretation of the Qur'an and the Hadith was deemed necessary because, while these sources addressed many practical issues, illustrating the relevance of the tradition to new social and political contexts required additional guidance. The connection between authoritative interpretation and legal pronouncement presents still more difficult issues. In chapter 13, "Islam and the Family in North America," Jane Smith notes that while family is a central component of Islamic life, debates have arisen among Muslims in the United States about how to understand key passages of the Qur'an that speak to the relationship between wives and husbands, parents and children. In such cases deeper study and new insights reveal understandings of marriage and gender relations that earlier interpretations may have missed or obscured.

ACCOMMODATION

Another strategy for confronting modernization combines features of both moderate acceptance and skeptical resistance. We call this *accommodation* because it displays an ambivalent, but mostly optimistic, relationship with modernizing tendencies. In particular, it accepts some of modernity's promises, such as better health, longer life, education, more wealth, and more freedom. However, the accommodation approach picks and chooses only those aspects of modernity judged to be valuable while selectively retaining and quietly rejecting various elements of its own traditional teachings.

One example of this strategy is found in chapter 3, "The Cultural Contradictions of Mainline Family Ideology and Practice." In this essay W. Bradford Wilcox and Elizabeth Williamson argue that, while many mainline Protestants praise the spousal equality that followed new interpretations of the Christian tradition, some do not choose to emulate this gender equality in their own marriage. This is partly because of the considerable "institutional distance" between church leaders and the laity in mainline denominations. This distance makes it possible for leaders to act favorably, even progressively, toward the trends of modernity while many laypeople remain more critical and resistant. A compromise between these two tendencies suggests that mainline Protestants follow an accommodationist strategy, intellectually accepting of family disruptions, divorce, and nonmarital births while actually enacting fairly traditional marital and family behaviors.

Another example of the accommodation strategy can be seen in the way Hindu families in America have maintained their familial identities within broader attempts to accommodate to the surrounding culture through traditional marriage ceremonies and international marriages, facilitated by the now relative ease of travel and communication. To some extent whether a tradition leans more toward accommodation or strategic limitation (discussed later) depends on that tradition's past attempts to engage modernizing influences and whether the community deemed them successful.

MODULATION OF DISTINCTIVENESS

Cultural distinctiveness often strongly characterizes the relationship between religious groups and the wider society. However, this distinctiveness has the capacity to take different forms at different times. More important is that this distinctiveness plays various roles in a religion's self-understanding and in the perceptions the wider society may form of a tradition. Some religions take distinctiveness as an important element in defining their response to modernization. Others find that cultural distinctiveness is an inherent part of what it means to be a member of that particular religious group. By *modulation of distinctiveness* we mean the incremental adjustment or tempering of distinctive aspects of religious identity in response to particular historical events or trends. Even when a religious tradition modulates the distinctiveness, determining how it should respond to the encroachment of modernity is still a challenge. Within the general strategy of modulating cultural distinctiveness, we have identified a continuum of specific refinements to this strategy, ranging from resistance on the one hand to capitulation on the other.

Modulating distinctiveness through resistance is particularly puzzling because it can take many forms. It might include refraining from culturally dominant ways of dressing, eating, dating, or marrying. It might also include actively using political and legal tools to reject cultural and legal intrusions into inherited family practices. While none of the traditions considered here can be neatly situated within this type, a case can be made that there is one long-standing and noteworthy approximation.

In chapter 5, "Native American Families and Religion," Raymond Bucko charts the history of the native peoples of North America through their interactions with cultural and legal institutions supported by the U.S. government.

With the help of churches, government attempted to forcibly assimilate Native American families into the dominant culture. The government and churches did this by laying claim to tribal lands, sending native children to Christian schools hundreds of miles from their parents, and coercively placing them for adoption in the homes of white citizens. Native Americans resisted these attacks on their families in various ways, which Bucko carefully details. Indeed, the extent to which Native American families remain intact at all can be taken as a sign of successful resistance to attempts to disrupt them. In this scenario it becomes increasingly difficult to see either modernization or democratization apart from Christianization. However, while Native American attempts to preserve cultural distinctiveness have resisted incursion by the surrounding culture, individuals and tribal leaders have also embraced elements of modernization, seeing education and the establishment of small businesses as ways of carving out a place in society where cultural distinctiveness might still survive.

Modulating distinctiveness through capitulation suggests that a tradition is significantly transformed by the surrounding culture, even to the point of losing its unique character. Religious traditions may contain elements that make a given religion particularly prone to embrace surrounding cultural models. However, these same traditions may also have historical precedents for defining themselves in opposition to prevailing cultural norms.

Jack Wertheimer, in chapter 9, "What Is a Jewish Family? Changing Rabbinic Views," argues that the distinctiveness of Jewish marriage has capitulated to the practices of the wider Christian and secular culture. Supported by what Wertheimer calls the "radicalization of rabbinic thinking," this conformity to surrounding practices is especially visible in the incursions of intermarriage into the ranks of the Jewish faithful. Wertheimer argues that Judaism is defined at its core by differences and distinctions that set it apart from other groups, traditions, and cultural trends. This capitulation, he claims, has not only diluted the distinctiveness of Judaism but has actually weakened its existence, viability, and capacity to survive. Wertheimer suggests that this problem is more severe and intricate than a model positing differing emphases within a single tradition can encompass. He points to strategies that Jewish organizations use to gain recognition and respect for Jews in American society. In an attempt to embrace the characteristic attitudes of modernity, he believes that these organizations have unwittingly opened Jewish communities to models of inclusivity that threaten the distinctiveness of Jewish identity. It should be clear, however, that certain Jewish communities will not agree with this assessment and may indeed see themselves as more closely using the resistance model. In other words, the interpretation that a particular Jewish community brings to the issue of intermarriage, and the place of cultural distinctiveness in its understanding of family practices, will significantly affect whether that community modulates identity mostly through resistance or capitulation.

TRANSFORMATION

A religious tradition's engagement with the surrounding culture has the potential to transform that culture. Yet it is equally possible that a new cultural context might significantly transform traditions that are welcomed into that culture. Both sides of this transformation are evident in the history of Buddhism in America as presented by Charles Prebish in chapter 11, "Family Life and Spiritual Kinship in American Buddhist Communities."

Throughout the history of Buddhism in its various Asian contexts, constructive tensions have existed between the lay and monastic communities and also between monastic leadership and dominant political forces. Layers of mutual interdependence characterized the religious and political alliances in the geographical regions to which Buddhism spread. As different strands of Buddhist teaching arose and circulated, lineages of ordained monks held together monastic and lay Buddhist communities. Some of these teachings gained prominence and challenged long-standing assumptions about the importance of traditional family structures and procreative goals.

The immigration of Buddhists to the United States marks the first time that all the major schools of Buddhist teaching and practice have coexisted in the same nation. Prebish points out that, as a result, the model of the spiritual family, on which Buddhist spiritual kinship is based, has had to adapt to the American environment, where the old model of monastic authority based on ordination lineage is no longer clear. As American practitioners of Buddhism attempt to integrate Buddhist teachings into their own family lives, they retain the model of the Buddha's spiritual family but struggle to identify which lineage or traditional teaching they should follow amid a plurality of authorities. Similarly, they struggle to understand what the Buddha's teaching means for contemporary gender relations. The unique circumstances of American Buddhism transform both the lay practitioners and the lineage of ordained monks.

STRATEGIC LIMITATION

The term *strategic limitation* denotes how a tradition uses its unique resources to limit the influence of potentially damaging but occasionally beneficial dominant cultural norms. It differs from the accommodation strategy in that strategic limitation more strongly positions itself against modernization as a dominant cultural form, and it differs from the strategy of modulating distinctiveness through resistance by being more selective in its rejection of modernity.

As Jeffery Meyer explains in chapter 10, "Confucian 'Familism' in America," Confucianism often served a "religious" role in the lives of Chinese immigrants. It taught a philosophy that held that respect for and duty to family was the highest form of right living. From one perspective this high valuation of family tradition makes Confucian groups resistant to the tradition-undermining dynamics of modernity. However, from another perspective the Confucian virtues of hard work and sacrifice for family coordinate well with the values of efficiency and advancement that modernization requires. Some Confucian traditionalists can do quite well in modernizing countries. At the same time Chinese as well as Indian immigrants often look to traditional family structures for solace from the dark side of modernization, which promotes individual isolation. The very traditions that some Confucian-influenced immigrant families use to preserve family unity, although of ancient heritage, also resemble modern values of hard work and efficiency. Even so, these groups are likely to disagree significantly with modern emphases on what ends these virtues ought to be used to pursue. The virtue of personal industry in the service of maintaining traditional patterns of family life, therefore, runs the risk of devolving into hard work for individual advancement, which challenges family cohesion.

For another example of this strategy we can look to the evangelical Protestant traditions. As Margaret Bendroth argues in chapter 4, "Evangelicals, Family, and Modernity," families associated with this strand of Christianity have often understood themselves as being in opposition to a dominant modern culture that is opposed to so-called family values. However, these same evangelical families value those aspects of modernization that emphasize freedom in personal matters—in this case the freedom of families to create a domestic space separate from the dangers of the outside world. These conservative Protestants are also quite eager to use the technological advances of modernity (radio, television, e-mail) that facilitate the spread of their resistance message. Those who use this moderate form of resistance appreciate those aspects of the dominant culture that enable them to communicate the Christian gospel effectively, but they also value the freedoms of modernity that permit a partial separation from that same culture.

Perhaps the most striking form of the strategic limitation response can be found in the story of the Church of the Latter-day Saints (LDS), told in chapter 8 by David Dollahite. Marriage, procreation, large families, lineage, intergenerational continuity, and the hoped-for community of loved ones in heaven are central values in this uniquely American denomination. Many people seem to find these values attractive: the LDS is also one of the most rapidly growing religions in the world. Although the LDS is an expression of Christianity, its high esteem for intergenerational family continuity may be more reminiscent of values in classic forms of Judaism, Islam, Hinduism, and Confucianism. At first glance the LDS might seem to be primarily an example of resistance to the individualistic and family-disruptive forces of modernity. And in many ways it is. But in addition, as Dollahite points out, the LDS understands itself as both prodemocracy and, in selective ways, promodernity. Democracy gives the LDS the religious freedom to both exist and thrive. Modernity provides the LDS with sophisticated means of communication (radio, television, and wireless phones) and travel (automobiles, trains, and airplanes), and these expressions of technical rationality make it possible for the LDS to spread its message aggressively and train its young people to preach its version of the Christian gospel and the importance of family life.

MODERNITY AND DISCRIMINATION

In one sense all minority religions are, either subtly or overtly, discriminated against by the dominant cultural and religious forces of a society. Protestant Christianity has been the dominant form of religion throughout the history of North America. Both Jewish and Catholic groups have been minorities, and because of this their families have suffered various forms of discrimination in American life. This is doubtless even more true, but less obvious, for smaller minority religions such as Hinduism, Buddhism, Islam, and various forms of Confucianism. But religions of black Americans and their families provide a vivid and tragic example of how the forces of modernization and the injustice of discrimination can interact to create devastating consequences for black families—their children, mothers, and fathers. Chapter 7, "Generative Approaches to Modernity, Discrimination, and Black Families," by Robert Franklin, shows how the two forces of modernity and discrimination have worked together to marginalize men and fathers, upset the balance between male and female relations in the black community, and undermine parental support and guidance of their children. At the same time he discusses various strategies that black religious communities have used to deal with these forces—strategies that run the gamut of the many forms of response that we have discussed in this introduction. More than the other communities, however, the analytic distinction between modernity and cultural discrimination, and the interaction of these two forces, proves useful to understanding the relationship of religion and family in the black community and is suggestive, in less dramatic ways, of forces that doubtless touch in various ways all the minority religions and families in the United States.

FAMILIES, RELIGIONS, AND MODES OF ENGAGEMENT

The contributors to this book have also helped us detect specific modes of engagement with the wider culture that serve to complement, nuance, and render these general strategies more practical. We offer here a selection of these modes of engagement, although many more no doubt can be identified.

CONSERVATIVE COUNTEREXAMPLES

As new waves of immigrants confront the challenges of family life, economic viability, and citizenship in the United States, they may enjoy more continuity than earlier immigrant groups with the cultural, national, and religious ideals prevalent in their countries of origin. As Paul Numrich points out in chapter 2, "Immigrant American Religions and the Family: New Diversity and Conservatism," the religions of recent immigrants may have a conservatizing effect on the public discussion about families in the United States. Attempts by immigrant groups to find social stability and family unity often constitute a conservative reaction against what they perceive to be excessively permissive models of marriage and family life in the American cultural mainstream.

ALTERNATIVE LEGAL MODELING

In chapter 14, "Religion and Modernity in American Family Law," Lee Teitelbaum suggests that the best model for interpreting the changing interactions among families, religion, and law is to understand families as complex systems, or "interactive communities," rather than as structures or units that relate to society as intact wholes. He posits that current laws governing marriage and family may not be sufficient to capture the complex realities of religiously motivated marriage and family practices. Many cultural traditions, often with religious support, envision the formation of new families as interfamilial alliances rather than as contractual relations between two independent, self-determining parties. Even some Christians are not satisfied with the current legal options for marital formation and dissolution and seek new models, sometimes in the form of additional barriers to marital entry and exit, that better reflect their theological reasons for marrying and raising families.

This complex situation may require adopting a bare minimum standard for legal marriage that would give a broad freedom for legal coupling without conferring the sanction of law on particular religious interpretations of marriage and definitions of family. Or it may eventually move in the direction of requiring different marriage laws for different religious and cultural traditions, all having equal legal standing. If the former development occurs, Americans may find themselves debating whether religious officials will continue to execute a minimal legal function in performing religious marriages. If the latter development occurs, the debates may include whether religious concepts, discussed and clarified inside religious traditions, will gain some form of legal standing in the secular world. This, in turn, could force the legal profession to take up the questions of what constitutes a religion and how the law identifies and interprets a "religious concept." How this would work in practice and under whose jurisdiction is an ongoing puzzle, but at the very least it presents reasons why family law may need to wrestle with the category of religion beyond the law's shallow understanding of professed allegiance to an ideological group.

CRITICAL AND COMPARATIVE SCHOLARSHIP

Religious traditions throughout the world are examining themselves both critically and comparatively on a broad scale. The increasing extent and depth of this activity places those working from within religious traditions in closer contact with scholars studying these same traditions from outside a confessional context. Partly as a result of the oversimplifications used by media, government, and popular writers, the comparative and critical study of religion is now seen as an increasingly relevant and necessary aspect of any public discussion about religious matters. As David Clairmont points out in chapter 15, "Comparative Religion, Ethics, and American Family Life," the significance of the comparative study of religion to debates about family life in the American religions derives in part from its ability to break apart oversimplifications. While religious traditions do have normative agendas, public debates about marriage and family run into problems when they assume that religions draw upon uniform ethical systems or that their textured personal interactions are easily reducible to their theoretical ethical stances.

Along with critical studies of foundational religious texts and philosophical systems, contemporary scholarship in religion emphasizes the place of ritual in the investigation of religious life. Raymond Williams, in chapter 12, "Hindu Family in America," notes the importance of religious ritual in the context of family activities for maintaining transnational family identity. Not only ritual but also other categories, such as narrative and authority, illuminate religious influences on family life that other methods have tended to ignore. The comparative study of religion has a role in public debate; its task is to communicate the complexity of these traditions and illustrate the diverse ways that these traditions have for justifying and implementing their family beliefs and practices.

ARTISTIC REENVISIONING

Groups that do not have access to the political and economic mainstream of a country often use various means of expression to make themselves heard in a wider cultural conversation. Several chapters consider how various literary genres and other forms of artistic activity give form to the changing experiences of family life that statistical analysis and conceptual argument cannot communicate. In chapter 10, "Confucian 'Familism' in America," Jeffrey Meyer points to several examples in poetry and autobiography that depict Chinese immigrants who are searching for a balance between traditional family obligations and the educational and economic mobility that became possible for increasing numbers of Chinese Americans.

TECHNOLOGICAL INGENUITY

Finally, the chapters in this book also draw attention to the enormous impact of technological developments on the American religions and their family teachings. Technology spans the realms of communication, travel, health, human reproduction, entertainment, and scholarship. All these realms bring people closer together at an alarming rate. For families this means that immigrants are able to keep in close contact (either through electronic media or travel) with relatives in other countries. For each of the American religions this means that new means are available to create and maintain religious communities in the absence of a central geographical location for religious authority or ritual life. It also means that the discussion about what constitutes a religious tradition, and whether a tradition has essential elements that migrate with its adherents from one context to another, is put into question. Charles Prebish notes the importance of the Internet in expanding and defining American Buddhist communities, while Raymond Williams examines the practice of many American Hindus of maintaining strong family ties despite great geographical distance, even to the point of staging extravagant transnational weddings. The ability of immigrant families to stay in contact with families and traditions in their countries of origin gives further support for Paul Numrich's claim that these new religions may have a conservatizing effect on American family life. In the future these groups could assimilate to modernization more slowly and with more of their identity intact.

FAMILIES AND RELIGIONS AS PUBLIC-PRIVATE DIALOGUES

Whether intentionally or as a product of media stereotyping, religion has and undoubtedly will continue to influence public discussions about families. Exactly how this is occurring and, more important, how religious traditions believe it ought to occur, is a recent question to which the chapters here are a response. The experience of democracy teaches us that voices that are intentionally ignored will find a way to be heard. Families are perhaps one of the few practical sites where religion and public life are forced to confront each other. For this reason we hope that the reader finds in this collection resources to *challenge* certain prevailing public notions about religion: that a tradition is something unchanging and impervious to criticism, that religion is primarily about what a person believes rather than about what one does, and that there exist sufficient resources to make a neat separation between the practice of religions and their public influence. We also hope that the reader finds, through these essays, that one can look neither to the earliest expression of a tradition nor to its most recent expression, if one wants to study the religions of the world, particularly in their American expressions. The study of religion is a much more interesting and complex affair.

Religious interpretations of family, as the following chapters make clear, do not often abide by a neat public-private dichotomy, perhaps because families occupy a space somewhere between public and private. Both families and religions eventually force their way into the public space precisely because they embody this public-private tension. Navigating personal convictions amid multiple visions of a common good is the work of families as much as it is the work of modern democratic government. The changing shape of American demographics is forcing these public-private dialogues to call upon the many resources of the various religious traditions, listening to their questions as well as their past and present answers.

NOTES

1. Max Weber, *The Protestant Ethic and the Spirit of Capitalism* (New York: Charles Scriber's Sons, 1958), esp. 47–78, 181–83. See also his *Methodology of the Social Sciences* (New York: Free Press, 1949).

2. Jürgen Habermas, *Reason and the Rationalization of Society*, Vol. 1 of *The Theory of Communicative Action* (Boston: Beacon, 1984); see especially Habermas's critique and further development of Weber, 143–271.

3. Recent scholarship has considered the phenomenon of globalization from many perspectives. In *Modernity at Large* (Minneapolis: University of Minnesota Press, 1996), Arjun Appadurai has described the role of imagination in spreading cultural influences around the globe, thereby identifying a form of modernization that, while relying on the products of technical rationality for its advancement, is nonetheless distinct from and has the capacity to critique the more instrumental forces of modernization. In *Global Transformations: Politics, Economics and Culture* (Stanford, Calif.: Stanford University Press, 1999), David Held and colleagues consider globalization as a series of interrelated processes rather than as a single condition, and they define it primarily in terms of the expanding magnitude and scope of human power (1–31). For a recent study of religious interpretations of these and other views of globalization, see the three-volume *God and Globalization: Theological Ethics and the Spheres of Life*, edited by Max L. Stackhouse, Peter J. Paris, Don S. Browning, and Diane B. Obenchain (Harrisburg, Pa.: Trinity International Press, 2000–2002).

4. See, for example, Carolyn Osiek and David L. Balch, *Families in the New Testament World: Households and House Churches* (Louisville, Ky.: Westminster John Knox Press, 1997), and, more recently, their *Early Christian Families in Context: An Interdisciplinary Dialogue* (Grand Rapids, Mich.: Wm. B. Eerdmans, 2003); John Witte Jr., *From Sacrament to Contract: Marriage, Religion, and Law in the Western Tradition* (Louisville, Ky.: Westminster John Knox Press, 1997), and his *Law and Protestantism: The Legal Teachings of the Lutheran Reformation* (Cambridge: Cambridge University Press, 2002); and Lisa Sowle Cahill, *Family: A Christian Social Perspective* (Minneapolis: Fortress Press, 2000).

CHAPTER 2

Immigrant American Religions and the Family: New Diversity and Conservatism

PAUL D. NUMRICH

The United States is once again a land of immigrants. The twentieth century's final decade surpassed its first, the historical high, in total legal admissions to the country. At the turn of the twenty-first century the number of foreign-born residents and their children—what immigration scholars call the first and second immigrant generations—stood at the highest level ever, fifty-six million people, or one in five U.S. residents, a figure "likely to rise in the future as recent immigrants form families."[1]

Since the relaxation of immigration restrictions in the 1960s, the ethnic face of America has diversified significantly. During the 1990s Latin American and Asian countries of origin accounted for 78 percent of the total immigrant flow, in contrast to 31 percent during the 1950s. During that same time period European immigration dropped from 53 percent of the total to a mere 15 percent.[2] Thus America's ethnic roots are becoming increasingly more Latin American and Asian, and less European: the Census Bureau projects that by the mid-twenty-first century, whites will account for slightly more than half of the total population (down from 72 percent today), while the combined percentage of Hispanics and Asians will more than double, reaching one-third of the total population.[3] The latest wave of immigrants is also more diverse socioeconomically than classical American immigrant cohorts, exhibiting a bimodal clustering at the high and low ends of occupational status and income levels. Whereas earlier immigrants tended to enter the U.S. economy at the lower socioeconomic strata, recent immigrants range from computer scientists and engineers to taxi drivers and day laborers.[4]

America's increasing ethnic diversity brings a new religious diversity to the cultural landscape. Long storied for its spiritual vitality and variety, the United States has become a "complex religious reality of encyclopedic dimensions," as the Pluralism Project's Diana L. Eck puts it in *A New Religious America: How a "Christian Country" Has Become the World's Most Religiously Diverse Nation.*[5] New diversity characterizes both Christian and non-Christian circles, as the sociologist R. Stephen Warner explains: "Millions of adherents of other religions—Islam, Hinduism, Buddhism, and more—have joined Jews to expand the boundaries of American religious pluralism to an extent unimaginable only forty years ago. At the same time, Christians from Asia, the Middle East, and Latin America are de-Europeanizing American Christianity."[6]

Some controversy has surfaced regarding the numbers of adherents of the major non-Christian religions in the United States, both overall and in the recent immigration wave. In particular, since the attacks of September 11, 2001, critics have challenged widely reported estimates making Muslims the nation's second-largest religious group after Christians, usurping the historically significant place of American Jews.[7] Findings from a survey of legal immigrants who arrived in 1996 may be representative of religious preferences in recent immigration generally: 65 percent Christian (from virtually every country in the pool), 8 percent Muslim, 4 percent Buddhist, 3.4 percent Hindu, 2.6 percent Jewish, and 1.4 percent "other." A substantial 15 percent of the sample reported no religious preference.[8]

This "numbers game" often involves political motivations, but it essentially misses the larger point of America's new religious diversity. No matter what the hard figures—which cannot be determined with certainty—perceptions of a significant new American religious diversity have become reality. Many Christian congregations and denominations have been diversified by the new immigration. A single mosque or temple on a religious landscape that previously contained only churches and synagogues registers in the public mind, as does interaction with neighbors, coworkers, and acquaintances professing unfamiliar faiths. It did not take large numbers of Jewish Americans to create the perception of a "Judeo-Christian" society. In recent decades America has acquired a sufficient quantitative critical mass and, more important, experienced the qualitative perceptual shift to become a multireligious society.

CONSERVATIVE CRITIQUE OF CONTEMPORARY AMERICAN SOCIETY AND FAMILY

Many new immigrant religious voices have raised serious conservative criticisms of contemporary American society, particularly regarding negative influences on the family. The following illustrations, from a wide variety of Christian and non-Christian sources, make the point.

First, from immigrant Christian circles. Leaders and members of several Houston churches in the Religion, Ethnicity and New Immigrants Research project expressed concern about the moral state of American society and its potentially harmful effects on immigrant family life. For instance, a pseudonymous Argentine evangelical church

> places a heavy emphasis on the family as both a fundamental religious and Hispanic value. Immigrants are, therefore, especially concerned with the second generation, worried that they may succumb to "American values" that include family dissolution. . . .
>
> Many aspects of the new land are revered, but there is a general perception on the part of both generations that Americans are not good role models in the area of family. Sermons frequently allude to increasing divorce rates in the U.S., sexual promiscuity, extra-marital affairs, homosexuality, reversal of "Biblical" gender roles, and difficult inter-generational relationships.[9]

The field researcher at a multiethnic Assemblies of God church in Houston reports that "most of the youth believed that their families come from societies that have much more conservative morals and values than the U.S. and where training children is a community rather than simply a family matter." A female Nigerian member of this congregation elaborated: "Well, my country's not perfect, but we believe in families and values a whole lot. We came from a country that was kind of secure in morals and values and then we moved to this country where there's absolutely none; where you can do whatever you want because you feel like doing it."[10] Similar reports of tension between morally conservative immigrant perspectives and perceived negative American moral influences come from a Korean Protestant church, a Hispanic Catholic parish, a storefront Hispanic Protestant church, a multiethnic Catholic parish, and a Chinese evangelical Protestant church in the Houston project.[11]

The sociologist Fenggang Yang, a researcher in the Houston project, has documented the generally conservative evangelical identity of Chinese Protestant churches in the United States. Yang notes that "intact and traditional marriage and family life are highly valued in the Chinese church," adding that "Chinese parents are in constant fear of bad influences in American society. . . . To guard against bad influences the parents rely on the church for meaningful and attractive youth activities. They also try to fill their children's schedules by sending them to camp meetings, pressing them to study the Chinese language, and bringing them to private music and sports classes. These efforts are quite successful. Some common problems in American society, such as drugs, teenage pregnancy, and homosexuality, have been very rare among the young people in Chinese Christian churches."

Yang reports that, although problems arise in immigrant Chinese families, these "are generally not made known to the public, and divorce cases have been rare."[12] Chinese evangelical Christians incorporate traditional Confucian teachings about the family into their moral agenda in America but reject Buddhist and Taoist components of their Chinese cultural heritage as incompatible with evangelical Christian beliefs.[13]

Korean Protestants, probably the most studied new immigrant religious group, share much in common with their Chinese counterparts. Researchers Kwang Chung Kim and Shin Kim draw a direct parallel between the conservative evangelicalism that predominates in both groups, providing "absolute belief and strict moral standards."[14] Kim and Kim report survey data on members, elders, and clergy of the Presbyterian Church (U.S.A.) that show that Korean respondents "strongly adhere to the sanctity of heterosexual marriage" and express significantly higher disapproval rates for homosexuality and extramarital cohabitation than either white or black Presbyterians.[15] The sociologist Pyong Gap Min's comments capture a recurrent theme among both Christian and non-Christian conservative immigrant religious groups, namely, that American society has departed from its Christian roots: "Many Korean pastors tend to think that American society, which originated from the Christian background, is turning against the Christian ideology. They argue that Korean traditional values such as respecting adult members are more consistent with Christian values than 'American individualism.' They frequently tie certain Korean traditional values to a paragraph from the Bible and preach church members to preserve those Korean values to live as sincere Christians."[16]

Church-going second-generation Korean Americans tend to agree with their immigrant elders, as the sociologist Kelly Chong's interviews of Chicago-area Koreans suggest: "Compared with non-church respondents, the church members hold far more strictly to traditional Korean views regarding sexual morality and gender relations, displaying a much more critical stance toward American culture and values such as individualism and liberal sexual morality."[17]

Non-Christian immigrant religious groups also experience tensions between traditional Old World family norms and American cultural influences. Describing how the Iranian Jewish community in Los Angeles is negotiating its tripartite identity as Iranians, Jews, and Americans, the ethnographer Shoshanah Feher explains that "although family values are prized highly, the family itself is suffering as a result of juggling identities. . . . The Los Angeles [Iranian Jewish] community is finding that, instead of maintaining the good aspects of American culture, their children are falling prey to the negative American norms."[18] During a recent Purim celebration at an Orthodox synagogue in Chicago, the guest speaker talked about the American Dream of success through hard work. After sharing a quaint tale about an illiterate Ukrainian Jewish immigrant who struck it rich in America during the old days, he cautioned the congregation: "It's a great story. It teaches us not to go shopping when we are hungry. You come to this country and you are hungry. But don't forget about what you have to do in the first place. Don't forget that you are Jews. Don't wait until your son brings a shiksa into your home. Don't wait until your daughter comes home with a belly button sticking out like Britney Spears. Come to [the synagogue] regularly, listen to [the rabbi], help him and his family to upkeep the synagogue, and the rest will follow."[19]

The ethnic Buddhist community in the United States includes both immigrants and refugees, the latter forced migrants who often face traumatic circumstances in coming to America. Wat Dhammaram, an immigrant Thai Buddhist temple in Chicago, established a Sunday school program in order to teach its second generation about Buddhism, Thai culture and language, and the dangers of "the social, teenager and criminal problems in the communities." As I reported in my study of this temple, "a group of young people from Wat Dhammaram told me that their parents have 'tried everything' to keep them 'Thai' rather than see them become too Americanized."[20] A Sunday school text written by one of the temple's monks includes lessons that promote traditional family relationships, such as respectful, grateful, and obedient children; a husband who adores his wife; and a wife who conscientiously performs her household and familial duties. These guidelines are presented as alternatives to Western/American culture, which "emphasizes individual independence over sharing and co-operation and mutual responsibility," attitudes that contribute to "current male-female relationships," which, we can assume, include unloving husbands and nondutiful wives.[21]

The extreme trauma experienced by Southeast Asian refugee Buddhist communities and families in the United States is well documented. Reports from the field show that Buddhist institutional, doctrinal, and moral resources are being marshaled to address this situation.[22] A Vietnamese temple in Houston is a microcosm of the socioeconomic diversity of America's latest immigrant wave, with members from all strata of educational and occupational attainment. One monk described the temple's role in members' lives in the new American context: "There are a lot of social pressures on them. Furthermore, the relationships within a family are loose. It is not a close-knit relationship like in Vietnam. Once conflict arises, the only place that they can rely on for help is the temple."[23]

On the whole, the South Asian immigrant community is socioeconomically better off than Buddhist refugees, but South Asians too face cultural and moral adjustments in American society. Immigrants from India and Pakistan, who make up the bulk of the South Asian community in the United States, practice a variety of religions, notably, Hinduism, Islam, Sikhism, Jainism, Christianity, and Zoroastrianism. "When asked what their major contribution to America might be," explains Raymond Williams, the foremost expert on these religious groups, "immigrants from India and Pakistan often reply, 'Our close family ties.' Family values are topics of many South Asian religious conferences and meetings. Immigrants from the Indian subcontinent . . . are suspicious of American family life and fearful of bad influences from their children's peers. Many believe that American children do not care for their parents and will desert them in their old age and that American families fail to inculcate morals in the children."[24]

In a study of immigrant Hindus the sociologist Prema Kurien observes that "Indian immigrants in the United States are often concerned that their children will pick up the negative aspects of teenage American culture, which they perceive to include sexual promiscuity, lack of respect for elders, violence, as well as drug and alcohol abuse." On their part second-generation Indian Hindus find it difficult to navigate between conservative parental expectations and peer pressures to rebel against those expectations. One of the local religious groups that Kurien studied, a small *bala vihar*, or child development organization, was established in order "to bring both children and their parents together as 'an extended family' to work through these issues."[25]

The Swaminarayan branch of Hinduism has established a transnational institutional infrastructure aimed at preserving and transmitting Indian/Hindu identity among Indians in the homeland and throughout the diaspora. The Swaminarayan moral code for householders (lay families) includes a vow to abstain from adultery, which is reinforced through gender separation in public settings and moderate sexual activity between spouses. As Williams summarizes, for Swaminarayan Hindus "marriage is one of the structures of society for the good of man and the protection of woman; thus the institution is protected by regulations associated with the prohibition of adultery."[26] A Swaminarayan temple in the Chicago area has instituted a program of "home assemblies" with daily activities designed to preserve the "sanctity of the family" and to keep communication lines within the family open. This temple's motto is "Save Our Heritage." A temple leader described how one slide in his PowerPoint presentation to other immigrants typically draws stunned silence: "Economic and Educational Success Without Cultural Preservation: Is It Worth It?"[27]

Conservative Muslim critiques of American society and family have been particularly pointed, perhaps partly in response to a sustained negative perception of Islam and Muslims that suffuses the larger American population (predating the events of September 11, 2001). In the late 1970s the Muslim sociologist Hammudah 'Abd al 'Ati challenged readers concerned with the contemporary crisis of the family in the West: "If the true structure of the family in Islam is successfully brought to their attention, they may well discover how the classic solutions of Islam can help to solve their modern problems."[28] In the 1980s the researchers Yvonne Haddad and Adair Lummis noted a growing perception among Muslims worldwide and in the United States that American society is in moral decline, as indicated by feminism, high divorce rates, sexual promiscuity, pornography, sexual explicitness in the media, crime, drugs, and a general abandonment of Christian moral roots.[29] In a pre-9/11 survey of leaders of 416 mosques nationwide, two-thirds of the immigrant respondents said that they either strongly or somewhat agreed with the statement that "America is an immoral, corrupt society."[30]

Early in its history one of Chicago's prominent immigrant mosques envisioned creating a Muslim neighborhood in order to "answer the challenge faced by the Muslim community in its efforts to lead a truly Islamic life in a non-Muslim environment." In 1977 a task force of the Muslim Community Center (MCC) proposed carving out a tract of approximately six square miles on Chicago's North Side that would include "a masjid [mosque], school, and facilities for assembly and meetings, health care, nursery, dorm, and cooperative investment projects," thus establishing a "Muslim neighborhood which would become a model community and a nucleus for the Islamic Da'wah [propagation of the faith] in the Chicago area."[31]

This ambitious plan never materialized, although the motivations behind the original Muslim neighborhood project continue to echo in MCC's programming. The statement of philosophy of MCC's full-time Islamic school, opened in a near north suburb in 1989, reads: "The school's foremost objective is to provide an Islamic environment for the education of young Muslims . . . [that] affirms in our children their identity and pride in the Islamic legacy. . . . As is widely accepted, the education of our children in an Islamic environment is the only genuine alternative to public school education to avoid their exposure to un-Islamic mannerism[s] and practices such as sexual permissiveness and undue emphasis on materialism."[32]

In a review of current research on Muslims in the United States, the anthropologist Karen Leonard summarized that "Many immigrant Muslims . . . uphold patriarchy and 'gender complementarity' (different male and female roles) in family and community. They perceive the dominant American values of gender equality and freedom of sexual expression as serious threats to a Muslim way of life, and indeed to all ordered social life. . . . These concerns with the maintenance of patriarchy and gender complementarity seem centrally connected to a fear of 'American individualism,' which is interpreted not as a moral ideal but as egoism, an amoral phenomenon and a sign of family and societal breakdown."[33]

Across the gamut of recent immigrant religions, concern is raised about the secular and material enticements of modern American society. What is gained, asks a Filipino Catholic, if immigrants "modernize ourselves but fail to fill the void?"[34] Williams writes of Swaminarayan Hindu temples that warn members about entering "a Mephistophelian pact under which, in exchange for *la dolce vita* of the American society, they have agreed, forever, to surrender their offspring to an alien culture."[35] In the survey of national Muslim leaders cited earlier, in which two-thirds of the immigrant respondents strongly or somewhat judged America to be "an immoral, corrupt society," 99 percent either strongly or somewhat agreed with the following statement: "America is a technologically advanced society that we can learn from."[36] The concern among many immigrant religious leaders is whether their constituents possess the moral discernment to make the right selections from America's many offerings.

The clash between American individualism and Old World communal and familial norms underlies much of the moral critique of American society coming from new immigrant communities.[37] Widely reported tensions and negotiations about the dating and marriage choices of the American-born second generation symbolize the issue. More is at stake here than group endogamy, although that certainly weighs heavily on the minds of many immigrant parents. The larger issue has to do with the proper relationship of individual to extended family to community, as reflected in Harlan and Courtright's observation about arranged marriages: "Because a marriage affects the status of the entire family and its lineage, it is deemed too important a decision to leave to the persons actually getting married. Rather, the decision rests with the heads of extended family units. Consequently, arranged marriages are the norm; marriages undertaken by the marrying parties themselves, so-called love marriages, are considered deviant, even dangerous."[38]

To summarize the conservative critique coming from many new immigrant religious groups, America has abandoned its original moral compass, and dissolute Americans today give in to passions and proclivities fueled by modern ideologies such as individualism, feminism, secularism, and materialism, with destructive consequences to the family. The litany is long, the effects on the traditional family disturbing to the critics—high divorce rates, sexual promiscuity, extramarital affairs, pornography and a general preoccupation with sex in popular culture, homosexuality, nontraditional gender roles, intergenerational tensions, neglect of family duties, substance abuse, crime, and violence. The fears of the immigrant generation find intense focus in efforts to protect their American-born offspring from these social ills by inculcating traditional Old World values through educational, cultural, and religious programs. It is not coincidental that recent immigrant communities typically established formal congregations as the second generation reached school age. The more informal religious associations that satisfied the needs of the pioneer immigrant generation were found inadequate to the task of passing on their ethnoreligious heritage to subsequent generations.

SOURCES AND FEATURES OF THE IMMIGRANT CONSERVATIVE RELIGIOUS CRITIQUE

The conservative sentiments described in the previous section probably characterize views of the majority of the recent immigrant population, particularly those immigrants for whom religious identity is important. But significant moderate and liberal crosscurrents exist as well. Among Muslim immigrants, for instance, many elite intellectual leaders emphasize the compatibility of Islamic and American models of social and political life.[39] In immigrant congregations across the board, a continuum of conservative, moderate, and liberal positions may be taken with regard to the adaptive question of how much of the transplanted religious heritage should be retained, how much jettisoned, and how much modified to fit the new circumstances in which immigrants find themselves in America.[40]

Still, moral conservatism is a common by-product of the immigration experience. In the historian Timothy Smith's memorable phrase, "migration was often a theologizing experience" for American immigrant groups, and their theologizing often produced an "immigrant Puritanism" (a phrase Smith borrowed from another historian of American immigration, Marcus Hansen). Immigrant Puritanism, Smith explained, is "a predictable reaction to the ethical or behavioral disorientation that affected most immigrants, whatever the place or the century of their arrival."[41] The specific objects of moral concern may vary from group to group, perhaps according to socioeconomic circumstances or doctrinal proclivities, but moral concern is ubiquitous in immigrant circles, especially among immigrant parents.[42]

The current critique of American society and family replicates that which was prevalent during the classical period of American immigration, from the 1800s to the severe restrictions placed on immigration flows in the 1920s. In the words of Oscar Handlin's epic narrative, *The Uprooted*, the immigrants of an earlier day "felt free to criticize many aspects of the life they discovered in the New World, the excessive concern with material goods and the inadequate attention to religion, the pushiness and restlessness of the people, the transitory quality of family relationships."[43] Handlin described many classical immigrant fears about the negative influences of American society that echo today, such as individualism, nontraditional gender roles, intergenerational tensions, romantic marriages, and subversive elements on the streets and in the public schools. "In their religious faith," wrote Maldwyn Allen Jones, the British historian of classical American immigration, "immigrants recognized almost the only pillar of the old life that had not crumbled in the course of the Atlantic crossing. To it, therefore, they clung both as a means of preserving their identity and as a source of security and solace in a bewildering world."[44] The same can be said of many who crossed the Pacific during the classical period of American immigration.[45]

In other words, Old World religious conservatism is nothing new in American immigrant history,[46] although it is best understood as Old World conservatism repackaged for New World life. Perhaps the sheer intensity and new variety of critical voices distinguish the current moral critique of American society and family from the earlier one. But more than this, the America of the new immigrants differs from that of the classical immigrants'. Beginning in the late 1960s, both American society and the global system of which it is a part have experienced qualitative changes with important moral implications. Economic globalization, urban transformation, political and cultural revolutions—

such powerful contemporary forces have not only exerted unprecedented pressures upon the family but also mobilized religious resources seeking to "reweave the torn social fabric," as one analyst of global evangelical Christianity puts it.[47] Although the divorce rate soared during the classical period of American immigration (from 1.2 to 4.5 per 1,000 marriages between 1860 and 1910), causing "widespread fears for the stability of the family," that increase did not approach the significance of the jump from fewer than 10 divorces per 1,000 marriages in the 1950s and early 1960s to 23 by 1979.[48] Other indicators of the current "ill health" of the traditional American family abound, including increases in single-parent units and juvenile delinquency.[49] Thus the new moral critique by immigrant religions addresses a new moral crisis in American society and family.

Whether another distinguishing feature of the contemporary situation exists deserves investigation. Is there today a relatively less strident "reverse" moral critique emanating from the indigenous majority population toward perceived negative immigrant influences on American society and family? In the classical period of American immigration, a strong animus toward southern and eastern Europeans and Asians, fueled by xenophobia and racism, included clear moral tones. Whether deemed fundamentally unassimilable to mainstream American ways or subjected to systematic "Americanization" or "Puritanization" campaigns, immigrants of a former era bore the brunt of heavy moral criticism.[50] Today's anti-immigration spokespeople seem driven more by economic and political motivations than moral ones.

The contemporary conservative critique of American society and family found in immigrant circles is clearly being sustained by growing conservative religious trends around the globe. For instance, as the historian and religious studies scholar Philip Jenkins observes, the critical mass of worldwide Christianity has shifted from the liberal northern regions of Europe and North America to the more traditional southern regions of Latin America, Africa, and Asia. "The most significant point," Jenkins stresses, "is that in terms of both theology and moral teaching, Southern Christianity is more conservative than the Northern—especially the American—version."[51] The majority of Christian immigrants to the United States today bring a conservative morality nurtured in the Global South and transmitted through transnational networks. A comparable conservatism characterizes other religions in the homelands and transnational networks of America's recent immigrants, such as conservative Islamic movements.[52]

IMPLICATIONS OF RECENT IMMIGRANT RELIGIOUS CONSERVATISM

The strong current of religious conservatism in the recent immigration carries some important implications for American religion, at least in the short term. After reviewing trends among African American and immigrant Christians,

Warner suggests that "American Christianity is becoming *ethnically more diverse, liturgically more populist, and doctrinally less modernist*."[53] We can certainly add *morally more conservative* to this list, especially with regard to family-related issues. Immigrant Christians have not only swelled the ranks of conservative denominations in the United States, they have also established conservative nondenominational congregations and formed conservative enclaves within liberal denominations. In Chicago evangelically oriented immigrant Indian Protestants have forged an informal network that crosses denominational affiliations. Randall Balmer, the historian of American evangelicalism, reports "some evidence that the evangelical subculture—or at least a part of the subculture—is available to those crossing the borders into the United States."[54] The significance of potential mutual influence between indigenous and immigrant evangelicalism is great. It remains to be seen whether conservative Christians will set aside historic doctrinal concerns in order to form interfaith networks around a conservative moral agenda in the U.S., along the lines of the recent "profamily" alliance of Catholics, Protestants, and Muslims at the United Nations.[55]

"In the short run, at least," suggests the sociologist Joseph Tamney after surveying current immigrant religious trends, "the libertarians may lose out to the social conservatives."[56] But the long run may show the opposite. Scholarly and anecdotal reports routinely describe conflicts between conservative Old World traditions and American alternatives within immigrant religious groups, often resulting in compromises favoring liberalism on a variety of issues, such as spousal procurement practices, gender roles, intergenerational roles and attitudes, dating, divorce, and individualism.[57] A palpable sense of resignation about the inevitability of adopting American ways is detectable. "What effect does living in America have on the Muslim family and individual Muslims in particular?" asked Haddad and Lummis in their 1980s study of Islamic values in the United States. "As we have seen so far," they said in summarizing their findings, "many of the stricter interpretations of Islam seem to decrease in proportion to one's stay in America, to interaction with non-Muslim Americans, and apparently as a general result of living in the American culture."[58] As a group of young adults in an Indian Christian congregation in Chicago explained, the longer their parents live in America, the more lenient they become with regard to dating and marriage restrictions, for example.[59] The future depends on how lenient the American-raised generations become.

Despite its scholarly detractors today, assimilation is still a powerful force affecting immigrant populations. It remains to be seen whether, following segmented assimilation or selective acculturation theories,[60] conservative immigrant religious groups will adopt other aspects of contemporary American society while maintaining their conservative moral compass or whether their moral conservatism will be modified by liberal American influences.

NOTES

1. U.S. Census Bureau, "1-in-5 U.S. Residents Either Foreign-Born or First Generation, Census Bureau Reports," *United States Department of Commerce News*, 7 February 2002. Also see Immigration and Naturalization Service (INS), *Statistical Yearbook of the Immigration and Naturalization Service* (Washington, D.C.: Immigration and Naturalization Service, 2000), table 2, 19–22.

2. INS, *Statistical Yearbook*, table 2.

3. U.S. Census Bureau, "Census Bureau Projects Doubling of Nation's Population by 2100," *United States Department of Commerce News*, 13 January 2000.

4. Paul D. Numrich, "Recent Immigrant Religions in a Restructuring Metropolis: New Religious Landscapes in Chicago," *Journal of Cultural Geography* 17, no. 1 (1997): 55–76.

5. Diana L. Eck, *A New Religious America: How a "Christian Country" Has Become the World's Most Religiously Diverse Nation* (San Francisco: Harper, 2001), 4.

6. R. Stephen Warner, "Immigration and Religious Communities in the United States," in R. Stephen Warner and Judith G. Wittner, eds., *Gatherings in Diaspora: Religious Communities and the New Immigration* (Philadelphia: Temple University Press, 1998), 4.

7. Tom W. Smith, "Estimating the Muslim Population in the United States," report for the American Jewish Committee, New York, 2001; Tom W. Smith, "Religious Diversity in America: The Emergence of Muslims, Buddhists, Hindus, and Others," *Journal for the Scientific Study of Religion* 41, no. 3 (2002): 577–85. The most widely cited pre-9/11 estimate of six to seven million U.S. Muslims comes from "The Mosque in America: A National Portrait," an April 2001 report from the Mosque Study Project, coordinated by the Hartford Institute for Religious Research under its larger Faith Communities Today study and released by the Council on American-Islamic Relations (available at www.cair-net.org/mosquereport/index.html).

8. Guillermina Jasso, Douglas S. Massey, Mark R. Rosenzweig, and James P. Smith, "Exploring the Religious Preferences of Recent Immigrants to the United States: Evidence from the New Immigrant Survey Pilot," in Yvonne Yazbeck Haddad, Jane I. Smith, and John L. Esposito, eds., *Religion and Immigration: Christian, Jewish, and Muslim Experiences in the United States* (Walnut Creek, Calif.: AltaMira Press, 2003), 217–53.

9. David Cook, "Iglesia Cristiana Evangelica: Arriving in the Pipeline," in Helen Rose Ebaugh and Janet Saltzman Chafetz, eds., *Religion and the New Immigrants: Continuities and Adaptations in Immigrant Congregations* (Walnut Creek, Calif.: AltaMira Press, 2000), 189.

10. Patricia Dorsey, "Southwest Assembly of God: Whomsoever Will," in Ebaugh and Chafetz, *Religion and the New Immigrants*, 318.

11. Chapters 5, 6, 7, 8, and 14 in Ebaugh and Chafetz, *Religion and the New Immigrants*. Only one of the eight chapters on Christian churches in Ebaugh and Chafetz is silent on the topic.

12. Fenggang Yang, *Chinese Christians in America: Conversion, Assimilation, and Adhesive Identities* (University Park: Pennsylvania State University Press, 1999), 113–14.

13. Ibid., 147–56.

14. Kwang Chung Kim and Shin Kim, "The Ethnic Roles of Korean Immigrant Churches in the United States," in Ho-Youn Kwon, Kwang Chung Kim, and R. Stephen Warner, eds., *Korean Americans and their Religions: Pilgrims and Missionaries from a Different Shore* (University Park: Pennsylvania State University Press, 2001), 92.

15. Ibid., 87.

16. Pyong Gap Min, "The Structure and Social Function of Korean Immigrant Churches in the United States," in Min Zhou and James V. Gatewood, eds., *Contemporary Asian America: A Multidisciplinary Reader* (New York: New York University Press, 2000), 383.

17. Kelly H. Chong, "What It Means to Be Christian: The Role of Religion in the Construction of Ethnic Identity and Boundary among Second-Generation Korean Americans," *Sociology of Religion* 59, no. 3 (1998): 270.

18. Shoshanah Feher, "From the Rivers of Babylon to the Valleys of Los Angeles: The Exodus and Adaptation of Iranian Jews," in Warner and Wittner, *Gatherings in Diaspora*, 81–82.

19. Dmitro Volkov, field researcher, fieldnotes, 26 February 2002, Religion, Immigration and Civil Society in Chicago Project, Loyola University Chicago.

20. Paul David Numrich, *Old Wisdom in the New World: Americanization in Two Immigrant Theravada Buddhist Temples* (Knoxville: University of Tennessee Press, 1996), 98, 107.

21. C. Phangcham, "Buddhism for Young Students," Wat Dhammaram, Chicago, 1990, 71.

22. See, for example, Penny van Esterik, *Taking Refuge: Lao Buddhists in North America* (Tempe: Arizona State University, 1992); Edward R. Canda and Thitiya Phaobtong, "Buddhism as a Support System for Southeast Asian Refugees," *Social Work* 37, no. 1 (January 1992): 61–67; Carl L. Bankston III, "Bayou Lotus: Theravada Buddhism in Southwestern Louisiana," *Sociological Spectrum* 17, no. 4 (1997): 453–72.

23. Thuan Huynh, "Center for Vietnamese Buddhism: Recreating Home," in Ebaugh and Chafetz, *Religion and the New Immigrants*, 54.

24. Raymond Brady Williams, "Asian Indian and Pakistani Religions in the United States," in Zhou and Gatewood, *Contemporary Asian America*, 402. Also see Williams, *Religions of Immigrants from India and Pakistan: New Threads in the American Tapestry* (New York: Cambridge University Press, 1988), and Padma Rangaswamy, *Namaste America: Indian Immigrants in an American Metropolis* (University Park: Pennsylvania State University Press, 2000).

25. Prema Kurien, "'We Are Better Hindus Here': Religion and Ethnicity among Indian Americans," in Pyong Gap Min and Jung Ha Kim, eds., *Religions in Asian America: Building Faith Communities* (Walnut Creek, Calif.: AltaMira Press, 2002), 109.

26. Raymond Brady Williams, *An Introduction to Swaminarayan Hinduism* (Cambridge: Cambridge University Press, 2001), 161.

27. Travis Vande Berg and Paul Numrich, field researchers, fieldnotes, 17 August and 15 March 2001, Religion, Immigration and Civil Society in Chicago Project.

28. Hammudah 'Abd al 'Ati, *The Family Structure in Islam* (Indianapolis: American Trust Publications, 1977), 283.

29. Yvonne Yazbeck Haddad and Adair T. Lummis, *Islamic Values in the United States: A Comparative Study* (New York: Oxford University Press, 1987), 124, 168–70.

30. Mosque Study Project, "Mosque in America," 31.

31. Masjid Planning Committee, "The Masjid and Community Development Project," Muslim Community Center, Chicago, January 1977, archived in the Islam in America collection, DePaul University Library, Chicago, 3, 10.

32. Quoted in Paul D. Numrich, "Recent Immigrant Religions and the Restructuring of Metropolitan Chicago," in Lowell W. Livezey, ed., *Public Religion and Urban Transformation: Faith in the City* (New York: New York University Press, 2000), 247–48.

33. Karen Leonard, "Muslims in the U.S.: The State of Research," unpublished essay, September 2002, 41.

34. Quoted in Kathleen Sullivan, "St. Catherine's Catholic Church: One Church, Parallel Congregations," in Ebaugh and Chafetz, *Religion and the New Immigrants*, 270.

35. Williams, *Introduction to Swaminarayan Hinduism*, 226.

36. Mosque Study Project, "Mosque in America," 31.

37. Paul D. Numrich, "Marriage, Family, and Health in Selected World Religions: Different Perspectives in an Increasingly Pluralist America," in John Wall et al., eds., *Marriage, Health, and the Professions: If Marriage Is Good for You, What Does This Mean for Law, Medicine, Ministry, Therapy, and Business?* (Grand Rapids, Mich.: William B. Eerdmans, 2002), 305–23. This normative clash is not unique to new immigrants. Comparable moral critiques of American individualism can be found in traditional Native American cultures (see chapter 5) and in indigenous conservative Protestantism (see the discussion in the last section of this chapter; on evangelical ambivalence in this regard, however, see chapter 4).

38. Lindsey Harlan and Paul B. Courtright, "Introduction: On Hindu Marriage and Its Margins," in Lindsey Harlan and Paul B. Courtright, eds., *From the Margins of Hindu Marriage: Essays on Gender, Religion, and Culture* (New York: Oxford University Press, 1995), 5. Although written in the context of Hindu marriage, this statement would apply in most immigrant contexts.

39. M. A. Muqtedar Khan, "Constructing the American Muslim Community," in Haddad, Smith, and Esposito, *Religion and Immigration*, 175–98.

40. Paul David Numrich, introduction to Gurinder Singh Mann, Paul David Numrich, and Raymond B. Williams, *Buddhists, Hindus, and Sikhs in America* (New York: Oxford University Press, 2001), 11–13.

41. Timothy L. Smith, "Religion and Ethnicity in America," *American Historical Review* 83 (1978): 1175, 1176.

42. Ebaugh and Chafetz, "Passing It On: The Second Generation," *Religion and the New Immigrants*, 433.

43. Oscar Handlin, *The Uprooted: The Epic Story of the Great Migrations that Made the American People* (New York: Grosset and Dunlap, 1951), 267.

44. Maldwyn Allen Jones, *American Immigration* (Chicago: University of Chicago Press, 1960), 136. Also see Will Herberg, *Protestant-Catholic-Jew: An Essay in American Religious Sociology* (New York: Doubleday, 1956), 23, and H. Richard Niebuhr, *The Social Sources of Denominationalism* (New York: Living Age Books, 1957), 222–23.

45. See, for example, Tetsuden Kashima, *Buddhism in America: The Social Organization of an Ethnic Religious Institution* (Westport, Conn.: Greenwood, 1977), and Ronald Takaki, *Strangers from a Different Shore: A History of Asian Americans*, updated and revised ed. (Boston: Little, Brown, 1998).

46. Marcus Lee Hansen, *The Immigrant in American History*, edited by Arthur M. Schlesinger (Cambridge, Mass.: Harvard University Press, 1940), 83, 91.

47. Manuel A. Vasquez, "Review Essay: Tracking Global Evangelical Christianity," *Journal of the American Academy of Religion* 71, no. 1 (March 2003): 171. Also see Livezey, *Public Religion and Urban Transformation*; Livezey et al., *Religion in the New Urban America* (forthcoming).

48. Maldwyn A. Jones, *The Limits of Liberty: American History, 1607–1992*, 2nd ed. (New York: Oxford University Press, 1995), 331; Barbara Dafoe Whitehead, "Dan Quayle Was Right," *Atlantic Monthly*, April 1993, 50.

49. Numrich, "Marriage, Family, and Health," 305–6.

50. Handlin, *Uprooted*, 278–79, 294–95; Hansen, *Immigrant in American History*, 120–21; Jones, *American Immigration*, 233–34; Takaki, *Strangers from a Different Shore*.

51. Philip Jenkins, "The Next Christianity," *Atlantic Monthly*, October 2002, 59.

52. John L. Esposito, ed., *Political Islam: Revolution, Radicalism, or Reform?* (Boulder, Colo.: Lynne Rienner, 1997); Martin E. Marty and R. Scott Appleby, eds., *Accounting for Fundamentalisms: The Dynamic Character of Movements*, vol. 4 of *The Fundamentalism Project* (Chicago: University of Chicago Press, 1994).

53. R. Stephen Warner, "Approaching Religious Diversity: Barriers, Byways, and Beginnings," *Sociology of Religion* 59, no. 3 (1998): 207; emphasis in original.

54. Randall Balmer, "Crossing the Borders: Evangelicalism and Migration," in Haddad, Smith, and Esposito, *Religion and Immigration*, 58.

55. Geoffrey Knox, ed., *Religion and Public Policy at the UN* (Washington, D.C.: Religion Counts, 2002).

56. Joseph B. Tamney, editorial, *Sociology of Religion* 59, no. 3 (1998): iii.

57. M. Christian Green and Paul D. Numrich, "Religious Perspectives on Sexuality: A Resource Guide," Park Ridge Center, Chicago, 2001, 66–92.

58. Haddad and Lummis, *Islamic Values in the United States*, 121.

59. Interview by author, 19 May 2003, Chicago.

60. Alejandro Portes and Ruben G. Rumbaut, *Immigrant America: A Portrait*, 2nd ed. (Berkeley: University of California Press, 1996); Alejandro Portes and Min Zhou, "The New Second Generation: Segmented Assimilation and Its Variants among Post-1965 Immigrant Youth," *Annals of the American Academy of Political and Social Sciences* 530 (1993): 74–96.

PART II

Family Traditions in the American Religions

CHAPTER 3

The Cultural Contradictions
of Mainline Family Ideology and Practice

W. BRADFORD WILCOX AND ELIZABETH WILLIAMSON

The last half-century has witnessed dramatic changes in American family life, marked by—among other things—increases in divorce, illegitimacy, and women's labor force participation and by declines in fertility. Family scholars from across the ideological spectrum argue that the United States is succumbing to the logic of what might be called family modernization, where the family is weakening as an institution in the face of social structural and cultural developments associated with late modernity (Bumpass 1990; Popenoe 1988). At the social structural level the family modernization perspective holds that the expansion of the market and the state means that functions once associated with the family—for example, food preparation, education, leisure, and the care of the infirm and elderly—are increasingly being delegated to the state and market. Moreover, developments in the cultural arena, such as the disestablishment of religion-rooted moral codes and the rise of an ethic of expressive individualism, have undercut the moral beliefs and norms that have traditionally bound individuals to their families. For instance, the collapse of popular support in the 1970s for religion-based prohibitions of premarital sex, which weakened the institution of marriage by permitting sex outside marriage, is one indication of the cultural changes associated with family modernization.

Larry Bumpass's 1990 presidential address to the Population Association of America is indicative of the way in which scholarly proponents of the family modernization perspective view the current state and future trajectory of American family life: "Family relationships occupy an important but ever shrinking space in our lives. . . . This is the continuation of a long-term process and is not confined to one country. Trends in cohabitation, marriage, fertility, and marital disruption are widely shared across Western industrial societies. To my mind, major causes include the individualizing tendency of participation in our economy and cultural values of individualization that both facilitate this process and are reinforced by it. There is no reason to think that these processes are exhausted or are likely to reverse" (Bumpass 1990:493).

Many religious institutions in the United States—especially conservative Protestant and Catholic ones—have played a central role in resisting the logic of family modernization, particularly cultural developments associated with family modernization. As Margaret Bendroth and Julie Hanlon Rubio argue in chapters 4 and 6, respectively, Catholic and especially evangelical Protestant churches, family organizations, and leaders have devoted a great deal of public and pastoral discourse—for example, sermons, books, radio shows, and pastoral letters—to the cause of family stability and family development (see also Wilcox 2004a).

The efforts of these religions on behalf of the family have been motivated in part by their traditions, which stress the sanctity of family life and the importance of maintaining fidelity to religion-grounded moral codes even if they become unpopular in the society at large (Wilcox 2004b). For instance, for almost a millennium the Catholic Church has taught that marriage is a sacrament that represents the covenantal relationship between Jesus and the church and conveys grace from God that enables spouses to grow in love for God and one another (May 1995; Witte 1997). The Catholic Church's collective self-understanding is oriented, in part, to a commitment to maintaining fidelity to its moral tradition. Moreover, its hierarchical organizational structure tends to reward clergy and bishops who maintain fidelity with this tradition. Consequently, the Catholic Church is willing to take unpopular stands on contested moral issues if its moral tradition seems to require those stands (Burns 1994; Chaves 1997). Thus, as Rubio observes in chapter 6, the Catholic Church's religious understanding of marriage, its regard for tradition, and its internal institutional character all help explain why this church has largely resisted the logic of family modernization on issues such as divorce, contraception, and premarital sex.

But religious institutions have also opposed the logic of family modernization because they benefit institutionally from strong and happy families. For instance, adults—especially men—who marry and have children are significantly more likely to attend religious services and involve themselves in religious congregations than adults who remain unmarried and childless (Stolzenberg, Blair-Loy, and Waite 1995; Wilcox 2002, 2005). Not surprisingly, other things being equal, religious traditions that include some type of familism in their moral belief system tend to flourish, more so than traditions that do not stress family values (Wilcox 2005). This helps to explain why so many religious rites and programs in religious traditions around the world focus on marriage, birth, and the moral formation of children. Accordingly, religious institutions have an institutional stake in strong families that often motivates them to resist the weakening of the family as an institution and to provide religious services to families.

Given the strong reciprocal relations of dependence between the institutions of family and religion, it is curious that mainline Protestantism, and especially its leading policy-making bodies, bureaucracies, and seminaries, has largely adopted an accommodationist stance toward family modernization. Neverthe-less, since the 1960s mainline institutions have generally welcomed or accepted gender egalitarianism and changes in family life—at least the ideological level (Browning 1995; Wilcox 2002).

The mainline approach to family and gender issues in the last half-century can be understood as a consequence of its religious orientation, its organiza-tional structure, and its membership. Throughout the twentieth century main-line Protestant denominations—which include the American Baptist Conven-tion, the Episcopal Church (USA), the Evangelical Lutheran Church of America, the Presbyterian Church (USA), the United Churches of Christ, and the United Methodist Church—have adapted a self-consciously progressive ori-entation to religious and moral truth. They have embraced a "modernistic mi-lieu" characterized by an openness to religious and moral change, a commit-ment to tolerance and civility in the face of religious and moral pluralism, respect for individual autonomy, and a high view of the intellectual assumptions associated with the Enlightenment (Riesebrodt 1993:87). This openness to the world, which these denominations regard as a willingness to see the Holy Spirit do a "new thing" in their churches, has encouraged mainline Protestant de-nominations and their leaders to embrace family diversity and the consequences of family modernization: stepfamilies, single parents, and—in most cases—divorce (Browning 2003a; Wilcox 2002).

Mainline Protestant accommodation to family change can also be under-stood as a consequence of its organizational structure and elite culture, as well as the sociocultural status of its members. The main line's centralized, repub-lican approach to authority and governance, which is clearly indebted to the democratic political culture of the United States, tends toward formally rational procedures and arguments, as opposed to the hierarchical, traditional approach to authority and government that largely orient Catholic institutions (Wilcox 2004b). This means that mainline leaders have no institutional ties to religious authorities who have a vested interest in the religious tradition itself or to au-thorities who hold a non-Western cultural outlook. Mainline leaders also tend to be well educated. The organizational structure of mainline churches and the educational background of mainline leaders help explain why these denominations tend to identify with the progressive family and gender ideologies articulated by elite cultural institutions in the United States (and, more generally, the West) such as universities, newspapers, and liberal advocacy organizations.

Finally, the progressive religious orientation of mainline Protestant churches has been largely congruent with the sociocultural profile of the mainline Protestant membership. For the latter half of the twentieth century, mainline Protestants tended to be better educated and more likely to come from the North and the east coast—factors that made them more open to a liberal social outlook (Roof and McKinney 1987; Wilcox 2004b). While lay members of mainline churches tend not to be as liberal as their clergy and denominational leaders, they do value tolerance and civility. Lay members also tend to be theologically liberal (Ammerman 1997). For these reasons mainline Protestant laity generally support or accede to the family- and gender-related innovations sponsored by their churches.

This is not to say that the main line's approach is entirely modern. In recent decades, at the congregational level, at the level of pastoral practice, the logic of "progressive familism" has emerged to replace the traditional familism that once oriented mainline churches (Wilcox 2002). This progressive familism is progressive in that it stresses equality between men and women and is familist in its pastoral focus on family life—especially the religious and moral education of children. Familism survives in the main line both because congregations have a measure of institutional distance from denominational bureaucracies and mainline seminaries and because family- and child-oriented programming and family-related pastoral discourse are key religious goods that mainline congregations have to offer their congregants.

Overall, the mainline approach to the family can be characterized as a form of Golden Rule liberalism, where much of the pastoral practice and discourse, especially at the congregational level, promotes a Golden Rule Christianity focused on family and community even as much of the main line's public discourse and some of its pastoral discourse, especially at the elite level, support a cultural logic of "expressive liberation" that rejects classical Protestant teaching on the family and promotes self-realization and the acceptance of a range of family configurations and sexual practices (Ammerman 1997; Wilcox 2002). In other words, the cultural contradiction at the heart of mainline Protestant family policy is that a child-centered, nuclear family orientation dominates the practical focus of congregational life even as mainline Protestant discourse is marked by a pronounced rejection of the familist ideology that has legitimated the child-centered, nuclear family in the United States for more than a century and a half. I outline this contradiction in greater detail as I first review the recent history of mainline Protestant discourse on family and gender, then summarize trends in attitudes toward family and gender among mainline Protestant laity, and conclude with an analysis of trends in divorce and maternal labor force participation among mainline Protestants.

INCLUSIVITY OVER FAMILISM

The 1950s marked the high-water mark of American familism, that is, the "set of both cognitive and normative assertions that interpret the family as *the* crucial social institution, both for the individual and the society as a whole" (P. Berger 1967:47). At the time the main line embraced this familism, which garnered support from virtually all sectors of society during this era. For instance, the 1956 Methodist General Conference described the family as the "bulwark of Christian faith" and celebrated increased family togetherness and rising birth-rates, even as it expressed concern about the church's failure to stem the surge in divorces following World War II. But when elite opinion turned against familism in the 1960s and 1970s, mainline seminaries, policy-making bodies, and bureaucracies also distanced themselves from the family-centered ideology that they had endorsed only a decade or two earlier. The main line's discursive rejection of familism can be understood in the context of its progressive orientation to social change, a commitment to inclusiveness and social justice sharpened by its involvement with the civil rights movement, its support for an egalitarian brand of feminism, and a therapeutic pastoral ethic that stressed personal fulfillment over adherence to traditional moral norms. Thus, in the wake of dramatic cultural and demographic shifts in family life in the late 1960s and the late 1970s, the main line moved quickly to demonstrate its commitment to a progressive approach to the changing American family—at least at the level of public discourse.

A 1976 pronouncement of the General Conference of the Methodist Church is indicative of the accommodationist public position that mainline Protestantism took to the logic of family modernization:

> We understand the family as encompassing a wider range of options than that of the two-generational unit of parents and children (the nuclear family), including the extended family, families with adopted children, single parents, couples without children. We urge social, economic, and religious efforts to maintain and strengthen families in order that every member may be assisted toward complete personhood. . . . In marriages where the partners are, even after thoughtful reconsideration and counsel, estranged beyond reconciliation, we recognize divorce and the right of divorced persons to remarry, and express our concern for the needs of the children of such unions. To this end we encourage an active, accepting, and enabling commitment of the Church and our society to minister to the needs of divorced persons.
>
> (*United Methodist Church Book of Discipline* 1976:71)

This statement is suggestive of the posture of acceptance and affirmation that the mainline Protestant churches were taking to family diversity. It also is indicative of the structural, rather than individual, stand it took to improving family life, insofar as the statement called for "social, economic, and religious efforts" but not individual efforts to strengthen family life. The statement also reflects changes in the Methodist Church's position on divorce over this period. Up to the 1960s the Methodist Church had allowed remarriage only in cases of adultery or abandonment. But by the time this statement was issued in 1976, the church had removed all pastoral barriers to divorce and remarriage and had committed itself to an "active, accepting, and enabling" ministry to the divorced (Morgan 1985). The theological and familistic categories of evaluation for family life that once oriented Methodist family policy were largely replaced by more progressive standards, which were influenced by the therapeutic and social justice currents of the period (Wilcox 2002).

This emphasis on acceptance and affirmation of family diversity has continued up to the present day. A 1999 survey of clergy in upstate New York found, for instance, that 85 percent of mainline clergy believed that "God approves of all kinds of families" (Edgell 2003). A 1999 survey of Presbyterian pastors found that 73 percent of these pastors think that the church should be "tolerant of family changes (divorce, remarriage, same-sex couples) now taking place" (Presbyterian Panel 1999). The main line's commitment to the liberal virtues of tolerance, inclusion, and equality, in addition to therapeutically motivated concerns about personal fulfillment and interpersonal authenticity, has also structured mainline discourse on sexuality, including homosexuality, along liberationist lines. One prominent example of this liberationist tendency in mainline thinking is the Presbyterian report "Keeping Body and Soul Together" (Special Committee 1991), which was drafted by a committee of leading clerics, seminary professors, denominational officials, and laypeople. In the name of "inclusive wholeness" and "justice-love," the report argued that a range of sexual relationships—from homosexual relationships to sexual friendships to heterosexual marriages—might embody the types of sexual and emotional intimacy, as well as equality, that meet its liberal and therapeutic standards of legitimacy. While this report and most proposals dealing with homosexuality have been rejected by churchwide legislative assemblies not yet ready to dispense with traditional Christian understandings of marriage, they do represent the thinking of key elites in the main line and of a substantial minority of clergy and laity. Thus the main line's embrace of elements of cultural modernity—tolerance, gender equality, the impulse to inclusion, and the therapeutic ethic—has led it to reject key dimensions of 1950s familism. Its acceptance of unconditional divorce and remarriage, as well as its affirmation of family pluralism, contradict the familist idealization of the nuclear family and its commitment to lifelong marriage.

This is not to say that the main line has entirely jettisoned the familistic logic. The main line also promotes a range of noncontroversial values that lend strength to the familial ethic of moral obligation that undergirds familism. Nancy Ammerman's extensive 1997 ethnographic study of mainline churches found that many of them foster a Golden Rule Christianity where noncontroversial values—honesty, kindness, and caring—are given social and supernatural sanction. The values associated with this Golden Rule Christianity fit well with the expressive character of contemporary family life. Moreover, mainline discourse about these values tends to anchor them in the context of family life, especially child rearing. In fact, one key reason that mainline Protestants attend church is to supply their children with exposure to religious and moral precepts that will lend meaning and purpose to their lives.

This child-centered focus is evident in a number of ways. More than 70 percent of mainline churches offer worship services especially designed to incorporate children into the corporate worship of the church—for example, biblical "story times" offered just before the main sermon (Wilcox 2002). This new interest in children's worship is indebted to the emphasis on inclusion in mainline churches, along with insights derived from developmental psychology (R. Browning and Reed 1998). According to the Christian educators David Ng and Virginia Thomas, "God's Kingdom is for all, and . . . God's love draws all together . . . children and adults worshiping together make the statement of faith" (R. Browning and Reed 1998:261). Virtually all mainline churches also offer Sunday school programs that impart basic religious and moral truths to children. In sum, the main line's embrace of cultural modernity in the wake of the social upheavals of the 1960s and 1970s led it to reject key aspects of 1950s familism—especially the notion that the "traditional" nuclear family is the cornerstone of a decent society—even as it has retained a Golden Rule ethical orientation and a child-centered focus that are largely congruent with the familism of the 1950s. This is partly why the mainline approach to the family might be described as exemplifying a kind of Golden Rule liberalism, where a caring, child-centered ethos coexists with ideological support for expressive liberation.

THE RISE OF EGALITARIANISM

Similar patterns can be seen in the main line's response to the changing status of women and, more generally, to the gender ideology that marked the latter half of the twentieth century. Although the main line had already moved away from a strong endorsement of male headship in the 1950s, it still supported clear distinctions between men's and women's roles in this period. The 1956 Methodist General Conference, for instance, expressed concerns about increases in working mothers (Wilcox 2002).

But in response to the rise of feminism in the late 1960s and early 1970s, and broader shifts in the status of women, the main line made a number of moves to signal its accommodation to the newly egalitarian ethos of the wider culture. Partly because the women's movement came to be seen as a logical extension of the civil rights movement, mainline churches were early and ardent supporters of key feminist goals, such as the Equal Rights Amendment and universal child care (Wilcox 2002). Perhaps more important, under pressure from internal feminist movements, mainline churches also reformed their internal life to promote greater gender equality. By 1976 all mainline churches had adopted policies in support of women's ordination, and the percentage of women in mainline seminaries surged more than 100 percent in the 1970s. This effort also extended to efforts to diversify mainline leadership: starting in the 1970s, women were elected to head mainline churches and institutions such as the United Presbyterian Church and the National Council of Churches (Chaves 1997).

This egalitarian commitment has also led mainline denominations to issue statements in support of gender equality in the home. Since 1972, for example, the United Methodist Church has passed a series of resolutions seeking the elimination of gender role stereotypes in work and family life (Schmidt and Murphy-Geiss 1996). In 1988 Methodist resolutions affirmed "shared responsibility for parenting by men and women" and rejected "social norms that assume different standards for women than for men in marriage" (Melton 1991:173). Judging by the survey of upstate New York clergy, this egalitarian ethic is also shared by mainline ministers: fewer than 10 percent of those surveyed agreed with a separate spheres ideology — "It's better for all if the man earns the money and the woman takes care of home/children" — or an explicitly patriarchal ideology — "It's God's will that the man is spiritual head of the family" (Edgell 2003:170).

This egalitarian drive in mainline Protestant churches has also affected the symbolic center of the Christian faith. The symbolic patriarchy of historic Christianity has been steadily deconstructed since the 1970s. Linguistic shifts in the world of mainline Protestantism signal the dramatic changes that have taken place in theology and pastoral practice. Churches in the mainline tradition are now much more likely to use gender-neutral language, and they are also more likely to incorporate images of God as mother into Sunday worship and everyday spirituality (Wilcox 2004b). For instance, the 1979 edition of the *Episcopal Book of Common Prayer* incorporated gender-neutral language and eliminated scriptural references to the subordination of women from its daily lectionary. Thus the main line has gone to great lengths to establish, symbolically at least, its commitment to gender equality.

Three cultural factors help account for this commitment. First, the main line has long maintained a self-conscious effort to adapt to important social changes. In this case mainline leaders believed that the dramatic increase in women's labor force participation and status meant that they had an obligation to recast the faith along egalitarian lines. In the words of the mainline social ethicist Max Stackhouse: "The rapid inclusion of women in the work force demands fresh attention to women's rights, to new patterns of shared responsibility in family life, and especially to those values which can guide women's newly discovered sense of extrafamilial vocation" (1985:997).

Second, the main line's commitment to a therapeutic ethic of self-realization and expressiveness has led it to reject gendered roles and hierarchies that might constrain the self or its interaction with others. This therapeutic emphasis can be seen in the Presbyterian report "Keeping Body and Soul Together," where egalitarian marriages are affirmed for their capacity to "enhance individual identity in the midst of deepening intimacy and interpersonal encounter" (Special Committee 1991:26). Most fundamentally, the main line's egalitarian stance toward gender flows from its commitment to the liberal project of modernity, especially the "notion that individuals have distinctive moral standing *qua individuals* and not as members of 'natural' groups [e.g., genders] . . . that possess certain 'natural' rights and functions" (Chaves 1997:192). Thus, once gender came to be framed as an illiberal and arbitrary criterion for discrimination in the broader society during the 1970s, the main line moved to recast its family-related gender discourse and its very symbolic foundations to signal its adherence to the canons of cultural modernity.

THE FAMILY-RELATED ATTITUDES AND PRACTICES OF MAINLINE LAITY

Mark Chaves has observed that often the official discourse of religious denominations is only "loosely coupled" to the beliefs and practices of the members of these denominations. Such discourse can function more as a source of collective identity, or as a signal to important internal or external constituencies in churches, than as a guide to the beliefs and practices of ordinary members of a denomination. In this case the main line's formal ideological commitment to gender egalitarianism and to an inclusive and accepting family ethic may have more to do with its desire to signal its commitment to the liberal project of modernity than to providing clear guidance to the beliefs and practices of its members.

Indeed, figure 3.1, which tracks the attitudes of mainline Protestants and average Americans to divorce from 1974 to 1998, suggests that the increasingly inclusive posture of official mainline institutions has not had much of an impact on their members. From 1974 to 1998 the percentage of mainline Protestants expressing the view that "divorce should be more difficult to obtain than it is now" rose from 49 percent to 54 percent. As the figure suggests, mainline views closely paralleled those of the population at large, which suggests that the mainline members are quite conventional in their approach to this family matter. Furthermore, active mainline Protestants (who attend several times a month or more) are markedly more familistic than average mainline Protestants (who simply indicate a mainline Protestant affiliation to survey interviewers). Thus, at least on this outcome, regular church attendance does not make mainline Protestants more tolerant of divorce, as we might expect. Rather, attendance is associated with higher levels of familism.

Figure 3.1 Trends in Attitudes toward Familism for Whole Population

Divorce should be more difficult to obtain than it is now (1974+)

	1970s	1980s	1990s
Active mainline Protestants	60	68	64
Mainline Protestants	49	58	54
National average (all Americans)	48	53	52

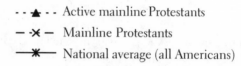

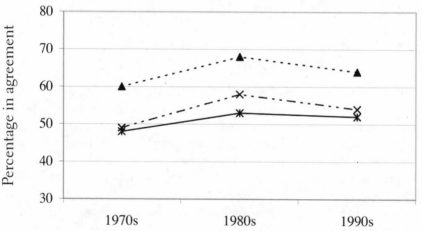

Sources: National Opinion Research Center 1972–98; Wilcox 2004b.

Figure 3.2, however, suggests that mainline Protestant views are moving in the direction of expressive liberation, a tendency suggested by at least some of the family-related discourse that has been coming from mainline leaders, intellectuals, and policy-making bodies. From 1972 to 1998 the percentage of mainline Protestants opposed to premarital sex fell from 30 percent to 21 percent. Indeed, mainline Protestants are more liberal on this measure of familism than average Americans. Once again, however, active mainline Protestants continue to be more familistic than mainline Protestants as a whole—with 34 percent of active mainline Protestants opposing premarital sex in the 1990s, compared to 21 percent of all mainline Protestants. Thus we have more evidence that church attendance does not make mainline Protestants less familistic; it seems to make them more familistic. Nevertheless, it still is striking that a

Figure 3.2 Trends in Attitudes toward Premarital Sex for Whole Population

Sexual relations before marriage is always wrong (1972 +)

	1970s	1980s	1990s
Active mainline Protestants	43	34	34
Mainline Protestants	30	23	21
National average (all Americans)	32	28	26

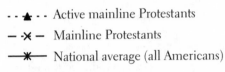

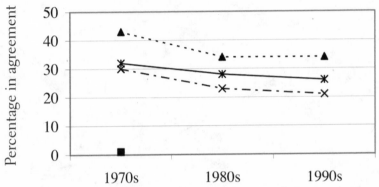

Sources: National Opinion Research Center 1972–98; Wilcox 2004b.

majority of active mainline Protestants openly reject the classical Protestant teaching on premarital sex.

Figure 3.3 provides evidence of a closer coupling between the official ideology promulgated by mainline Protestant institutions and the views of the men and women in the pews. From the 1970s to the 1990s mainline Protestants became markedly less likely to support the notion that it is "better if the man is the achiever outside the home and the woman takes care of the home and family"—with 68 percent of mainline Protestants holding this view in the 1970s and 35 percent taking this view in the 1990s. Obviously, their views closely followed the national pattern during this period, providing more evidence of the conventional character of mainline Protestant thinking regarding family and gender. Figure 3.3 also suggests that active mainline Protestants were slightly less egalitarian than average mainline Protestants in the 1980s and 1990s. Thus, despite the pronounced support for egalitarianism from mainline leaders,

Figure 3.3 Trends in Attitudes for Gender Role Traditionalism for
Whole Population

Better if the man is the achiever outside home and the woman takes care of
home/family (1977+)

	1970s	1980s	1990s
Active mainline Protestants	67	47	40
Mainline Protestants	68	42	35
National average (all Americans)	66	46	37

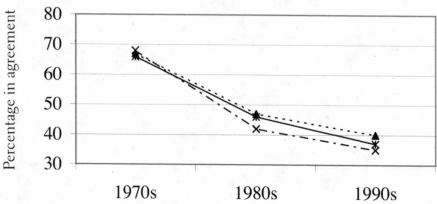

Sources: National Opinion Research Center 1972–98; Wilcox 2004b.

the most active mainline Protestants are slightly less likely to take an egalitarian position on the household division of labor.

Figure 3.4 also suggests that the attitudes of mainline Protestants have become closely coupled with the official ideology of mainline institutions in recent years—at least when it comes to gender attitudes. In the 1970s, 70 percent of mainline Protestants affirmed the belief that "a preschool child is likely to suffer if his or her mother works," but by the 1990s only 44 percent of mainline Protestants took this view. As the figure shows, the attitudinal trends for this outcome among active mainline Protestants and average Americans parallel those found among mainline Protestants as a whole. This provides additional evidence that mainline Protestant gender attitudes are quite conventional.

In sum, figures 3.1 through 3.4 suggest that the familist attitudes of mainline

Figure 3.4 Trends in Attitudes toward Working Mothers for Whole Population
Agree that a preschool child is likely to suffer if his or her mother works (1977 +)

	1970s	1980s	1990s
Active mainline Protestants	72	52	47
Mainline Protestants	70	51	44
National average (all Americans)	67	51	45

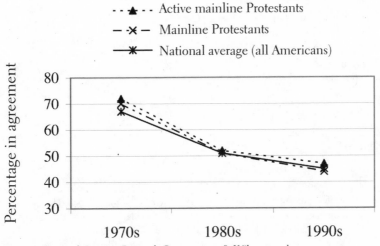

Sources: National Opinion Research Center 1972–98; Wilcox 2004b.

Protestants are only loosely coupled to the official ideology promoted by main-line institutions, especially because they are markedly more conservative on divorce than the public pronouncements of mainline elites and policy-making bodies would suggest, and that active mainline Protestants tend more toward familism than average mainline Protestants. However, when it comes to gender role ideology, mainline Protestants have moved strongly toward egalitarianism in ways that are in keeping with the official positions of their denominations. But for both familism and gender role traditionalism, the trends displayed in figures 3.1 through 3.4 suggest that broader trends in society have influenced mainline attitudes more than the pronouncements of their churches. In other words, mainline Protestants seem to be governed more by social convention than their churches when it comes to their family and gender views.

What about practice? Model 1 in table 3.1 suggests a striking pattern. It turns out that average mainline Protestants and active mainline Protestants have the *lowest* divorce rates of any large religious or secular group in the United States.

Table 3.1 Percentage Change in Likelihood of Divorce
by Religious Tradition (1987–1994)

	Model 1 Without controls	Model 2 With controls[a]
Mainline Protestant	-39^*	-20
Conservative Protestant	-21	-10
Catholic	-35^{**}	-18
Jewish	-33	39
Other	-45^{**}	-41^{***}
Active mainline Protestant	-54^*	-35^{**}
Nominal mainline Protestant	-37^{***}	-11
Active conservative Protestant	-44^*	-35^{**}
Nominal conservative Protestant	15	20
Active Catholic	-50^*	-31^{***}
Nominal Catholic	-13	-5
Active Jewish	-99	-97
Nominal Jewish	-23	53
Active other	-53^{**}	-48^{***}
Nominal other	-31	-29

$^*\ p < 0.1;\ ^{**}\ p < 0.05.;\ ^{***}\ p < 0.01.$

[a]These models control for age, gender, race, ethnicity, education, and region.

Note: Approximately 9 percent of married Americans divorced from 1987 to 1994. The comparison category here is unaffiliated married Americans. Table values are percentage changes in odds associated with each religious tradition as derived from logistic regression analyses $(\exp(B) - 1) \times 100$. Active religious affiliation refers to attending several times a month or more. Nominal religious affiliation refers to respondents who attend less than several times a month or more.

Source: Sweet and Bumpass 1996.

Using data from two waves of the National Survey of Families and Households (1988–93), I find that they are, respectively, 39 percent less likely and 54 percent less likely to divorce than unaffiliated Americans. (Note that 9 percent of married Americans divorced from 1988 to 1993, according to this survey.) Average conservative Protestants and active conservative Protestants are, respectively, only 21 percent and 44 percent less likely to divorce than unaffiliated Americans. And average Catholics and active Catholics are, respectively, 35 percent and 50 percent less likely to divorce than unaffiliated Americans.

But model 2 of table 3.1 suggests that distinctive mainline divorce patterns are largely a consequence of the superior socioeconomic status of its members. Once I control for socioeconomic factors, the mainline religious edge disappears. Nevertheless, it is still the case that active mainline Protestants are 35 percent less likely to divorce than unaffiliated Americans, after controlling for socioeconomic factors. Here, however, they have no significant edge over their Catholic and conservative Protestant peers.

Why does mainline Protestants' superior socioeconomic status help account for their lower divorce rates? The literature on the family suggests that people with more education and income are less likely to experience the stresses (poverty, unemployment, job difficulties) that can undermine a marriage (Schoen et al. 2002). This literature also suggests that men and women with higher levels of education have better communication skills (Kohn 1977). So, one of the primary reasons that mainline Protestants are more likely to enjoy marital stability than other Americans is that they benefit from higher levels of socioeconomic status. Still, this pattern is striking because mainline institutions take the *most* permissive stand on divorce of any large religious tradition in the United States.

Similar patterns are apparent in table 3.2, which examines the association between religious tradition and the odds of full-time work among married mothers with children aged eighteen and younger at home. (Note that about 39 percent of married American women with children worked full time from 1992 to 1994, according to the National Survey of Families and Households.) Model 1 of table 3.2 suggests that married Catholic and mainline Protestant mothers are both more than 25 percent less likely to work full time than unaffiliated mothers. Once I control for socioeconomic differences in model 2, mainline and conservative Protestant mothers are both about 30 percent less likely to work full time than unaffiliated Americans. So, for both outcomes, married mainline Protestant mothers come close to registering the lowest rates of full-time work of any large religious or secular group of married mothers.

The pattern becomes even more pronounced when we look at active mainline Protestant married mothers. With and without controls for socioeconomic status, they are the group of married mothers consistently the least likely to work full time outside the home. In model 1 active mainline Protestant mothers are 43 percent less likely than unaffiliated mothers to work full time—whereas 27 percent of active conservative Protestants and 33 percent of active Catholics are less likely than unaffiliated mothers to work full time. In model 2, which controls for socioeconomic status, active mainline Protestant mothers are 48 percent less likely to work full time than unaffiliated mothers—compared to active conservative Protestants (40 percent) and active Catholics (29 percent), who are, respectively, 40 percent and 29 percent less likely that unaffiliated mothers to work outside the home. Thus table 3.2 conveys the striking pattern that mainline Protestant women who are married and have children—especially women who attend church several times a month or more—are significantly less likely to work full time than are women from some other large religious and secular groups. This is striking, of course, in light of the pronounced institutional and lay support for gender equality found in mainline Protestant churches.

Table 3.2 Percentage Change in Likelihood of Married Mothers Working Full
Time, by Religious Tradition (1992–1994)

	Model 1 Without controls	Model 2 With controls[a]
Mainline Protestant	−26[*]	−29[*]
Conservative Protestant	−20	−31[*]
Catholic	−27[*]	−18
Jewish	−52[*]	−48[*]
Other	−29[***]	−34[*]
Active mainline Protestant	−43[**]	−48[**]
Nominal mainline Protestant	−3	−1
Active conservative Protestant	−27[*]	−40[**]
Nominal conservative Protestant	4	−1
Active Catholic	−33[*]	−29[*]
Nominal Catholic	−14	4
Active Jewish	−55	−47
Nominal Jewish	−50[*]	−48[*]
Active Other	−23	−29
Nominal Other	−37	−39

[*] $p < 0.05$; [**] $p < 0.01$; [***] $p < 0.1$.
[a]These models control for age, gender, race, ethnicity, education, income, and region.

Note: Approximately 39 percent of married American women with children worked full time during the survey period (1992–94). The comparison category here is unaffiliated married Americans. Table values are percentage changes in odds associated with each religious tradition, as derived from logistic regression analyses ($\exp(B) − 1$) × 100. Active religious affiliation refers to attending several times a month or more. Nominal religious affiliation refers to respondents who attend less than several times a month.

Source: Sweet and Bumpass 1996.

WALKING RIGHT, TALKING LEFT

In recent years a number of intellectuals who generally support the project of liberal modernity—from the theologian Don Browning to the political theorist William Galston to the sociologist Brigitte Berger—have argued that political and civic liberalism depends, in part, on strong families (Browning 2003b; B. Berger 2002; Galston 1991). Pointing to a wide range of social scientific studies on children and families, they note that children are much more likely to acquire the virtues of self-control, deliberation, independence, and solidarity that liberalism requires if they grow up in a child-centered, intact, married family. Indeed, Brigitte Berger (2002:xiii) argues that the "conventional [nuclear] family, with its emphasis on personal autonomy, responsibility, [and] individual freedom," has played and continues to play a central role in the growth of freedom, equality, and opportunity in the West.

As we have shown, mainline Protestants—especially active ones—seem also to recognize implicitly that the best way they can serve their children and their communities is by staying married and investing heavily in child rearing. In the way that they approach marriage and parenting, they also appear to be drawing on the mores and examples of their forebears, who, like them, drew heavily on the moral rectitude associated with mainline Protestantism's Golden Rule Christianity. As one recent Presbyterian report on family life observed, "Most Presbyterians . . . were once children in the white, middle- and upper-income families of the 1950s and have been able to repeat that family form themselves" (Browning 2003a:8). Finally, mainline Protestants are also able to live a comparatively traditional, family-centered lifestyle because they have the education and the material resources to do so.

The irony is that mainline Protestant laity and especially mainline Protestant institutions generally do not preach what they practice. As we have shown, the public discourse from mainline Protestant churches on family- and gender-related issues has moved sharply away from the familistic and traditional tenor of the 1950s. While the mainline laity has become slightly more conservative on divorce since the 1970s, it has otherwise adopted a progressive approach to sexual morality and gender issues. Thus at the ideological level mainline Protestantism has largely accommodated itself to the logic of family modernization. The symbolic liberalism of mainline Protestant churches can be understood by their regional ties to the North and the East Coast, the high levels of socioeconomic status found among their clergy and laity, the nationally oriented representative character of their institutions, and their modernist religious orientation. All these factors foster a progressive family outlook among mainline clergy and laity.

Thus the Golden Rule liberalism found in mainline Protestant churches is marked by deep cultural contradictions between family practices and family-related ideologies. Mainline Protestants take a fairly traditional approach to family life, an approach that ensures that they, their children, and their communities garner the social, economic, and civic benefits associated with strong families. But they do not embrace the ideology of familism because it has fallen out of favor in the social and intellectual circles they travel in. As Wade Clark Roof has observed, mainline churches "are open theologically to family diversity yet on the whole are bastions of familism" (Roof 1999:251). As demographic change and family controversies continue to roil American society, it will be interesting to see whether and how mainline Protestant churches attempt to address the tension between their progressive ideological commitments and their traditional family practices.

REFERENCES

Ammerman, Nancy Tatom. 1997. "Golden Rule Christianity: Lived Religion in the American Mainstream." In *Lived Religion in America: Toward a History of Practice*. Edited by David Hall. Princeton, N.J.: Princeton University Press.

Berger, Brigitte. 2002. *The Family in the Modern Age: More Than a Lifestyle Choice*. New Brunswick, N.J.: Transaction.

Berger, Peter. 1967. "Religious Institutions." In *Sociology: An Introduction*. Edited by Neil Smelser. New York: John Wiley and Sons.

Browning, Don. 1995. "Religion and Family Ethics: A New Strategy for the Church." In *Work, Family, and Religion in Contemporary Society*. Edited by Nancy Tatom Ammerman and Wade Clark Roof. New York: Routledge.

———. 2003a. "Empty Inclusivism." *Christian Century*, 28 June, 8–9.

———. 2003b. *Marriage and Modernization: How Globalization Threatens Marriage and What to Do about It*. Grand Rapids, Mich.: Eerdmans.

Browning, Robert L., and Roy A. Reed. 1998. "Families and Worship." In *The Family Handbook*. Edited by Herbert Anderson, Don Browning, Ian Evison, and Mary Stewart Van Leeuwen. Louisville, Ky.: Westminster John Knox Press.

Bumpass, Larry L. 1990. "What's Happening to the Family? Interactions between Demographic and Institutional Change." *Demography* 27:483–98.

Burns, Gene. 1994. *The Frontiers of Catholicism: The Politics of Ideology in a Liberal World*. Berkeley: University of California Press.

Chaves, Mark. 1997. *Ordaining Women: Culture and Conflict in Religious Organizations*. Cambridge, Mass.: Harvard University Press.

Edgell, Penny. 2003. "In Rhetoric and in Practice: Defining 'the Good Family' in Local Congregations." In *The Handbook for the Sociology of Religion*. Edited by Michelle Dillon. New York: Cambridge University Press.

Galston, William. 1991. *Liberal Purposes: Goods, Virtues, and Diversity in the Liberal State*. New York: Cambridge University Press.

Kohn, Melvin L. 1977. *Class and Conformity: A Study in Values*. Chicago: University of Chicago Press.

May, William E. 1995. *Marriage: The Rock on Which the Family Is Built*. San Francisco: Ignatius Pres.

Melton, J. Gordon. 1991. *The Churches Speak on Sex and Family Life*. Detroit: Gale Research.

Morgan, Richard Lyon. 1985. *Is There Life after Divorce in the Church?* Atlanta: John Knox Press.

National Opinion Research Center. 1972–98. General Social Survey. www.norc.uchicago.edu/projects/gensoc.asp.

Popenoe, David. 1988. *Disturbing the Nest: Family Change and Decline in Modern Societies*. Hawthorne, N.Y.: Aldine de Gruyter.

Presbyterian Panel. 1999. "Public Role of Presbyterians." Office of Research, Presbyterian Church of the United States of America, Louisville, Ky.

Riesebrodt, Martin. 1993. *Pious Passion: The Emergence of Modern Fundamentalism in the United States and Iran*. Translated by Don Reneau. Berkeley: University of California Press.

Roof, Wade Clark. 1999. *Spiritual Marketplace: Baby Boomers and the Remaking of American Religion*. Princeton, N.J.: Princeton University Press.

Roof, Wade Clark and William McKinney. 1987. *American Mainline Religion: Its Changing Shape and Future*. New Brunswick, N.J.: Rutgers University Press.

Schmidt, Jean Miller and Gail E. Murphy-Geiss. 1996. "Methodist: 'Tis Grace Will Lead Us Home." In *Faith Traditions and the Family*. Edited by Phyllis D. Airhart and Margaret Lamberts Bendroth. Louisville, Ky.: Westminster John Knox Press.

Schoen, Robert et al. 2002. "Women's Employment, Marital Happiness, and Divorce." *Social Forces* 81(2): 643–62.

Special Committee on Human Sexuality. 1991. "Keeping Body and Soul Together." Report to the 203rd General Assembly, Presbyterian Church USA, www.pcusa.org/ogaresources/human-sexuality1991.pdf.

Stolzenberg, Ross M., Mary Blair-Loy, and Linda J. Waite. 1995. "Religious Participation in Early Adulthood: Age and Family Life Cycle Effects on Church Membership." *American Sociological Review* 60:84–103.

Sweet, James A. and Larry L. Bumpass. 1996. The National Survey of Families and Households—Waves 1 and 2: Data Description and Documentation. Center for Demography and Ecology, University of Wisconsin–Madison, www.ssc.wisc.edu/nsfh/home.htm.

United Methodist Church Book of Discipline. 1976. Nashville, Tenn.: Cokesbury.

Wilcox, W. Bradford. 2002. "For the Sake of the Children? Mainline Protestant Family-Related Discourse and Practice." In *The Quiet Hand of God: Faith-Based Activism and the Public Role of Mainline Protestantism*. Edited by Robert Wuthnow and John H. Evans. Berkeley: University of California Press.

———. 2004a. "Focused on the Family? Religious Traditions, Family Discourse, and Pastoral Practice." *Journal for the Scientific Study of Religion* 43:491–504.

———. 2004b. *Soft Patriarchs, New Men: How Christianity Shapes Fathers and Husbands*. Chicago: University of Chicago Press.

———. 2005. "Together Bound: Church, Sect, and the Family." In *Handbook of Religion and Social Institutions*. Edited by Helen Rose Ebaugh. New York: Springer.

Witte, John. 1997. *From Sacrament to Contract: Marriage, Religion, and Law in the Western Tradition*. Louisville, Ky.: Westminster John Knox Press.

CHAPTER 4

Evangelicals, Family, and Modernity

MARGARET BENDROTH

For many evangelicals family defines their sense of separation from—and of belonging to—the modern world. Indeed, if the rhetoric of groups like Focus on the Family, Promise Keepers, and Concerned Women for America is any indication, to be evangelical in American society today is to be "profamily." Though that term is sometimes ill defined, it has proved itself to be an immensely useful badge of evangelical identity, allowing conservative Protestants to proclaim their rejection of mainstream American society and at the same time to emphatically embrace the values of the heartland.

It was not always thus, of course. In the larger scheme of things, evangelicals are relative latecomers to the family agenda; historically, a public commitment to Christian domesticity has been much more typical of twentieth-century mainline Protestants. From the late-nineteenth century on into the midtwentieth, the pious Christian home aptly symbolized the mainstream position of white liberal denominations in American society. Faith in happy families reached an apotheosis of sorts in the 1950s, when countless mainline books and sermons proclaimed a causal link between Christian faith and domestic tranquility. In stark contrast, up through the 1960s conservatives celebrated the "old-fashioned" home mostly as a bulwark against immorality, always insisting on the primary importance of individual salvation.[1] The modern evangelical movement and its profamily agenda did not emerge on the national stage until the mid-1970s, with the election of Southern Baptist layman Jimmy Carter and the rise of the New Right in Ronald Reagan's 1980 campaign for the presidency.

But the perception that conservative Protestants were sole owners of family-related issues also reflected increasing disillusionment with the traditional family agenda among socially active mainline Protestants. As liberals moved away from familist theology and practice, evangelicals became increasingly identified in the public mind, and in their own perception, as ardent culture warriors, united in their dedication to the preservation of traditional family values against long cultural odds.

Given this recent history, it is tempting to paint American evangelicals as a model of resistance to secular individualism, especially in contrast to the more accommodating response of theological and social liberals. Certainly their family ethic is not hard to identify: most Americans know that "family values" describes a nexus of conservative positions on abortion, homosexuality, and the role of women. And certainly many evangelicals see themselves in this same antithetical mold. For many conservative Protestants there is simply no denying that, as one author put it, "the political arena is brimming with secularists seeking every opportunity to defame Christ and deny Christians their rights."[2] Though in terms of income and education most evangelicals are now solidly middle class, they often act as though they are still the poorer cousins of mainline Protestant churches. On their own mental maps, at least, evangelicals remain socially marginal, trudging doggedly against the grain of the dominant culture.

But a great deal of recent scholarly work has called this confrontational image into question. The current picture is broader and more nuanced than popular stereotypes allow, and it emphasizes the deep contradictions in the evangelical stance toward modern culture. The most obvious example concerns the use of electronic media, especially the technologically sophisticated web of satellite and cable television programming, syndicated radio broadcasting, and Internet resources that evangelicals have used to proclaim their nostalgia for the traditional family. Moreover, as recent scholarship has shown, evangelical resistance has taken different forms, depending on the issue at hand. Sometimes conservative Protestant leaders use vigorously confrontational rhetoric aimed at overturning federal laws countenancing abortion and homosexuality. And at other times evangelicals sound almost libertarian, demanding private space to raise and educate their children without governmental intrusion.

This chapter focuses on two important reasons why this is so, tracing the historical experience of evangelicals in modern American society and the movement's ongoing struggle to define and maintain its boundaries. Both dynamics make it clear that evangelicals are neither cultural resisters nor capitulators; they are in fact an odd combination of both, reflecting the famously difficult biblical call to be "in the world but not of it." As other chapters in this book make clear, conservative Protestants are not the only religious group in the United States to fill this ambiguous slot. Jeffrey Meyer's chapter on Chinese immigrants and Raymond Williams's description of "transnational" Hindu families (chapters 10 and 12, respectively) depict the complex struggles of people caught quite literally between two worlds. But by virtue of their historically influential role in twentieth-century American religious institutions, evangelicals have become a leading voice in the ongoing family debate. Their contribution is not always easily received: as the final section of this chapter suggests, the ambivalence of conservative Protestants toward American culture has made them difficult partners in large-scale national debates about marriage, sexuality, and the future of the traditional family.[3]

DEFINING EVANGELICALS

It is now customary to begin any discussion of present-day evangelicals with a ritual stab at defining them. They represent a broad range of American Protestant denominations and parachurch groups, about fifty million Americans.[4] Minimally, evangelicals hold to four basic theological propositions: the primacy of biblical authority, the necessity of conversion, the exclusivity of salvation through Jesus, and a mandate for activism in the world. The definition is theologically neat but otherwise cumbersome, lumping together rural Mennonites, suburban Dutch Calvinists, urban black Pentecostals, and Southern Baptists (and catching a surprising number of mainline Protestants and Roman Catholics in the process). Moreover, in the United States today evangelical ranks also contain a growing number of nonwhite and non-Western adherents, reflecting a long history of missionary outreach as well as a deep resonance in many immigrant communities with conservative Protestant ideals. Any simple definition is further complicated by the fact that evangelicalism is not a denomination or a single institution but a movement with a shifting center, constantly giving rise to a seemingly endless variety of megachurch and parachurch organizations.[5]

The largest patch of common ground is probably historical, centering on a shared sense of grievance against the perceived secular trajectory of American society. This adversarial relationship to American culture is a legacy of the movement's fundamentalist past. Fundamentalism emerged in the late nineteenth century as a coalition of like-minded and mostly northern white Protestants who were frustrated with the accommodationist tilt toward Darwinism and the higher criticism of the Bible within their home denominations. In the first few decades of the twentieth century, the movement failed to eradicate theological modernism in established Protestant institutions, with the Scopes trial of 1925 marking a significant public defeat. But in the long run fundamentalism proved itself a durable, and increasingly popular, alternative to religious liberalism. During the 1930s and 1940s conservative Protestant schools, missionary agencies, and evangelistic institutions grew apace, creating a vigorous religious subculture, beyond the purview of most cultural elites. Indeed, as the historian George Marsden has noted, fundamentalist ambivalence toward the dominant culture made it a congenial form of Americanism for many immigrant groups in the early twentieth century, drawing in allies among Swedish Baptists, Dutch Reformed, and German Missouri Synod Lutherans.[6]

The modern evangelical movement is a diverse coalition of like-minded conservative Protestants, and many—especially those from Holiness and Pentecostal denominations or more recent immigrant groups—have no direct historical connection to early twentieth-century fundamentalism. Yet to a large degree the general cross section of present-day evangelicals remains deeply affected by that movement's separatist spirit. Many conservative Protestants are not, of course, technically outsiders—they are generally white and middle class, in many ways the heirs of the great tradition of nineteenth-century Protestantism. But they are historically ambivalent toward American culture, which they see as both a doomed, sinful enterprise and occupying a land uniquely blessed by God. Consequently, when evangelicals talk about national affairs, they sometimes use a language of ownership and sometimes one of denunciation—a contradiction that the historian Mark Noll describes as "proprietary sectarianism." Put more simply, evangelicals may wish to be left alone, but they will not tolerate being ignored.[7]

GREAT REVERSALS

This ambiguity, and the absence of strong institutional borders, means that symbolic boundaries have proved enormously important in shaping evangelical identity in recent decades. Since the 1970s a succession of social as well as ecclesiastical and theological issues—the inerrancy of the Bible, the question of speaking in tongues, women's ordination, opposition to abortion, and now the nature of God's sovereignty—have constantly roiled evangelical churches. The almost ritualized nature of regular theological combat suggests that evangelical public controversy serves a productive purpose, as a means of winnowing the faithful and strengthening their allegiance to the larger cause. In this respect the profamily movement has played a central role in defining what it means to be an evangelical in modern secular society.

During the 1970s and 1980s family issues headed a new political agenda that propelled evangelicals into the public spotlight. Much of the impetus came as a reaction to the 1973 *Roe v. Wade* decision legalizing abortion, read as a signal that the U.S. government was no longer willing to place limits on sexual morality. In 1980 antiabortion leaders sparked the "profamily" movement by staging a walkout from Jimmy Carter's White House Conference on American Families. Objecting to the plural form of the noun (the demand was for a name change to the singular, that is, the American *family*), they launched an enormously successful campaign to fight the inroads of secular humanism in American public institutions.[8]

The overall tone was negative but hardly antimodern. Religious conservatives had been organizing opposition to sex education curricula since the early 1960s, and by the 1970s they had become adept at using the latest communications technology to spread their moral message. In many ways this technological sophistication was a direct function of the movement's religious zeal and social alienation. Fundamentalist preachers had made wide use of radio since its birth in the 1920s and 1930s; just as quickly, missionaries realized the power of gospel radio to transcend physical barriers that had once limited their access. In the television era, when preferential treatment to mainline Protestants blocked conservatives' access to federally mandated free air time, angry outsiders learned to become expert fund-raisers. By the 1970s vigorous entrepreneurs like Pat Robertson and Oral Roberts were among the first to enter the emerging cable television market. By 1975 Robertson's CBN programming was reaching an estimated 110 million viewers on about twelve hundred cable systems. Two years later CBN became one of the first cable networks in the country to own its own satellite and began offering a twenty-four-hour schedule of evangelistic programming. Not surprisingly, moral and political issues soon began to dominate the evangelical airwaves, creating a ready constituency for the political mobilization of conservative Protestants in the 1980s.[9]

The political successes of the religious right in the Reagan era marked a distinct departure for the normally quiescent evangelical rank-and-file. But the long-term trajectory of this so-called great reversal was open to question. The New Right campaign, led by Jerry Falwell, Pat Robertson, and an array of Washington-based political action committees, peaked with the election of Ronald Reagan in 1980 but came to a fairly decisive halt when Robertson, who rode a desk during the Korean War, claimed to have been a "combat marine." The embarrassment (as well as the financial and sex scandals involving the televangelists Jim Bakker and Jimmy Swaggart), coupled with the relative lack of concrete results during the Reagan era, especially in regard to *Roe v. Wade*, led to some deep rethinking of political strategy. In particular, the publication of Ed Dobson and Cal Thomas's internal jeremiad, *Blinded by Might: Can the Religious Right Save America?* signaled persistent doubts about the moral ambiguities of secular politics, misgivings probably first formed in the movement's fundamentalist past.[10]

Evangelical disillusionment with American public institutions found vigorous expression in the homeschooling movement. The 1972 Supreme Court decision in *Wisconsin v. Yoder*, recognizing the right of Amish parents to exempt their teenagers from attending high school, opened the way for evangelical parents to exercise more direct control over the intellectual and social environment of their young children. By 2000 an estimated one million students, the vast majority of them from evangelical families, were being educated at home.[11] Though Christian schools also grew at a rapid clip in the 1980s and 1990s, accounting for about 35 percent of all American schools by the 1990s, they did not satisfy most homeschooling advocates, who argued that even a specially designed curriculum could never replace direct parental oversight. As the historian Colleen McDannell has noted, military metaphors appear frequently in homeschool curricula, reflecting parents' sense that they are engaged in a pitched battle against the forces of secularism for the hearts and minds of their children. But in practice homeschooling does not simply replace secular subjects with religious ones; as McDannell explains, home-based education allows parents to "redefine humanistic, secular values" into categories that Christians can affirm. Home operates as a cultural filter, separating children from the world and shaping their intellectual understanding within a quietly separate space, protected from the insistent push of secular institutions.[12]

When Ronald Reagan left the White House, the evangelical political agenda was far from finished. Survey evidence suggests that the 1990s saw a successful political mobilization of conservative white Protestants, a constituency that was already heavily Republican but generally far less active than its nonreligious counterparts. A new wave of evangelical political involvement began with the rebirth of the Christian Coalition during that decade. Under more patient, savvy leadership, coalition leaders began a long-term grassroots effort aimed at maintaining a conservative Christian voice in the public realm. They have also broadened the profamily agenda to include economic issues and some forms of social welfare advocacy. The Christian Coalition has even attempted to reach out to conservatives within the African American, Jewish, and Roman Catholic communities, though with more limited success.[13]

Undeniably, family issues have energized a powerful shift in the evangelical political and social agenda. By the late 1990s conservative Protestants appeared to be far more enthusiastic about civic engagement than their mainline and liberal counterparts, a surprising reversal of their historical positions. According one recent sociological study, 68 percent of evangelicals agreed that "religion should speak to public issues," while only 48 percent of main liners and 37 percent of religious liberals were similarly convinced. Evangelicals are not, however, simply moving to the center and assuming the cultural prerogatives that main liners once enjoyed. Social engagement among conservatives has a definite edge, a sense of embattlement against the perceived intrusion of government and popular culture into two key areas of private life, the sanctity of the home and the education of young children.[14]

Today in the public realm evangelicals still cut a fairly clear profile on family matters. The Web sites of groups like Concerned Women for America and Focus on the Family target a predictable range of "below the belt" issues: pornography, homosexuality (specifically, domestic partner benefits), and abortion rights. Evangelicals also promote a more positive roster of causes, including funding for public education, the protection of free religious speech and the rights of homeschoolers, and faith-based efforts to promote marriage. In their present form many evangelical organizations are not directly confrontational;

they regularly monitor doings on Capitol Hill and work primarily through Internet resources, mass mailings, books, and magazines to educate and mobilize their constituency. Most often they advocate rather low-level forms of political action, such as writing to members of Congress or starting study groups. Still, it would be difficult to identify just one mode of evangelical engagement in public issues; depending on the circumstances, they may be intensely committed to a wholesale moral reworking of American society or, just as emphatically, thoroughly disillusioned with the entire project.

SOFTER, KINDER EVANGELICALS?

But by an even more concrete form of measurement—money—political warfare is not a top evangelical priority. In a major assessment of budget figures from conservative Protestant institutions, the historian Michael Hamilton notes that "for every dollar evangelicals spend on political organizations, they spend almost $12 on foreign missions and international relief and development; they spend another $13 in evangelical book and music stores; they spend almost $25 on evangelical higher education; and they spend almost $31 on private elementary and secondary schools." Making the point even more plainly, Hamilton concludes that "evangelicals spend more on summer camps than on politics, more on urban rescue missions than on politics, and more on youth programs than on politics."[15] Like most Americans, perhaps, evangelicals prefer to use voluntary and charitable solutions to moral and social problems, not legislation.

Current sociological research reaffirms this softer profile of evangelical social engagement. In his study of so-called ordinary evangelicals, the sociologist Christian Smith finds significant differences between the rank-and-file churchgoer and the leadership of the New Right. The "vast majority" of the self-identified evangelicals interviewed by Smith's team held to a "civil, tolerant, and noncoercive view of the world around them." Indeed, Smith argues that "relatively few ordinary evangelicals, though they are clearly traditionalists, have any serious interest in culture wars." "In the end," he writes, most of them "believe and invest in building personal relationships, sharing their faith politely, setting good examples, and hoping the unbelieving world will see the truth and voluntarily respond with a changed heart."[16] Other studies by Smith and his colleagues have failed to unearth much passion for a narrowly defined family-values agenda among evangelicals or a lock-step unity in beliefs about the structure and purpose of godly families.

Part of the reason for the lack of unity is that evangelicals tend to prefer individualistic solutions to social problems. This dichotomy emerges most clearly in the evangelical understanding of racial prejudice, which was documented by a recent study by Christian Smith and Michael Emerson. Most respondents agreed that racism was a matter best handled through interpersonal means, by being kind and polite to people of different racial backgrounds—not by political confrontation. Though this predilection doesn't necessarily distinguish evangelicals from the majority of white Americans, the tendency to minimize racial issues by personalizing them suggests that on some social issues, evangelicals find it difficult, if not impossible, to oppose the status quo.[17]

They are far more aggressive on family matters. Indeed, according to the most recent research data, being evangelical makes a definite difference in the theory and practice of family life. Conservatives, for example, are demonstrably less prone to divorce than are other Protestants, though evangelicals have become increasingly tolerant of divorced people who wish to remarry or assume positions of church leadership. The difference mounts among those who are the most actively involved in church activities. Only 4 percent of self-proclaimed evangelicals interviewed in a major study during the mid-1990s were divorced, compared with 7 percent of mainline and 10 percent of liberal Protestants. Allowing for social factors like income and education, at least part of the reason for the difference was a strongly articulated ethic against divorce for reasons of personal fulfillment. In fact, about 70 percent of divorced evangelicals surveyed would not countenance marital separation on purely emotional grounds. Not only are evangelical marriages statistically strong, they also show high commitment to parenting. Evangelical fathers, for example, tend to be more actively involved in their children's lives than other Protestant dads, and the evangelical men do so because they believe that raising children is a responsibility shared by husbands and wives. Although most Americans might assume that evangelical distinctiveness would emerge most clearly around moralistic prohibitions of abortion, homosexuality, or divorce, the private realm of interpersonal family relationships is actually where the lines are drawn most clearly.[18]

RHETORIC AND REALITY

What accounts for the differences? Is there a connection between the proclamation of strict moral guidelines and evangelical success in promoting cohesive families? Are evangelical families different because they have internalized the strict rules set forth by their leadership? Perhaps, the cynic might conclude, the moralistic family-values agenda is mostly aimed at winning public attention; it's meant to fill press releases, not to be taken at face value by the faithful or by the public at large.

In many respects the commitment to family reveals more about the internal dynamics of the evangelical movement than does its public political agenda. In fact, Christian Smith argues that a lot of the aggressive speech is really what Deborah Tannen has called "rapport talk," a form of communication whose fundamental purpose is to build and maintain a collective identity, not to propel the rank-and-file into political action, and certainly not to coerce outsiders into particular behaviors. Family-values talk is really a vocabulary intended for insiders, to cement their loyalty and sense of distance from the outside world.[19]

One good example of how this works lies in the real and symbolic meaning of "male headship." In large proportions—90 percent in one recent study—evangelicals affirm that the husband is the divinely appointed leader of the family, chosen by God to be the spiritual leader of his wife and children.[20] This is not just a sentimental suggestion: in 1998 the Southern Baptist Convention passed a resolution on family that became part of the denomination's core document, "Baptist Faith and Method." The statement emphasized the wife's duty to "submit herself graciously to the servant leadership of her husband, even as the church willingly submits to the headship of Christ." As Page Patterson, wife of the SBC's president, famously affirmed, "Even when it comes to submitting to my husband when I know he's wrong, I just have to do it."[21]

Although her statement elicited a collective social gasp, no one really believed that Page Patterson routinely kowtowed to her husband. In fact, the growing consensus within historical and sociological literature on the subject affirms just the opposite. In terms of employment, education, and even clothing styles, evangelical women are hardly distinguishable from their middle-class friends and neighbors.[22] Nor are their marriages visibly different, despite the words they may use to describe the relationship. "Most of the time," the sociologist Sally Gallagher writes, "couples engage in a range of strategies that allow them to practice partnership without violating the 'rules' associated with husbands' headship."[23] In practice, though they may avow the husband's spiritual leadership, nearly all evangelical couples take a firmly pragmatic approach to working out the details of housework, child care, and outside employment.

To an outsider this may seem a bit unnecessary. Why insist on conservative ideals that most people do not practice? As Christel Manning argued in a 1999 book about women in conservative religious cultures, actual behavior is not as important as stated belief. In other words, it's far more critical for an evangelical woman to say that she is "not a feminist," that is, not given to selfish, materialistic goals of personal fulfillment, than it is to be uniformly obedient to her husband.[24] The same symbolic equation holds true for the parallel issue of women's ordination. According to the sociologist Mark Chaves, American Christians tend to read a conservative position on gender roles as a larger commitment to moral separation from the secular world; conversely, a liberal position means, at its most fundamental level, a full capitulation to the forces of secularization.[25]

As Gallagher explains, the language of headship—and its particular understanding of gender roles—is important for symbolic reasons, as a means of defining what it means to be an evangelical. In contrast to the predominant secular view that gender differences are largely learned and therefore negotiable, the headship ideal assumes that biology is "a metaphor for being." Thus, according to traditionalists, women are spiritually drawn toward more passive, supportive roles because their bodies are constructed to bear and nurture infants. Similarly, men's superior physical strength means that they are divinely destined to assume spiritual leadership. The complementarity between the sexes is written into the fabric of the universe; to deny it would invite chaos. In Gallagher's view the countercultural implications of this model—its rejection of mainstream egalitarian values—are the essence of its appeal among evangelicals. Headship language is an unusually potent form of marking difference, of feeling embattled even if in reality one is affirming some fairly traditional values. Egalitarianism, Gallagher says, "does no cultural work in helping to identify or maintain religious boundaries."[26]

Certainly outsiders have done their share to reinforce the evangelical sense of embattlement. From the dystopian fundamentalist world of Margaret Atwood's *Handmaid's Tale* to the editorial page garment-rending in the wake of the 2004 election, examples of outsiders' distrust and bafflement are not hard to come by. Observed from a distance, evangelicals often look far more united and more belligerent than they actually are.

In many ways, however, these misunderstandings reflect the comparative newness of conservative Protestants to family issues and their relative lack of theological heft in public debate. Not so very long ago evangelicals were a fairly isolated religious subculture, concerned primarily with individual conversion and biblical prophecies pointing toward Jesus's triumphal second coming.

The story of the Promise Keepers illustrates the shallow roots of much evangelical social concern. There are, of course, powerful historical precedents for the manly rhetoric characteristic of the evangelical men's movement. Turn-of-the-century evangelists like Dwight Moody, J. Wilbur Chapman, and Billy Sunday all preached a strong appeal for masculine piety, claiming that orthodox belief was a sure sign of virile character. Leaders of the fundamentalist movement similarly championed manly religion, openly suggesting that liberalism could have no appeal for anyone other than women and children. But these early-twentieth-century conservative leaders did not offer a sustained theological rationale for godly fatherhood. It was enough for a man to swear off drink, work hard in his job, and seek to evangelize the lost. Family issues remained primarily women's business.

In the 1990s the Promise Keepers moved the discussion forward a few notches, attempting to engage men in the long-term commitments that "Christian fatherhood" required. Speakers at huge, emotionally charged rallies, and a busy stream of books and magazines urged evangelical men to become the spiritual leaders of their families—sometimes in language that implied that women would be forcefully moved into second place. But observers who worried that the Promise Keepers signaled a political backlash against feminism have found those fears mostly groundless. As the movement faded in the late

1990s, its primarily spiritual character emerged in sharp relief. In keeping with its pietistic evangelical roots, the Protestant men's movement has preached a gospel of personal transformation—honoring promises to wives and children, spending more time at home, being a regular churchgoer—not large-scale social change. In fact, in 1996 the Promise Keepers canceled a Capitol Hill rally to avoid the appearance of being too political.[27]

But there are other indicators about the future. Especially since the 1980s American society—and conservative Protestant churches—have become increasingly diverse, both ethnically and religiously, fed by large-scale immigration from many parts of the developing world. For evangelicals the influx of new Americans from Asia, Africa, and Central America raises mixed possibilities. On the one hand, many new immigrants are conservative, often Pentecostal, Christians for whom white evangelical concerns about family and social morality resonate deeply. The historian Philip Jenkins finds this potential allegiance "doubly valuable" for the public agenda of evangelical Christians, "since conservative positions stand a much better chance of gaining a hearing in the mainstream media when they are presented by African or Asian religious leaders rather than the familiar roster of White conservatives." Yet ethnic diversity may work the other way for evangelicals determined to press religious values in the public square. As Jenkins asks, "Would those Christians who want school prayer or other displays of religion really make the same demands if they were forced to listen to Muslim prayers, to see Asian Buddhist shrines on the public grounds?"[28]

Recent decades have proved repeatedly that evangelicals are good at defining issues around family, marshaling resources, and motivating people to act. They are good at caring for their own. And, without doubt, evangelicals have played a key role in stimulating important social discourse about difficult questions: the definition of a family, role of fathers, ethics of life and death. There is no question that they deserve a seat at the table in any discussion of social policy regarding the family. Indeed, within the plural framework of American society, they play an invaluable role—like the proverbial canary in the mine shaft, they often raise an alarm about important problems ahead.

But they are also lightning rods. The freewheeling pluralism of American culture presents challenges for a group determined to be "in the world but not of it," people who may be ardently patriotic in one instance and fervently denouncing national sinfulness in the next. In order to remain a viable subculture, evangelicalism requires controversy; it thrives on its own sense of embattlement. Is it possible, then, for evangelicals to embrace social policies aimed at the common good of many different sorts of Americans? Can they abide strategic compromise? In the years ahead the answers to these questions will say much about the character of the evangelical movement in American society. For many decades conservative Protestants have defined themselves in opposition to the dominant culture while declaring themselves the champions of mainstream

American values. Their history suggests that closer access to political power will create as many new problems as it solves; certainly, for a group that has long styled itself an alienated minority, the contradictions will not sit easily.

NOTES

1. On evangelicals, mainline Protestants, and family issues, see David Harrington Watt, *A Transforming Faith: Explorations of Twentieth-Century Evangelicalism* (New Brunswick, N.J.: Rutgers University Press, 1991), 84–91; Margaret Bendroth, *Growing Up Protestants: Parents, Children and Mainline Churches* (New Brunswick, N.J.: Rutgers University Press, 2002), 119–43; W. Bradford Wilcox, *Soft Patriarchs, New Men: How Christianity Shapes Fathers and Husbands* (Chicago: University of Chicago Press, 2004).

2. Marty Pay and Hal Donaldson, *Downfall: Secularization of a Christian Nation* (Green Forest, Ark.: New Leaf Press, 1991), 50.

3. The scholarly and popular literature of evangelicalism has followed this basic dichotomy, that is, that evangelicals are fundamentally antimodern or are consummate capitulators to modernity. The first view owes much to Dean Kelley's groundbreaking *Why Conservative Churches Are Growing* (San Francisco: Harper and Row, 1977), and the popular model of "culture wars," for example, that depicted in James Davison Hunter, *Culture Wars: The Struggle to Define America* (New York: Basic Books, 1991). To a degree, George Marsden's characterization of the fundamentalist movement as "militant antimodernism" in *Fundamentalism and American Culture* (New York: Oxford University Press, 1980) has shaped understanding of current evangelicalism, even though there is considerable debate about the degree to which the modern movement is a direct descendent of fundamentalism. The critique of evangelical capitulation to modern culture probably originated with Richard Quebedeaux, *The Young Evangelicals: Revolution in Orthodoxy* (New York: Harper and Row, 1974), and was affirmed by Douglas Frank, *Less Than Conquerors: How Evangelicals Entered the Twentieth Century* (Grand Rapids, Mich.: Eerdmans, 1986). Recent work by Christian Smith [*American Evangelicalism: Embattled and Thriving* (Chicago: University of Chicago Press, 1998] and a host of others stresses the commonalities between conservative Christian subcultures and dominant American cultural values.

4. George Marsden, Understanding Fundamentalism and Evangelicalism (Grand Rapids, Mich.: Eerdmans, 1991), 5.

5. See discussion in Mark A. Noll, *American Evangelical Christianity: An Introduction* (Oxford: Blackwell, 2001), 29–43. The exact proportion of evangelicals in the U.S. population has varied somewhat, depending on the means of identifying them. Early studies often depended on theologically oriented questionnaires about beliefs (James Davison Hunter, *American Evangelicalism: Conservative Religion and the Quandary of Modernity* [New Brunswick, N.J.: Rutgers University Press, 1983]); however, one major recent study of evangelicals relies on a combination of participants' self-identity and affiliation with evangelical institutions (Smith, *American Evangelicalism: Embattled and Thriving*).

6. Marsden, *Fundamentalism and American Culture*, 194–95, 204–5.

7. Noll, *American Evangelical Christianity*, 195.

8. A good description of these and other related events is found in William Martin, *With God on Our Side: The Rise of the Religious Right in America* (New York: Broadway Books, 1996). See also Clyde Wilcox, *Onward Christian Soldiers? The Religious Right in American Politics* (New York: Westview/HarperCollins, 1996); Robert Wuthnow, *The Restructuring of American Religion: Society and Faith since World War II* (Princeton, N.J.: Princeton University Press, 1988).

9. On evangelical mobilization in the 1960s see Martin, *With God on Our Side*, 100–43. On broadcasting see David Edwin Harrell Jr., *Pat Robertson: A Personal, Political and Religious Portrait* (New York: Harper and Row, 1987), 59–84, and Margaret Bendroth, "Fundamentalism and the Media, 1930–1980," in Daniel Stout and Judith Buddenbaum, eds., *Religion in the Mass Media: Audiences and Adaptations* (Thousand Oaks, Calif.: Sage, 1996).

10. Ed Dobson and Cal Thomas, *Blinded by Might: Can the Religious Right Save America?* (Grand Rapids, Mich.: Zondervan, 1999).

11. "From Home to Harvard," *Time*, 11 September 2000, 55.

12. Colleen McDannell, "Creating the Christian Home: Home Schooling in Contemporary America," in David Chidester and Edward Linenthal, eds., *American Sacred Space* (Bloomington: Indiana University Press, 1995), 187–219. On Christian schools see Alan Peshkin, *God's Choice: The Total World of a Fundamentalist Christian School* (Chicago: University of Chicago Press, 1986); Susan Rose, *Keeping Them out of the Hands of Satan: Evangelical Schooling in America* (New York: Routledge, 1988).

13. Steve Bruce, *Rise and Fall of the New Christian Right: Conservative Protestant Politics in America, 1976–1988* (New York: Oxford University Press, 1988); Mark J. Rozell and Clyde Wilcox, *God at the Grass Roots, 1996: The Christian Right in the American Elections* (Lanham, Md.: Rowman and Littlefield, 1997). On recent mobilization see C. Wilcox, *Onward Christian Soldiers*, 102.

14. Mark Regnerus and Christian Smith, "Selective Deprivation among American Religious Traditions: The Reversal of the Great Reversal," *Social Forces* 76 (June 1998): 1356, 1365.

15. In all, Hamilton estimates that evangelicals spend about $160 million annually on various aspects of public presence. See Michael Hamilton, "More Money, More Ministry: The Financing of American Evangelicalism Since 1945," in Larry Eskridge and Mark A. Noll, eds., *More Money, More Ministry: Money and Evangelicals in Recent North American History* (Grand Rapids, Mich.: Eerdmans, 2000), 129–31.

16. Christian Smith, *Christian America? What Evangelicals Really Want* (Berkeley: University of California Press, 2000), 48, 49.

17. See, for example, John Bartkowski, *Remaking the Godly Marriage: Gender Negotiation in Evangelical Families* (New Brunswick, N.J.: Rutgers University Press, 2001). On the evangelical social agenda see also Christian Smith and Michael Emerson, *Divided by Faith: Evangelical Religion and the Problem of Race in America* (New York: Oxford University Press, 2000). Recent literature on evangelical college students also suggests that they are more cautious about political involvement than their peers in the 1980s were. See James M. Penning and Corwin E. Smidt, *Evangelicalism: The Next Generation* (Grand Rapids, Mich.: Baker Academic, 2002), 143–53.

18. Sally K. Gallagher, *Evangelical Identity and Gendered Family Life* (New Brunswick, N.J.: Rutgers University Press, 2003), 69–70, 215n3, 116–18; Wilcox, *Soft Patri-*

archs, 77–82. See also John Bartkowski and Xiaohe Hu, "Distant Patriarchs or Expressive Dads? The Discourse and Practice of Fathering in Conservative Protestant Families," *Sociological Quarterly* 41 (2000): 465–85.

19. Smith, *Christian America?* 56.

20. Gallagher, *Evangelical Identity,* 70–77.

21. "SBC Approves Family Statement," *Christian Century,* 17–24 June, 1998, 602–3; Gustav Niebuhr, "Southern Baptists Declare Wife Should 'Submit' to Her Husband," *New York Times,* 10 June 1998, A1.

22. Robert Woodberry and Christian Smith, "Fundamentalism et al.: Conservative Protestants in America," *Annual Review of Sociology* 24 (1998): 25–56; Bartkowski, *Remaking the Godly Marriage;* R. Marie Griffith, *God's Daughters: Evangelical Women and the Power of Submission* (Berkeley: University of California Press, 1997).

23. Gallagher, *Evangelical Identity,* 100.

24. Christel Manning, *God Gave Us the Right: Conservative Catholic, Evangelical Protestant, and Orthodox Jewish Women Grapple with Feminism* (New Brunswick, N.J.: Rutgers University Press, 1999), 35–60.

25. Mark Chaves, *Ordaining Women: Culture and Conflict in Religious Institutions* (Cambridge, Mass.: Harvard University Press, 1997).

26. Gallagher, *Evangelical Identity,* 126, 167, 169–70; the quote is on p. 170.

27. Mary Stewart VanLeeuwen, "Weeping Warriors: The Changing Message of Manly Religion," *Books and Culture* 3 (November–December 1997): 9–11; Dane Claussen, "What the Media Missed about the Promise Keepers," in *Standing on the Promises: The Promise Keepers and the Revival of Manhood* (Cleveland, Ohio: Pilgrim Press, 1999), 17–33.

28. Philip Jenkins, *The Next Christendom: The Coming of Global Christianity* (New York: Oxford University Press, 2002), 202, 104.

CHAPTER 5

Native American Families and Religion

RAYMOND A. BUCKO

When speaking of the importance of self-government and self-determination for Native American peoples, the noted Indian law expert Felix Cohen used this striking metaphor: "For us, the Indian tribe is the miners' canary and when it flutters and droops we know that the poison gasses of intolerance threaten all other minorities in our land. And who of us is not a member of some minority?" (1960:313–14).

The same metaphor can be fruitfully applied to the essential issue of the relationships among civil law, religions, and family in the United States. As Cohen insightfully points out, the liberty of one group represents the liberty of all. In particular, the experience of one group, Native Americans, illustrates the dangers of exclusive governmental control of family issues and the problematic of control of policy in nineteenth-century America by the then-dominant Christian faith community (see also chapter 14). Federal civil law and majority Christian religious views were rigorously imposed on native peoples in an assimilation program that began during the presidency of Thomas Jefferson. The federal government largely ignored the religious rights of native communities and families, to detrimental effect.

Native Americans represent a unique case in a multicultural nation of immigrants. They are the only group that did not immigrate to North America subsequent to Columbus's arrival. Despite the wide use of such terms as *New World* and *unexplored wilderness*, North America was neither before the arrival of Europeans and other cultural groups. Natives were present when the great waves of immigration began in the fifteenth century. These waves of immigration continue even today, whereas the original native population remains a distinct but small minority.

In discussing Native American families, it is essential to emphasize that they live in the present. Although social scientists have been preoccupied with pre-contact social and familial structures of native peoples, and Hollywood, artists, and authors have frozen and stereotyped the image of Indians in the nineteenth century on the Great Plains, family and religion remain central in the lives of contemporary Indian peoples.

Today most Natives Americans enjoy what amounts to dual citizenship as United States citizens and as legal members of federally recognized tribes (not all Native Americans are registered in tribes, and not all groups that consider themselves tribes are recognized as such by the federal government). Historically, as I will show, the dominant culture generally has deprived native peoples of their liberty and right to self-determination with regard to matters of religion and family. Nevertheless, the remarkable resiliency of the first inhabitants of this land is evident in their struggle to maintain religious and family institutions and, in some instances, to revive, reconstruct, and strengthen those institutions today. As Lee Teitelbaum suggests in chapter 14, religions continue to have an important role, but people belonging to minority religions do not follow a single dominant religious model for family structure. As Numrich points out in chapter 2, minority religions grow more conservative and oppositional to a now-liberal government. Native American groups, on the other hand, seek to free themselves from being wards of the government and return to the religious kinship-based culture that the government and mainline churches sought to dissolve.

Native American cultures are heterogeneous, as are Native American family structures, languages, economics, ecological conditions, and belief systems. What Native Americans do share is a common identity defined in opposition to that of the European invaders. Native American cultures are unique and both legally and symbolically separate from the dominant and other minority cultures surrounding them. Native peoples themselves debate even the use of the term *Native American*. Most groups prefer to identify themselves first by using their historical term, such as *Lakota* or *Anishnabe*, from their own language, and secondarily identify with other native groups as *Indians* or *Native Americans* or *indigenous* or, more commonly in Canada, *First Nations*.

European outsiders have characterized Native American cultures or peoples as marginalized or backward and acted coercively to re-create native peoples in their own image, both legally and religiously. Native Americans counter this by asserting that the dominant culture is the dysfunctional culture. The most common critique offered by Native Americans of the cultures around them is that non-Indians do not take care of their family. Native people consistently defend the integrity of their own way of life and charge that anthropological and sociological literature has contributed to the image of Native American families as marginal and, in the extreme, incapable (Medicine 1981:13). Native Americans also point out that churches and independent service agencies try to pump up their budgets by promoting the negative image of Native American society.

At the time of first European contact the total Native American population of North America is estimated to have been 1.2 to 10 million individuals (Henige 1998; Thornton 1987; Thornton and Marsh-Thornton 1987; Uberlaker 1976, 1988). In 1900 the Native American population reached its nadir, its numbers estimated at 350,000. When the 2000 census allowed people to check off more than one racial category, 2.5 million people identified themselves exclusively as American Indian and Alaska Native (0.9 percent of the population). An additional 1.6 million people (0.6 percent) identified themselves as either American Indian or Alaska Native *and* one or more other "races" (a problematic category rejected by anthropologists but perpetuated by the government in the census document). Thus 4.1 million individuals, or 1.5 percent of the total population of the United States, identify themselves in some way as American Indian (Ogunwole 2002). Of that total 3.1 million specified the tribe to which they belong (U.S. Census Bureau 2002a). Using census categories, the "Native American" population appears to have grown by 26 percent, while the "Native and other race" group increased by 110 percent in the ten years since the 1990 census, when it wasn't possible to designate mixed race. The total U.S. population grew by 13 percent in the same ten years (Ogunwole 2002).

The 2000 census counted 936,000 Native American families, 63 percent of whom were married couples, with 56 percent including nonadopted children younger than eighteen. In comparison with the U.S. medians, Native Americans are younger (28.7 years vs. 35.3) and poorer (24.5 percent vs. 11.7 percent living below the poverty level) (U.S. Census Bureau 2002b, 2002c).

Census figures like these demonstrate crucial problems in estimating Native American populations and representing Native American family structure. Leaving aside the issue of undercounts due to low census response rates among minorities, the very definition of who is a Native American differs among government agencies and within Native American populations themselves. The federal government counts as Native American only those individuals legally enrolled in one of the 562 federally recognized tribal entities (Bureau of Indian Affairs 2002), although many other groups have applied for formal tribal recognition. The Census Bureau applies a different standard: "self ascription," which simply means that a person considers himself or herself to be Indian. Federally recognized Indian tribes have the right to determine their own membership criteria, but inability to prove eligibility or failure to follow procedures prevents others from enrolling. Even though Native Americans have the highest birthrate of all the minority populations, birthrate alone does not account for the apparent increase in the Native American population.

Furthermore, government definitions of marriage and family presume that the dominant culture's norms are universal. Among Native Americans, marriage can be as informal as simple cohabitation but still be tribally or culturally recognized and sanctioned as a valid marriage. Native people consistently define their family structure as "extended," whereas the Census Bureau collects household data only on "nuclear families." Marshal Sahlins once defined a nuclear family as a mother, father, two children, and a bomb shelter; in Indian Country a Native American extended family is defined as a mother, father, four grandparents, seven aunts and uncles, six children, and an anthropologist. In the past, Native American identity was a negative attribute, often hidden; today Native American identity is more openly expressed and positively valued. Thus people are more likely to self-identify as Native American for the census takers. Years ago a Lakota friend explained to me the depth of his shame at being Indian and how he did not want to acknowledge his heritage. He said his friends were that way too and that, when they played "Cowboys and Indians" on the reservation, none of them wanted to be the Indians. A Mohawk friend who critiqued this chapter laughed at this and commented that, where she came from, there were no cowboys.

Given the cultural, linguistic, and geographic diversity of Native Americans and their enduring cultural uniqueness, broad statements about contemporary Native American identity and behavior are likely to be problematic (Medicine 1981:14–15). Tribal and geographical groups differ from one another externally and exhibit internal heterogeneity. This is also true for religious belief. Individuals within groups may follow what are generally termed "traditional religions." Others are Christian. Still others follow both Christian and traditional ritual and belief patterns, as is the case among the Pueblo peoples or within the Native American Church (Forbes 2000). Similarly, Native American groups and individuals choose to incorporate varying degrees and elements of the dominant culture into their lives, identifying themselves as "traditional" and "progressive." Differences are sometimes expressed genetically, with "full bloods" distinguished from "mixed bloods," although the critical determinant tends to be behavior rather than biology.

Anthropologists reconstructed genealogies of Native American families from the oral histories passed along by the oldest members of these groups. These histories are set in the ethnographic present, the idealized time of Native American life just before contact with Europeans. These data describe a wide variety of family structures based on descent, kinship alliance, residence, inheritance, and religion. While these are separate categories to anthropologists, to Native Americans they are tightly interwoven cultural realities. Groups such as the Iroquois were and continue to be organized into clans, with membership inherited through the mother. Clans might be further organized into moieties, with a number of clans divided into two "sides," which occurs among many northwest coast tribes, with marriage prescribed between moieties and proscribed within them. Other groups, such as the Lakotas and Utes, are structured by extended family patterns based in blood, marriage, social alliance, and location of residence. Many tribes have religious ceremonies to adopt outsiders (Native American and, in some cases today, non-native) into their clan or extended family structures. What is consistent throughout Native America is that family and kinship have historically been conterminous with political structure and religious practice.

In addition to the variety and flexibility of Native American family structure, there is a further dynamic based on migration and seasonal activity. Historically, hunting and gathering, fishing, and farming distant fields resulted in fluctuating family size and structure throughout the year. Today a variation on that pattern has Native American people moving between their home reservations and cities or military stations. In the 1950s a government relocation program displaced many Native American families from the reservations and resettled them in urban areas, in a continued program of mandated assimilation. Since then, many people have returned to the reservations, but outmigration continues to urban areas, and extended family members often move back and forth. The majority of Native Americans reside in urban areas today (Fixico 2000). The use of multiple residences in urban and reservation locations helps Native Americans to maintain family relationships over a broad geographical range.

Using a variety of models, many social scientists have analyzed contemporary variation in Native American family configuration. Each model suggests a range of classificatory types based on behavioral choices along a continuum between traditional Native American culture and the dominant culture. Thus one model suggests that families may be (1) a traditional group that overtly adheres to culturally defined styles of living; (2) a nontraditional bicultural group that appears to have adopted many aspects of non–American Indian styles of living; and (3) a pantraditional group that overtly struggles to redefine and reconfirm previously lost cultural styles of living (Red Horse et al. 1978:69; Stubben 2001:1467–69).

These choices are dynamic and ongoing, and the dominant trend today clearly is to shift in the direction of tradition. Nevertheless, it is possible to describe some broad commonalities in the way Native Americans conceptualize themselves today. Despite tribal differences and sometimes-heated internal divisions, Native American people consider themselves ultimately related and identify with one another as a group. Also, tribes are increasingly acting in concert, politically and economically. The greater mobility of Native American groups through boarding schools, military service, and relocation to urban areas has strengthened this wider identity and unity.

Native Americans today have a general sense of pride in their culture, although at times this may be marked by ambivalence that stems from conflict with the persistent negative outside stereotyping. Native Americans recognize the importance of their traditions and beliefs and stress the importance of the group over the individual while holding to the importance of respect for personal choice. They share a common historical experience of missionization, forced assimilation, loss of resources, and geographic displacement. Many Native Americans speak of this experience as a "historical trauma" and a "soul wound" in need of healing (Brave Heart 1995a).

Native American families are in at least some way structurally extended, in contrast to the nuclear family assumed to be the norm by the dominant culture. Children, elders, and the family in general are respected and often deemed sacred. Family dynamics are marked by humor and expectations of communal participation and cooperation. The often-used image of "seven generations" stresses the importance of intergenerational continuity and responsibility, as well as the multigenerational family structure common to Native American groups. Reciprocity is essential both within and among these extended family groups. Families practice "noninterference," generally not intervening in the activities of other family members (John 1988: 330–36; Stubben 2001:1472–74; Weaver and White 1997:69–71).

In order to understand the situation within many Native American families today, it is essential to understand the history of Indian-white contact and subsequent actions on the part of the U.S. government and the Christian and Mormon churches. This history of contact between whites and Native Americans, as all know, has been a tragic one. Native American people lost land and resources and were either restricted in their land bases or removed to other territories. The government pursued a dual policy of apartheid (removal) and assimilation but ultimately pursued an assimilationist policy. This was particularly true in the 1880s, when the government, in cooperation with the churches, undertook vigorous assimilation campaigns against Native American peoples. The government divided native lands into allotments assigned to "nuclear families," selling off their remaining lands to non-natives. Kinship-based tribal governments were devalued, undermined, and later ignored and dissolved by the United States, which assumed that Native Americans would become citizens once they became competent in "civilization." Children were sent to boarding and day schools, where they were "taught to be civilized" in the hope of transforming an entire generation of Native Americans into "Americans"—the final solution to the "Indian problem."

The government and churches also actively suppressed elements of Native American religious culture, particularly dances and other public religious ceremonies, in an attempt to replace Native American with Western culture. No provisions were made for religious liberty for Native American peoples (Prucha 1984a:524–25). While these prohibitions were eventually narrowed to religious customs considered directly in conflict with the norms of the dominant economic and religious culture, not until John Collier became the administrator of the Office of Indian Affairs in 1933 was full religious liberty for Native American peoples recognized, in "Indian Religious Freedom and Indian Culture," Circular No. 2970, issued 3 January 1934 (Prucha 1984b:800–3, 951).

Although detribalization of Native American communities ended in the 1930s with a series of reforms known as the Indian Reorganization Act, under the new legal regime many tribal governance structures were reorganized into democratic tribal councils, a form that did not reflect earlier kinship-based governance systems. Also, government policy remained assimilationist and became even more so after the Roosevelt administration implemented the "termination movement," which attempted to dissolve the legal and political relationship between the federal government and Indian tribes, and relocation, a government program designed to move Indians away from their own land base to assimilate them into cities.

Perhaps the most egregious wound was inflicted between the 1930s and 1950s, when the U.S. government and various Christian organizations assumed legal and moral authority over the Native American family. This usurpation began earlier with the boarding school system and allotment but evolved into a widespread practice of removing Native American children from their families for adoption into non–Native American families under the fallacious assumption that Indian families were simply not competent to raise their own children. Under a joint effort by the Bureau of Indian Affairs and the Child Welfare League of America, 25 percent to 35 percent of all Indian children were adopted by non–Native American families (Paulson 1999, cited in Halverson, Puig, and Byer 2002). This practice was intended to strike at the heart of Native American cultures. To remove children from their families was to undermine the foundation of Native American culture.

While church- and government-sponsored forced assimilation has radically reshaped Native American culture and family structure (by the proscription of polygamy, for example), Native Americans were and are not simply the passive victims of white encroachment and government policy. One need not ignore, excuse, or diminish past and even ongoing historical injustices to recognize that Native American peoples made and continue to make their own choices and decisions, sometimes with great difficulty, and continue to interact with other cultures and political systems on their own terms, as do other cultural groups in the United States. Despite the adversity, Native American families have remained resilient and have in many instances restructured themselves according to traditional extended patterns. They have also reincorporated traditional belief systems in their social and political structures. Through resistance, accommodation, and innovation Native American peoples have continued to use their own resources as well as the structures of the government and, at times, the churches that surround them to maintain their identity and integrity. This return to tradition and rejection of a variety of external religious and civil structures is echoed by recent immigrant groups that are striving to retain their religious and cultural context (see chapter 2).

The 1978 Indian Child Welfare Act (ICWA—25 U.S.C. § 1901 et seq.) was a response to the dire situation of Native American families that were losing children to adopters outside their tribal and ethnic structure. The law was designed to protect the cultural rights of tribes by giving them jurisdiction over the adoption of tribal members, ideally placing children with other relatives or other tribal members rather than allowing them to be adopted out and thus alienated from their families, religions, and cultures. This legislation was essential to the preservation of Native American families by giving tribes sovereignty over their own members (Gale, cited in Kawamoto 2001:1491) and by assuming that the Native American extended family itself is a strength, not evidence of cultural deficiency (Red Horse et al. 2000:18–19). Even so, the nuclear family remains the dominant model, and the dominant culture sees extended multigenerational families as a problem (Red Horse et al. 2000:29—30). For example, when parents are unable to care for their offspring, adoption agencies prefer to place a child in a nuclear family, whereas some native groups prefer that grandparents or aunts take over as primary caregivers. In addition, coordination among tribal and nontribal social workers and legal systems is essential for ICWA's success and difficult to achieve. While the law was intended to strengthen Native American families, a more recent piece of child welfare legislation, the Adoption and Safe Family Act of 1997 (42 U.S.C. § 1305), sometimes conflicts with the goals of ICWA. The 1997 act, for example, stresses the permanent placement of children, which usually includes full termination of parental rights, a concept that many Native American communities eschew (MacEachron et al. 1996; Barth, Webster, and Lee 2002).

Key to the implementation of all such well-meaning legislation is an understanding of and respect for Native American family structures (Brown et al. 2001). Adoption, gift giving, and the exchange of labor remain ways to strengthen families socially and economically, although Native American peoples recognize that such traditions may also enable dysfunction among noncontributing members of communities (Medicine 1981:18–19). Healing of historical trauma through both ancient religious ritual as well as counseling is another important movement that is affirming and strengthening Native American families (Brave Heart 1995a–b, 1998, 1999a–b, 2000, 2003, 2004a–b; Brave Heart and De Bruyn 1995, 1998; Brave Heart, Duran, and Duran 1998a–b; Weaver and Brave Heart 1999; Duran and Duran 1995; Red Horse et al. 2000:14; Rhine and Moreno 1991). Reinvigoration of Native American families through tradition remains paramount in this process, whether carried out in a clinical or ritual context. Indeed, clinical and ritual are frequently combined by Native Americans seeking to use their own models of healing instead of working according to Western paradigms. This choice reflects a conservatism and reliance on their own faith-based values and symbols (Native Americans are more likely to refer to this configuration as traditional). It is telling that the majority of published literature on the contemporary Native American family is in the area of social work, a very Western non–Native American institution at base, yet this material consistently advocates using internal cultural resources and institutions to heal the family.

Native American families have been further supported by a piece of federal legislation called the Native American Graves Protection and Repatriation Act (Mihesuah 2000). This act (25 U.S.C. § 3001 et seq.) establishes tribal sovereignty over human remains and sacred objects that have been stored in museums and other research centers and mandates their return. While to Western eyes this legislation seems to deal with archaeology, it is at root a family and religious initiative. Native American justifications for these returns are religious, based on the sacredness of the dead and the importance of religious objects to the ongoing well-being of the cultural group. Indeed, the physical returns are carried out in the context of religious rituals, beginning at the museums and concluding on the reservations. Strengthening the tribal unit in this way *is* isomorphic with strengthening the family. The repatriation act recognizes the rights of Native American individuals and families, as well as tribes, in asserting claims to human remains and cultural patrimony. Thus government intervention in Native American life is historically ambivalent. Measures like the child welfare and repatriation acts, which increase tribal sovereignty and bolster cultural rights, are positive, in counterpoint to a long history of government control and detribalization.

Just as cultural variations across and even within Native American groups can be wide, responses to the issues of modernization and encroachment of Western culture are varied and different. The U.S. government used removal of Indians to expand its territorial holdings, but some Native American groups voluntarily moved farther from settlers' holdings to insulate themselves from outside influence. Selective isolation remains a solution for some groups, such as the Hopi and Onondaga, who close their reservations to outsiders during ceremonial times and generally restrict visiting and the outflow of information about their cultures. Many tribes now have an Office of Cultural Resources that academics must consult before they may conduct research and publish the resulting data.

Native American people have also consistently relied upon religious inspiration to bolster tradition and familial unity while reconstructing families devastated by warfare, disease, displacement, and famine. Handsome Lake, Wovoka, and John Slokum are among many Native Americans who have revitalized Native American family structure through their religious vision, charismatic preaching, and moral example. The militant social protests of the 1970s, such as the occupations of Alcatraz, the Bureau of Indian Affairs, and Wounded Knee, transformed Native American consciousness and shook the complacency of non–Native Americans throughout the United States while making existing Native American cultures more visible internationally and more positive about their futures.

Peaceful political change is another measure that Native American cultures use to resist outside influence. The U.S. government tried to impose itself on Native Americans through the selection and recognition of chiefs friendly to its policies, but Native American societies themselves have historically reorganized politically to maintain their independence. The most notable example of this is the Cherokees, who combined traditional and Western forms of governance in their political system during their early contact with Europeans and Americans. These structures incorporated American political institutions while continuing to recognize and incorporate traditional family structures. The Cherokees were nevertheless removed from the east coast to Oklahoma.

In response to the insistence of Native American peoples that their cultures be respected and preserved, health care and social workers have become more culturally sensitive and responsive to their clients (Garwick, Jennings, and Thiesen 2002; Halverson, Puig, and Byer 2002). Tribes themselves have employed social workers directly and hired others to study issues of family and mental health (Gayle 1994; Kawamoto 2001). Native American people have themselves developed therapeutic processes specific to Native American issues. For example, Maria Brave Heart's regime for the healing of historical trauma among Native American peoples involves "(a) heightened awareness of historical trauma and the historical trauma response, (b) facilitation of a trauma resolution process, and (c) stimulation of recathexis (re-attachment) to traditional Lakota values that positively influence parenting" (Brave Heart 1999b:110).

In general, contemporary Native American cultures focus on integrating or, in many cases, regaining and reintegrating traditional religion, family structure, culture, and language. Currently, the main tensions within Native American cultures stem from the need to negotiate the interplay of tribal traditions and contemporary American norms. Specific Native American groups and individuals in the present, as in the past, may split over accepting a Christian identity. Thus religion does not always serve as a source of unity, although contemporary Native Americans generally prioritize group solidarity over religious difference, particularly at the kinship level. Religion can also create new divisions or solidify older differences. Many questions remain unanswered: Should tribes accept the form of governance promoted by the Indian Reorganization Act or resume traditional patterns of government that are more in tune with traditional extended family structure? Should Native Americans participate in the American pattern of working to accumulate money and goods or revive economic patterns based in the traditional ethos of redistributing goods among family and tribal members, however broadly defined? Should Christian Native Americans continue to pray in the church or return entirely to traditional religious practices? While the churches are more tolerant of multiple participation by Native American people, more Native Americans are moving toward religious exclusivism despite their history of religious eclecticism (Steinmetz 1998). Some Native Americans hold today that being Christian is incompatible with being Native American, while others continue as Christians or participate in both religious forms.

Native American critics of Western society can be found within academe, where voices such as Beatrice Medicine's (2001), Vine Deloria Jr.'s (1969, 1970, 1983, 1999; Deloria and Lytle 1984), Ward Churchill's (1994, 1998, 2004, 2005), Devon Mihesuah's (1998; Mihesuah and Wilson 2004), and Angela Wilson's (2005) speak of the uniqueness of Native American cultures and the problems of Western culture. In newspapers the best-known voice is that of Tim Giago (1978, 1984). Other critiques of Western culture appear in the very large genre of "told to" books. This kind of social critique of Western and American society goes back to the time of first contact. A conversation between a Jesuit and a Huron in the seventeenth century is illustrative: "And when we preach to them of one God, Creator of Heaven and earth, and of all things, and even when we talk to them of Hell and Paradise and of our other mysteries, the headstrong savages reply that this is good for our Country and not for theirs; that every Country has its own fashions" (Brébeuf 1897:117).

My own work has been with the Lakota (Sioux) peoples of western South Dakota, particularly on the Pine Ridge Reservation. It is clear, as Lakota authorities themselves have pointed out (Brokenleg 1998; Brokenleg and Middleton 1993; E. Deloria 1944; Medicine 1969, 1981, 1987, 1994; Mohatt and Eagle Elk 2000; Red Shirt 1998, 2002; Sneve 1995; Standing Bear 1975, 1988; Young Bear and Theisz 1994), as have various anthropologists (Bolz 1984; Bucko 1998; Bucko and Brokenleg 2000; DeMallie 1972, 1979; Kurkiala 1997; Miles and Lovett 1994; Petrillo 2001; M. Powers 1986; W. Powers 1975), that family remains the key value among these people.

Ella Deloria, herself a tribal member and scholar, as well as an advocate for her people, best summed up the centrality of kinship to Lakota (Dakota) life: "Kinship was the all-important matter. . . . By kinship all Dakota people were held together in a great relationship that was theoretically all-inclusive and co-extensive with the Dakota domain. Everyone who was born a Dakota belonged to it; nobody need be left outside. . . . In the last analysis every other consideration was secondary—property, personal ambition, glory, good times, life itself. Without that aim and the constant struggle to attain it, the people would no longer be Dakota in truth. They would no longer even be human" (1944: 24–25).

Lakota family life has reasserted itself despite the earlier threats, such as the restriction of land base and economic livelihood, the assault on the traditional tribal structure based in kinship, institutionalization by both government and the churches, deliberate suppression of social structure and religious activity, the boarding school system, displacement into urban areas, and today the allure of modernity (not to mention postmodernity) itself. Extended family remains the organizing social structure both on the reservation and in urban areas. Families are increasingly returning to traditional religious patterns, celebrated in events like the sun dance and vision quest. These events are kinship based and are organized and attended by groups related by blood, marriage, residence, and social alliance. The majority of Christian churches, repentant of the days of rejecting Native American cultures, are more open to Native American ritual and belief within their own spiritual traditions and ceremonial structures. They also encourage Native American leadership rather than providing outside governance by non-Indians.

Lakota religious belief stresses the kinship of all creation, exemplified by the phrase used to end Lakota prayers, "Mitakuye Oyas'in" (for all my relatives). This kinship orientation has allowed families to survive dire economic circumstances (Pine Ridge is located in the poorest county in the United States) and to retain their cultural heritage. The centrality of kinship has also allowed the Lakotas to vigorously interact with the rest of the inhabitants of the United States, and indeed the entire world, while maintaining a distinct identity.

While nineteenth-century social scientists predicted the demise of Native American culture and indeed even the disappearance of Native American people themselves, Native American populations are on the rise, and Native American culture and religious practice are experiencing a resurgence. The Pine Ridge Reservation holds an increasing number of public rituals such as the sun dance and sweat lodge. The buffalo sing ceremony, a rite of passage that prepares a young girl for the duties of family life as a mature woman, has been revived in some areas, and ceremonial societies have also been revived or made public. At all these ceremonies one will hear speeches encouraging participants to care for their families and devote themselves to communal needs by placing "the people" above themselves.

Lakota people, who are ecumenical in their religious approach, stress religious experience over doctrinal purity and continue today to work to strengthen their families through a variety of approaches: prayer with traditional spiritual leaders and/or Christian leaders, social services, family "doings," healing and reconciliation services, protests, dialogues, and whatever else will help bring families together and continue the rich legacy of a tradition that has always been centered on and nurtured in the extended family.

Before sitting down to write the initial draft of this chapter, I was invited to a sweat lodge ceremony by a Lakota friend. I accepted—it presented a good way to pray as well as a good way to prepare for the spiritual discipline of writing this piece. After the sweat, another Jesuit and I shared a meal with the small group of Lakota participants, who first carefully traced their relationship to one another through various families. The conversation then turned to the importance of returning to the traditional religion, which was suppressed by the government and the church. Despite the presence of two priests at the table, and despite the raising of such potentially volatile topics as boarding schools and other assimilation attempts, the conversation was gentle and congenial.

That evening, and many other evenings that I have spent on the Pine Ridge and Rosebud reservations, where I have done the majority of my scholarly work, confirmed to me the importance of scholarly research in the service of people and of continuing my own social and in some cases familial relationships with

Native American people. Over the years I have learned from my Native American teachers to be respectful. A respectful person does not speak for others but, rather, shares reflections and thoughts. In this paper, and in all my dealings, I have tried to honor that essential Native American value, and in that spirit, I share this research for the good of the people, as well as for the understanding of all.

As a "miner's canary," Native American families can tell us a lot about the danger of forced assimilation, government usurpation of family roles and responsibilities, disregard for cultural integrity, and the tragedy of the misguided paternalism and cultural myopia that sanctioned the imposition of Christianity. These families also tell us of the danger of religious coercion, suspension of religious liberty, and the problems of forced change rather than free choice. That the "canary" of Native American family life has not expired but has emerged from the mine of historical trial with renewed vigor and vitality speaks volumes of the strength of Native American family and tradition, the resilience of cultural and religious patterns, and the ability of heterogeneous peoples united by a common history and identity to continue to integrate themselves with the world around them yet maintain their distinctive familial and religious identities.

I would like to thank the participants of the American Religions and the Family consultation who made valuable suggestions when the first version of this chapter was read, and Kateri Mitchell, a Mohawk, and Marie Therese Archambault, who is Lakota; they read various versions of this paper and made valuable suggestions.

REFERENCES

Barth, Richard P., Daniel Webster, and Seon Lee. 2002. "Adoption of American Indian Children: Implications for Implementing the Indian Child Welfare and Adoption and Safe Families Acts." *Children and Youth Services Review* 24 (3): 139–58.

Bolz, Peter. 1984. "Ethnic Identity and Cultural Resistance: The Oglala-Sioux of the Pine Ridge Reservation Today." In *North American Indian Studies*. Edited by Pieter Hovens, 2:204–24. Gottingen, Germany: Edition Herodot.

Brave Heart, Maria Yellow Horse. 1995a. "The Return to the Sacred Path: Healing from Historical Trauma and Historical Unresolved Grief among the Lakota." Ph.D. diss., Smith College School for Social Work.

———. 1995b. "So She May Walk in Balance: Integrating the Impact of Historical Trauma in the Treatment of American Indian Women." In *Racism in the Lives of Women: Testimony, Theory and Guides to Antiracist Practice*. Edited by Jeanne Adelman and Gloria Enguidanos, 345–68. New York: Haworth.

———. 1998. "The Return to the Sacred Path: Healing the Historical Trauma Response among the Lakota." *Smith College Studies in Social Work* 68 (3): 287–305.

———. 1999a. "Gender Differences in the Historical Trauma Response among the Lakota." In *Health and the American Indian*. Edited by P. A. Day and H. N. Weaver, 1–21. New York: Haworth.

———. 1999b. "Oyate Ptayela: Rebuilding the Lakota Nation through Addressing Historical Trauma among Lakota Parents." *Journal of Human Behavior in the Social Environment* 2 (1/2): 109–26.

———. 2000. "Wakiksuyapi: Carrying the Historical Trauma of the Lakota." *Tulane Studies in Social Welfare* 21–22:245–66.

———. 2004a. "The Historical Trauma Response among Natives and Its Relationship with Substance Abuse: A Lakota Illustration." In *Healing and Mental Health for Native Americans: Speaking in Red*. Edited by Ethan Nebelkopf and Mary Phillips, 7–18. Walnut Creek, Calif.: AltaMira.

———. 2004b. "Incorporating Native Historical Trauma Content." In *Education for Multicultural Social Work Practice*. Edited by Lorraine Gutierrez, Maria Zuniga, and Doman Lum, 201–11. Alexandria, Va.: Council on Social Work Education.

———. 2003. "Morning Star Rising: Healing in Native American Communities— The Historical Trauma Response among Natives and Its Relationship with Substance Abuse: A Lakota Illustration." *Journal of Psychoactive Drugs* 35 (1): 7–15.

Brave Heart, Maria Yellow Horse and L. M. De Bruyn. 1995. "So She May Walk in Balance: Integrating the Impact of Historical Trauma in the Treatment of American Indian Women." In *Racism in the Lives of Women: Testimony, Theory and Guides to Antiracist Practice*. Edited by Jeanne Adelman and Gloria Enguidanos, 345–68. New York: Haworth.

Brave Heart, Maria Yellow Horse and L. M. De Bruyn. 1998. "The American Holocaust: Historical Unresolved Grief among Native American Indians." *National Center for American Indian and Alaska Native Mental Health Research Journal* 8 (2): 56–78.

Brave Heart, Maria Yellow Horse-Davis, Eduardo Duran, and Bonnie Duran. 1998a. "Healing the American Indian Soul Wound." In *International Handbook of Multigenerational Legacies of Trauma*. Edited by Yael Danieli, 341–54. New York: Plenum.

———. 1998b. "Native Americans and the Trauma of History." In *Studying Native America: Problems and Prospects of Native American Studies*. Edited by Russell Thornton, 60–76. Madison: University of Wisconsin Press.

Brébeuf, Jean de. 1897. "Relations of What Occurred among the Hurons in the Year 1635." In *The Jesuit Relations and Allied Documents*. Edited by R. G. Thwaites, 8:67–151. Cleveland, Ohio: Burrows Brothers.

Brokenleg, Martin K. 1998. "A Native American Perspective: 'That the People May Live.'" In *Preaching Justice: Ethnic and Cultural Perspectives*. Edited by C. M. Smith, 26–42. Cleveland, Ohio: United Church Press.

Brokenleg, Martin K. and David Middleton. 1993. "Native Americans: Adapting, Yet Retaining." In *Ethnic Variations in Dying, Death and Grief: Diversity in Universality*. Edited by D. P. Irish, K. F. Lundquist, and V. J. Nelsen, 101–12. Washington, D.C.: Taylor and Francis.

Brown, Eddie F. et al. 2001. "Title IV-B Child and Family Service Plans: An Evaluation of Specific Measures Taken by States to Comply with the Indian Child Welfare Act (ICWA)." Casey Family Programs and the National Indian Child Welfare Association, Portland, Oregon.

Bucko, Raymond A. 1998. *The Lakota Ritual of the Sweat Lodge: History and Contemporary Practice*. Lincoln: University of Nebraska Press.

Bucko, Raymond A. and Martin K. Brokenleg. 2000. Introduction to *Dakota Cross-*

Bearer: The Life and World of a Native American Bishop, xi–xx. Lincoln: University of Nebraska Press.

Bureau of Indian Affairs. 2002. "Department of the Interior: Indian Entities Recognized and Eligible to Receive Services from the United States Bureau of Indian Affairs; Notice." *Federal Register* 67 (134): 46328–33.

Churchill, Ward. 1994. *Indians Are Us? Culture and Genocide in Native North America*. Monroe, Me.: Common Courage Press.

———. 1998. *Fantasies of the Master Race: Literature, Cinema, and the Colonization of American Indians*. San Francisco: City Lights Books.

———. 2004. *Speaking Truth in the Teeth of Power: Lectures on Globalization, Colonialism and Native America*. Oakland, Calif.: AK Press.

———. 2005. *Since Predator Came: Notes from the Struggle for American Indian Liberation*. Oakland, Calif.: AK Press.

Cohen, Felix S. 1960. "Indian Self-government." In *The Legal Conscience: Selected Papers of Felix S. Cohen*. Edited by L. K. Cohen, 305–14. New Haven, Conn.: Yale University Press.

Deloria, Ella C. 1944. *Speaking of Indians*. New York: Friendship Press.

Deloria, Vine Jr. 1969. *Custer Died for Your Sins: An Indian Manifesto*. New York: Macmillan.

———. 1970. *We Talk, You Listen: New Tribes, New Turf*. New York: Macmillan.

———. 1983. *God Is Red*. New York: Dell.

———. 1999. *For This Land: Writings on Religion in America*. New York: Routledge and Kegan Paul.

Deloria, Vine Jr. and Clifford Lytle. 1984. *The Nations Within: The Past and Future of American Indian Sovereignty*. New York: Pantheon.

DeMallie, Raymond J. Jr. 1972. "Teton Dakota Kinship and Social Organization." Ph.D. diss., University of Chicago.

———. 1979. "Change in American Indian Kinship Systems: The Dakota. In *Currents in Anthropology: Essays in Honor of Sol Tax*. Edited by R. Henshaw, 221–41. The Hague: Mouton.

Duran, Eduardo and Bonnie Duran. 1995. *Native American Postcolonial Psychology*. Albany: State University of New York Press.

Fixico, Donald L. 2000. *The Urban Indian Experience in America*. Albuquerque: University of New Mexico Press.

Forbes, Bruce David. 2000. "Which Religion Is Right? Five Answers in the Historical Encounter between Christianity and Traditional Native American Spiritualities." *Neihardt Journal* 2:18–26.

Garwick, Ann, Jennifer M. Jennings, and Darch Theisen. 2002. "Urban American Indian Family Caregivers' Perceptions of the Quality of Family-Centered Care." *Children's Health Care* 31 (3): 209–22.

Gayle, N. 1994. "What Is Post-traumatic Stress?" *News from Indian Country: The Nation's Native Journal*, November, p. 24.

Giago, Tim A. Jr. 1978. *The Aboriginal Sin: Reflections on the Holy Rosary Mission School (Red Cloud Indian School)*. San Francisco: Indian Historian Press.

———. 1984. *Notes from Indian Country*. N.p.: K. Cochran.

Halverson, Kelly, Maria Elena Puig, and Steven Byer. 2002. "Culture Loss: American

Indian Family Disruption, Urbanization, and the Indian Child Welfare Act." *Child Welfare* 81 (2): 319–36.

Henige, David P. 1998. *Numbers from Nowhere : The American Indian Contact Population Debate*. Norman: University of Oklahoma Press.

John, Robert. 1988. "The Native American Family." In *Ethnic Families in America: Patterns and Variations*. Edited by Charles H. Mindel, Robert W. Habenstein, and Roosevelt Wright, 325–63. New York: Elsevier.

Kawamoto, Walter T. 2001. "Community Mental Health and Family Issues in Sociohistorical Context: The Confederated Tribes of Coos, Lower Umpqua, and Siuslaw Indians." *American Behavioral Scientist* 44 (9): 1482–91.

Kurkiala, Mikael. 1997. *Building the Nation Back Up: The Politics of Identity on the Pine Ridge Indian Reservation*. Uppsala, Sweden: Uppsala University.

MacEachron, A. E. et al. 1996. "The Effectiveness of the Indian Child Welfare Act of 1978." *Social Services Review* 70 (3): 451–63.

Medicine, Beatrice. 1969. "The Changing Dakota Family and the Stresses Therein." *Pine Ridge Research Bulletin* 9:1–20.

——. 1981. "American Indian Families." *Journal of Ethnic Studies* 8 (4): 13–23.

——. 1987. "Indian Women and the Renaissance of Traditional Religion." In *Sioux Indian Religion: Tradition and Innovation*. Edited by Raymond J. DeMallie and Douglas R. Parks, 159–71. Norman: University of Oklahoma Press.

——. 1994. "Families." In *Native America in the Twentieth Century: An Encyclopedia*. Edited by M. B. Davis, 193–95. New York: Garland.

——. 2001. "Learning to Be an Anthropologist and Remaining Native." In *Learning to Be an Anthropologist and Remaining "Native": Selected Writings*. Edited by Beatrice Medicine and Sue-Ellen Jacobs, 3–15. Urbana: University of Illinois Press.

Mihesuah, Devon A., ed. 1998. *Natives and Academics: Researching and Writing about American Indians*. Lincoln: University of Nebraska Press.

——. 2000. *Repatriation Reader: Who Owns American Indian Remains?* Lincoln: University of Nebraska Press.

Mihesuah, Devon A. and Angela Wilson, eds. 2004. *Indigenizing the Academy: Native Academics Sharpening the Edge*. Lincoln: University of Nebraska Press.

Miles, Ray and John R. Lovett. 1994. "The Pictorial Autobiography of Moses Old Bull." *American Indian Art Magazine* 19 (3): 48–57.

Mohatt, Gerald Vincent and Joseph Eagle Elk. 2000. *The Price of a Gift: A Lakota Healer's Story*. Lincoln: University of Nebraska Press.

Ogunwole, Stella U. 2002. "The American Indian and Alaska Native Population: 2000." *Census 2000 Brief*, February.

Petrillo, Larissa S. 2001. "Contemporary Lakota Identity: Melda and Lupe Trejo on 'Being Indian.'" Ph. D. diss., University of British Columbia.

Powers, Marla N. 1986. *Oglala Women*. Chicago: University of Chicago Press.

Powers, William K. 1975. *Oglala Religion*. Lincoln: University of Nebraska Press.

Prucha, Francis P. 1984a. *The Great Father: The United States Government and the American Indians*. Vol. 1. Lincoln: University of Nebraska Press.

——. 1984b. *The Great Father: The United States Government and the American Indians*. Vol. 2. Lincoln: University of Nebraska Press.

Red Horse, John G. et al. 1978. "Family Behavior of Urban American Indians." *Social Casework* (February): 67–72.

———. 2000. *Family Preservation: Concepts in American Indian Communities*. Seattle: Casey Family Programs.

Red Shirt, Delphine. 1998. *Bead on an Anthill: A Lakota Childhood*. Lincoln: University of Nebraska Press.

———. 2002. *Turtle Lung Woman's Granddaughter*. Lincoln: University of Nebraska Press.

Rhine, Gary and Fidel Moreno, directors. 1991. *Wiping the Tears of Seven Generations*. Videocassette.

Sneve, Virginia Driving Hawk. 1995. *Completing the Circle*. Lincoln: University of Nebraska Press.

Standing Bear, Luther. 1975. *My People the Sioux*. Lincoln: University of Nebraska Press.

———. 1988. *My Indian Boyhood*. Lincoln: University of Nebraska Press.

Steinmetz, Paul B. 1998. *Pipe, Bible, and Peyote among the Oglala Lakota: A Study in Religious Identity*. Syracuse, N.Y.: Syracuse University Press.

Stubben, Jerry D. 2001. "Working with and Conducting Research among American Indian Families." *American Behavioral Scientist* 44 (9): 1466–81.

Thornton, Russell. 1987. *American Indian Holocaust and Survival: Population History since 1492*. Norman: University of Nebraska Press.

Thornton, Russell and J. Marsh-Thornton. 1987. "Estimating Prehistoric American Indian Population Size for United States Area: Implications of the Nineteenth-Century Population Decline and Nadir." *American Journal of Physical Anthropology* 55 (1): 47–53.

Uberlaker, Douglas H. 1976. "Prehistoric New World Population Size: Historical Review and Current Appraisal of North American Estimates." *American Journal of Physical Anthropology* 45 (3, pt. 2): 661–65.

———. 1988. "North American Indian Population Size, AD 1500 to 1985." *American Journal of Physical Anthropology* 77 (3): 289–94.

U.S. Census Bureau. 2002a. "American Indian/Alaska Native Heritage Month: November 2002," press release, 21 October, *U.S. Census Bureau Facts and Features*, www.census.gov/Press-Release/www/2002/cb02ff17.html.

———. 2002b. Geographic Comparison Table: GCT-P7. Households and Families: 2000. Geography: American Indian and Alaska Native Area, and Alaska Native Regional Corporation. *Census 2000 Summary File 2 (SF 2) 100-Percent Data*.

———. 2002c. "Poverty Rate Rises, Household Income Declines, Census Bureau Reports." Press release, 24 September. www.census.gov/Press-Release/www/2002/cb02-124.html.

Weaver, Hilary N. and Barry J. White. 1997. "The Native American Family Circle: Roots of Resiliency." *Journal of Family Social Work* 2 (1): 67–79.

Weaver, Hilary N. and Maria Yellow Horse Brave Heart. 1999. "Examining Two Facets of American Indian Identity: Exposure to Other Cultures and the Influence of Historical Trauma. In Weaver, *Voices of First Nations People*, 109–26.

Wilson, Angela. 2005. *Remember This! Dakota Decolonization and the Eli Taylor Narratives*. Lincoln: University of Nebraska Press.

Young Bear, Severt and Ron D. Theisz. 1994. *Standing in the Light: A Lakota Way of Seeing*. Lincoln: University of Nebraska Press.

CHAPTER 6

Marriage, Family, and the Modern Catholic Mind

JULIE HANLON RUBIO

WHAT'S WRONG WITH MODERNITY?

In 1965 the bishops of Vatican II opened the groundbreaking document "Pastoral Constitution on the Church in the Modern World" with an empathetic understanding of the "joy and hopes, the griefs and anxieties" of the modern age.[1] *Gaudium et Spes*, as the document is also known, exemplifies the standard methodology of contemporary Catholic magisterial documents in that it begins with an analysis of what might be called "the situation" before turning to theological reflection. However, in this document the analysis is more inductive and historically conscious than in most church documents and paves the way for a more thorough engagement with the modern world.[2] Contemporary popes and theologians have, to varying degrees, continued and extended this practice of confronting and responding to the social situation. Much of recent Catholic theology, then, can be seen as an encounter with modernity.

However, the Magisterium (the teaching office of the church) and lay theologians encounter modernity differently.[3] The bishops of Vatican II, like many others, characterize modernity as an age of industrialization, urbanization, technology, change, and advancement, but they also focus on spiritual poverty, false notions of freedom, and flawed understandings of the self.[4] The bishops' concern about the relationship between social change and religious beliefs and practices is typical of Catholic thought. With respect to marriage and family, even as the bishops try to appreciate the gifts of modernity, their writings are marked by a fear that dangerous trends in modern thought (especially individualism) support practices (i.e., divorce, contraception, consumerism, etc.) that are ultimately destructive to human beings.[5] Worry about how modern thought undermines the family is a key piece of the Magisterium's larger concern with the excesses of modernity.

Lay theologians immersed in the modern world see things somewhat differently. Though they often share with the Magisterium a suspicion of modern individualism and a related respect for the demands of the common good, they tend to be much more accepting in practice of the sort of respect for the experiences of individuals that worries church leaders. In the work of lay Catholic theologians one finds support for the Magisterium's social ethics alongside a critique of its personal ethics. While the Magisterium and lay theologians join in critically responding to the social problems that modernity has spawned, they part company in the realm of the family, where the Magisterium continues to criticize the culture, while many lay theologians turn and criticize the church. In this chapter I will outline these differences before suggesting that this divide in Catholic thought undermines the ability of the church to confront modernity and must be overcome if the church is to speak prophetically in modern society.

THE CATHOLIC CHURCH IN MODERN AMERICA

Before considering contemporary Catholic dilemma in America, it is necessary to understand that the problem can be traced to the late 1800s, when great numbers of Catholics began to enter the United States. Germans and Irish comprised the majority of the first wave of Catholic immigrants (1860–80). Southern and eastern Europeans (especially Italians and Poles) came in great numbers between 1880 and 1920. In 1860 only three million Catholics lived in America, but by 1930 there were twenty million, representing one-sixth of all Americans.[6]

During the immigrant years ordinary Catholics struggled primarily with the problem of assimilation. Like other minority groups, Catholics had to decide to what extent they would conform to American culture rather than retain a distinct identity.[7] The predominantly Protestant culture viewed Catholic faith with suspicion. Acceptance of papal authority, frequent confession, domestic devotions involving rosaries or statues of saints, and processions organized to venerate Mary seemed foreign to Protestants, whose religious life centered on the reading and interpretation of scripture. Still, immigrant Catholic communities held on to the significant parts of their "unwashed faith," even when second-generation Catholics pressured them to worship in more modern, American ways.[8]

   Progressive Catholic leaders eventually came into conflict with the Vatican, which supported the traditional faith of immigrants and energetically resisted theologians' attempts to modernize Catholic faith.[9] In the late 1800s Pope Leo XIII taught that because, ideally, the state should support the church, the American experiment was flawed. He also praised American immigrant Catholics for maintaining their distinctive practices. In contrast, more liberal priest theologians favored less emphasis on devotions, more openness to political liberalism (particularly the idea of church-state separation), and other modest changes in Catholic faith and practice. Rome responded with a condemnation of what Pope Leo called "Americanism." In response to a growing body of theologians who believed that America offered an excellent place for the church to adapt to modernity, Pope Leo XIII claimed, "It would be very erroneous to draw the conclusion . . . that it would be universally lawful or expedient for the State and Church to be, as in America, dissevered and divorced."[10] Theologians charged that they had been mischaracterized, but the tension remained. The controversy worsened in 1907 when Pius X issued his condemnation of modernism, arguing against those who sought to adapt Catholicism in response to modern historical and critical studies.[11] The Vatican won the battle in the short term, as the church continued to oppose the separation of church and state, and priest theologians largely abandoned attempts to liberalize Catholic teaching.[12] Still, the struggle between a Vatican critical of and resistant to modernity and American theologians open to adapting their Catholic faith was far from over.

   The Vatican's critique of modernity existed on two fronts—the personal and the social.[13] Two major documents of Pope Leo XIII's— *Arcanum*, an encyclical on Christian marriage, published in 1880, and *Rerum Novarum*, the first of the papal social encyclicals issued in 1891—provide an interesting contrast. In the former Pope Leo extols the church as the protector of true marriage and ridicules the notion that governments should maintain jurisdiction over marriage.[14] Leo characterizes Christian marriages as relationships marked by mutual love, the headship of the husband, and willing obedience of the wife and children.[15] Leo concentrates his criticism on divorce, claiming, "It is easily seen that divorces are in the highest degree hostile to the prosperity of families and States, springing as they do from the depraved morals of the people."[16] Leo also refers to the evils of cohabitation, interreligious marriage, and civil marriage.[17] From beginning to end the tone is triumphant and the norms are uncompromising, as Leo shows how modern corruption of marriage endangers both the fabric of society and the souls of the faithful.

   Rerum Novarum shares *Arcanum*'s triumphal tone and critical evaluation of modernity. It was written in part in response to requests for guidance from American church leaders of working-class Catholics who wanted the pope to weigh in on the rise of labor unions.[18] Pope Leo's response assumed the continuing existence of capitalism and affirmed the right to private property. Yet the document's ringing calls for justice were rooted in its empathetic depiction of workers unjustly treated.[19] While Leo condemns the socialist solutions to the problem because they fail to respect the individual's right to property, he promotes workers' rights (including the right to a just wage—one that enables a worker to support a family), acknowledges the need for limited amount of state intervention to ensure justice for workers, and encourages generous giving to the poor, after a family has spent enough to maintain its station in life.[20] What *Arcanum* does in the personal sphere, *Rerum Novarum* does in the social sphere, challenging the excesses of modernity and calling for structural change, church control, and personal conversion.[21]

How did American Catholics respond to these documents? While Leo XIII encouraged emerging movements of socially conscious Catholics on social justice issues and "provided a doctrinal challenge to the apathy and indifference of middle-class and affluent Catholics, including the clergy,"[22] on family issues he confirmed the ideas of laity. The first pope to seriously confront modernity, Leo XIII took a less defensive stance than his predecessors but attacked what he saw as threatening social trends,[23] giving hope to progressive theologians and working-class Catholics while challenging the middle and upper classes. His analysis of family issues, which affirmed the beliefs of most Catholics, provoked far less interest.

This style of confronting modernity on two fronts—the social and the personal—continued with Pope Pius XI, author of *Quadragesimo Anno* and *Casti Connubii* (both issued in 1931). Both documents respond to the excesses of modernity. The pope wrote the latter, his encyclical on marriage, to correct "modern fallacies," such as cohabitation, birth control, abortion, adultery, divorce, and "false liberty and unnatural equality with the husband." [24] Similarly, he wrote *Quadragesimo Anno* because with modern industrialization, "the number of non-working poor has increased enormously and their groans cry to God from the earth."[25] The reception of these documents was similar to that of *Rerum Novarum*. By this time groups of socially conscious Catholics, such the Catholic Worker movement started by Dorothy Day and Peter Maurin, and the Friendship Houses founded by Catherine de Hueck, had begun to gain strength.[26] In addition, the theologian John Ryan had written his influential book, *A Living Wage: Its Ethical and Economic Aspects*, and had spent years formulating the American bishops' 1919 Program of Social Reconstruction, which advocated the institution of a minimum wage and child labor laws.[27] Thus many were encouraged by the social justice message of *Quadragesimo Anno*, even as some criticized it for not going far enough. *Casti Connubii* received little critical commentary and seems to have been largely accepted by the Catholic masses.

This early period of conflict between the Magisterium and the theologians gave rise to three trends. First, liberal American theologians found their attempts to embrace modernity and adapt Catholicism to the American environment thwarted by the Vatican. Second, by the end of the nineteenth century both the Vatican and the U.S. bishops had begun to issue social documents that called into question modern social changes and structures. These documents were well received by socially conscious theologians and working-class Catholics but were questioned by the middle and upper classes. Third, magisterial documents addressing the problems of the modern family were far less controversial, eliciting little criticism from theologians or lay Catholics. The first two trends continue through the contemporary period, but when married theologians began to measure teaching on the family against their own experience, they found some of the Vatican's critique in that area to be wanting.

GENDER AND THE MODERN CATHOLIC MIND

More open than many of his predecessors, John Paul II confronted the modern world with a mixture of praise and critique and saw in it "an interplay of light and darkness." Still, while highlighting modern contributions such as greater respect for individual freedom, increased attention to marital relationships, and promotion of the dignity of women, he mourned an "excessive independence" between spouses, the decline of parental authority, as well as what he called "a truly contraceptive mentality," rooted in consumerism and unsubstantiated fear about the future, and evident in a declining respect for life. At the core of these problems, according to the pope, is a mistaken conception of freedom divorced from truth and used as an excuse for selfishness.[28]

The pope's theology of gender was a prime example of his argument with modernity.[29] Certainly, John Paul II's theology in this area was more progressive than the overtly sexist theologies of his predecessors, including Pius XI, who, in *Casti Connubii* (1931) called feminists "false teachers," advocated that the husband should rule the wife as the head rules the heart, and affirmed that "a certain inequality and due accommodation . . . is demanded by the good of the family."[30] John Paul II offered instead his theology of the body, according to which men and women are equal in dignity and similarly called to total self-giving but given different roles in the family. The pope based his theology on a distinctive reading of the Genesis creation stories that led him to affirm that all human beings become who they are meant to be by giving of themselves in love. However, women and men are distinct. Like Eve, women come to men as gifts; they give themselves first and fully. Like Adam, men receive women as gifts and respond with the gift of themselves.[31] The theology of body makes self-giving central for all but emphasizes women's particular role as givers in marriage.

Mulieris Dignitatem (1988) built on the pope's earlier theology of the body. According to John Paul, all women are naturally more able to give, and pregnancy deepens this capacity. Because women are physically, psychologically, and even ontologically different from men, their call to parent is primary and they answer it naturally. Men, in contrast, learn their fatherhood from women and stand somewhat outside the mother-child dyad, even as they direct the family's spiritual and social life. Men give themselves to the work of supporting the family first and to parenthood second.[32] Though in his later writing, especially *The Genius of Women* (1995), John Paul affirmed women's right to work and celebrated "the unique role women have in humanizing society," he still emphasized the complementary nature of men and women and the primacy of the vocation to motherhood.[33] In his claims about gender differences and his celebration of total self-giving in the family, the pope stood apart from modern advocates of freedom and equality in marriage.

While some conservative Catholic scholars find John Paul's views compelling,[34] the majority of academic theologians find his rejection of modern ideas about marital relationships problematic, primarily because they find that the experience of married people calls ideals of difference and self-sacrifice into question. It is important to point out here that the use of experience in moral theology is not without its problems, for experience differs across time and culture, and even among people. Moreover, when individuals make judgments based on their experience, they may falsely believe that the way they live is normative, which may limit their ability to imagine that life could or should be otherwise.[35] Yet, as Timothy O'Connell rightly notes, Catholic moral theology recognizes the validity of a natural law method that is experientially based, meaning that "moral evaluative judgements are conclusions derived from concrete perceptions of human reality, of what truly helps or hurts human persons."[36] O'Connell suggests that if moral judgments were unrelated to the experience of people, they would make little sense. While modern theologians are careful to balance their analysis of experience with attention to scripture, church teaching, and reason, they nonetheless remain committed to the idea that, ultimately, their moral theories should correlate with human experience. John Paul himself, in his early work, *Love and Responsibility*, asserted that he "fears nothing from experience" and invites readers to compare their own experience of love with his analysis of its hidden dimensions.[37]

Theologians responding to John Paul II's theology of gender in *Mulieris Dignitatem* attempt to do just that. Lisa Cahill argues that the ideal of motherhood celebrated in the document is inconsistent with men's and women's experiences in marriage.[38] Similarly, Cahill writes, Margaret O'Brien Steinfels finds the pope's "'idealized image' of women's 'nurturing, maternal qualities' to be 'strangely implausible,' [and] she observes that it is 'separated as by a chasm from the ordinary experience of an increasing number of women and men.'"[39] Other critics claim that the pope should consider women's public work as a vocation or good in itself.[40] All question the pope's emphasis on women's self-sacrificial nature and his insistence that motherhood defines women so profoundly that it makes all other callings peripheral. Critics claim to know from their experience that women and men both give and receive, that women and men can be both parents and contributors to public life.[41] For many Catholic theologians modern individualism is not the problem. Rather, the Magisterium itself stands in the way of needed adaptation to modern understandings of men, women, and married love.

SEXUALITY AND THE MODERN CATHOLIC MIND

If modern Catholic theologians are suspicious of magisterial teaching on gender, they are even more so with regard to Catholic sexual ethics. For John Paul II love, self-sacrifice, and openness to children lie inextricably intertwined at the center of a theology of sexuality. In his theology of the body he affirmed the centrality of procreation, claiming that spouses who "become 'one flesh,' . . . subject, in a way, their humanity to the blessing of fertility."[42] The pope saw sex as an expression of total self-giving that is the purpose of human existence. He believed that it is "the interior freedom of the gift—the disinterested gift of oneself—[that] . . . enables them both, man and woman, to find one another."[43] The pope contrasted his vision of spouses who come to see who they really are through the gift of self in the sexual act with the modern idea of sex as pleasurable give and take, for he believed that this view reduces human beings to objects and is rightly called lust.[44] Elsewhere he argued that the total self-giving that is necessary to sex cannot occur outside marriage or with artificial birth control.[45] According to John Paul II, sex in its essence is union through the disinterested giving of self and acceptance of the other, totally open to the gift of life, a sacramental sign of the ultimate human vocation of total self-giving. Moreover, he was convinced that respecting what sex is in its essence can only enhance marital love.[46] There can be no conflict between truth and experience.

Nevertheless, modern Catholic theologians have largely rejected key aspects of this understanding of sexuality as at odds with the experience of married people. In an article entitled "Can We Get Real about Sex?" Lisa Cahill "disagree[s] that sexual and marital experience necessarily confirm all current church teaching."[47] Cahill's alternative is an experientially based argument that sexuality involves mutual physical pleasure, intimacy, and procreative potential, not in each and every sexual act but in "the ongoing relationship of a couple."[48] For Cahill "getting real" about sex means measuring the Magisterium's norms against the experience of married couples who see sexual drive and pleasure as good, who believe that when they set aside the procreative potential of sex for a time, they are not compromising their commitment to life, and who know intimacy as the primary meaning of sexuality. Cahill ends up criticizing modern sexual norms as well, for she advocates only slight modifications in the Catholic position, advocating the acceptance of birth control for married couples but closing the door to casual sex, nonprocreative sexual relationships, and certain infertility treatments.[49] She attempts to modestly adapt Catholic teaching to the modern sexual experience in order to help the church regain its credibility as a speaker in the modern public square.

Christina Traina's trenchant critique of the pope's sexual ethics goes even further. Her argument is notable for its insistence that what seems natural often looks different when viewed "from the ground" of married life. Traina sets out to test the pope's theology of the body against her own experience as a married woman. She finds that the pope's thinking resonates with her in that "procreative sex sometimes achieves the relational or 'unitive' goods of love-making better than intercourse that is not aimed at procreation," for there is "a shared delight in a common project that really is a 'total self-gift' to each other and our hoped for future child."[50] Still, Traina claims that this sort of sex is rare, while nonprocreative sex is common and good in a different way.[51]

In her defense of nonprocreative sex Traina questions the pope's insistence that artificial birth control hinders total self-giving. She writes, "For me contraception does not impede self-gift but, like pregnancy, allows it the freedom to proceed unworried by consequences." Yet contraceptive lovemaking does not exclude children, for sex "involves our whole selves, including and especially our parental selves."[52] Thus while the pope claims that contraceptive sex constitutes something less than complete self-giving, Traina argues that contraception makes total personal, spousal, and even parental self-gift possible.[53]

Traina's critical insights are rooted in a modern sensitivity to the need for theology to speak the truth about experience. She and many others point out the failure of John Paul II's theology to resonate with the experience of most Catholic married couples who practice contraception but do not see themselves as having nongiving, let alone objectifying, sex. Traina and Cahill do not speak for all Catholic couples, for certainly some practice natural family planning and claim that periods of abstinence are difficult but ultimately enriching for their marriage.[54] Still, these couples are a distinct minority in the church today, and while their experience should be valued, it seems that modern theologians are right to pay careful attention to the experiences of the majority of the faithful as well.[55]

MODERN GAINS AND MODERN LOSSES

Most Catholic theologians would agree that the criticisms of scholars like Cahill and Traina on gender and sex are most often on the mark, and many are grateful for the powerful witness of those theologians who use experience to question the contemporary Catholic theology on the family. The growing body of this kind of theology is testimony to the modern valuing of experience.

However, the cost of this focus in Catholic thought is that the radical personalism of the Magisterium is muted and its powerful critique of the dehumanization in the modern world is hard to hear. John Paul II made defense of the dignity of the human person the centerpiece of his papacy and built much of his moral theology around the fundamental claim that all people are valuable in themselves and must be treated accordingly. Yet the church's wisdom about life in the modern world is drowned out by the voices of theologians and ordinary Catholics who question its claim to speak the whole truth about married love. Because the church is not "real" about sex or gender, it has found it difficult to be recognized as a prophetic critic of modernity. Only in the area of social ethics has the church been able to effectively proclaim a countercultural model.

DOMESTIC POLICY, DOMESTIC CHURCH, AND THE MODERN CATHOLIC MIND

In its social teaching the Magisterium ordinarily addresses political issues such as international human rights, war, and the role of state, but most social documents also include some attention to what might be called a social ethic of the family.[56] Recall that *Rerum Novarum* (1891), the first modern social encyclical, addresses the obligation of employers to pay employees a just wage. This norm is rooted in a condemnation of modern economic theories that view the worker as a commodity. Catholic teaching insists that work is inherently personal because it is done by a person and necessary because remuneration for work provides for the basic needs of workers and their families. Thus the worker who is paid unjustly "is the victim of violence against which justice cries out."[57]

Catholic teaching on just wage is rooted in four general principles: the state must intervene when the rights of a human being are violated, the family has priority over the state and possesses certain rights that the state must respect, work is for the person, and the health of the family (and ultimately the good of human beings) depends on a harmonious balance of work and family.[58] These principles constitute the basis for a significant part of the Catholic critique of modern society.

The radical potential of the first becomes clear when Catholic notions of human rights are spelled out in greater detail.[59] If all people have the right not only to marry but also to live in the social and economic conditions that make marriage possible, the right to work in conditions that do not hinder the well-being of the family, the right to decent housing, and so on, the state seems to have many unmet responsibilities to human beings. The second principle makes clear the priority of the good of the family in society and the political duty of the state to recognize family rights. The third principle obligates employers to treat workers as people rather than instruments and may relate to family leave policies and the availability of options such as job sharing and flex time. The last principle suggests that employers whose long hours lead to imbalance for their employees are contributing to the decline of families and, ultimately, society itself. Thus Catholic teaching on just wage is a piece of a larger understanding of how people, families, work, and the state fit together. It has profound implications for those with power in the work world and in government.

The Catholic social ethic of the family includes both social policy analysis and a consistent call for Christian families to move beyond the domestic sphere into the world. Against the modern idea of the privatized family's providing a haven to comfort its members when they return from the harsh, cold world, contemporary Catholic teaching insists that families are "the first cell of society" with a mission to humanize modern culture.[60] In contrast to those who want to save the world by focusing on the family, John Paul II argues that Christian families have four tasks. First, they must become communions of love. Second, they must serve life, first by welcoming children into their home but also by teaching their children to live counterculturally and by practicing hospitality, especially toward those whom society rejects. Third, Catholics are to serve society by living simply, doing charity, and working for justice in the political realm. Finally, they should be called "domestic churches," because, like the larger church, their mission is both to become communities of love and to bring love to the world.[61]

The claim that families must serve a good larger than their own serves to militate against idolization or sacralization of the family. Unlike other religious traditions in which family plays the central role, family in the Catholic tradition is properly understood as a community in which the Christian commitment to love is lived out through relationships between family members, service to the community, and action for justice in the world.[62]

Catholic theologians do not criticize the church's teaching on the social rights and social mission of the family. Instead, lay theologians affirm both the social policy agenda and the prophetic call for families to involve themselves in the work of charity and justice. Barbara Andolsen's book, *The New Job Contract: Economic Justice in an Age of Insecurity*, uses Catholic social teaching to rethink workers' rights in a new economic situation.[63] Her work is representative of many similar analyses of Catholic social teaching on the family. The official teaching on the social mission of the family is also celebrated by Catholic theologians like Lisa Cahill, who insists that "the Christian family defines *family values* as care for others, especially the poor."[64] Florence Caffrey Bourg's work on the domestic church is notable for a similar favorable response to papal teaching and a commitment to make that teaching concrete by reflecting on the every day practices through which families work toward a realization of the ideal.[65] Other thinkers focus on the problem of consumerism and ask how families can live "a spirituality of resistance" in the face of overwhelming pressure from a market economy that values things over people.[66] Catholic theologians join the Magisterium in affirming the responsibility of the state to support families and asking families to care for the poor, cultivate social virtues, combat consumerism, and engage in the work of justice.

Certainly, one can imagine experiential arguments against the social mission of the family similar to those raised by married theologians who are critical of papal teaching on sex and gender. Some thinkers call for more emphasis on the natural bonds among family members, question the wisdom of asking vulnerable modern families to do one more thing, or worry about what the family will lose when it enters the public sphere,[67] but in most cases they are not Catholic thinkers. When the church responds to the individualism of modern life with a radically communal social ethic, lay theologians immersed in modern family life concur. This means that though the contemporary Catholic Church is divided and weakened when it addresses gender relations or sexuality, it speaks with one voice on the need for families to counter the negative effects of modern life with community and solidarity.

TOWARD AN INTEGRATED RESPONSE TO MODERNITY

The Catholic critique of modernity has its roots in the late nineteenth century, when the Catholic Church began to address what it saw as modern evils. The Magisterium of the contemporary Catholic Church attempts to deal with modernity in many different ways: in the gender sphere the church offers an ethic of total self-giving to counter the modern emphasis on the self, identifies women as the primary self-givers, and upholds their irreplaceable work of love in the home. In the sphere of sexuality the church celebrates the potential of married sexual love to be a mutual self-gift of husband and wife but claims that contraception makes self-gift impossible. In the social sphere the church calls the state to recognize the rights of families and promotes the ideal of the family as a domestic church with responsibilities to inculcate its members with social virtues, live counterculturally, and work for justice in the world. All three aspects of the official response to modernity can be linked to a fundamental respect for human beings and a belief that people are called to give themselves in love to others in all areas of their lives.

The response to Catholic teachings on modernity has varied. In the earlier period liberal theologians supported the Vatican's critique of both social and personal excesses of modernity. However, today's theologians are more suspicious of official teaching on the family. While lay theologians affirm the personalist emphasis of recent Catholic teaching, and agree with the modern link between families and social justice, they are more apt to bring their own experiences as married people to bear in a critique of the Magisterium's views of sex and gender and are more likely to call for adaptation of church teaching in this area. The divide between the Magisterium and theologians undermines the effectiveness of the Catholic critique of modernity because it shifts the focus of theological energy away from social analysis and critique to internal debate.

Not surprisingly, conservatives and liberals disagree about how to move forward. Some conservative Catholics contend that the Magisterium's theology must be embraced as a whole, for it involves a total understanding of people in relation to the world. There is, as one advocate has argued, a fundamental connection between chastity and justice.[68] Meanwhile, some liberal Catholics want to move beyond the Magisterium's teaching because they see that teaching as fundamentally flawed. One critic charges that the tradition is so weakened by its gender divide that it fails to advance any compelling alternative to modernity.[69]

Perhaps a middle position can be advanced. On the one hand, the consistent refusal of recent Catholic teaching to separate the public from the private offers much of value. A clear focus on the dignity of people and a call to total self-giving pervades both social teaching and family teaching. In a world where the value of people can seem negotiable, the church refuses to compromise. Liberal critics seem to be less than fully appreciative of the church's prophetic, countercultural affirmation of people, evident in recent critiques of capital punishment, the rush to war in Iraq, and the sexual exploitation of women. On the other hand, the church's insistent emphasis on gender complementarity and the illegitimacy of artificial birth control limits its critique in important ways. When women seem to bear the burden of self-giving in the family, the value of their public callings is diminished, and the necessity of men's self-giving in the home becomes less obvious. When the church places artificial birth control alongside abortion, euthanasia, and capital punishment, and calls them all violations of human dignity, its claim to be a prophetic critic of modernity is rendered suspicious.

At the same time, when theologians allow their disagreement with the Magisterium on these issues to blind them to the great gifts of the tradition, something is lost. Surely, there is much to celebrate in a tradition that takes seriously the ways in which people are valued or used in every realm of human existence, in a church that stands for human life despite the cost. Given the low probability that the specific, problematic teachings in the areas of sex and gender will change in the near future, it seems prudent to pull out the more prophetic threads of the Catholic critique of modernity and weave them into a strong defense of the person both inside and outside the home.

If Catholic theologians were to do this, they might find themselves in a fruitful dialogue with those from other religious traditions who also struggle with the need to adapt to good modernist impulses and the desire to challenge modern evils. Surely, American families in immigrant Muslim and Buddhist communities would identify with the bishops of Vatican II who wrote in 1965 of the "joy and hopes, and griefs and anxieties" brought by modernity. While their specific struggles may differ, all families are potentially liberated by a world that offers them new choices and potentially threatened by a world that often ignores the good of people. All have an interest in joining together in dialogue and action promoting human dignity in a modern world pregnant with both liberating and dehumanizing potential.

NOTES

1. *Gaudium et Spes*, in Austin P. Flannery, ed., *The Conciliar and Post Conciliar Documents, Vatican Council II*, rev. ed. (Northport, N.Y.: Costello, 1975), #1. Vatican II was a council called by Pope John XXIII to bring the Catholic Church into the modern age by updating its teachings. Bishops from all over the world met from 1962 to 1965 and wrote documents addressing different aspects of Catholic theology.

2. Marvin L. Krier Mich, *Catholic Social Teaching and Movements* (Mystic, Conn.: Twenty-Third Publications, 1998), 125.

3. I will refer to lay theologians throughout most of the chapter because the contributions of married theologians who write about marriage have been especially significant since Vatican II. This is not to deny the reality that priest-theologians may have much in common with their lay colleagues.

4. *Gaudium et Spes*, #6.

5. Ibid., #47.

6. George M. Marsden, *Religion and American Culture* (Fort Worth, Texas: Harcourt, Brace, Jovanovich, 1990), 132.

7. Ibid.

8. In *The Madonna of 115th Street: Faith and Community in Italian Harlem, 1880–1920* (New Haven, Conn.: Yale University Press, 1985), Robert Orsi brilliantly shows how a traditional Italian Catholic festival honoring the Madonna of Carmel eventually became embarrassing to Irish and German Catholic clergy who had adapted to their American Protestant environment (57).

9. Orsi notes that Pope Leo XIII crowned the Madonna of Carmel (a statue of Mary brought from Italy and used in traditional processions and devotions in an Italian neighborhood in New York City). The coronation symbolized Rome's recognition of the favors granted by the Madonna and her popularity. Leo's coronation of the Madonna in 1903 showed his approval of traditionalism rather than modernism in American Catholic life. See Orsi, *Madonna of 115th Street*, 60–61.

10. Leo XIII, *Longinqua Oceani*, quoted in Sydney Ahlstrom, *A Religious History of the American People* (New Haven, Conn.: Yale University Press, 1972), 837. This 1895 document, addressed to the American church, was designed to quell modernist impulses. When the theological argument continued, Leo issued *Testem Benevolentiae* in 1899, specifically condemning Americanism. See Ahlstrom, *Religious History of the American People*, 835–39.

11. Ibid., 839.

12. Ahlstrom claims that after this rebuke, American theologians abandoned attempts to adapt and turned instead to practical matters. See *Religious History of the American People*, 840.

13. Though Brad Wilcox and Elizabeth Williamson are correct to point out, in chapter 3, that the Catholic Church "has largely resisted the logic of family modern-

ization on issues like divorce, contraception, and premarital sex," I believe that it is important to acknowledge that the church also defends the family in its strong critique of unfettered capitalism. The church faults both modern personal ethics and modern social systems for the ways in which they fail to respect human dignity.

14. Leo XIII, *Arcanum* (1880), in Claudia Carlen, ed., *The Papal Encyclicals, 1878–1903* (Raleigh, N.C.: McGrath, 1981), #19.

15. Ibid., #11 and 12. This model seems similar to both the Buddhist understanding of marriage as a union in which spouses minister to each other by performing specific, gender-related tasks and to the traditional Muslim view of male authority in marriage, which is linked to the husband's role as provider. See also chapters 11 and 13.

16. Leo XIII, *Arcanum*, #29.

17. Ibid., #44, 43, 18.

18. Mich, *Catholic Social Teaching and Movements*, 17–18.

19. Leo XIII, *Rerum Novarum*, in Michael Walsh and Brian Davies, eds., *Proclaiming Peace and Justice: Papal Documents from* Rerum Novarum *through* Centesimus Annus, rev. ed. (Mystic, Conn.: Twenty-third Publications, 1991), #42.

20. Mich, *Catholic Social Teaching and Movements*, 20–21.

21. *Rerum Novarum's* brief analysis of the family constitutes more attack on the personal front of modernity. The document reaffirms woman's primary role as mother and discourages employment outside the home (#60). The gender roles assumed in *Arcanum* carry over, expounding upon the father's governing role in the family (#20). Even the just wage is premised on the norm of a male worker who is supporting a family.

22. Mich, *Catholic Social Teaching and Movements*, 26–27.

23. Ibid., 26.

24. Pius XI, *Casti Connubii, Five Great Encyclicals* (New York: Paulist, 1939), #74.

25. Pius XI, *Quadragessimo Anno, Five Great Encyclicals*, #59.

26. Mich, *Catholic Social Teaching and Movements*, 65–72.

27. Ibid., 48–56.

28. John Paul II, *Familiaris Consortio* (Washington, D.C.: U.S. Catholic Conference, 1981), #6.

29. I have chosen gender and sex as illustrations of the divide between theologians and the Magisterium, but similar analyses could be done using divorce and homosexuality, among other issues.

30. Pius XI, *Casti Connubii, Five Great Encyclicals*, #74, 27, and 76, respectively.

31. John Paul II, *Original Unity of Man and Woman: Catechesis on the Book of Genesis* (Boston: Daughters of St. Paul, 1981), 131–34.

32. John Paul II, *Mulieris Dignitatum* (Washington, D.C.: U.S. Catholic Conference, 1988), #18.

33. John Paul II, *The Genius of Women* (Washington, D.C.: U.S. Catholic Conference, 1995), 40, 52, and 25. The pope also worries that women's "sensitivity" will diminish with the advent of new roles (28) but advocates "flexible and balanced solutions" so that work and motherhood can exist in harmony (33).

34. See, for instance, Leonie Caldecott, "Sincere Gift: The Pope's 'New Feminism,'" in Charles E. Curran and Richard A. McCormick, eds., *John Paul II and Moral Theology* (New York: Paulist, 1998), 216–34; Mary Ann Glendon, "What Hap-

pened at Beijing," *First Things*, January 1996, 30–36; Janet E. Smith, "John Paul II and the Family," in Gregory R. Beabout, ed., *A Celebration of the Thought of John Paul II on the Occasion of the Papal Visit to St. Louis* (St. Louis: St. Louis University Press, 1998), 85–103.

35. For example, middle-class Americans surrounded by large houses and ever-increasing consumption of consumer goods may be unable to see that their experience is atypical in a global context, let alone choose to live differently in order to practice solidarity with Third World neighbors. Thanks to Brad Wilcox for this suggestion.

36. Timothy O'Connell, *Principles for a Catholic Morality* (San Francisco: Harper and Row, 1976), 146. For a more recent discussion see Todd Salzman, *What Are They Saying about Catholic Ethical Method?* (New York: Paulist, 2003), 48–79. Muslim scholars are beginning to do something similar as they bring "local custom" in America into dialogue with the more traditional teachings of the Qur'an and Sunna (see Smith, chap. 13). Mainline Protestants who value "openness to the world," are also using experience as a source of moral reasoning (see Wilcox and Williamson, chap. 3).

37. Karol Wojtyla, *Love and Responsibility*, translated by H. T. Willetts (New York: Farrar, Straus, and Giroux, 1981; 1st Polish ed., 1960), 10, cited in Christina Traina, "Papal Ideals, Marital Realities: One View from the Ground," in Patricia Beattie Jung, with Joseph Andrew Coray, eds., *Sexual Diversity and Catholicism* (Collegeville, Minn.: Liturgical 2001), 269.

38. Lisa Cahill, *Women and Sexuality* (New York: Paulist, 1992), 54.

39. Ibid.

40. Gregory Baum, "Bulletin: The Apostolic Letter *Mulieris dignitatem*," in Elisabeth Schüssler and Anne Carr, eds., *Motherhood: Experience, Institution, Theology* (Edinburgh: Clark, 1989), 149. See also Lisa Cahill, who argues that even the progress made in *The Genius of Women* is limited by the continuing insistence on women's special capacity for giving in relationships and an unwillingness to reconsider teachings on contraception. Christians are left with "a vision of women in the home, a private, autonomous sphere of love, in which the mother is constantly prepared for the arrival of another birth, and where she above all others exemplifies empathy and devotion" (Cahill, *Family: A Christian Social Perspective* [Minneapolis: Fortress, 2000]), 94.

41. I would assume that many mainline Protestants embrace equality for these substantive reasons, and not simply, as Wilcox and Williamson argue in chapter 3, because traditional ideas have "fallen out of favor in the social and intellectual circles they travel in" or because they embrace "a therapeutic ethic of self-realization and expressiveness." As they note, a suspicion of constraining gender roles may not yet correlate with egalitarian marriages in which both spouses live out vocations to home and world, but surely contemporary marital relationships differ in ways that are hard to measure in sociological studies. In addition, it may take more than a generation for those deeply committed to family and public life to work out how to practice what they have come to believe is best.

42. John Paul II, *Original Unity*, 111.

43. Ibid., 116.

44. Ibid., 130–32.

45. John Paul II, *Familiaris Consortio*, #32.

46. Ibid., #33.

47. Lisa Cahill, "Can We Get Real about Sex?" in Kieran Scott and Michael Warren, eds., *Perspectives on Marriage: A Reader* (New York: Oxford University Press, 1993), 208.

48. Ibid., 213.

49. Ibid.

50. Traina, "Papal Ideals, Marital Realities," 274.

51. Ibid.

52. Ibid., 279.

53. Ibid.

54. See Paul Murray, "The Power of 'Humanae Vitae': Take Another Look," *Commonweal* (15 July 1994): 14–18, and National Conference of Catholic Bishops, *Parenthood* (Washington, D.C.: U.S. Catholic Conference, 1990), 23–28.

55. See Julie Hanlon Rubio, "Beyond the Liberal Conservative Divide on Contraception: The Wisdom of Practitioners of Natural Family Planning and Artificial Birth Control," *Horizons* 32, no. 2 (fall 2005): 270–94.

56. See my dissertation, "A Catholic Social Ethic of the Family," University of Southern California, Los Angeles, 1995.

57. Leo XIII, *Rerum Novarum*, 44.

58. See Leo XIII, *Rerum Novarum*, #33–37, on state intervention; John Paul II, *Charter on the Rights of the Family* (Washington, D.C.: U.S. Catholic Conference, 1983), 6, on family rights; John Paul II, *On Human Work* (Washington, D.C.: U.S. Catholic Conference, 1981), #6, on work and the person; and John Paul II, *On the Family*, #23, and *Genius of Women*, 43, on balancing work and family.

59. See John XXIII, *Pacem in Terris* (Washington, D.C.: U.S. Catholic Conference, 1963), and John Paul II, *Charter*.

60. John Paul II, *Familiaris Consortio*, #42.

61. Ibid., #17.

62. It is useful to note that nothing in the Christian tradition would parallel this statement of the Prophet Muhammad: "The best of you are those who are best to their families."

63. Barbara Andolsen, *The New Job Contract: Economic Justice in an Age of Insecurity* (Cleveland, Ohio: Pilgrim, 1998).

64. Cahill, *Family*, 135.

65. Florence Caffrey Bourg, "Domestic Church: A New Frontier in Ecclesiology," *Horizons* 29, no. 1 (spring 2002): 51, and *Where Two or Three Are Gathered: Family as Domestic Church* (Notre Dame, Ind.: University of Notre Dame Press, 2004). More practical work in this area has been done by James McGinnnis and Kathleen McGinnis, cofounders of the Parenting for Peace and Justice Network, a support group for parents who want "to act for justice without sacrificing our children and to build family community without isolating [them]selves from the world." See their *Parenting for Peace and Justice* (Maryknoll, N.Y.: Orbis, 1990), 2. This seems similar to the current American Muslim emphasis on raising children in an American society that is hostile to Muslim values (see Smith, chap. 13, and Wilcox and Williamson, chap. 3), and to the emerging immigrant Buddhist interest in distinctive ways of Buddhist parenting (see Prebish, chap. 1).

66. Kieran Scott, "A Spirituality of Resistance for Marriage," in Kieran Scott and Michael Warren, eds., *Perspectives on Marriage: A Reader* (New York: Oxford University Press, 2001), 208–9.

67. See Jean Bethke Elshtain, "The Family and Civic Life," in David Blankenhorn, Steven Bayme, and Jean Bethke Elshtain, eds., *Rebuilding the Nest: A New Commitment to the American Family* (Milwaukee: Family Service America, 1990), 141.

68. Gregory R. Beabout and Randall Colton, "If You Want Justice, Work for Chastity," unpublished paper, 2003. Beabout and Colton analyze John Paul II's *Evangelium Vitae* (1995) and conclude that the pope rejects the social values of efficiency and convenience, which characterize the modern "culture of death," but upholds chastity and justice, virtues of a countercultural embrace of life. See also the work of John Kavanaugh, who seeks to hold together the personal and social aspects of Catholic teaching, in *Following Christ in a Consumer Society*, rev. ed. (Maryknoll, N.Y.: Orbis, 1991).

69. Christine Guforf, "Renewal or Repatriarchalization? Responses of the Roman Catholic Church to the Feminization of Religion," in Joann Wolski Conn and Walter E. Conn, eds., *Horizons on Catholic Feminist Theology* (Washington, D.C.: Georgetown University Press, 1992), 75–76.

CHAPTER 7

Generative Approaches to Modernity, Discrimination, and Black Families

ROBERT M. FRANKLIN

African American discourse about rationality in public life and modernization occurs within the context of profound suspicion about the capacity of "right reason" to form and guide the moral will, particularly in relation to acknowledging the equal dignity of all people. When blacks saw that Thomas Jefferson, father of the American Enlightenment, had trouble with practicing racial equality, they knew that the ordinary whites with whom they had to deal were unlikely to be more virtuous than the nation's most "enlightened" public leaders.

To the extent that modernization offered promise of a break with a racist status quo, it was a welcome phenomenon. It inspired African American hope that America could change and dispose of its wretched history of race group interactions. But modernization unfolded within the context of a larger and more powerful, even primitive, cultural force, namely, racism. Modernization was filtered and compromised by the dehumanization and enslavement of a particular group of humans, based on observable genotypic features (skin color) for the purpose of generating wealth for their owners. And no amount of religious rhetoric appeared to have sufficient force to budge racism very much.

So African Americans recognized that they had to formulate their own strategies of response to modernization and discrimination. The black community's most influential institutions, its houses of worship, sponsored these responses. But the churches and mosques also had secular counterparts, as I will attempt to illustrate. Indeed, it is possible to say that African Americans have used at least five distinct religious responses to the dual phenomena of modernization and discrimination. Before reviewing these responses, I will provide a brief overview of the religious traditions that African Americans have developed. After sketching the five religiously sponsored responses to modernity and discrimination, I illustrate how these varying responses are reflected in their respective strategies of dealing with family challenges and particularly the challenge of sustaining male investment in marital, parental, and familial obligations.

AN OVERVIEW OF BLACK RELIGION

Like their Native American counterparts, African people were sustained by vital religious beliefs and practices that predate the birth of the American colonies. Also akin to Indian traditions, African traditional religions were oral rather than founded upon a revealed text, communal rather than individually oriented, did not draw a strict distinction between the sacred and secular, and were strongly oriented to the land and rhythms of nature.[1]

In 1619 the first Africans were brought to Jamestown, Virginia, for the purpose of serving as indentured servants. Following a specified period of labor they were granted freedom. This small nucleus of free blacks gave rise to a politically and economically significant community of free persons of color who would later agitate on behalf of abolition and other progressive causes (W. E. B. Du Bois was born free in Great Barrington, Massachusetts). By the mid 1600s slavery had become a permanent status in several colonies, setting the pattern for slavery in America.

For the first hundred years the white population did not carefully monitor the spiritual life of blacks. Some black people worshipped in the same churches as their masters. Others, preferring the spiritual traditions they brought with them from West Africa, avoided the suspect versions of Christianity that slaveholders practiced. But by the 1740s, with the spread of the Great Awakening, tens of thousands of black people were converted to Westernized Christianity. The historian Albert Raboteau reminds us that blacks began to craft a complex and unique pragmatic faith made up of at least four sources: African traditional religion; Roman Catholic popular piety, with its elaborate collection of saints, candles, and colorful vestments; Protestant evangelicalism, with its egalitarian message that slaveholders and slaves were equal sinners before God; and Islam, a faith that many Africans had embraced back home.

By the 1770s separate black congregations began to emerge in both North and South. Before the dawn of the nineteenth century blacks could be found in most Protestant denominations as well as the Catholic Church. And, as the twentieth century progressed, blacks would become devotees of Judaism (especially in New York) and an indigenous version of Islam (Sunni, Sufi, and the sectarian Nation of Islam). Indeed, the remarkable religious diversity within the African American population is often misrepresented by those who oversimplify by using the concept of the black church as a proxy for all religiosity in black America.

Let me fast-forward the narrative to what I suggest are five distinct approaches to modernity and discrimination within a very diverse black religious community. Each response reflects a slightly different view of the family in modern society.

FIVE TRADITIONS OF RELIGIOUS RESPONSE

The first response of black religion to modernization and discrimination can be characterized as progressive accommodationism. Led by optimistic leaders such as Booker T. Washington and his religious counterparts, including Rev. Elias Camp Morris (founding president of the National Baptist Convention, the nation's largest black denomination) and most bishops of the African Methodist Episcopal Church, progressive accommodationists sought to embrace the cultural changes associated with modernization and to work in incremental, nonconfrontational ways to eradicate discrimination. Sometimes this meant accommodating black aspirations to the dominant ideology of "separate but equal," an ideology that came to be the nation's legal and social status quo up to the civil rights movement.

Majority black Baptists and Methodists, and blacks in mainline denominations, were progressive insofar as they regarded change to be positive and exploited opportunities to subvert and replace American racial prejudices and practices. Even the simple gesture of having personal and family photographs taken while dressed in their Sunday best and displaying, sometimes publishing, them in black-owned newspapers, was a quiet rebuke against racists who believed that blacks were uncivilized and could not maintain "normal" families. But these blacks were also accommodationist in their willingness to tolerate rather than mount a full offensive against a status quo predicated on their subordination. The accommodationists concentrated on building black institutions such as the one hundred or so historically black colleges and universities, black businesses, and, of course, black families. Booker T. Washington mounted a relentless campaign to establish black colleges in the tradition of Hampton (his alma mater) and Tuskegee Institute, schools that promoted industrial and vocational education over classical liberal arts education. Mainline black Christian denominations provided what the ethicist Peter Paris of the Princeton Theological Seminary refers to as a "surrogate world" in which blacks could maintain their own parallel universe of social institutions, customs, and values.[2]

Although developed throughout the eighteenth, nineteenth, and twentieth centuries, the progressive accommodationist orientation is alive and well today as it seeks to renew black family life. Black families were stronger, more numerous, and more durable during the era of de jure segregation. The weakening of black family life seemed to correlate with black community preoccupations with politics and social concerns rather than family life, moral values, and personal responsibility. Family decline seemed to accelerate after the civil rights movement. Hence blacks must retrieve their preintegration practices and outlooks about interpersonal dependency and personal responsibility.

Second, the prophetic progressives were led by religious leaders such as Martin Luther King Jr. and "secular moralists" such as W. E. B. Du Bois and America's first black feminist, Anna Julia Cooper. They believed that America must conform to the ethical principles of its constitutive documents and of universal reason. Rather than accommodate to an unjust status quo, blacks and whites must join forces in attacking legal and political barriers to the full integration of blacks. Anna Julia Cooper insisted that racism and male domination were of the same fabric and that both had to be eradicated, an analysis that Du Bois, black America's most "Enlightened" leader, did not immediately embrace. In black communities denominations like the Progressive National Baptist Convention cohered around Dr. King's more radical strategies of confronting racism. Also, civil rights organizations like the National Association for the Advancement of Colored People (NAACP) and the Southern Christian Leadership Conference (SCLC) were established in 1910 and 1957, respectively, to mount a multiracial, interfaith challenge to the status quo. Du Bois was among the few nationally recognized African Americans on the governing board of the NAACP. The radical sector of the black religious community was open to critically examining the inherited traditions of black family life. Although not antagonistic toward the traditional family, the progressives recognized that egalitarianism between men and women would become the new reality with which black families must grapple. In effect, they were more open to modernity, although not dramatically so, than their more conservative accommodationist counterparts.

Third, the redemptive nationalists insisted that blacks voluntarily separate and insulate themselves from white American norms of political, social, and family life. Led by Marcus Garvey, Elijah Muhammad, and his most famous disciple, Malcolm X (pre-1964), the nationalists expressed vigorous opposition to integrating into American culture. Today this tradition is sometimes embraced by various and sundry "Afrocentric" cultural and religious organizations to justify reappropriating (not always in a critical manner) gender role and communal norms and practices associated with West Africa or even ancient Egypt. This orientation is sustained by religious communities like the Shrine of the Black Madonna (Detroit and Atlanta), some black megachurches with an Afrocentric emphasis, and the various splinter groups that identify themselves as authentic expressions of the original Nation of Islam. Although the splinter groups articulated a strong ethic of reclaiming black men and reinstalling them as the "heads of their households," to the chagrin of women who had held together families and communities, most of these groups are now revising their approach to embrace gender equality. Recall that it was this segment of the black religious community that sponsored the Million Man March in October 1995 and not the traditional accommodationist black churches. Today the national representative of Minister Farrakhan, Imam Ava Muhammad, is a woman, an attorney who bears the title of imam, a phenomenon that has been challenged by Imam Warith Deen Muhammad, a Sunni Muslim and son of Elijah Muhammad. And, in October 2005 the Nation of Islam reconvened an impressive number of women and men, straight and gay, for what they called the "Millions More Movement."

Fourth, grassroots pietists firmly reject modernity and work for a return to the simpler days of tradition. But, unlike the nationalists, the pietists advocate a return to tradition not for purposes of ethnic separation but to establish an environment in which individual moral purity may flourish in isolation from the corrosive and seductive effects of capitalism. The pietists conceptualize discrimination as another manifestation of Satan's reign in this world and do not offer social or systemic responses. Rather, they see the key to social change as individual conversion and personal holiness. This response has been shaped by a variety of charismatic, evangelistic leaders over time, including William J. Seymour (father of modern black Pentecostalism), Bishop Charles Harrison Mason (founder of the Church of God in Christ), and other evangelical, Holiness, and Pentecostal groups that have flourished in poor and urban communities. Somewhat similar to the nationalists, the pietists individualize human fulfillment and regard the moment of conversion as the real start of the authentic life. Conversion should inaugurate the journey toward accepting traditional biblical norms of family and personal uprightness.

Finally, the positive thought materialists embrace modernization and its many material benefits. Like the pietists, they do not attempt to address or confront discrimination as a systemic social problem but insist upon their own individual liberty to maximize the acquisition of material goods. Led by Depression-era messianic figures like Daddy Grace and Father Divine, and, more recently, the New York "Reverend Ike," they were precursors to contemporary exponents of a "prosperity gospel" that is rooted in a quasi-biblical theology of "health, wealth, and success." This orientation appears to cohere around a theory of "ethical egoism" and does not regard marriage or other kinship connections to be intrinsically important or central to the Bible's moral teachings.

With this religious map in place I'd like to turn to illustrating the way these various groups view the challenge of promoting marriage and fatherhood in contemporary black communities.

LIVING WITH AMERICA'S ORIGINAL SIN

It might be useful to summarize the debate about the lingering effects of slavery on black family structure. When the famed Howard University sociologist E. Franklin Frazier argued that slavery was responsible for the troubles and instability of black families, many social scientists embraced his perspective. Indeed, the late Daniel Patrick Moynihan's infamous report trumpeting the pathology of black families was essentially following Frazier's lead. As a white policy maker and academic, Moynihan was an easier target than his African American mentor; however, more recent research has challenged Frazier's perspective. Relying on census data, historians have shown that the two-parent, nuclear family was the predominant family form in the late nineteenth and early twentieth centuries for blacks as well as whites. Herbert Gutman found that 70 to 90 percent of black households were "male-present" and that a majority of them in the counties he examined were nuclear families.[3] Scholars of the African American family such as Andrew Billingsley have tried to replace the usual focus upon black deficits with the family assets and strengths that African Americans developed and retain, such as the extended family, fictive kin, and the veneration of grandmothers.[4]

Again, the picture is complex. Black women and men were marrying and attempting to build strong families, but significant social and economic forces were impeding their efforts. Given the migration of the black population between 1940 and 1970, perhaps I should say that African Americans were headed into the jaws of modernity.

In a powerful study of African American gender relations titled *Rituals of Blood: Consequences of Slavery in Two American Centuries*, the Harvard sociologist Orlando Patterson acknowledges that the black community must not overemphasize slavery as an explanation (as Frazier did), but intellectual honesty and rigor require an understanding of its most important features: "After two hundred fifty years of forced adaptation to the extreme environment of slavery, African-American men and women developed a distinctive set of reproductive strategies in their struggle to survive. Tragically, the strategies that were most efficient for survival under the extreme environment of slavery were often the least adaptive to survival in a free, competitive social order."[5]

Patterson notes that the most devastating impact of the "centuries-long holocaust of slavery" was the "ethnocidal assault on gender roles, especially those of father and husband, leaving deep scars in the relations between African-American men and women."[6] He then traces the manner in which male slaves found it rational and expedient to have as many children as possible in order to "leave progeny who might survive to adulthood."[7] Male slaves experienced the separation of two important processes that have been almost universally observed together in parenting, that is, calculating the number of children one could support financially, on one hand, and then carefully proceeding to limit one's family size accordingly, on the other. During slavery black men were prevented from exercising moral agency to participate in this parenting process; after slavery they were not encouraged or rewarded for doing so.

Patterson presents a chilling analysis of how newly freed young black men and women began to have large numbers of children, which suited them perfectly but almost sentenced them to long-term dependence upon the southern sharecropping economy and "farm tenancy rather than farm ownership."[8]

He declares that "Afro Americans and American society at large (like Afro-Caribbean and Afro-Latin societies) are *still living with the devastating consequences* of this male attitude toward reproduction."[9] Together with the phenomenon of much earlier marriages among African Americans than in other groups, and extremely high fertility rates, he notes that "this pattern was a recipe for chronic and persistent poverty."[10] Whether Patterson's interpretation is firmly supported by the data may be a matter of perspective and presupposition. But he has highlighted factors and dynamics from the slave past that have not been adequately theorized, and he has thereby served the conversation well. Going forward, academics should be attentive to these factors without engaging in deterministic analysis of human behavior.

INTO THE JAWS OF MODERNITY

In his best-selling book, *The Promised Land: The Great Black Migration and How It Changed America*, Nicholas Lemann observes that "between 1910 and 1970, six and a half million black Americans moved from the South to the North; five million of them moved after 1940, during the time of the mechanization of cotton farming. The black migration was one of the largest and most rapid mass internal movements of people in history—perhaps the greatest not caused by the immediate threat of execution or starvation. In sheer numbers it outranks the migration of any other ethnic group—Italians or Irish or Jews or Poles—to this country."[11]

Growing up in a working-class household in Chicago in the 1950s, I used to enjoy listening to the migration stories of my parents and extended family. Most of the adults whom I knew and loved were born in rural Mississippi, where they struggled to thrive amid the economic challenges of the sharecropping system and the social boundaries of Jim Crow. On occasion, relatives moved to Detroit or Chicago in search of better job opportunities or in desperate efforts to escape the terror of local white citizens who meant to do them harm. Most folks traveled by train or bus, but I can recall a couple of cousins and neighbors who claimed to have been smuggled out by cover of darkness in the trunks of automobiles driven by well-dressed and respected black pastors, a latter-day version of the underground railroad rarely heard about.

My parents heard the stories of those northern relatives who were living well, thanks to the abundant work opportunities in heavy industries of the North. My extended family (grandmother and her eight young adult offspring) moved to Chicago's South Side en masse, and all my aunts and uncles soon were gainfully employed. They all became members of the Roberts Temple Church of God in Christ, the congregation whose membership included Sister Mamie Till and her family. Emmett Till, her son and soon-to-be man-child martyr, was several years older than I. You can imagine how the little boys in my church felt when the story of his chilling murder circulated and echoed around Chicago. What kind of people would do this to one of us mischievous but harmless kids?

My father worked his way up the ladder to management at the Campbell's Soup Company's West Side plant. All the adults worked, and they all married. All had children but not quite as many as their own parents, who had relied upon child farm labor to make ends meet. Already my parents and their siblings were learning an important adaptive lesson: large families were no longer an economic necessity; indeed, they could prove to be a liability.

William Julius Wilson reminds us that the earliest detailed national census information about family structure is available from the 1940 census: "In 1940, female-headed families were more prevalent among blacks than among whites, and among urbanites than among rural residents for both groups. Yet, even in urban areas, 72 percent of black families with children under eighteen were male headed. Moreover, irrespective of race and residence, most women heading families were widows."[12]

Although African Americans had embraced marriage once they were free to do so, especially between the 1890s and the 1940s, something began to change after the 1950s. I witnessed this change, learning and observing painful lessons as the women of my family whispered about how a neighbor or relative had been laid off, started drinking, and stopped coming home to his wife. During the 1950s we learned a new word, *divorce*. African American women began to marry later than their white counterparts, resulting in a "post-sixties reversal in which the proportion of single African-American women significantly exceeded that of single Euro-American women."[13] We had no way of anticipating what the 1960s and its many revolutions would bring.

Wilson's explanation for family and community decline emphasizes economic factors. Important as they may be, the explanation is incomplete without due consideration of the role of demographic and cultural factors. Wilson's Harvard colleague, Orlando Patterson, offers such a complementary perspective. Underscoring the impact of macroeconomic changes on black families that had survived slavery and sharecropping, only to arrive in northern ghettos, Wilson stresses that between 1947 and 1972 the central cities of the thirty-three most populous metropolitan areas lost 880,000 manufacturing jobs, while manufacturing employment in their suburbs grew by 2.5 million positions. The same cities lost 867,000 jobs in retail and wholesale trade even as their suburbs gained millions of such positions. Wilson argues persuasively that society cannot ignore the impact of joblessness on the desire of men to pursue marriage.[14]

Orlando Patterson begins with these statistics: "There has been a sizable decline in the marriage rate of African-American men since the forties. In 1940, the overall marriage rate of black men under twenty-four exceeded that of their white counterparts, as did the percentage of black men under thirty who were married. After 1950, the rate at which black men married plunged, although it still remains significantly higher than that for black women."[15]

Patterson then sets the stage for an animated debate by putting forth three provocative questions: Why are blacks refusing to get married? Why, when they do get married, do their marriages collapse at such unusually high rates? And why do African Americans choose to remain single when the social, psychological, and economic rewards of marriage or stable partnering are, especially in their case, so substantial?[16]

Various scholars offer three frequently cited explanations. First, the "male marriage pool" thesis, developed by Wilson, suggests that black marriage rates deteriorated in the 1970s because of declining job prospects. Most women, unless they are social workers in search of new cases, are not interested in relationships with men who enter the relationship as an economic dependent. As a popular blues tune sung by a female artist used to declare, "I can do badly all by myself, I don't need no one to help." Second, Patterson writes, "the 'female independence' thesis argues that the improved economic situation of women since the 1950s has made all women more independent of men. Women delay marriage in order to pursue their careers or because they do not feel as pressured to secure a marriage early, and when they do get married they are less reluctant to walk away from unhappy circumstances."[17] And third, the "school enrollment" hypothesis maintains that "increased school enrollment accounts for the delay in marriage. Young black people are pursuing their education instead of going directly into the work force and getting married, as they might have done during earlier periods when there were fewer educational opportunities," Patterson declares.[18] I can think of innumerable black female professionals who recall with some frustration the dual messages from their mothers: Stay in school, get as much education, and then earn as much as you can without depending on a man, but also hurry and marry a good man and provide me with grandchildren before your biological time clock runs out. This may constitute a normative crisis in which equally desirable goods compete for a woman's preference.

Although Patterson uses demographic data to challenge and qualify each of these common explanations, for him the bottom line is that black men and women are "moving on very *different socioeconomic trajectories*":

> Black women do considerably better than men on all the vital demographic indicators of health and physical survival. And, they are fast closing the income gap between the genders and are already significantly ahead of African-American men in the acquisition of educational and occupational skills and positions.[19]

This parallel trajectory leaves Patterson close to despair about the future of black marriages, at least what traditionally constitutes a "black marriage." He offers a variety of additional data and insights documenting this discrepancy that are worth reviewing and must certainly be discussed throughout African American communities, including:

- 83 percent of divorced or separated black men believe that a woman can do just fine bringing up a boy, but only two-thirds of divorced or separated black women think so.
- Black men and women hold significantly different attitudes toward sexual morality. Much of the difference is traceable to the higher rate of female participation in the church, resulting in a more conservative sexual ethic. Since so many divorces are the result of infidelity, it is significant that black women live by a norm of marital fidelity (83 percent had never been unfaithful to their spouse, compared with 57 percent of men, a 26-point gap).[20]

Ultimately, Patterson has advice to give. And here he shifts from social-scientific explanation to normative discourse:

> I urge African-Americans, especially African-American women, to engage more in out-marriage. This would immediately help to solve the marriage squeeze of African-American women. And with the sexual and marital competition of men from other ethnic groups, African-American men may well be prompted to alter their own attitudes and behavior. Given that African-Americans are only thirteen percent of the population, even if only one in five men who are not African-Americans are interested in inter-marrying with them this would immediately double the market of available spouses for them. Hence, African-American women *should immediately* . . . extend the equal opportunity principle to the marriage market.[21]

Of course, African Americans for many decades have engaged in interracial partnering, especially males. Consider such celebrated multiracial offspring such as Tiger Woods and Halle Berry. However, this path remains emotionally charged and politically complicated for many blacks, although anecdotal evidence suggests that earlier patterns of caution are changing. Whatever one thinks about Patterson's substantive recommendation, it is unusual and interesting to see a respected sociologist abandon dispassionate, objective distance to engage in moral, almost pastoral, counsel for the good of those whom he studies. If there is a trend lurking here, perhaps it is more collaboration between social scientists and theologians.

CULTURAL CHANGE

The third significant factor affecting the environment for black marriage and parenting was the changing nature of social, cultural, and moral codes. During and immediately after the slave period, the black community did not stigmatize female-headed households. Who knew why such a woman was now alone? Who would dare judge her for this status if her fiancé or husband had been lynched? Or perhaps she was with child because the master had raped her. Other women were abandoned by husbands who migrated north, promising to send for the rest of the family, but ultimately were consumed by the streets of the city. The economists Ronald B. Mincy and Hillard Pouncy observe, "At certain times in the painful history of race relations in this country, desertion and victimization were as likely causes of single motherhood as moral failure. In any individual case, who could know? Who would ask? In response, the black community developed a tradition of embracing all of its children, even the fair-skinned ones. Under these circumstances, stigmatizing unwed births was impossible."[22]

The famed sociologist Kenneth Clark noted how this change of moral code correlated with class identity:

> In the ghetto, the meaning of the illegitimate child is not ultimate disgrace. There is not the demand for abortion or for surrender of the child that one finds in more privileged communities. In the middle class, the disgrace of illegitimacy is tied to personal and family aspirations. In lower-class families, on the other hand, the girl loses only some of her already limited options by having an illegitimate child: she is not going to make a "better marriage" or improve her economic and social status either way. On the contrary, a child is a symbol of the fact that she is a woman, and she may gain from having something of her own.[23]

This practice is complex and merits more attention than I can provide here. However, I should note that the ethic of toleration and acceptance of single-parenthood that was developed by the larger community has always lived in tension with the more traditional family agenda of middle-class black church culture. The churches believed that the causes of out-of-wedlock birth and divorce could be changed. The larger community, however, assimilated the dominant culture's myths of individualism and moral relativism and made no special efforts to intervene.

PUBLIC POLICY

In addition to the impacts of slavery, as well as economic and cultural change, on families, public policy has been an important factor. Here I will be exceedingly brief in noting that the black family has been acted upon with varying effects by a long history of law and public policy. Blacks have had to endure the indignity of a social system that did not permit legal marriages and contract making among enslaved people. Blacks would not be recognized as citizens before the law until passage of the Thirteenth and Fourteenth Amendments to the U.S. Constitution in 1865 and 1868, respectively. Later, the welfare system was implemented in ways that penalized women for allowing a man to be present in the household. Law and policy have been enemies of the black family for a long time. Perhaps they can now lend their authority and resources to strengthening fragile families.

THE MARRIAGE MYSTERY

Mincy, of Columbia University, and Pouncy, of Rutgers University, have investigated what they refer to as the "marriage mystery," namely, "given the significant advantages to marriage for black adults and, with qualifications for children, why is this institution relatively underused by blacks?"[24] One would expect self-interested, economically rational agents to select life plans that represent good investments and life choices. Why is that not happening among many educated, upwardly mobile black people who make smart decisions in other areas of their lives? Mincy and Pouncy ask: "Does marriage offer enough advantages to adults to motivate them to marry and remain married so that the interests of their children are also secured?"[25] Another way to ask this question is, *has the best case for marriage been made to young African Americans?* And, if not, *who will make it?* Who is going to pitch marriage to a skeptical audience? I have already shown my cards. I think that the church can and must take up this challenge.

A growing body of research on marital assets is useful for making the case. Mincy and Pouncy summarize some of it:

- Married people are economically better off when they pool their resources.
- Married men earn significantly more than their never married, cohabiting, and widowed peers (the efficiencies, scales, and bargains of marriage almost always benefit men more than women).
- Married people live longer and enjoy better health than singles.
- Married people enjoy more frequent sex and are happier with their sex lives than single people.
- The children of married people tend to fare better in life, especially in educational attainment and avoiding risky behaviors.

In 2001 the popular weekly black magazine *JET* weighed in on the subject of differential benefits with an article titled "Who Benefits More from Marriage—Men or Women?" Nearly all the scholars who provided sound-bite comments concurred that men are the winners (especially economically) in marriage. The Howard University sociology professor Florence B. Bonner explained,

Women may benefit from the resources being brought to the relationship like finances and status; however, in a dual-working family, women still end up with more of the responsibility for children, less of an opportunity to advance their careers than do men, and a lot more stress engaged in both at work and at home, because they are trying to negotiate those two spaces. If you document the number of things that women do within a week to help support a man's career, it is obvious that marriage benefits males in terms of career advancement. If you are working six to seven days a week, then you have almost no time to do laundry, make the trip to the cleaners or do grocery shopping. Men can step in and do that, and we treat it as if it's a wonderful example of progress, but they do not do that consistently.[26]

Despite the premium for men, Dr. Joyce A. Ladner argues that "men and women need companionship, they need to be loved, to have someone to care about them and someone who is there for them."[27] Hence both women and men are beneficiaries of marriage, even if in different ways. However, Patterson's research suggests that men value companionship at a considerably higher rate than women (49 percent of men versus 19 percent of women), while women seem more focused on the "instrumental aspects of marriage" such as financial security.[28]

These data recall for me a haunting question raised by the theologian Jacquelyn Grant. Noting the variety of ways in which women are exploited and excluded by organized religion, she asks, "Is religion good for women's health?" She urges women to reexamine the goods they derive from faith and to begin negotiating with religious authorities for more inclusive and just practices. Society might ask the same kinds of questions about marriage: Is marriage good for women? Do women really need marriage? These are other provocative questions that the black community will need to discuss honestly and patiently.

Examining an early draft of this chapter, my wife observed that I had failed to include the "sister networks" that function as husband-father surrogates. She listed the various small groups of women who gather with their children to carpool, share babysitting needs, lend money, offer counsel and advice, share meals, and generally offer sisterhood and empathic support to one another. When these networks work well, women (including married ones) get at least some of the support they need, without a man nearby. Given such sister networks, how can the case for marriage succeed?

CREATING GENERATIVE ADULTS

With greater sobriety about precisely who benefits from marriage, let us consider its benefits for children. Ron Mincy and Helen Oliver insist that society and adult men and women should privilege the well-being of children as they make decisions for or against marriage and divorce: "Central to the debate surrounding the next phase of welfare reform are two basic questions: what types of families are *best for children*, and what can government do to encourage these beneficial arrangements?"[29]

They ask, why do black children have less access to their fathers than other children? The answer is simple and painful: Black marriage rates are low and divorce rates are high. Meanwhile, 70 percent of black children are born to single mothers. More obvious and just as painful, a staggering number of men and fathers are in prison. Consequently, the deck is stacked against black youngsters' having any time with their fathers.

Despite this dismal picture, there is some good news: 45 percent of the children in single-parent homes see their fathers at least once a week. Forty percent of all black children live in households with both parents; however, the visiting arrangements for the children of unwed parents are fragile and generally do not last beyond the ages of five to eight. It is in the long-term best interest of society at large and, certainly for these children, to find ways to support fathers who wish to remain involved in their children's lives and to create incentives for fathers who currently have nothing to do with their children. A capitalist society should not underestimate the power of cash payments to motivate fathers to do what they should do for the right reasons. And who knows? Perhaps the behavior that is initially rewarded with monetary benefits might continue as those benefits are progressively reduced and terminated.

The sociologist Brad Wilcox has noted that the "failure of civil society to hold back the tidal wave of divorce and out-of-wedlock births that swept across the United States after the 1960s" has led many marriage proponents to advocate vigorous public action on behalf of marriage.[30] Early in its second term the Bush administration was moving forward with a concern expressed by the 105th Congress, namely, ensuring that our welfare system reflects traditional family values. Among Congress's welfare reform proposals is the effort to "encourage the formation and maintenance of two-parent married families." It also dedicates $300 million in federal and matching funds to support marriage promotion efforts. "Unfortunately," writes Mincy, "the plan only pays lip service to responsible fatherhood and provides no dedicated federal funds to support such efforts."[31] The inclusion of the word *married* in this goal represents a shift proposed by the Bush administration.

Mincy sees challenges ahead for African Americans who are trying to increase responsible fatherhood. Since the mid-1990s fatherhood advocacy organizations have "expanded their services to help fathers make positive contributions to their children, even while unmarried, and to position themselves to assume the responsibilities . . . to one day sustain happy marriages. The new services focus on job retention, wage and career growth, and job placement [as well as] legal, educational, team-parenting, substance-abuse, child-support, health, mental-health, spouse-abuse, and other services to meet the needs of clients and their families."[32] Mincy worries that these important efforts could be discouraged by heavy-handed marriage-promotion initiatives, especially those that enjoy the backing of the government. He further proposes a metaphor about father involvement in children's lives, regarding it as a ladder that begins with "no father-child contact" and moves to "some father-child contact," then to cohabitation and marriage.

Based on his collaborative research with a team comprised of Columbia and Princeton researchers, Mincy points to what scholars know about increasing the probability that people will move up the ladder. The upward climb is most likely to occur when

- Fathers are employed.
- Men and women avoid having children with multiple partners.
- Employment services are available.
- Education about preventing out-of-wedlock pregnancy is accessible.[33]

Based on my own experience, observations, and practice of ministry, I think that I would add to this list:

- Both individuals possess, or are willing to develop, basic respect and care for each other. In other words, estranged lovers and relative strangers can learn and can try to become friends.

Whether or not the focus upon increasing fathers' involvement in children's lives becomes an integral part of the government's current efforts to energize traditional family values, it will certainly be the centerpiece for an increasing number of African American nonprofit organizations such as the National Center for Strategic Nonprofit Planning and Community Leadership and for voluntary associations such as fraternities, 100 Black Men, mosques, and churches.

These are just a few of the groups that are stepping up to the challenge of ensuring that every child has a responsible and caring adult in her or his life. In most cases it would be ideal for the father to be one of the caring adults in the child's life. But when that is not possible or desirable, fallback options are available.

I would like to offer a brief comment about the need for all communities to develop "generative adults." I first came across this phrase when reading the work of Don S. Browning when I was a graduate student at the University of Chicago. Browning was building on the wise and profound work of the psychologist Erik Erikson. Erikson noted that as adults approach the end of the human life cycle, they should demonstrate the capacity to care for the next generation. When adults are able to look back upon their lives without great regret, and with an abundant sense of gratitude for "what had to be," they can look outward and forward to add their final touches to the canvas of life. On the other hand, when adults approach the end of life with resentment about all that they did not get to do, or all that they were entitled to but did not receive, and when they are obsessed with their own failing health or declining retirement resources, they are people burdened by despair, the opposite of generativity.

I believe that effective congregations can and should create generative people, people who are willing to sacrifice some of their own happiness for the good of the next generation. Generative adults are people who are willing to remain in marriages, even if they are not ecstatically happy, in order to offer certain goods to their children and community. Generative adults need not be martyrs or live in misery, but they should be urged to consider the consequences of their actions and decisions upon the next generation. Generative fathers would commit themselves to remaining responsibly active, caring, and resourceful people in the lives of their own children and in the lives of those who need them.

WHO HELPS TROUBLED FAMILIES?

To this point, I have reviewed various dimensions of the father-absence challenge. I noted that the legacy of slavery cannot be ignored in this discussion as it established social conditions under which blacks developed adaptive reproductive strategies to preserve the group. Unfortunately, those same strategies quickly became maladaptive in a relatively free society with increasing economic and educational opportunities.

I followed the line of argument elaborated by Orlando Patterson to appreciate the divergent socioeconomic trajectories of black women and men since the first half of the twentieth century. I have also reviewed the impact of economic dislocation, cultural change, and public policy on black families. I cited the challenges surrounding the case for marriage in a milieu in which women benefit less than men and in which both men and women underuse the institution. It is patently unfair that black children are deprived of their fathers because of the choices and behavior of adult men and women. Hence my call for congregations and the larger culture to take seriously the cultural work of creating "generative adults."

I believe that African American congregations and their leaders are the natural coordinators and catalysts for an ongoing conversation about the future of black marriages, families, and children's well-being. The United States has more than seventy thousand black churches and mosques. They possess a variety of assets necessary to sponsor a series of conversations. These include meeting space, talented leaders, armies of potential volunteers, track records of service and effectiveness, community credibility and trust, financial assets, and the moral authority to instruct, admonish, and empathically guide people in regard to that which is right and wrong, good and bad, blameworthy and praiseworthy.

As Ron Mincy said recently: "I don't believe the marriage and fatherhood agenda will go very far without a religious foundation. The black community expects that moralizing will have religious roots. But the failure of the black church to get out front and speak up hampers the efforts of other professionals who wish to help black kids."[34]

As I noted at the beginning, the five responses to modernization and discrimination may yield differing responses to the most prominent challenges facing black families today. The accommodationists continue to encourage marriage and family formation but without creativity and vigor. Their approaches generally do not capture the interest of the young people in their congregations. The progressives, led by some of the black church's best-educated clergy, have shown innovation and a willingness to experiment with communicating concern about the black family. Some have developed "male academies," where they teach sexual ethics and male responsibility. They have championed the concept of mentoring and taken the initiative in assisting single mothers with parenting boys. But these ministries tend to be limited to the innovative churches in which they began and have not translated into a national movement.

Long ago the nationalists recognized that the black family was in crisis. And, as the Million Man March illustrated, the nationalists were among the few community leaders willing to sponsor dramatic, headline-making activities to call attention to the family crisis. They tended to diagnose it as a crisis within capitalism and modernity that devalues familial relationships and overvalues material acquisition, individual mobility, and sexual liberty. Sometimes this legitimate analysis was compromised by lodging it within a conspiracy theory of white society's deliberate efforts to destroy black families, a notion that continues to have resonance for some blacks. But the theory seems less persuasive when one considers the decline of white families and families of other ethnic groups in our postmodern era, a theme explored by other authors in this book.

The pietists have individualized the family challenge and continue to diligently work on saving the family one by one, an effort that is doomed by lack of scale and scope. But they do correctly call attention to the need for personal commitment, reform, and effort to sustain marriages and families. In the view of the pietists, personal commitment, not policy, is the most critical factor in renewing families.

Finally, the materialists tend to see family commitments as incidental and not central to a full life. Like the pietists, materialists individualize social problems. Less distressed about the decline of black families, they focus on helping individuals adopt "new thinking" that is positive and upwardly mobile. Most individuals are not ready for the demands of marriage. Only after they have had a proper intellectual conversion can they begin to assess their readiness and need for a like-minded (positive-minded) mate.

What is interesting to me is that none of the traditions, with the possible exception of the progressives and nationalists (Rev. Jeremiah Wright and Minister Louis Farrakhan), has mounted a fierce and urgent response to the decline of black marriage and parenting. If the momentum for a national campaign is to emerge, it will require the leadership and sponsorship of dynamic and creative leaders. And it will be important for their visions to be open to mutual criticism and revision as a more diverse black community seeks to take up the challenges ahead. My hope is that a villagewide conversation about the future of black families will soon begin this campaign. This is a project to which I will devote my energies in the coming years.

DO NOT DISTURB: VILLAGE DIALOGUE IN PROGRESS

How would such a conversation begin? Congregations, all of them, need *training* and user-friendly materials to inform their perspectives on the complex issues of marriage and family formation in contemporary society. The village dialogue will cover material that is emotionally charged, intellectually demanding, and theologically complex. This work will demand study and the discipline of listening carefully.

Congregations will need a curriculum or discussion materials in order to focus the dialogue and ensure that it is properly informed, for example, a version of the Morehouse Research Institute report with expanded analysis of religious and moral dimensions of sexuality, marriage, parenting, and childhood.[35]

Congregations should consider employing a collaborative leadership model and cosponsor community-based dialogues in order to share the burdens of such community service among many resource people.

Congregations should regard this as an opportunity for healing the community, and they must do everything possible to *practice an ethic of hospitality, patience, and reconciliation*. They must restrain themselves in love, so that they do not simply reimpose traditional stigmas or moral judgments on those who have experienced moral failure of various sorts. A great deal of healing could come from church leaders and members courageously admitting their own shortcomings and failures in this arena of life.

Finally, congregations would benefit from role models that demonstrate how and why the dialogue is important and valuable. Media personalities, sports stars, Hollywood glitterati, and artists could attend to dramatize and celebrate the process of having a conversation about difficult topics. For example, during the Million Man March in October 1995, a great number of such luminaries were present to lend credibility to the ongoing work of "atonement," which was the selected focus of the day. Their blessing helped to inspire local stars and grassroots leaders to sustain the good work initiated in the mass meeting.

I would recommend that discussion, preparation, and planning start now to prepare for a series of conversations that might begin within eighteen months. I would recommend further that either Black History Month or the season of Lent be used as a symbolically appropriate time to hold the conversation over a several-week period. Congregations could organize and localize the conversation to reflect their unique histories and circumstances. Organized philanthropy could be called upon to assist in supporting this critical process.

At a conference on black fathers sponsored by Morehouse College, the Pulitzer Prize–winning columnist William Raspberry posed a provocative question:

> Are Black fathers necessary? You know, I'm old and I'm tired, and there are some things that I just don't want to debate anymore. One of them is whether African-American children need fathers. Another is whether marriage matters. Does marriage matter? You bet it does. Are Black fathers necessary? Damn straight we are.[36]

I believe that African Americans have sufficient resources within and outside the community to reverse the current trend of declining marriage, rising divorce, and out-of-wedlock births. If the most respected and influential leaders of the most powerful institution in the black community can be persuaded that this is God's work for this time and place, miracles can happen.

Let us see if they will heed the call.

NOTES

1. For a more detailed discussion of African traditional religions, see John S. Mbiti, *African Religions and Philosophy*, 2nd rev. ed. (Portsmouth, N.H.: Heinemann, 1990), and Albert Raboteau, *Slave Religion: The "Invisible Institution" in the Antebellum South*, updated ed. (New York: Oxford University Press, 2004).

2. Peter Paris, *The Social Teachings of the Black Churches* (Minneapolis, Minn.: Fortress Press, 1992).

3. William Julius Wilson, *The Truly Disadvantaged: The Inner City, the Underclass, and Public Policy* (Chicago: University of Chicago Press, 1987), 64; Herbert Gutman, *The Black Family in Slavery and Freedom, 1750–1925* (New York: Vintage, 1977).

4. Andrew Billingsley, *Climbing Jacob's Ladder: The Enduring Legacy of African-American Families* (New York: Augsberg Fortress Press, 1992).

5. Orlando Patterson, *Rituals of Blood: Consequences of Slavery in Two American Centuries* (Washington, D.C.: Civitas/CounterPoint, 1998), 41.

6. Ibid., 25.

7. Ibid., 41.

8. Ibid., 48.

9. Ibid., 43.

10. Ibid., 47.

11. Nicholas Lemann, *The Promised Land: The Great Black Migration and How It Changed America* (New York: Alfred A. Knopf, 1991), 4.

12. Wilson, *Truly Disadvantaged*, 65.

13. Ibid., 56.

14. Ibid.

15. Patterson, *Rituals of Blood*, 56.

16. Ibid., 62.

17. Ibid., 63.

18. Ibid.

19. Ibid., 160 (emphasis added).

20. Ibid., 63.

21. Ibid., 165.

22. Ronald B. Mincy and Hillard Pouncy, "The Marriage Mystery: Marriage, Assets and the Expectations of African American Families," unpublished paper delivered at the Morehouse Research Institute, Summer 2001, 22.

23. Kenneth B. Clark quoted in Wilson, *Truly Disadvantaged*, 73.

24. Mincy and Pouncy, "Marriage Mystery," 22.

25. Ibid., 22.

26. Malcolm West, "Who Benefits More from Marriage—Men or Women?" *JET*, June 2001, 15.

27. Ibid.

28. Patterson, *Rituals of Blood*, 165.

29. Ronald B. Mincy and Helen Oliver, "Age, Race, and Children's Living Arrangements: Implications for TANF Reorganization," policy brief for the Urban Institute, Washington, D.C., April 2003, 1 (emphasis added), www.urban.org/Uploaded PDF/310670_B-53.pdf.

30. W. Bradford Wilcox, "Sacred Vows, Public Purposes: Religion, the Marriage Movement and Marriage Policy," Institute for the Advanced Study of Religion, Yale University, May 2002, 26.

31. Ronald B. Mincy, "What about Black Fathers?" *American Prospect* 13, no. 7 (8 April 2002), www.prospect.org/print-friendly/print/V13/7/mincy-r.html.

32. Ibid.

33. Ibid.

34. Ronald Mincy, interview by author, telephone, 23 March 2003.

35. David Blankenhorn, Obie Clayton, and Ronald Mincy, "Turning the Corner on Father Absence: A Statement from the Morehouse Conference on African American Fathers," Morehouse Research Institute, Atlanta, and Institute for American Values, New York, 1999, www.americanvalues.org/turning_the_corner.pdf.

36. Ibid., 4.

CHAPTER 8

Latter-day Saint Marriage and Family Life in Modern America

DAVID C. DOLLAHITE

The Church of Jesus Christ of Latter-day Saints (LDS, Mormon) is considered by its adherents to embody all the doctrines and authority that were present in the church that Christ established (Matthew 16:18–19) but that subsequently were lost through an apostasy that took hold after the original apostles were martyred. Latter-day Saints consider their faith to be a modern restoration of ancient truths and practices accomplished through modern revelation given by the Lord to modern prophets.

While in some ways Mormonism appears to be an exceedingly modern American faith that adopts the latest technologies to assist in its efforts, in other ways it evokes religious institutions of the Old and New Testaments. In fact, Mormonism is among the few faiths with a strong combination of the paradoxical features of firm adherence to traditional doctrinal understandings and moral standards *and* extensive and enthusiastic adoption of modern technologies and organizational ideas to further its work.

In many ways Mormonism thrives and grows *because* of the social, emotional, geographical, and familial confusions and dislocations caused by modernization and globalization; in other ways modern and postmodern culture presents the church with significant challenges to its core values and practices. Although U.S. Latter-day Saints tend to be patriotic Americans who are disproportionately involved at high levels in a variety of American institutions (education, business, government, military), in other ways some core features of modern American culture are antithetical to Mormonism.

In this chapter I will discuss some major ways that modernization in America interacts with and affects LDS family life, how the LDS Church and its members cope with the negative aspects of modernization, and how it and they thrive despite or even because of modernization. I begin with a demographic view of the LDS Church in America and then discuss LDS thought about America and about how the Saints view the modern era. The bulk of the chapter focuses on core LDS doctrines and practices regarding children, marriage, and family life, along with discussion of a number of ways that American-style modernization conflicts with LDS doctrine and practice on marriage and family life.

I am a qualitative scholar who believes in giving people their own say to the fullest extent possible. Latter-day Saints greatly value and rely on the teachings of their leaders, whom they sustain as modern prophets and apostles. Therefore I quote LDS scriptures and leaders extensively in order to provide the reader with an in-depth inside look at how Latter-day Saints frame Mormonism, marriage, and family in the modern era.[1]

DEMOGRAPHIC PROFILE

Founded by Joseph Smith in 1830 in upstate New York with six original members, the Church of Jesus Christ of Latter-day Saints now has more than twelve million members in 165 nations.[2] More than half of current church members are converts from other faiths (or no faith).[3] With about 5.5 million American members, the LDS Church is now the fourth-largest and the fastest-growing major religious denomination in the United States.[4] Maps of the distribution of religious adherents in the United States in 2000 show that in addition to being the dominant faith in Utah (70 percent), Latter-day Saints constitute a significant minority of religious adherents in parts of several states in the intermountain West.[5] And while LDS members represent a much smaller percentage of the religious population in the rest of the country, continual growth is occurring in these regions as well.[6]

The sociologist of religion Rodney Stark drew on demographic analyses of the rapid and accelerating worldwide growth of the church during its first 150 years and declared that, based on growth patterns and on its unique doctrine and practice, Mormonism was a "new world faith." Stark projected a worldwide LDS Church membership of more than fifty million by the year 2040 and perhaps as many as 265 million members by 2080.[7] Indeed, although often referred to by non-LDS scholars as an "American church" in fact less than half of the LDS Church's members live in the United States and more Latter-day Saints speak Spanish than English (Portuguese is the third language of the church). The church is growing fastest in Latin America, the Philippines, and Africa. And while most American Latter-day Saints are white, middle class, and live in suburban areas, the church is experiencing rapid growth among ethnic minorities and urban populations as well.

MORMONISM, AMERICA, AND THE WORLD

It would be difficult to overstate the importance of America to Mormons. Latter-day Saints believe that nineteenth-century upstate New York was the birthplace of a religious movement that will spread across the earth and have profound influence for good throughout the world and throughout eternity. The church was founded on American soil by an American prophet, in the generation after the American Revolution. Former church president (and U.S. secretary of agriculture during the Eisenhower administration) Ezra Taft Benson stated: "I love this nation of which we are a part. To me it is not just another nation, not just a member of a family of nations. It is a great and glorious nation with a divine mission and it has been brought into being under the inspiration of heaven. It is truly a land choice above all others. I thank God for the knowledge which we have regarding the prophetic history and the prophetic future of this great land of America."[8]

From the beginning the Latter-day Saints have had a complex relationship with America. Although Mormonism has been called "quintessentially American" by various scholars of religion, early LDS people rejected core aspects of American life (e.g., rugged individualism and unrestrained capitalism), and the Mormons were rejected by one set of Americans after another—often violently.

Joseph Smith taught that the U.S. Constitution was an inspired document; in LDS revelation the Lord declares that "for this purpose have I established the Constitution of this land by the hands of wise men whom I raised up unto this very purpose, and redeemed the land by the shedding of blood (D&C 101:80).[9] An LDS Article of Faith states, "We believe . . . that Zion (the New Jerusalem) will be built upon the American continent." So America (past, present, and future) is sacred soil to Latter-day Saints.

Yet in the early years of the church's existence, America was a hostile environment. After reviewing—and finding wanting—arguments made by various scholars of religion about how much Mormonism was supposedly derivative of American culture, the LDS historian Richard Bushman stated:

> The problem is further complicated by Mormonism's estrangement from American society. For a movement that purportedly incorporated so many elements from the surrounding culture, Mormonism found itself at odds with that culture over and over again. I don't mean arguments, I mean violence. None of the Saints' American neighbors accepted them for very long. Wherever the Saints settled in the nineteenth century, they were rejected like a failed kidney trans-

plant. In New York, Missouri, Illinois, and even Utah, the Saints were attacked by force and compelled to change or die. Far from being fundamentally American, something about Mormonism repulsed large numbers of Americans.

Every attempt to assimilate the Restoration into some [American] schema has to face the possibility that Mormonism was more un-American than American. There is more evidence of Mormonism's alienation from the nineteenth-century United States than of its being a natural outgrowth of American culture. The American connection grows ever more tenuous as Mormonism is increasingly viewed as a world religion. If Mormonism is so American, why the immediate success in nineteenth-century Europe and the rapid twentieth-century growth in Latin America and the Philippines?[10]

Thus, while much of their early history is centered in America, Latter-day Saints believe their church is not "an American church" and that it is the destiny of the church to continue to move far beyond American borders and culture to ultimately spread throughout the earth and prepare the inhabitants of the earth for the return of Jesus Christ.

Latter-day Saints consider their church to be the kingdom of God on Earth and believe it will fulfill the scriptural prophecy as the "stone which is cut out of the mountain without hands [that] shall roll forth, until it has filled the whole earth" (see Daniel 2:34, 45; D&C 65:2). About the ultimate destiny of the Church of Jesus Christ of Latter-day Saints, Joseph Smith stated: "The standard of truth has been erected; no unhallowed hand can stop the work from progressing; persecutions may rage, mobs may combine, armies may assemble, calumny may defame, but the truth of God will go forth boldly, nobly, and independent, till it has penetrated every continent, visited every clime, swept every country, and sounded in every ear, till the purposes of God shall be accomplished and the great Jehovah shall say the work is done."[11]

When Joseph Smith made this statement, the church had only a few thousand members in a few scattered communities. The Saints consider this statement a prophecy of a glorious future, and it helps them look beyond the fact that most Latter-day Saints throughout the earth live in areas where they find themselves members of a misunderstood minority faith.

MORMONISM AND MODERNIZATION

Latter-day Saints believe that the current era represents the "last days" preceding the second coming of Jesus Christ. The Saints believe they are called to build Zion—a holy society that will prepare the world for the return of Jesus. They believe that, as Jesus said, no man knows "the day or the hour" of his coming but that many of the biblical "signs of the times" have been and are being fulfilled and so that event can happen soon.[12] Thus Latter-day Saints have a clear and strong—indeed, unabashedly triumphalist—sense that the time in which they live will be momentous and troubling for individuals, families, and nations and yet ultimately glorious and triumphant for the Latter-day Saints and all those who honestly serve God and strive to prepare themselves for the coming of Jesus Christ.

Latter-day Saints believe that the founding of America was guided by divine providence in order to establish a fit nation in which to restore the Church of Jesus Christ—a nation with religious freedom (absence of a state church), with openness to new ideas, and with abundant human and natural resources from which to develop the wealth needed to support the spread of the restored gospel throughout the earth. Commenting on the way historians have viewed Mormonism in the context of American historical forces, the LDS historian Richard Bushman stated: "In fact, Latter-day Saints are inclined to reverse the order and place American history in the history of the gospel. We think that Western civilization has been shaped in preparation for the Restoration. The breakup of the medieval church, the rise of learning and free inquiry, the separation of church and state, even a technology like printing are seen as providential preparation for the Restoration. The United States, in the Mormon view, was founded to make a home for the Church."[13]

Unlike other "high tension" religious communities that reject nearly all aspects of modern technology and culture (e.g., the Amish, Hasidic Judaism), Latter-day Saints, while maintaining significant boundaries with certain aspects of modernism, are not only quite comfortable with many aspects of modern life but consider modern technology to be divinely inspired.[14]

Latter-day Saints consider modern technologies to be gifts from God to help them spread the gospel and allow the leaders of the church to communicate with and travel to the millions of members spread across the earth, thus allowing the church to remain pure in doctrine and practice and not fall away, as did the "primitive church" established by the original apostles. In his concluding remarks at the LDS General Conference in April 2005, church president Gordon B. Hinckley stated, "Through the miracle—and it is a miracle—of modern technology, these proceedings have been broadcast worldwide. Ninety-five percent of the membership of the Church in all the world could have participated with us."[15] In commenting on this statement, the LDS Church News opined, "Indeed, it is amazing to witness how the Lord has made technologies available to govern and unify His Church in this last dispensation, revealing them as quickly as Church growth makes them necessary."[16] So what other religionists may see as a dizzying, almost out-of-control, technological revolution spurred only by human creativity and greed, Latter-day Saints typically see as a divinely inspired and guided process designed to aid the spread of Mormonism (and other good works and worthy influences) throughout the earth.

The ecological, political, economic, and social upheavals of contemporary life, while to some extent troubling to Latter-day Saints, do not surprise them and in some respects provide faith-validating evidence of the truthfulness of prophecies of great tribulations in the last days found in the Bible (e.g., Matt. 24; 2 Tim. 3:2) and in modern LDS scripture (e.g., D&C 45:26–75; Moses 7:61–66). Indeed, Mormonism appears not merely to survive but to thrive under the kinds of challenging conditions brought about by modernization and globalization. The sociologist John Jarvis concluded in regard to Mormon success in France, "My findings suggest that rather than succeeding in France *despite* the stresses of globalization, Mormonism's success there is *due* to these stresses and to the reassuring answers the Church provides to them."[17]

MODERN PROPHETS FOR MODERN TIMES

The Church of Jesus Christ of Latter-day Saints is "built upon the foundation of the apostles and prophets, Jesus Christ himself being the chief corner stone" (Eph. 2:20). The highest leaders of the church (First Presidency and Council of Twelve Apostles) are considered as having literally the same calling and authority as the ancient prophets and apostles. Perhaps the most distinguishing feature of how Latter-day Saints cope with and thrive under the challenges to family life stemming from modernization is the overall sense that God continues to speak through prophets to give divine guidance in troubled times.

Latter-day Saint leaders and families are well aware of the social forces weakening marriage and family ties and have taken significant steps to try to stem this tide. In 1981 then–LDS church president Spencer W. Kimball predicted that "many of the social restraints which in the past have helped to reinforce and to shore up the family are dissolving and disappearing. The time will come when only those who believe deeply and actively in the family will be able to preserve their families in the midst of the gathering evil around us."[18] Latter-day Saints consider this statement a modern prophecy that is being literally fulfilled. The belief in modern prophets and apostles brings great comfort and confidence to Latter-day Saints, who believe that their leaders provide access to God's will in today's challenging and changing times, times in which marriage and family bonds have been increasingly loosened and threatened.

One important example of this is that church leaders first initiated the now well-known LDS Family Home Evening program in 1918 and encouraged families to set aside an evening each week and reserve it for family religious devotion and family recreational activity. The church began to strongly reemphasize this program in the 1960s, and it is now fully enshrined as an important LDS religious practice. Latter-day Saints consider this program, which was revealed by modern prophets long before the crisis of family that has gripped America since the 1960s, to be one of many clear evidences of the reality and blessing of divinely inspired prophetic counsel for current needs, and they believe that those families who faithfully practice home evenings will be much better prepared to fend off the various forces that have wreaked havoc on contemporary families.[19]

PROPHETIC PROCLAMATION ON FAMILY

Although LDS prophets and apostles have spoken frequently about the eternal importance of marriage and family from the beginning of the church, teaching about family life has increased dramatically since the mid-1970s and was highlighted by the issuance in 1995 of the authoritative proclamation called "The Family: A Proclamation to the World."[20] Church president Gordon B. Hinckley stated: "Why do we have this proclamation on the family now? Because the family is under attack. All across the world families are falling apart. The place to begin to improve society is in the home. Children do, for the most part, what they are taught. We are trying to make the world better by making the family stronger."[21]

This 604-word proclamation clearly and concisely sets forth fundamental LDS doctrine on marriage and family life.[22] This document approaches the status of scripture for Latter-day Saints, who believe that "whatsoever [church leaders] shall speak when moved upon by the Holy Ghost shall be scripture, shall be the will of the Lord, shall be the mind of the Lord, shall be the word of the Lord, shall be the voice of the Lord, and the power of God unto salvation" (D&C 68:4). Every LDS chapel and temple and many LDS homes display framed copies of the "family proclamation." While the thrust of the family proclamation is an affirmative moral call to strengthen marriage and family life through revealed doctrine and practice, a concluding paragraph states, "We warn that individuals who violate covenants of chastity, who abuse spouse or offspring, or who fail to fulfill family responsibilities will one day stand accountable before God. Further, we warn that the disintegration of the family will bring upon individuals, communities, and nations the calamities foretold by ancient and modern prophets."

REJECTING RELATIVISM

Latter-day Saints accept a set of highly distinctive doctrines and live a unique set of practices relating to marriage and family life. In so doing they face numerous challenges to those beliefs and practices from a modern American culture steeped in moral relativism, since church doctrine makes no concessions to changing morals and cultural values when it comes to core doctrines, practices, and standards of conduct. Indeed, most American Latter-day Saints likely would agree with Pope Benedict XVI when (just before his election as pope in April 2005), he warned that "we are moving toward a dictatorship of relativism which does not recognize anything as for certain and which has as its highest goal one's own ego and one's own desires."[23] In 1995 LDS apostle Neal A.

Maxwell stated that "Heavenly Father loves his children perfectly, but he knows our tendencies perfectly, too. To lie, steal, murder, envy, to be sexually immoral, neglect parents, break the Sabbath, and to bear false witness—all occur because one mistakenly seeks to please himself for the moment regardless of divine standards or human consequences. As prophesied, ethical relativism is now in steep crescendo: 'Every man walketh in his own way, and after the image of his own god, whose image is in the likeness of the world'" (D&C 1:16).[24] The modern American cultural climate encourages all citizens to create and practice their own personal religion—what Robert Bellah and his colleagues called "Sheilaism," or what can be called a "denomination of one" approach to religion.[25] One way that unchanging beliefs and high standards of personal and family morality help LDS couples and families avoid the relativistic character of modern America is by providing a sense of stability and moral clarity.

DOCTRINES ON MARRIAGE, FAMILY, AND CHILDREN

About the status of marriage and family in LDS doctrine, the sociologist John Jarvis correctly stated, "It is this family focus, a veritable 'theology of the family,' that must be understood before one can understand . . . Mormonism."[26] One recent church president stated, "The family is the most important organization in time or in eternity. Our purpose in life is to create for ourselves eternal family units."[27] Another LDS leader taught, "Marriage, the family, and the home are the foundation of the Church. Nothing is more important to the Church and to civilization itself than the family!"[28] Indeed, when teachings and practices about the role of marriage and family in this life and beyond are considered, the LDS church has one of the most explicitly and strongly family-oriented doctrine, practice, and culture among religious institutions.[29]

FAMILY IS CENTRAL IN GOD'S PLAN OF HAPPINESS

The LDS emphasis on marriage and family comes from the central place of the family in the "plan of happiness," which is a set of core beliefs regarding the underlying divine purposes of life and existence. The Saints believe that before being born, all human beings existed in a "premortal" state as "spirit sons and daughters" of God the Eternal Father and that mortal experience is the next stage in humans' eternal quest to become more godlike.

LDS children begin singing and memorizing the LDS hymn "I Am a Child of God" when they are very young, and this core identity is a powerful orientation for LDS children, youth, and adults. The family proclamation succinctly summarizes Mormons' understanding of God's plan of happiness: "In the premortal realm, spirit sons and daughters knew and worshiped God as their Eternal Father and accepted His plan by which His children could obtain a physical body and gain earthly experience to progress toward perfection and ultimately realize his or her divine destiny as an heir of eternal life." The doctrine of a premortal existence brings comfort and hope to families struggling with problems incident to mortality. Apostle Neal A. Maxwell said:

> Without an understanding of premortality, it is no wonder that mortals often fail to take account of what is perhaps mortality's most prominent feature — its stern proving and tutoring dimensions. Some then use life's trials as an argument against God, instead of accepting these trials as being something "common to man," or as the needed tutorials which, though rigorous, last "but for a small moment" (1 Corinthians 10:13; D&C 122:4). Mortality is properly designed to permit us only limited vision. Without the perspective of premortality, instead of understanding that "all these things shall give thee experience" (D&C 122:7), we can become drenched in doubt and be wrenched by adversity and irony, lamenting, "Why me? Why this? Why now?"[30]

Latter-day Saints believe that the quality of one's soul and the status of one's marriage and family after mortal life are influenced by the extent to which one is willing to make sacred covenants and keep them faithfully. For those who have made and kept the sacred covenants of the holy temple, the prospects for their ongoing association in marriage and family relationships are assured. The family proclamation states that "the divine plan of happiness enables family relationships to be perpetuated beyond the grave. Sacred ordinances and covenants available in holy temples make it possible for individuals to return to the presence of God and for families to be united eternally."

Thus the plan of happiness (a) provides LDS families with a sense that earth life and all its vicissitudes are part of a divine plan; (b) helps them make sense of both personal and global events; (c) brings great comfort in times of death since birth, life, and death are all part of this divine plan; and (d) is the eschatological paradigm or sacred worldview for Latter-day Saints. The family proclamation states: "We . . . solemnly proclaim that marriage between a man and woman is ordained of God and that the family is central to the Creator's plan for the eternal destiny of His children. . . . The family is ordained of God. Marriage between man and woman is essential to His eternal plan." So this plan teaches that marriage and family life is ordained of God, central to God's purposes, and potentially eternal.

DOCTRINE OF ETERNAL MARRIAGE

Among the most important and distinctive LDS doctrines is that the plan of happiness provides that marriage is not intended only for this life but rather was designed to be an eternal relationship.[31] In a revelation to the Prophet

Joseph Smith (D&C 132:19–20) the Lord declared: "And again, verily I say unto you, if a man marry a wife by my word, which is my law, and by the new and everlasting covenant, and it is sealed unto them by the Holy Spirit of promise, by him who is anointed, unto whom I have appointed this power and the keys of this priesthood . . . shall be of full force when they are out of the world" (D&C 132:19).

Latter-day Saints who have made the "new and everlasting covenant" of eternal marriage have been "sealed," or eternally bound, by priesthood power in holy temples and believe they will be married not only until death but throughout eternity. The Apostle Paul taught that "neither is the man without the woman, neither the woman without the man, in the Lord" (1 Cor. 11:11), and Jesus taught that "what therefore God hath joined together, let not man put asunder" (Mark 10:9).[32] The temple "sealing" that unites couples eternally is conditional on continued worthiness and faithfulness on the part of both spouses.

One unique aspect of LDS temples is the vicarious saving ordinances such as baptism and confirmation, and exalting ordinances such as marriage for a person's deceased ancestors, that are performed there.[33] After obtaining their own sealings, Latter-day Saints can go to the temple and be sealed "for and in behalf of" their deceased progenitors whom they have known or have discovered through genealogical research (it is believed the deceased person may chose to accept or reject this ordinance). This "temple work" allows a married couple to attend the temple together and remember and renew their own marriage covenants by acting as a proxy for those who did not have a chance to be sealed eternally to their spouse in mortality but have now passed beyond mortal life.

Temples are peaceful and spiritual, and the work done there is deeply meaningful to Latter-day Saints, so this opportunity to periodically be together in this sacred setting helps couples cope with the stresses and strains of modern married life. Church leaders frequently urge the Saints to be involved in temple worship and service both to help fulfill the divine mandate to make these ordinances available to those who have died without receiving them *and* to obtain the spiritual and relational blessings available to those who perform this sacred temple work together. LDS couples who engage in regular temple worship report feeling protected and empowered in the face of the gathering storms of marital failure so prevalent in modern society. President James E. Faust (counselor in the First Presidency) taught: "Those who cherish their family have a compelling reason to claim the transcendent blessing of being sealed for eternity in the temples of God. For all grandparents, parents, husbands, wives, children, and grandchildren, this sealing power and authority is a crowning principle, a pinnacle in the restoration 'of all things' through the Prophet Joseph Smith."[34]

Other significant resources are made available to assist couples to make their marriage strong, including Sunday school classes, periodic lessons and talks in church meetings, written materials, and counseling from church leaders. LDS

Family Services, a social service agency, provides professional counseling for those who desire it. Divorce is allowed though strongly discouraged, and perhaps it is warranted when the quality of the marriage is "nothing less serious than a prolonged and apparently irredeemable relationship which is destructive of a person's dignity as a human being."[35]

The importance placed on making and keeping the marriage covenant is demonstrated by demographics: LDS men and women typically marry three to four years younger and at a significantly higher rate than the general U.S. population, yet LDS couples experience a very low divorce rate compared with the national average. Scholars working from publicly available data suggest that the divorce rate for LDS "temple marriages" (the type most commonly entered into by two active Saints) may be as low as 10 percent but is likely no higher than 15 percent.[36] The divorce rate for nontemple LDS marriages is similar to the national average of 40 to 50 percent, and the divorce rate for LDS/Non-LDS interfaith marriages is even higher.[37]

So, although Latter-day Saints, like most Americans, are troubled by the very high national divorce rates, and although the rate of LDS divorce has increased since the 1970s, the knowledge that LDS temple divorce rates are relatively low likely helps LDS singles and couples avoid the tendency of many in modern society to possess a deep and often debilitating cynicism about their personal potential to experience marital happiness and permanence. However, LDS leaders and members are deeply concerned about the continuing trend of increasing age at first marriage among LDS couples. Many see this as an indication of increasing individualism and materialism among LDS young adults— or as the influence of "the world" on LDS courtship and marriage behavior.[38]

DOCTRINE OF CHILDREN

Mormon theology includes the unique doctrine that all human beings are the spiritual offspring of heavenly parents. The family proclamation states, "All human beings—male and female—are created in the image of God. Each is a beloved spirit son or daughter of heavenly parents, and, as such, each has a divine nature and destiny." Therefore Latter-day Saints take quite literally the biblical statement that "God created man in his own image, in the image of God created he him; male and female created he them" (Gen. 1:27). Current LDS apostle M. Russell Ballard stated:

> In the spring of 1820, a pillar of light illuminated a grove of trees in upstate New York. Our Heavenly Father and His Beloved Son appeared to the Prophet Joseph Smith. This experience began the restoration of powerful doctrinal truths that had been lost for centuries. Among those truths that had been dimmed by the darkness of apostasy was the stirring reality that we are all the spirit sons and daughters of a loving God who is our Father.

We are part of His family. He is not a father in some allegorical or poetic sense. He is literally the Father of our spirits. He cares for each one of us. Though this world has a way of diminishing and demeaning men and women, the reality is we are all of royal, divine lineage. In that unprecedented appearance of the Father and the Son in the Sacred Grove, the very first word spoken by the Father of us all was the personal name of Joseph. Such is our Father's personal relationship with each of us. He knows our names and yearns for us to become worthy to return to live with Him.[39]

Although Latter-day Saints follow the pattern set by Jesus by praying only to their Father in Heaven, the doctrine that all human beings also have a Mother in Heaven occupies a place of honor in LDS belief.[40] This doctrine gives many LDS women and men the sense of earthly life's being patterned after heavenly life and gives LDS women the sense that their eternal destiny and potential is coequal with men's—to someday become like their heavenly parents. Thus for LDS women the calling of wife and mother, and for LDS men the calling of husband and father, are preparation for a glorious eternal destiny together, doing what the most glorious and powerful beings in the universe do—rather than merely human or earthly social roles.

Mormon families tend to be larger than the national average because Latter-day Saints believe it is part of God's plan that all his spirit children come to Earth to gain a physical body, to experience opposition and thus grow spiritually through making moral choices, and make and keep sacred covenants with God (e.g., baptism and marriage). While many American LDS families have large numbers of children and the relative size of LDS families to the U.S. population historically has remained fairly constant (about two to one), one of the perceived negative consequences of modernization is a reduction in the overall size of LDS families.[41]

DOCTRINE OF PARENTAL RESPONSIBILITY

Latter-day Saints believe that their two most important responsibilities are to make and keep the covenant of eternal marriage and to bear children and parent them effectively. The family proclamation states:

> The first commandment that God gave to Adam and Eve pertained to their potential for parenthood as husband and wife. We declare that God's commandment for His children to multiply and replenish the earth remains in force. . . . Parents have a sacred duty to rear their children in love and righteousness, to provide for their physical and spiritual needs, to teach them to love and serve one another, to observe the commandments of God and to be law-abiding citizens wherever they live. Husbands and wives—mothers and fathers—will be held accountable before God for the discharge of these obligations.

The church provides extensive educational programs to help parents teach children the gospel.[42] LDS parents draw heavily on their beliefs, practices, and faith communities to meet the challenges they face.[43] Much teaching by LDS local and general leaders focuses on the ways that parents can best fulfill their important obligations. Often this counsel addresses the mounting challenges of parenting in a culture dominated by strong pulls toward overinvolvement in paid work, media entertainment, personal hobbies, and various other distractions that pull parents away from children (and spouses away from each other).

While many parenting responsibilities outlined in the family proclamation are similar for both parents, Latter-day Saints also believe in some distinction of responsibilities for fathers and mothers. The family proclamation states: "By divine design, fathers are to preside over their families in love and righteousness and are responsible to provide the necessities of life and protection for their families. Mothers are primarily responsible for the nurture of their children. In these sacred responsibilities, fathers and mothers are obligated to help one another as equal partners."

Contrary to popular perception, the LDS Church teaches complete equality between men and women, husbands and wives, fathers and mothers. In LDS parlance "presiding over" involves loving leadership and service, not domination. A church leader taught that "every father is to his family a patriarch and every mother a matriarch as coequals in their distinctive parental roles."[44] A group of LDS scholars who carefully analyzed the teachings of LDS scripture and prophetic teaching on the issue stated:

> The patriarchal priesthood is not so called to imply a hierarchy between men and women. Instead, as President Ezra Taft Benson taught, it is called patriarchal because in ancient days it was handed down from faithful father to faithful son, and today frequently still is (D&C 107: 40–42). (*Patri* is Latin for father.) President Benson also taught that the patriarchal order is the family order of government, presided over by mothers and fathers. One of the most revolutionary aspects of the restored gospel is its ability to help us envision difference without hierarchy, distinctiveness without inequality. This is what the Proclamation calls upon us to hold as the ideal relationship between husbands and wives.[45]

This clear sense of distinct but equal sacred responsibilities helps LDS women and men avoid the gender role confusion that pervades modern American culture and American marriages and families.

FAMILY WORSHIP

The LDS church constantly stresses the importance of family-based religious activity. Home-based family worship includes practices such as family prayer and father's blessings, family fasting and giving offerings for the poor, family scripture study, family musical expression, family Sabbath observance, and family home evening.[46] Having regular patterns of family religious activity helps many LDS families avoid the increasing levels of family chaos and dysfunction prevalent in modern society. While not all LDS families consistently practice all these family devotions, they typically feel that they ought to. Most try to implement such practices to the best of their ability and according to the family situations they face.

IN MODERN AMERICA,
BUT NOT OF MODERN AMERICA

Together these beliefs and practices make Latter-day Saints quite distinct in contemporary America. LDS leaders have expressed that the church and the world are on increasingly divergent paths. In modern America, with the dramatically increasing rates of out-of-wedlock birth and cohabitation, the link between marriage and childbearing has been severely weakened. That link remains strong for LDS culture. The age at first marriage in modern America continues to rise, yet for LDS couples it remains three to four years younger than the national average. The amount of sexual content continues to rise in contemporary media, while LDS leaders increase the frequency and intensity of their pleas to the Saints to avoid pornographic and sexual content in all its manifestations. The culture of divorce continues unabated, while LDS leaders and members increase the church's educational efforts to prepare for and strengthen marriage and counseling services to help troubled couples.[47]

Thus it is accurate to characterize the contemporary American Mormon situation by using the worn but apt phrase "in the world, but not of the world."[48] This is particularly true of the culture of youth and young adulthood, as LDS youth increasingly find themselves on the front lines of the cultural wars engulfing America. Interestingly, in a recent national study of religiosity in 3,370 youth from various faith communities, the sociologists Christian Smith and Melinda Lundquist Denton found that Mormon youth reported the highest degree of religious vitality and salience, and they reported that "Mormon teens are the most likely among all U.S. teens to hold religious beliefs similar to their parents'."[49] Probably partly in response to this study, President Gordon B. Hinckley recently stated: "It is wonderfully refreshing to see the faith and faithfulness of our young people. They live at a time when a great tide of evil is washing over the earth. It seems to be everywhere. Old standards are discarded. Principles of virtue and integrity are cast aside. But we find literally hundreds of thousands of our young people holding to the high standards of the gospel. They find happy and uplifting association with those of their own kind. They are improving their minds with education and their skills with discipline, and their influence for good is felt ever more widely."[50]

On many important issues, particularly those concerning marriage and family matters, there is a great chasm between the powerful and pervasive culture of modern America and the even stronger and deeper culture of Mormonism. The Latter-day Saint counterculture is conscious and passionate. LDS scripture and modern prophets have called the Saints to "go ye out of Babylon" (D&C 133:7) and be a "chosen generation, a royal priesthood, an holy nation, a peculiar people" (1 Peter 2:9). Or, as a current member of the church's First Presidency, said, "We have always been regarded as a peculiar people. . . . Being spiritually correct is much better than being politically correct. Of course, as individuals and as a people we want to be liked and respected. But we cannot be in the mainstream of society if it means abandoning those righteous principles which thundered down from Sinai, later to be refined by the Savior, and subsequently taught by modern prophets. We should only fear offending God and His Son, Jesus Christ, who is the head of this Church."[51]

CHALLENGES FOR LDS FAMILIES: CONFLICTS WITH MODERNIZATION

Despite the doctrinal clarity of LDS theology regarding marriage and family life, many aspects of modernization and postmodern thought and practice are highly problematic and difficult for LDS families, particularly the changing social norms and practices pertaining to courtship, sexuality, marriage, and family life. To many Saints the social trends in modern culture directly conflict with Latter-day Saint doctrine and practice pertaining to marriage and family life. This brings a sense of confirmation that these are indeed the "great and dreadful" last days, and it also presents serious challenges to LDS families trying to be "in the world but not of the world." Let me briefly sketch some of the central conflicts.

SEXUAL ISSUES

The sexual revolution of modern Western cultures radically conflicts with LDS teaching on complete chastity before marriage and complete fidelity in marriage. The family proclamation states: "God has commanded that the sacred powers of procreation are to be employed only between man and woman, lawfully wedded as husband and wife. We declare the means by which mortal life is created to be divinely appointed. . . . Children are entitled to birth within the bonds of matrimony, and to be reared by a father and a mother who honor marital vows with complete fidelity." LDS leaders and parents work hard to teach their children and youth about the importance of remaining sexually chaste before marriage (no sexual relations of any kind) and maintaining "complete fidelity" in marriage. Chastity and fidelity are requirements to receive the weekly Sacrament of the Lord's Supper, to serve a mission, to be married in the temple, hold a "church calling" in the congregation, and to hold a "temple recommend," which allows a person to participate in sacred temple ordinances.

Of course, not all LDS youth or adults are chaste before marriage or faithful in marriage, and church leaders both teach preventative measures and counsel with those who have not lived up to these standards. The standard for sexual purity is the same for men and women and is a requirement of full church participation, which sends a very clear message that, despite what is allowed or encouraged in modern society, male and female Latter-day Saints are equally expected to keep themselves "unspotted from the world" (James 1:27).

While church doctrine rejects homosexual conduct (and all other sexual relationships outside marriage), President Gordon B. Hinckley has repeatedly taught that there must be respect and love shown for those who "struggle with same-sex attraction." These Latter-day Saints often feel that they are faced with having to deny either their religious beliefs or their sexual orientation. Many struggle valiantly and need and desire the love, understanding, and respect of other Latter-day Saints—particularly their parents and other family members. The church provides support groups and trained professionals for Saints striving to live an LDS life despite same-sex attraction, and bishops (pastors of local congregations) are also often involved in trying to help.

GENDER FEMINISM

An important strain in modern gender feminism posits few innate distinctions between men and women, places the source of observed gender variation on culture and upbringing, and suggests that most gender differences can and should be minimized or even eliminated. These ideas conflict with LDS teaching that "gender is an essential characteristic of individual premortal, mortal, and eternal identity and purpose" (family proclamation). Latter-day Saints believe the human spirit (what many refer to as the soul) is gendered, that some divinely mandated core gender distinctions influence earth life, and that our resurrected bodies will be gendered—just as God's is.[52]

These views do affect gender roles both in the church and in the family. Indeed, some view LDS women as "oppressed" because they do not hold the priesthood, are more likely to marry and have children than non-LDS women, and are more likely to defer education and career for family reasons. Conversely, most Latter-day Saints think that LDS women are fortunate or "blessed" because they are considered equal partners with LDS men, with equal earthly and eternal potential; LDS theology includes belief in a Heavenly Mother; the highest (temple) covenants and ordinances of the LDS Church (marriage sealing) can be received only by a woman and man together; LDS doctrine considers marriage and parenthood the highest and holiest callings that women *and* men will ever have; and LDS men and women labor together in families, local congregations, and holy temples.

Latter-day Saints value what occurs in homes and temples more than what occurs in chapels (i.e., formal ecclesiastical structure). Husband and father or wife and mother are considered completely equal roles and eternally meaningful responsibilities. Because Latter-day Saints do not reveal the specific nature of temple work publicly, those who have not participated in temple ordinances are not aware of the extent to which men and women work side by side, doing the same essential exalting priesthood work in the holy temple. Thus the fact that LDS women are not ordained to the priesthood and serve as bishops or as apostles does not detract from the sense of empowerment from God, the church, and the family that most LDS women experience in their most highly valued religious responsibilities and activities. Of course, some LDS women and men struggle with these "traditional" gender expectations and some leave the church over this issue.

SUBSTANCE USE AND ABUSE

Modern culture and media tend to normalize and even glorify alcohol and drug consumption. Such portrayals and promotions are unfortunate because these images sharply conflict with data that link alcohol and drug abuse with higher rates of disease, criminality, death, and family abuse and dysfunction. Indeed, most family violence involves substance abuse. Use of alcohol and recreational drugs conflicts with LDS belief and practice. In 1833 Latter-day Saints were given a revelation known as "the Word of Wisdom," which proscribed the use of alcohol, tobacco, coffee, and tea. Among other things, it said: "Behold, verily, thus saith the Lord unto you: In consequence of the evils and designs which do and will exist in the hearts of conspiring men in the last days, I have warned you, and forewarn you, by giving unto you this word of wisdom by revelation—That inasmuch as any man drinketh wine or strong drink among you, behold it is not good, neither meet in the sight of your Father" (D&C 89:4–5).

In the same way that keeping kosher distinguishes observant Jewish families from their nonobservant or non-Jewish friends and associates, observing the Word of Wisdom has served to distinguish active LDS families from their non-LDS friends and family members. This provides a sense of family identity and unity, as LDS youth and families often are singled out for their unique habits. At the end of the revelation known as the Word of Wisdom is a promise: "And all saints who remember to keep and do these sayings, walking in obedience to the commandments, shall receive health in the navel and marrow to their bones; and shall find great treasures of knowledge, even hidden treasures; And shall run and not be weary, and shall walk and not faint, And I, the Lord, give unto them a promise, that the destroying angel shall pass by them, as the children of Israel, and not slay them" (D&C 89:18–21).

An abundance of modern scientific evidence demonstrates the health hazards of smoking, alcohol consumption, and drug use. Research has shown that Latter-day Saints enjoy lower rates of cancer and significantly longer life and better physical health than their non-LDS counterparts.[53] These health and longevity benefits contribute to LDS grandparents' being much more likely to see their grandchildren and great-grandchildren grow up and to be there to support them. In this respect the Word of Wisdom is a law of marriage and family well-being in addition to a law of physical and spiritual well-being. Thus adherence to the Word of Wisdom helps LDS families avoid one aspect of modern life that is very damaging to healthy marriages and families—the widespread use and abuse of harmful addictive substances.

INTERNET PORNOGRAPHY

While the Saints consider the invention of the computer and the Internet to be part of the ongoing technological inspiration needed to preach the gospel to every person in every land on Earth, fulfill the divine mandate to search out their ancestors, and allow church leaders to quickly and easily communicate with the Saints throughout the earth, the Internet also poses tremendous challenges to LDS families, particularly in easy access to pornography. Apostle M. Russell Ballard said: "We see a rapid increase in cyberporn, involving sexual addiction over the Internet. Some become so addicted to viewing Internet pornography and participating in dangerous online chat rooms that they ignore their marriage covenants and family obligations and often put their employment at risk. Many run afoul of the law. Others develop a tolerance to their perverted behavior, taking ever more risks to feed their immoral addiction. Marriages crumble and relationships fail, as addicts often lose everything of real, eternal value."[54] LDS leaders repeatedly warn adults and youth about the dangers to personal purity and marital fidelity that are lurking only a mouse-click away. LDS bishops counsel with those who have become involved with or addicted to pornography, and the church provides other resources such as professional counselors trained to help people overcome this malady. Usually, in the twice-yearly General Conference at least one speaker will address this issue and urge the Saints to avoid "the plague" of pornography.

POPULAR CULTURE

Jesus taught his disciples to "seek ye first the kingdom of God and his righteousness" (Matt. 6:33), but modern secular, materialistic, and hedonistic culture urges adults and children, men and women to have it all right now. So LDS parents face an uphill battle to choose spiritual things and help their children to do so as well, when all are enticed with an ever-growing cornucopia of material wonders. So LDS parents try to teach their children to "choose the right," reject the enticements of the world, and make the sacrifices their faith invites them to make. Recent research suggests that they are being quite successful—American LDS teens tend to be more involved in and more committed to their faith than teens from most other faiths and more likely to make personal sacrifices for religious reasons.[55]

MEDICAL ISSUES AND FAMILY MATTERS

The Saints view modern medicine in the same way as other technological advances—as divinely inspired blessings for humanity. Those holding the higher (Melchizedek) priesthood can anoint the sick with oil and bless them by the laying on of hands to be healed (see James 5:14–15), and the Saints do believe that divine intervention can bring healing. However, use of medical care is also enjoined, and there is no sense that using modern medicine is incompatible with faith in the divine power to heal.

The Saints strongly oppose elective abortion except when the woman's life is in danger or when the pregnancy resulted from rape or incest. Church policy is that these are not necessarily automatic reasons to abort, but the woman should prayerfully decide what to do. While the church encourages couples not to avoid having children or limit family size for purely selfish reasons, birth control is allowed, and decisions about when to conceive and how many children to have are left to each couple to prayerfully decide. Church policy allows fertility treatments and discourages permanent sterilization. The church is opposed to euthanasia (mercy killing), but decisions about whether to remove life-sustaining medical treatment are left to individuals and families. Thus while the church is clearly pro-life and pro-natal, it places a strong emphasis on the prayerful exercise of individual moral agency in these difficult and personal matters of life and death.

MORMONISM AND TECHNICAL RATIONALITY

As this collection makes clear, technical rationality is a major feature of modernization that can influence faith communities in negative ways, especially when fueled by the cultural values of individualism. Like all contemporary faiths, Mormonism is forced to deal with one especially challenging aspect of technical rationality: the one that entices individuals to make personal choices based mainly on a rational calculation of (often immediate) personal satisfaction in the context of meanings influenced by an overwhelming culture. And that culture is characterized by increasingly radical secularism, hedonism, individualism, materialism, and sexuality. Decisions based in such meanings often lead to actions that harm both faith and family life and include pre- and extramarital sexual activity, abortion, divorce, abuse, substance abuse, careerism, and limiting family size based on selfish motivations.

A science-dominated and education-oriented culture can be considered another aspect of technical rationality that can be threatening to religious groups and individuals. Religious individuals and groups with a traditional, orthodox, or fundamentalist approach may find some aspects of a science-oriented culture (e.g., rational explanations of miracles, evolution versus creation) that challenge or contradict a religiously oriented worldview.

Because Latter-day Saint theology requires the search for all truth, Latter-day Saints have an expansive approach to education and to scientific knowledge. Indeed, American Latter-day Saints obtain more education than the national average, and the most highly educated Latter-day Saints are also the most religiously devout and active.[56] And Latter-day Saints are not bothered by some of the scientific issues that concern other highly religious groups. For example, they believe that the creation of the earth was accomplished in six "creative periods" of indeterminate length (called "days" in Genesis), so scientific evidence of the great age of the earth does not call into question LDS theology.[57]

In the area of marriage and family relations, rather than relying exclusively on sacred texts to help couples and families, the church maintains an extensive church-based higher-education system (including Brigham Young University, with campuses in Provo, Idaho, and Hawaii) with scientific/professionally oriented books and classes as well as the LDS Family Services organization, which provides professional counseling on a range of relationship issues. This approach helps Latter-day Saints respond to modernization by knowing that they have the power of scripture, the timely help from the teachings of modern living prophets, and the best that science and professional practice have to offer that is consistent with sacred sources.

MORMONISM AND AMERICAN-STYLE DEMOCRACY

Mormonism has flourished in the American political system and most American Latter-day Saints are patriotic, freedom-loving citizens. Although the majority of contemporary American Saints live outside Utah and Idaho and thus constitute a political minority, the gathering of the Saints, practiced from the beginning of Mormonism, has had the practical result that the Saints have often held political influence where they have had numerical concentrations.[58] Thus American-style democracy has allowed the Saints to have a great deal of influence over their political destiny.

Church leaders repeatedly encourage the Saints to be involved in the political process, and data show that Latter-day Saints are highly involved, including disproportionate representation in Congress. A political profile of American Latter-day Saints suggests that the Saints have been largely ignored by scholars as a political force, even though their high concentration of members in several states, their cohesive nature, their political distinctiveness, and their willingness to mobilize for causes articulated by their leaders make them a political force to be reckoned with.[59]

For example, recent social and political efforts to legitimize homosexual behavior and orientation by changing the definition of marriage to include homosexual couples conflicts sharply with LDS teaching, that heterosexual marriage is the only divinely legitimate expression of sexuality. Indeed, since LDS doctrine explicitly outlines marriage as ordained by God, the church clearly rejects the modern idea of marriage as a malleable social institution that should be adapted to fit changing human cultures. The church has officially declared that it is in favor of a constitutional amendment explicitly defining marriage as a relationship only between a man and a woman,[60] and the church has been in the forefront of legal and political efforts to preserve the definition of marriage as a relationship between a man and a woman.

MORMONISM AND OTHER FAITHS

Mormonism has some interesting similarities with and differences from other faiths that influence matters of marriage and family. I briefly mention a few.

Like Catholicism, Mormonism is hierarchical in structure and culture; the authority to declare doctrine and policy clearly resides in church leaders. Thus, for the word of the Lord on matters of marriage and family life, the Saints look to the prophets and apostles in Salt Lake City, just as their more traditional Catholic friends look to the pope in Rome.

Like evangelical Christians and Jehovah's Witnesses, Latter-day Saints believe strongly in the written word of God and in the importance of expending significant effort studying and sharing the word with others near and far. Thus Latter-day Saints are likely to search the scriptures for personal answers to family challenges and are likely to invite their friends and neighbors to find answers to their family struggles in Mormonism.

Like Catholics, Orthodox Christians (i.e., Eastern Orthodox), and Anglicans, Latter-day Saints believe they are the possessors of an essential and unbroken line of ecclesiastical authority and power (in the case of Latter-day Saints, priesthood authority restored by angelic visitations of the resurrected ancient apostles Peter, James, and John to the Prophet Joseph Smith). Thus Latter-day Saints grant those who hold this priesthood and lead their congregation unique spiritual authority to assist them in dealing with the challenges of contemporary marriage and family life.

Like Orthodox Jews and Seventh-day Adventists, Latter-day Saints believe strongly in the sanctity of the Sabbath day, and generally choose not to work, make purchases, or seek entertainment on Sunday. Thus active Latter-day Saints typically spend the entire Sabbath day involved in personal and family activities of a religious character.

Like Muslims, Latter-day Saints believe God revealed many great and important things to a prophet hundreds of years after Christ and believe that the scripture revealed to that prophet joins the canon of holy writ. Thus, as Muslims look to the Qur'an and the Hadith (sayings) of the Prophet Mohammed, Latter-day Saints look to revelations received by Joseph Smith and to his successors for teachings on marriage and family.

INTERNAL CRITICISM AND MORMONISM

Since Latter-day Saints believe their prophets and apostles have the same religious authority as, for example, Moses or Peter, Mormonism has no long-standing culture of internal criticism. In fact, while it is understood that the highest leaders of the church may have varying perspectives on a variety of nondoctrinal issues, because LDS revelations stress the importance of unity in decision making and following the living prophet, LDS leaders act only in concert and usually after much deliberation. The Saints are encouraged to seek personal spiritual confirmation of prophetic counsel and not to practice blind obedience. There is no tradition of public criticism, lobbying, politicking, or other approaches similar to the decision making or influencing of church policy that is seen in many other American churches.

However, since the mid-1980s a vocal culture of critical discontent has arisen among some Latter-day Saints and former Latter-day Saints. Articles in two publications (*Dialogue* and *Sunstone*) edited and written by those known variously as "Mormon intellectuals" or "liberal Mormons" are often critical of LDS leaders and policies. These critics usually wish LDS leaders were more progressive or in other ways more in step with the modern or postmodern views held by less orthodox Saints (or former Saints). In the past these publications included a broader array of views and were probably more influential with some LDS leaders than they are today, but since the mid-1980s they have become so strident and critical that they have a much smaller readership and likely little to no influence with church leaders.

Evidence from a variety of sources has led many scholars and commentators to refer to Mormonism as perhaps the greatest modern American religious success story. Data showing dramatic domestic and international numerical growth, astounding economic strength, disproportionate and increasing influence in business and government, cultural influence over large geographic areas, significantly better mental and physical health than other Americans and, most relevant to this essay, higher likelihood of success and happiness in marriage and family life (in terms of lower divorce rates and greater marital and family well-being) seem to support these assessments. This essay suggests some reasons why Mormonism has been so successful despite—or perhaps even because of— the constellation of forces called modernization.

Latter-day Saint couples and families believe they are living in the final dispensation of time and have a responsibility to strive to perfect their lives, strengthen their marriages and families, teach the gospel to others, and do vicarious ordinances that bind them to their deceased ancestors—all this to help prepare all the children of God for the triumphant return of the Savior of the world. They use whatever modern technologies, ideas, or resources they believe will assist them in this work. They also face significant opposition from a modern culture that undermines many of their core values and purposes. They are able to cope with and even thrive on the challenges of modernization by following the counsel of living prophets and apostles who lead the church; by making and keeping sacred covenants—especially the covenant of eternal marriage; and by exercising faith in the Lord Jesus Christ as they strive to follow God's plan of happiness for individuals, couples, and families.

NOTES

1. I believe it is important for readers to know something about the perspective that an author has on his or her subject. I am an active Latter-day Saint and so provide a believing insider's perspective on Mormonism. I was converted to the faith when I was nineteen, then served as a full-time missionary for two years, and married a fifth-generation LDS woman in the Salt Lake Temple; we are raising our seven children in the faith. In sum, I strongly believe in and happily practice Mormonism. I am also a social scientist and honor the scholarly values of evidence, academic honesty, the scientific method, reasoned criticism, and effort at objective treatment of the subject of one's scholarship. While I am certainly *not* objective about either Mormonism or my fellow Latter-day Saints, I believe I can accurately and honestly report the basic beliefs and practices of LDS families and the ways they compare and contrast with the values and practices of modern America. Of course, the thoughts expressed are my own and do not necessarily reflect the views of the Church of Jesus Christ of Latter-day Saints or other Latter-day Saints.

2. First Presidency and Council of the Twelve Apostles of the Church of Jesus Christ of Latter-day Saints, "The Family: A Proclamation to the World," *Ensign*, November 1995, 76. *Ensign* is the official LDS church magazine.

3. Henry B. Eyring, "Hearts Bound Together," *Ensign*, May 2005, 77.

4. E. W. Lindner, ed., *Yearbook of American and Canadian Churches* (Nashville, Tenn.: Abingdon, 2005).

5. D. E. Jones et al., *Religious Congregations and Membership in the United States, 2000* (Nashville, Tenn.: Glenmary Research Center, 2002). See esp. maps on 547 and 562.

6. Latter-day Saints constitute the majority (more than 50 percent) of adherents in southern Idaho and make up a substantial minority (5 percent to 25 percent) of adherents in northeastern Nevada, northern Arizona, southwestern Wyoming, south-

western Washington, northwestern New Mexico, eastern Colorado, and southwestern Montana, and they have a strong presence in certain parts of southern California.

7. Rodney Stark, "The Rise of a New World Faith," *Review of Religious Research* 26 (1984): 18–27. See also a reprint of this article in J. T. Duke, ed., *Latter-day Saint Social Life: Social Research on the LDS Church and Its Members*, 9–27 (Provo, Utah: Religious Studies Center, Brigham Young University, 1998). This chapter tests Stark's prediction after ten years and finds that in every year actual growth of the LDS church was substantially higher than his predictions. Also see Rodney Stark, "The Basis of Mormon Success" (originally published in 1998) on pages 29–70 of this same book. The historian Jan Shipps refers to Mormonism as a "new religious tradition" (see Shipps, *Mormonism: The Story of a New Religious Tradition* [Urbana: University of Illinois Press, 1985]).

8. Latter-day Saints use certain titles for church leaders (e.g., elder, president) and formal names (full or middle initial), and I adhere to that practice in this essay. The quote is from Donald B. Cannon, ed., *Latter-day Prophets and the United States Constitution* (Provo, Utah: Religious Studies Center, Brigham Young University, 1991), 166.

9. In LDS parlance D&C stands for Doctrine and Covenants, a set of revelations given to the prophet Joseph Smith. All citations to the Bible are from the King James Version, the authorized text of the LDS Church. All citations to the Book of Mormon are given, like those for the Bible, with the name of the book, chapter, and verses.

10. Richard L. Bushman, *Believing History: Latter-day Saint essays*, edited by R. L. Neilson and Jed Woodwroth (New York: Columbia University Press, 2004), 272.

11. Quoted in Daniel H. Ludlow, ed., *Encyclopedia of Mormonism*, 5 vols. (New York: Macmillan, 1992), 4:1754.

12. However, one prophesy of the last days includes Jesus's statement that "this gospel of the kingdom shall be preached in all the world for a witness unto all nations; and then shall the end come" (Matt. 24:14.), so Latter-day Saints believe they have much missionary work yet to do before the restored gospel is preached in all nations.

13. Bushman, *Believing History*, 270.

14. The term *high tension* comes from Rodney Stark and Roger Finke, *Acts of Faith* (Berkeley: University of California Press, 2000).

15. Gordon B. Hinckley, *Ensign*, May 2005, 102.

16. *LDS Church News*, 9 April 2005, 24. A fundamental doctrine for Latter-day Saints is that God creates and also inspires human beings to create while Satan (Lucifer, the devil) destroys and perverts what God has created or inspired and urges human beings to destroy and pervert. Thus Latter-day Saints consider many aspects of modern life (freedom, technology, democracy, America, abundance) to be inspired by God but acknowledge that all these can be destroyed or perverted by evil influences. Latter-day Saints believe that God inspired the creation of computers to facilitate God's work (for example, genealogical research throughout the earth). But Latter-day Saints also believe that Satan has perverted these technologies to increase, for example, the spread of pornography.

17. Emphasis in original. John Jarvis, "Mormonism in France," in S. K. Houseknecht and J. G. Pankhurst, eds., *Family, Religion, and Social Change in Diverse Societies* (New York: Oxford University, 2000), 239.

18. Spencer W. Kimball, "Families Can Be Eternal," *Ensign*, November 1980, 4.

19. About the crucial need for modern revelation, Latter-day Saints like to say that "the Lord didn't command Moses to build an ark," meaning that the Lord gives each prophet counsel and commandments for current circumstances, so a modern prophet will give the Lord's counsel and warnings unique to this age.

20. D. C. Dollahite, "The Proclamation as Prophetic Guidance for Strengthening the Family," in D. C. Dollahite, ed., *Strengthening Our Families: An In-Depth Look at the Proclamation on the Family* (Salt Lake City, Utah: Bookcraft, 2000), 1–6; First Presidency and Council of the Twelve Apostles of the Church of Jesus Christ of Latter-day Saints, "The Family: A Proclamation to the World," *Ensign*, November 1995, 102.

21. Gordon B. Hinckley, *Teachings of Gordon B. Hinckley* (Salt Lake City, Utah: Deseret Book, 1997), 209.

22. C. H. Hart, L. D. Newell, E. Walton, and D. C. Dollahite, eds., *Helping and Healing Our Families: Principles and Practices Inspired by* "The Family: A Proclamation to the World" (Salt Lake City, Utah: Deseret Book, 2005). See also D. C. Dollahite, "Proclamation as Prophetic Guidance."

23. "'Dictatorship of Relativism,'" Vatican Watch: Latest from Rome and Beyond, MSNBC, 20 April 2005, http://msnbc.msn.com/id/7516788/page/9.

24. Neal A. Maxwell, "Deny Yourselves of All Ungodliness," *Ensign*, May 1995, 66.

25. Robert N. Bellah et al., *Habits of the Heart: Individualism and Commitment in American Life* (Berkeley: University of California Press, 1996).

26. Jarvis, "Mormonism in France," 245.

27. Joseph Fielding Smith, "Counsel to the Saints and to the World," *Ensign*, July 1972, 27.

28. Boyd K. Packer, "The Standard of Truth Has Been Erected," *Ensign*, November 2003, 25.

29. Dollahite, *Strengthening Our Families*.

30. Neal A. Maxwell, *A Wonderful Flood of Light* (Salt Lake City, Utah: Deseret Book, 1990), 38.

31. Orthodox Christians also believe that marriage can endure beyond the grave; Jehovah's Witnesses believe that if a couple is married when Jesus returns, they will stay in that state in the new order of things; and Muslims believe that they will enjoy family relations in the next world. What sets LDS doctrine apart is that the new and everlasting covenant of marriage promises that couples who keep the covenant will together inherit all that God has, become literally like God, and will have eternal offspring, or what LDS scripture calls a "continuation of the seeds forever" (D&C 132:19).

32. Latter-day Saints interpret the words of Jesus in Mark 12:25—"For when they shall rise from the dead, they neither marry, nor are given in marriage; but are as the angels which are in heaven"—to mean that all eternal marriages must be entered into *before* the resurrection since Jesus said that "when [after] they rise from the dead," they will not marry. Thus Saints search out their ancestors to perform eternal marriages (sealings) for couples that had been married on Earth "till death do us part" so they may be vicariously sealed in LDS temples *before* the resurrection.

33. LDS doctrine includes the concept that the atonement of Jesus Christ provides that all human beings will receive a bodily resurrection and, in addition, that all those

baptized by proper authority (either on this earth or by vicarious work done in LDS temples) may be saved and inherit the celestial or highest kingdom of glory but that only those who have been baptized and married for eternity through the sealing powers (available only in LDS temples) will be exalted to the highest degrees of the celestial kingdom and enjoy eternal marriage relationships.

34. James E. Faust, "Lord, I Believe; Help Thou Mine Unbelief," *Ensign*, November 2003, 19.

35. James E. Faust, "Father, Come Home," *Ensign*, May 1993, 36–37.

36. R. J. McClendon and B. A. Chadwick, "Latter-day Saint Families at the Dawn of the 21st Century," in Hart et al., *Helping and Healing Our Families*, 32–43. The LDS church does not release temple divorce statistics, so the percentages cited here are estimates based on the best recent available data.

37. E. L. Lehrer and C. U. Chiswick, "Religion as a Determinant of Marital Stability," *Demography* 30 (1993): 385–403.

38. T. B. Holman, A. Viveiros, and J. S. Carroll, "Progressing toward an Eternal Marriage Relationship," in Hart et al., *Helping and Healing Our Families*, 44–49.

39. M. Russell Ballard, "The Atonement and the Value of One Soul," *Ensign*, May 2004, 86.

40. Gordon B. Hinckley, "Daughters of God," *Ensign*, November 1991, 97.

41. McClendon and Chadwick, "Latter-day Saint Families."

42. D. C. Dollahite and L. D. Marks, "Teaching Correct Principles: Promoting Spiritual Strength in LDS Young People," in K. M. Yust, A. N. Johnson, S. Eisenberg Sasso, and E. C. Roehlkepartain, eds., *Religious Perspectives on Spirituality in Childhood and Adolescence* (Lanham, Md.: Rowman and Littlefield, 2006), 394–408.

43. D. C. Dollahite, "Fathering for Eternity: Generative Spirituality in Latter-day Saint Fathers of Children with Special Needs," *Review of Religious Research* 44 (2003): 237–51; L. S. Marks and D. C. Dollahite, "Religion, Relationships, and Responsible Fathering in Latter-day Saint Families of Children with Special Needs," *Journal of Social and Personal Relationships* 18, no. 5 (2001): 625–50.

44. James E. Faust, "The Prophetic Voice," *Ensign*, May 1996, 6.

45. A. J. Hawkins et al., "Equal Partnership and the Sacred Responsibilities of Mothers and Fathers," in Dollahite, *Strengthening Our Families*, 66.

46. D. C. Dollahite, "Family Worship at Home" in S. R. Klein and E. J. Hill, eds., *Creating Home as a Sacred Center: Principles for Everyday Living* (Provo, Utah: Brigham Young University Press, 2005), 191–202. LDS fathers hold the holy patriarchal priesthood, which allows them to give father's blessings by laying their hands on the heads of their children and speaking inspired words of comfort, counsel, and direction.

47. Hart et al., *Helping and Healing Our Families*.

48. In referring to the relatively more "worldly" or cosmopolitan ski town of Park City, Utah, where Robert Redford's Sundance Film Festival is held, some say that Park City is "in Utah but not of Utah."

49. Christian Smith and Melinda Lundquist Denton, *Soul Searching: The Religious and Spiritual Lives of American Teenagers* (New York: Oxford University Press, 2005), 35.

50. Gordon B. Hinckley, "The Church Grows Stronger," *Ensign*, May 2004, 4.

51. James E. Faust, "Search Me, O God, and Know My Heart," *Ensign*, May 1998, 17.

52. LDS teachings on the nature of God are distinct from the other Abrahamic faiths'. Latter-day Saints view God as having a literal, tangible, gendered body of flesh and bones. They view God the Father and his son, Jesus, as separate and distinct beings, one in purpose and power but distinct in personality and body. The third member of the godhead, the Holy Ghost, is a personage of spirit, also in complete unity with the Father and the Son but distinct in person. All LDS prayers call on the Father in the name of Jesus Christ, most ordinances are done in the name of Jesus Christ, but a few ordinances (baptism, temple sealings) are done in the name of the Father, the Son, and the Holy Ghost.

53. E. Enstrom, "Health Practices and Mortality Rates among Active California Mormons, 1980–1993," in Duke, *Latter-day Saint Social Life*, 461–71; S. R. Simmerman, "The Mormon Health Traditions: An Evolving View of Modern Medicine," *Journal of Religion and Health* 32 (1993): 189–96.

54. M. Russell Ballard, "Let Our Voices Be Heard," *Ensign*, November 2003, 16.

55. Smith and Denton, *Soul Searching*.

56. Stan L. Albrecht and Tim B. Heaton, "Secularization, Higher Education, and Religiosity," *Review of Religious Research* 26 (September 1984): 43–58.

57. Ludlow, *Encyclopedia of Mormonism*, 3:1270.

58. The Prophet Joseph Smith taught the Saints to gather in certain parts of America (Kirtland, Ohio; Nauvoo, Illinois) and prophesied that the Saints would later gather at the "everlasting hills" (see Gen. 49:26) or the "tops of the mountains" (see Isa. 2:2), a prediction that Latter-day Saints believe was fulfilled by the settlement along the various mountain ranges of the American West (from Canada to Mexico).

59. On Mormon disproportionate representation in Congress, see Robert Booth Fowler, Allen D. Hertzke, and Laura R. Olson, *Religion and Politics in America: Faith, Culture, and Strategic Choices* (Boulder, Colo.: Westview, 1999), 123–31. The profile is David E. Campbell and J. Quin Monson, "Dry Kindling: A Political Profile of American Mormons," in J. Matthew Wilson, ed., *From Pews to Polling Places: Faith and Politics in the American Religious Mosaic* (Washington, D.C.: Georgetown University Press, 2007).

Eighty-eight percent of Mormons voted for George W. Bush in 2000. In 2005 Senator Harry Reid (D-Nev.), an LDS member, served as the Democratic whip and thus the highest-ranking Democrat; Mitt Romney, governor of Massachusetts, one of the most liberal states in the nation, is also a Latter-day Saint; and Senator Gordon Smith, also a Saint, is a two-term Republican from Oregon, another very liberal state. While the church scrupulously maintains strict political neutrality, church leaders believe it is their right and duty to call on the Saints to become involved in what they consider clearly moral issues (such as the Equal Rights Amendment in the late 1970s and recent battles over gay marriage and gambling).

The political scientists David E. Campbell and J. Quin Monson ("Dry Kindling") found that, according to self-reports from the three groups, Mormons were far less likely than Southern Baptists or Catholics to have received any political information or influence at their places of worship.

60. First Presidency Statement issued 7 July 2004. Text available online: www.lds.org/news/article/0,5422,116–19733,00.html.

CHAPTER 9

What Is a Jewish Family?
The Radicalization of Rabbinic Discourse

JACK WERTHEIMER

Although no one can gainsay the fluidity of family life over the long course of Jewish history and in the many social and cultural environments inhabited by Jews, several fundamental assumptions about what constitutes a Jewish family and what ought to be sanctioned and encouraged by Jewish religious institutions have remained relatively stable at least since the emergence of rabbinic Judaism about two thousand years ago—until our own time. Since the last decades of the twentieth century, changing social patterns within the American Jewish community have prompted a reconsideration of profound questions concerning the nature of the Jewish family—its raison d'être, composition, and proper roles. As has been the case in American society at large, the questioning of long-held assumptions and religious practices has occasioned considerable turmoil within Jewish denominations and has sparked culture wars between religious movements.[1]

By virtue of their roles as the guardians and interpreters of Judaism, rabbis have stood at the front lines of such skirmishes. They have been pressed to defend or amend Jewish religious teachings regarding family matters, and, even more directly, rabbis themselves have been challenged to reconsider their own religious policies within the synagogue sanctuary and school, and under the marriage canopy. Not surprisingly, rabbinic discourse has shifted considerably in recent decades: new types of analyses have been brought to bear; the rhetoric has shifted; and long-standing assumptions have eroded, even among traditionalists. Symptomatic of the radicalization of discourse is the difficulty experienced by contemporary rabbis—including those within the same religious movement—to find a common language of religious conversation when they address certain questions related to the Jewish family.

For nearly two millennia rabbis have based their decisions about family law upon a vast body of Jewish literature, beginning with the biblical text and continuing with rabbinic works such as the Mishna and Talmud; subsequently, rabbis also drew upon later Jewish legal codes and exegetical works—all of which had much to say about family life. The Pentateuch itself, the formative text of the Jewish religious tradition, after all, devotes considerable attention both to the family narratives of Israel's patriarchs and matriarchs and contains an extensive set of commandments and prohibitions. Among the most important of the former are that men are to marry,[2] men and women are to procreate (some rabbinic works considered procreation to be the first of the commandments),[3] and they are obligated to teach their children about the religious traditions of Israel. Also, women, as conceived by rabbinic Judaism, are to attend to their children above all and therefore are exempt from time-bound ritual obligations. The biblical text and subsequent rabbinic Judaism also elaborate upon prohibitions affecting family life: certain types of sexual acts are forbidden; even sexual relations between husband and wife are regulated by laws of menstrual purity; and certain types of marriages, including exogamous marriages, are forbidden. (Divorce, however, is sanctioned and regulated.) Together, these do's and don'ts were understood by rabbinic Judaism to hold *legal force*, either as religious duties or religious prohibitions.

While a vast corpus of rabbinic literature developed to address these family matters, many additional concerns were not regulated by Jewish religious law but rather were subject to local custom. Recent research has especially illuminated the changeability of those family arrangements that were governed by custom rather than law: the age of marriage and childbearing has varied greatly; arranged marriages were more popular in some environments than in others; the roles of women inside the home and in the marketplace have undergone changes; views of the parental role in the disciplining of children have varied; conceptions of proper sexual modesty have changed, and so too have attitudes about the enjoyment of sexual pleasure within marriage. Circumstances and custom also shaped the relationship between the nuclear and extended family.

In the modern era new cultural perspectives and legal and social circumstances further accelerated changes within the Jewish family during the past 250 years.[4] The ideal of romantic love triumphed over arranged marriages, so much so that Jewish Enlightenment figures took up the cause of freedom of choice in the selection of a spouse.[5] Fertility rates plummeted in all modernizing Jewish communities.[6] Thanks to the decline in their family size and their embourgeoisement, upwardly mobile Jews could afford child care and the luxury of doting on their children.[7] Migration, a disruptive experience undergone by most Jewish families in the modern era, upended family relationships, casting children as educators of their parents and wives as the "breadgivers" who supported their families.[8] Jewish assimilation also increased the numbers of Jews who lapsed in their religious behavior. Rates of intermarriage soared in the late nineteenth and early twentieth centuries in much of western and central Europe, and when communism triumphed in Russia and later in other parts of Eastern Europe, intermarriage became the norm in those environments. But while rabbinic and communal leaders certainly scrambled to address a host of legal and communal issues prompted by such massive changes, the fundamental religious understanding of what constituted a Jewish family remained unchanged. During the last two decades of the twentieth century, new questions about family life have prompted the adoption of radically new approaches and policies toward families by various branches of American Judaism. What follows is a thumbnail sketch of the four most contentious issues and the arguments advanced by proponents of change.[9]

WHO IS A JEW?

Until quite recently Jews of different religious denominations, whatever their theological disagreements, could agree on who was a member of the Jewish community. Early in the common era rabbinic Judaism determined that a Jew was one who either had been born to a Jewish mother or had converted to the Jewish faith.[10] Not only was the rabbinic standard universally accepted, but the barriers to intermarriage created by internal Jewish taboos as well as by Gentile hostility saw to it that the standard was fairly easily maintained. But with today's massive increase in exogamy, some have been prompted to reconsider traditional definitions.

The first and most obvious target has been the doctrine of matrilineal descent.[11] Why, some have asked, should a child with only one Jewish parent be treated differently by the official religious community if that parent happens to be the child's father rather than mother? Should not community and synagogue alike embrace such children and thereby encourage "interfaith" families to identify themselves as Jews? Is it not self-destructive to risk the loss of hundreds of thousands of children solely to maintain a principle that, whatever may be said for it historically, no longer suits our circumstances?

In 1983 the Reform movement, currently the denomination with which the plurality of American Jews identifies, formally rejected the traditional definition of Jewish identity by adopting a resolution accepting any child with at least one Jewish parent as a Jew—provided that child engaged in public acts of Jewish religious participation. In the rabbinic debate about the resolution, proponents argued that the shift would merely recognize the de facto policy already practiced within the Reform movement; the patrilineal policy, moreover, ameliorated the condition of Jewish fathers who wished to raise their children as

Jewish; and it continued the process of equalizing the status of males and females, since it avoided giving preferential treatment either to Jewish mothers
or to Jewish fathers.[12] As one rabbi put it, the new policy was more equitable,
as it gave "the father's religion a vote."[13] In short, the redefinition of Jewish
identity was justified in the name of gender equality.[14]

Though often described as a policy on patrilineality, the Reform document
in fact was equable in its approach to Jewish identity: no longer was descent
from a Jewish mother a necessary condition. Nor, for that matter, was formal
conversion to Judaism. Rather, the child's Jewish identity was to be redefined
as an act of personal choice, the only proviso being that the "presumption" of
Jewish status was "to be established through public and formal acts of identification with the Jewish faith and people."[15] The consequence of this decision
has been the intentional severance of the link between the family and Jewish
identity: rather than base membership in the Jewish community primarily upon
descent from a Jewish family, the patrilineal decision added or substituted personal choice and acts of identification as considerations.[16] Hence the proud
embrace of the slogan "We are all Jews by choice," by a range of Jewish groups,
a slogan that itself reflects a radical break from earlier Jewish thinking, which
conceives of Jewish identity as inherited and fixed, an ascribed rather than freely
chosen characteristic.

This ruling has been duly rejected by the Conservative and Orthodox movements, both of which maintain the traditional rabbinic position on Jewish identity and regard Jews who intermarry as having broken a fundamental taboo. As
a consequence the Jewish community does not agree about who is a Jew, a
dispute that has important social repercussions, particularly because it revolves
around a question of personal status. Not long ago an Internet forum for Reform
rabbis was buzzing with stories of Conservative rabbis who do not allow the
teenagers in their synagogues to fraternize with their peers from local Reform
temples, on the ground that this could lead to dating young people not considered Jewish according to traditional criteria. Or consider the dilemma of a
Conservative rabbi asked by a female congregant to officiate at her marriage to
a young man who is Jewish only according to Reform's patrilineal dispensation.
A rabbi who acquiesces will be committing an act punishable by expulsion
from the organization of Conservative rabbis; a rabbi who declines will end up
alienating at least two families on account of "intolerance." We are rapidly approaching the time, moreover, when there will be rabbis who are themselves
offspring of interfaith families and who will not be recognized by their colleagues
as Jews. This state of affairs actually has some historical precedents: various Jewish
sects did erect high social barriers that discouraged social mingling and marriages
with members of competing religious groups that they deemed to be misguided
Jews. But it is more difficult to find examples of a time when adherents of Jewish
groups could not marry one another because they disagreed about the very definition of what is necessary to be counted as a Jew.

WHAT IS THE RELIGIOUS STATUS
OF INTERFAITH FAMILIES?

As rates of intermarriage have soared since the 1960s, reaching nearly 50 percent of all Jews who marry in this country, religious institutions have been challenged to formulate policies vis-à-vis the huge population of interfaith families.[17] To begin with, rabbis must decide whether they will officiate at wedding ceremonies at which a Jew marries a non-Jew. The fundamental question is whether the traditional ceremony, with its assumption that both partners adhere to "the religion of Moses and Israel" (as the traditional formula puts it), makes any sense when one partner is not an adherent of that religion. Beyond that, a rabbi may be asked to incorporate aspects of two religious traditions in the ceremony and to co-officiate with clergy of another religion. Rabbis must decide whether such syncretistic ceremonies in any sense can be called Jewish or can conform to any recognizable understanding of what makes for a Jewish wedding.[18] On a deeper level a rabbi needs to reconcile his or her participation at such a wedding with biblical and subsequent Jewish prohibitions against exogamy, such as the explicit statement in Deuteronomy: "You shall not intermarry with them."

Several hundred Reform, Reconstructionist, and nondenominational rabbis participate in such ceremonies, convinced that their presence will draw interfaith families closer to the Jewish community and encourage them to raise their children as Jews. As a cantor who has performed hundreds of such weddings put it, "I feel I have a calling. God wants me to help his people stay in the Jewish fold. . . . A Jew is entitled to a Jewish wedding."[19] Officiation at "interweddings" is justified in a number of ways: it is a Jew's right to be married according to a Jewish rite; families wishing for such a service are entitled to it; and the long-term effect will be positive, as it leaves the door open to the interfaith family's future participation in Jewish life. Significantly, the rabbinic organizations of the Reform and Reconstructionist movements do not apply any sanctions to such rabbis, deferring instead to their "autonomy," their right to decide for themselves.

But quite a few Reform and Reconstructionist rabbis nevertheless desist from officiating at such ceremonies. As one Reform rabbi explains: "I don't perform weddings between Jews and non-Jews because the *berachot* (blessings) don't apply if both people aren't Jewish. I would have to perform a non-Jewish ceremony—and I wasn't ordained to do non-Jewish weddings." Another Reform rabbi explains his position even more directly: "Jewish tradition says I can't do this. And I don't feel comfortable doing it because it's contrary to my tradition."[20] Both views sum up the positions of Orthodox and Conservative rabbinic organizations, which are on record as firmly opposed to such ceremonies and claim they would expel a member who officiated at an "interwedding."

A different set of questions arises when interfaith families make contact with Jewish religious institutions and wish to participate in religious services. When the child of such a union reaches the age of bar or bat mitzvah, should the non-Jewish parent be permitted to utter a Jewish prayer in public during the relevant religious service? And what if the Gentile parent would like to offer a Christian, Islamic, or Buddhist prayer? Are such prayers to be included in a synagogue service? The deeper question, as Rabbi Michael Wasserman has written, is the "authentication as Jewish families [and] easier access to the rituals by which the Jewish community defines its boundaries."[21] Here too some synagogues have bent, welcoming non-Jews to lead public prayer and partake of Jewish religious services. The rationale offered is that the synagogue wishes to honor parents who participate positively in the Jewish education of their children. Synagogues pride themselves, moreover, on their inclusiveness, their openness to many different types of families, both the conventional and the unconventional. As a liberal Conservative rabbi has put it in the course of explaining his policies on such matters: "Given a choice between a note of welcome or a message of distance, [my synagogue] prefers the arms that are open to the hand that is closed."[22]

Finally, religious institutions grapple with the question of whether they should explicitly encourage interfaith families to make a decision in favor of an unambiguous Jewish identification. Communal leaders of the so-called secular agencies of the Jewish community shy away from exerting any pressure in such a direction, lest they seem insufficiently inclusive. What is noteworthy, however, is the extent to which some rabbis subscribe to this approach. As one rabbi puts it, "The right thing to do is not to be judgmental about a decision that has already been made. . . . The question is 'how can we help you work through it.'"[23] In other words, some Jewish religious leaders favor a therapeutic approach, preferring to help couples who are "working through" any difficulties in their relationship and to remain studiously "nonjudgmental," rather than encourage interfaith families to become . . . Jewish.

Not long ago the leader of the Reform movement conceded that this way of thinking permeates many synagogues. Writing in the pages of the house organ of Reform Judaism, Rabbi Eric Yoffie, the president of the congregational arm of the Reform movement, described how "conversations with both rabbis and lay leaders lead me to believe that in most instances we do not encourage conversion by non-Jewish spouses in our synagogues. Perhaps this bespeaks a natural reluctance to do what we fear will give rise to an awkward or uncomfortable situation. Or perhaps we have been so successful in making non-Jews feel comfortable in our congregation that we have inadvertently sent the message that we neither want nor expect conversion."[24] It is worth noting that in Yoffie's analysis, the key to understanding his movement's inaction is concern for "comfort," a further symptom of the therapeutic role that synagogues are now expected to play.

In catering to the population of intermarried Jews and their families, synagogues and community centers have created an unprecedented new lobby.

Congregations now often *require* their rabbis to officiate at interfaith weddings, often alongside Christian clergy, and discourage rabbis from speaking about or urging conversion to Judaism.[25] Agencies of Jewish philanthropy employ a cadre of social workers to help keep intermarried families intact. In religious schools run by synagogues, teachers can no longer utter a word in favor of endogamy or prevent Jewish youngsters from being exposed to the jumbled religious views of their dual-faith classmates who, often "confused about which religion is which" (as one observer has reported), have trouble telling "who is Jesus and who is Moses."[26]

Still, defenders of change argue the virtues of an open, hospitable synagogue. They exhort congregations to engage interfaith families and do what is necessary to ensure their comfort. These are standard features of Reform and Reconstructionist congregational life, but, interestingly, some rabbis in the more traditional camps of the Conservative and Orthodox movements also have begun to worry about putting forth a more inviting welcome sign: a recent Conservative publication has gone so far as to urge the involvement of "non-Jews in the Torah service [which] may offend certain members but it allows loving family to continue to be part of their children's and grandchildren's lives."[27] Even some Orthodox rabbis have been pressed by congregants to "extend a *mazal tov* [congratulations] to a recently intermarried couple" and have begun to explore how intermarried Jews should be treated when it comes to synagogue services.[28]

Gone are the days when a rabbi, let alone a sociological researcher, would flatly declare, as Milton M. Barron did some two generations ago, that 90 percent of intermarriages are unsuccessful and only "undermine the stability of the home . . . and bring children into the world with a rift in their souls that can never be healed." Or a Rabbi Dangelow, who opined based on his forty-one years in the rabbinate: "Mixed marriages are rarely happy."[29] Or a researcher like Louis Berman who claimed in 1961 that

> intermarriage is classically viewed as an act of rebellion against social authority. Intermarrieds include more than their share of the headstrong, the rebels, those who think of themselves as "exceptions" to the ordinary rules of society. Perhaps their unwillingness to yield to society's disfavor of intermarriage reappears as an unwillingness to yield to each other's conflicting interests in the day-by-day drama of married life. Furthermore, attitudes which predispose a person to flout society's opposition to intermarriage should also help him flout society's opposition to divorce. How could it be otherwise? In each case the individual is guided by the dictum that his marital state is a private affair.[30]

By the end of the twentieth century, such voices had been silenced by the sheer size of the intermarried population and the concern about hurting the feelings of interfaith families.[31] Moreover, the impulse to create a warm hospitable con-

gregational environment had trumped long-standing taboos, even in more traditional religious circles. In a telling chapter in a new book, a Conservative
rabbi, in fact, exhorts his movement's congregations to "love the intermarried"[32]—a remarkable reversal, considering that intermarried Jews had long
been regarded as outcasts and renegades.

WHAT IS A JEWISH WEDDING?

The sexual revolution that began in the 1960s has prompted a reconsideration
of sexual ethics, ranging over such issues as premarital sex, multiple sex partners,
extramarital relationships, and homosexuality. What is perhaps most noteworthy
is the absence of serious public discussion in the Jewish community about some
of these issues. Whereas Jewish religious teachings have had much to say about
sexual ethics, it appears that few Jews bother to consult rabbis about such matters. A study of Modern Orthodox Jews claimed that even within this relatively
traditional sector of the Jewish community, attitudes toward premarital sex had
liberalized considerably within the rank-and-file, though not the rabbinate.[33]
Somewhat belatedly, rabbinic organizations have published pamphlets to clarify
their understanding of some of these issues.[34]

One issue that has garnered a good deal of press attention since the mid-
1980s is the religious status of homosexuals and lesbians. All Jewish religious
movements outside the Orthodox world have gone on record in their opposition
to civil discrimination against gays (although they differ on whether the state
should recognize gay marriages). Rabbinic leaders have also addressed the question of whether openly gay and lesbian Jews ought to be ordained as rabbis and
whether same-gender relationships should be sanctified through a religious ceremony conducted by a rabbi. In the debates that have ensued, no one has
argued that precedent exists for either; the argument in favor of change revolves
around new understandings of sexuality and the family, as well as proper respect
for other human beings.

What is fascinating in these debates is the extent to which the partisans have
been able to find no common language to bridge their differences. The point
is illustrated in a religious responsum issued by the Reform rabbinate in 1996
in reply to an inquiry about whether "a Reform rabbi [may] officiate at a wedding or 'commitment' ceremony between two homosexuals," and whether
"such a union qualifies as *qiddushin* from a Reform perspective." (The term
qiddushin refers to a sanctified Jewish marriage; precisely what that means was
at the heart of the debate, because a rabbi does not sanctify a Jewish marriage;
rather, the bride is sanctified to her husband during the ceremony, according
to the traditional rabbinic view, or the couple sanctify each other, in the more
liberal view.) The responsum began with a lengthy explanation of the tortured
process by which the committee arrived at an answer:

This question . . . has been an extraordinarily difficult one for our Committee. This is not only because we disagree as to its answer. . . . The difficulty in this case arises from the fact that argument itself, understood as the joint deliberative attempt to reach a common ground through persuasive speech, has broken down and proven impossible. On this *sheelah* [question], we have discovered that we no longer share a language of argument. . . . We have split into two or more camps, each framing the issue in a language or argument which the other side finds foreign, indecipherable, and obtuse."[35]

The majority ruled against rabbinic officiation at such marriages; the minority ruled in favor. Within two years, however, this decision was deemed so intolerable that the Reform rabbinate, through a plenum vote at its convention, overturned the findings of its own Responsa Committee, authorizing rabbis to follow the dictates of their conscience on the matter.[36]

There are, of course, many complex nuances to the debate about homosexuality, but for my purposes a few aspects of the discussion are especially salient. First, the debate about gays and lesbians has prompted a reconsideration of Jewish attitudes toward sexual expression. A recent pronouncement by a Conservative rabbi deeply unhappy with his movement's current stance on homosexuality illustrates how willing some rabbis are to break radically with earlier Jewish religious thinking about matters of sexuality: "We don't give a damn," he declared, "what they do when they go to bed."[37] This pithy outburst gives clear expression to the wish of many to privatize sexual ethics: it is no one's business what two consenting adults decide to do in private. Whether this judgment applies only to gays and lesbians or to all Jews, it surely represents a significant departure from traditional Jewish thinking about sexuality, if only because the Bible and subsequent rabbinic texts most certainly did take a strong interest in what Jewish people "do when they go to bed." Indeed, some rabbis took these prohibitions so seriously that they selected the Torah portion of Leviticus 18, which deals with forbidden sexual relationships, for public reading on the afternoon of the Day of Atonement.

Rabbis who favor officiating at gay commitment ceremonies have rejected earlier positions of the rabbinate quite self-consciously. Indeed, some have also rethought the nature of Jewish wedding ceremonies. As a practical matter, they have rewritten the traditional ceremony, dropping references to the act of sanctification (*quiddushin*) and some of the other traditional blessings.[38] In their place they have come to substitute newly composed liturgies. Moreover, some rabbis have also rethought the very purpose of the ceremony. One Conservative rabbi, for example, has asserted his willingness to "create an appropriate liturgy for any two people wanting to enter into a covenantal relationship, whether they be roommates, business partners, or a gay or lesbian couple."[39] The downgrading of the wedding ceremony could not be more clear: it is now regarded as a private affair that affirms the "covenant" between two people entering into *any* kind of relationship.

DOES JUDAISM CONTINUE TO VALUE MARRIAGE?

The debate about homosexuality—and also the emergence of nontraditional family constellations—has indirectly led to the rethinking of the very institution of marriage and its relationship to the Jewish family, as is evidenced by two documents issued by the Reform and Reconstructionist rabbinates during the 1990s. The first of these, "A Statement on Human Sexuality," drafted by the Reform rabbinate, explicitly acknowledges the change in thinking:

> In our age, the traditional notion of family as being two parents and children (and perhaps older generations) living in the same household is in the process of being redefined. Men and women of various ages living together, singles, gay and lesbian couples, single parent households, etc., may be understood as families in the wider, if not traditional sense. "Family" also has multiple meanings in an age of increasingly complex bio-technology and choice. While procreation and family are especially important as guarantors of the survival of the Jewish people, all Jews have a responsibility to raise and nurture the next generation of our people. The importance of family, whether biologically or relationally based, remains the foundation of meaningful human existence.

This statement radically expands the definition of a Jewish family to encompass all kinds of relationships. Quite dramatically, it also omits one element previously thought to be the sine qua non of Jewish sexual expression and family life—marriage. Indeed, this document on the Reform Jewish view of human sexuality "encourages adults of all ages and physical and mental capabilities to develop expressions of their sexuality that are both responsible and joyful," but it never once encourages Jews to marry![40]

A second document, issued by the Reconstructionist rabbinate, also avoids an endorsement of marriage as a Jewish ideal. The framers of the document list a series of values that "undergird our stance on homosexuality," including equality; loving, caring relationships; stable family and community life; personal freedom; inclusive community; democracy; physical pleasure; and spiritual health. Marriage is absent from this list but not from the document, where it is described as historically a relationship of "two unequal parties." By contrast, the document extols today's ideals: "Contemporary liberal Jews affirm the equality of both partners and understand that it is the obligation of each partner to treat the other with dignity. It is the qualities of mutual respect, trust, and love that we consider the fundamental attributes of loving partnerships"—not, however, marriage. Similarly, when discussing "stable family life," the document affirms its "commitment to preserving the traditional primacy of family because we understand the family as the primary, stable unity of intimacy." But the document is quick to add that "many old and new kinds of families can fulfill these values."[41] Here, then, are two documents on human sexuality and on the family issued by major rabbinic organizations, and neither endorses marriage as the necessary context for the expression of sexuality and the construction of Jewish family life.[42]

The astonishing radicalization of rabbinic thinking that has taken hold within ever expanding sectors of the Jewish community is all the more remarkable given the rapidity with which traditional religious policies have been overturned. Consider the following: In the early 1980s the Reform rabbinate was asked to address the following questions: Should we extend temple membership to the non-Jewish member in a mixed married family? Should a young unmarried uncouple be permitted to join a temple as a family unit rather than as individuals? Should a congregation engage a known homosexual as a religious school teacher or executive secretary? In all three cases the Responsa committee of the Reform rabbinate said no. Within a few years all these decisions were rejected, either through a formal decision or "on the ground" by a great many Reform rabbis and congregations.[43]

HOW ARE WE TO EXPLAIN CHANGING RABBINIC PERSPECTIVES ON THE FAMILY?

To begin with, the rejection of traditional views of the family by sectors of the Jewish community is part of a larger trend within American society to rethink "family values." Whereas the question of "who is a Jew" and the proper treatment of interfaith families may have few parallels outside the Jewish world, battles do rage in Christian denominations about questions of homosexuality and the proper ordering of family life. The broader sexual revolution and the rapidly changing social realities have forced most religious communities to scrutinize their religious traditions, and some of the more liberal Christian denominations have altered their policies in ways that parallel their counterparts within American Judaism.

Still, the Jewish community is even more apt to reconsider its position on family matters than are other religious groups. For one thing, as constituents of a voluntary community that is losing adherents, Jewish institutions are scrambling to be as inclusive as possible. With only 40 to 45 percent of American Jews affiliated with a synagogue at any given moment, Jewish congregations are under enormous pressures to institute "inclusive" policies to demonstrate just how welcoming they are. Most conclude they can ill afford to draw boundaries that will exclude potential members. Recent research has demonstrated, moreover, that large numbers of Jews make religious decisions based solely upon the inclinations of the "sovereign self."[44] Religious leaders are, therefore, under enormous pressure to bow to consumer demands, rather than work to convince individual Jewish families to surrender any of their autonomy. Hence Jewish religious and communal leaders prefer to bend rather than break.

Jews, moreover, are especially susceptible to the types of arguments made in favor of change. As past victims of intolerance, Jews are especially vulnerable to an argument framed in terms of civil rights, nondiscrimination, and inclusiveness. Proponents of change understand this and shape their case accordingly. To cite a particularly striking example: Urging his colleagues to support the introduction of civil legislation to legitimize same-sex marriages, one rabbi drew a parallel between the struggle for homosexual rights in our own time and the battle for racial equality in the middle of the twentieth century: "We were there then," he declared. "We have no choice [but] to be there now."[45] The implication is clear: opponents of same-sex marriages are bigots. Given such a reading, how can a rabbi possibly side with foes of civil rights? Similarly, those who oppose the unequal treatment of interfaith families in the synagogue bemoan such policies as discriminatory and exclusive, and opponents of the matrilineal policy stigmatize it as not egalitarian because it regards as Gentile the children of interfaith marriages whose fathers are Jewish.

A study guide issued by the Reconstructionist movement, in fact, ups the ante even further by linking the "mistreatment and negative stereotyping directed at Jews and [at] gay and lesbian people." The guide encourages group discussion within synagogues designed to foster an understanding of "the nature of groups targeted by a people and the parallels between antisemitism and the mistreatment of gays and lesbians."[46]

It is unthinkable for most American Jews, let alone their rabbis, to resist such arguments. American Jews, after all, have for decades registered the view that anti-Semitic discrimination poses the greatest threat to Jewish life in the United States. The official representatives of Jewish organizations accordingly have embraced the cause of civil rights and fought for an end to any form of discrimination, as they marched under the banner of American egalitarianism. Given these deeply entrenched tendencies, there is little prospect that the American Jewish community will long resist those who challenge fundamental teachings about Jewish family life and obligations as long as those challenges invoke ideals such as equality, privacy, inclusiveness, and pluralism—precisely the framing ideals used in numerous battles against anti-Semitism.

In a more positive vein, proponents of change also link their causes to past struggles in which Jews have played an active and successful role as agents of change. I have already noted the parallel drawn between the struggle for black equality and gay rights. In a similar vein proponents of homosexual equality link their cause with the struggle against gender discrimination. When the Women's Rabbinic Network, the organization of Reform women rabbis, led the campaign to overturn their movements' negative responsum on homosexual marriages, one leader of the group proudly observed that this effort "once again highlight[ed] the link between the ordination of women as rabbis and gay and lesbian issues."[47] The implication here too is clear: just as gender equality has won wide acceptance among Jews, the struggle for parity for homosexual liaisons with heterosexual relationships also must triumph.

Perhaps, just as important, the changing rhetoric and policies within Jewish religious circles in the United States reflect the internalization by Jews of contemporary American sensibilities. Religion has come to be defined as a matter of choice, and participants in religious activities expect to have a "meaningful experience." Religious leaders, in turn, are valued for their understanding and compassion, not for their teaching of a perspective at odds with contemporary cultural assumptions. "There is a reluctance to judge, to assert a language of responsibility and a posture of authority," contend the sociologists Charles S. Liebman and Sylvia Barack Fishman.[48] Religion, instead, is expected to offer therapy, to help people feel "comfortable," to attend to the personal needs of the individual rather than the collective needs of the group.[49]

As rabbis continue to adapt to this new climate, they will be hard pressed to reconcile current religious sensibilities with Judaism's long-standing commandments and prohibitions. With the passage of time rabbis, as guardians of the vitality and integrity of Jewish religious expression, will undoubtedly encounter new challenges posed by the continuing disparity between American ideals and the imperatives of Judaism. Ultimately, even the most open-minded will need to draw a line in the sand. American egalitarianism, after all, seeks to level distinctions between peoples, to efface categories and boundaries. Judaism, by contrast, has been a distinction-making religion that distinguishes between Jews and Gentiles, men and women, heterosexuality and homosexuality, and between the married and the unmarried.

In the short term, though, rabbis have underplayed the dissonance and have reshaped Judaism to fit American egalitarian ideals. It remains to be seen how well the new rabbinic thinking will serve the Jewish religion—and the Jewish family.

NOTES

1. On the heightened religious polarization among American Jews that has marked recent decades, see Jack Wertheimer, *A People Divided: Judaism in Contemporary America* (New York: Basic Books, 1993), and Samuel G. Freedman, *Jew vs. Jew: The Struggle for the Soul of American Jewry* (New York: Simon and Schuster, 2000).

2. In the traditional formulation these requirements apply to males only. One of the critical legal shifts occurred when Ashkenazic rabbis formally banned polygamy about a thousand years ago. We do not know how widespread nonmonogamous marriages were before the ban or in lands where this ban was not accepted.

3. "The duty of procreation," writes David M. Feldman, "has the popular distinction of being called the 'first mitzvah [commandment]' of the Torah" (*Marital*

Relations, Birth Control, and Abortion in Jewish Law [New York: Schocken Books, 1974], 46).

4. For an overview of these changes see Paula E. Hyman, "The Modern Jewish Family: Image and Reality," in David Kraemer, ed., *The Jewish Family: Metaphor and Memory* (New York: Oxford University Press, 1989), 179–93.

5. See Jacob Katz, "Marriage and Sexual Life among the Jews at the End of the Middle Ages" (Hebrew), *Zion* (1944): 21–54.

6. See Paul Ritterband, ed., *Modern Jewish Fertility* (Leiden, The Netherlands: Brill, 1981).

7. See, for example, Marion A. Kaplan, *The Making of the Jewish Middle Class: Women, Family and Identity in Imperial Germany* (New York: Oxford University Press, 1991).

8. See the depiction of this process in Irving Howe with Kenneth Libo, *The World of Our Fathers* (New York: Schocken, 1989). See also Anzia Yezierska's *Breadgivers* (New York: Doubleday, 1925) for a fictional account of the new roles played by immigrant women.

9. Because this essay focuses on changing attitudes, it devotes less attention to the arguments of traditionalists.

10. The historian Shaye J. D. Cohen has traced this process of clarification to the first five centuries of the common era. See *The Beginnings of Jewishness: Boundaries, Varieties, Uncertainties* (Berkeley: University of California Press, 1999).

11. Some also question whether conversion is necessary today and instead favor self-identification with the fate of the Jewish people as a sufficient qualification for acceptance as a Jew. See, for example, Egon Mayer, "Love Means Never Having to Be Proactive," *Sh'ma*, October 1999, 1–3.

12. As early as 1947 the Reform rabbinate had defined informal guidelines for accepting as a Jew the child of a Jewish father and a non-Jewish mother; these guidelines were included in a rabbi's manual produced in 1961. See Ellen Jaffe-Gill, "Patrilineality: Creating a Schism or Updating Judaism," *Moment*, December 1998, 71.

13. Ibid., 71.

14. A summary of the debate appears in the *CCAR Yearbook* 93 (1983): 14–60. To be sure, proponents justified the change by referring to the Hebrew Bible's patrilineal approach to the matter of tribal identity (i.e., an Israelite was of the same tribe as his father) and observed that only with the codification of the Mishna in the third century was matrilineal descent deemed determinative for Jewish identity. But the rationale offered for change was based on the conviction that fathers and mothers must be treated equally.

15. The document appears in Walter Jacob, ed., *American Reform Responsa: Jewish Questions, Rabbinic Answers* (New York: Central Conference of American Rabbis, 1983), 547–50. The small Jewish Reconstructionist movement had made a similar decision fifteen years earlier. I should note that the Reform rabbinate has never formulated a definition of what constitutes "public and formal acts" marking Jewish identity.

16. It has been a subject of some debate whether "acts of formal identification" are required of all Reform Jews or only those born to non-Jewish mothers. See Jaffe-Gill, "Patrilineality," 96.

17. The precise national figure for intermarriage has been hotly debated for more

than a decade. In the early 1990s the National Jewish Population Study claimed an intermarriage rate of 52 percent for Jews who married between 1985 and 1990. Using a different method, a study conducted in 2000–2001 reduced the figure for those years to 43 percent but claimed that between 1995 and 2000, 47 percent of marriages involving a Jew were intermarriages. See pp. 16–20 in "The National Jewish Population Survey 2000–2001: Strength, Challenge and Diversity in the American Jewish Population," a United Jewish Communities Report in cooperation with the Mandell L. Berman Institute—North American Jewish Data Bank, September 2003. .

18. While many rabbis may grapple with these questions of religious principle and authenticity, some are more preoccupied with a more mundane question: "How can we create a wedding ceremony that includes aspects of both traditions without offending anyone?" In reply, one Reform rabbi opined: "It is not only possible, but it is easier to achieve than you might think." Remarkably, her formula for success includes an admonition to "avoid saying prayers in Jesus' name," as if such a ceremony might not offend Christians. The operative concern, of course, is to avoid giving offense, not religious authenticity and coherence. See Devon A. Lerner, "One Rabbi's Approach to Interfaith Wedding Ceremonies," InterfaithFamily.com, 4 February 1999, www.interfaithfamily.com/article/issue7.lerner.htm.

19. Alan H. Feiler, "Will You Marry Me? Rabbis and Cantors Who Say 'I Do' to Interfaith Couples," *Baltimore Jewish Times*, 6 August 1993, 50.

20. Andrea Jacobs, "'Interweddings': Should Rabbis Officiate?" *Intermountain Jewish News*, 27 December 2002, www.ijn.com.

21. Michael Wasserman, "Intermarriage and Jewish Continuity: The Rabbinic Double Bind," *Conservative Judaism*, spring 1996, 8.

22. Rabbi Mark Loeb, "From the Rabbi: A Concern to Draw People Near," *Bulletin*, Beth El Congregation of Baltimore, February 1996.

23. Ami Eden, "Should the Walls Come Tumbling Down? The Jericho Project Seeks to Help Intermarried Families Find Their Way," *Philadelphia Jewish Exponent*, 4 May 2000, 54–56.

24. Eric H. Yoffie, "A Call to Outreach," *Reform Judaism*, Fall 1999, 32–33.

25. For specific cases see Gabriel Kahn, "Wanted: Rabbi Who Does Intermarriages," *Forward*, 9 February 1996.

26. Quoted in "Reform Rabbis Confront Issues of Intermarriage," *Jewish Post and Opinion*, 12 December 1999, 3.

27. Federation of Jewish Men's Clubs, *Building the Faith: A Book of Inclusion for Dual-Faith Families* (New York: Federation of Jewish Men's Clubs, 2001), 17.

28. Meryl Ain, "Re-Examine Intermarriage, Orthodox Rabbis Urged," *(New York) Jewish Week*, 7–13 February 1992, 4.

29. Both are quoted by Louis Berman, *The Jews and Intermarriage: A Study in Personality and Culture* (New York: Thomas Yoselof, 1968), 176–77.

30. Ibid., 178–79.

31. The massive increase in intermarriages has also provided more than sufficient evidence that such relationships are not doomed, even though they continue to be prone to higher divorce rates than inmarriages. Divorce rates for intermarried Jews consistently exceeded those for in-married Jews during the last sixty years of the twentieth century, although the gap has narrowed considerably in recent decades. See the forthcoming report of Bruce Phillips for the United Jewish Communities.

32. Dan Isaak, "Love the Intermarried," in Federation of Jewish Men's Clubs, *Let's Talk About It . . . A Book of Support and Guidance,* (New York: Federation of Jewish Men's Clubs, 2003),

33. Samuel Heilman and Steven M. Cohen, *Cosmopolitans and Parochials: Modern Orthodox Jews in America* (Chicago: University of Chicago Press, 1989), chap. 5.

34. See the pamphlets issued by the Reform and Reconstructionist movements cited later in this chapter, as well as "A Letter on Intimate Relations," issued by the Conservative rabbinate in February 1995 and available through the Rabbinical Assembly in New York.

35. "On Homosexual Marriage," *CCAR Journal: A Reform Jewish Quarterly,* Winter 1998, 5.

36. "Resolution on Same Gender Officiation," 111th Convention of the Central Conference of American Rabbis, March 2000. www.ccarnet.org. On the Reconstructionist position see Jewish Reconstructionist Federation and Reconstructionist Rabbinical Association, "Homosexuality and Judaism: The Reconstructionist Position: The Report on the Reconstructionist Commission on Homosexuality," the 1993 revised edition of a bound typescript distributed by the Jewish Reconstructionist Federation of Elkins Park, Pennsylvania. This report also offers a helpful survey of how this topic was discussed by Jewish groups across the denominational spectrum (see pp. 32–36). In late 2002 pressure built within the Conservative movement to reexamine its decade-old "consensus statement," which prohibited gay ordination and opposed rabbinic officiation at gay commitment ceremonies (Elliot Dorff, "Jewish Norms for Sexual Behavior: A Responsum Embodying a Proposal," Committee on Jewish Law and Standards of the Rabbinical Assembly, 25 March 1992, http://keshetjts.org/sources/Dorff-sexuality.pdf).

37. Abby Cohen, "Conservative Rabbis Here Ask Movement to Liberalize Policy on Gays," *(San Francisco) Jewish Bulletin,* 28 February 2003. This publication is now called the *Jewish News Weekly of Northern California;* its Web site is located at www.jewishsf.com.

38. Alexandra J. Wall, "Conservative Rabbis Here Defy Movement's Ban on Gay Nuptials," *Jewish Bulletin of Northern California,* 30 March 2001, www.jewishsf.com.

39. Ibid.

40. Ad Hoc Committee on Human Sexuality, report to the Central Conference of American Rabbis, June 1998. Only at the very end of this report is there any reference to marriage and then only the invocation of "the traditional unique status of heterosexual, monogamous marriage in Judaism." But that is a descriptive comment about the past, not a prescription for the future. Even more significantly, the actual report makes reference to the "convenantal relationship" as a major ground for "sexual expression in human relationships" and the need to "ground" these in "fidelity and the intention of permanence" but avoids any reference to marriage. The report's authors freely concede that "the value systems of liberal Jews are based upon contemporary secular norms."

41. Jewish Reconstructionist Federation and Reconstructionist Rabbinical Association, *Homosexuality and Judaism,* esp. 12–13.

42. For a different perspective see "This Is My Beloved, This Is My Friend: A Rabbinic Letter on Intimate Relations" issued by the Conservative rabbinate's Rab-

binical Assembly in February 1995. This document explicitly declares, "Judaism posits marriage as the appropriate context for sexual intercourse." It also declares, "Contrary to the contemporary notion that my body belongs to me, our tradition teaches that our bodies belong to God." Still, the document has occasioned controversy for offering guidelines for "non-marital sex."

43. Jacob, *American Reform Responsa*, 45–54. All the decisions were rendered by the committee in the early 1980s. As I have already noted, the Responsa committee's ruling on gay marriages was also overturned.

44. Steven M. Cohen and Arnold M. Eisen, *The Jew Within: Self, Family, and Community in America* (Bloomington: Indiana University Press, 2000).

45. "Reform Rabbis Approve of Same Sex Marriages," *Jewish Post and Opinion*, 3 April 1996, 1.

46. Mark Gluck, *Homosexuality and Judaism: A Reconstructionist Workshop Series* (Wyncote, Pa.: Reconstructionist Press, 1993), 52–53.

47. Denise L. Eger, "Embracing Lesbians and Gay Men: A Reform Jewish Innovation," in Dana Evan Kaplan, ed., *Contemporary Debates in American Reform Judaism* (New York: Routledge, 2001), 186–90.

48. Charles S. Liebman and Sylvia Barack Fishman, "Jewish Communal Policy toward Outmarried Families," *Journal of Jewish Communal Service*, Fall 2000, 25.

49. On this theme see Bernard Susser and Charles S. Liebman, *Choosing Survival: Strategies for a Jewish Future* (New York: Oxford University Press, 1999).

CHAPTER 10

Confucian "Familism" in America

JEFFREY F. MEYER

Wong Chin Foo was an educated spokesperson for Chinese Americans in the late nineteenth century, traveling around the country and giving about eighty lectures in major cities. He was described by *Harper's Weekly* as an "intelligent, cultured gentleman, who speaks English with ease and vivacity, and has the power of interesting his audiences." Having seen first hand how Chinese were murdered, robbed, and discriminated against, he resolutely refused to be lured into any Christian denominations, inviting instead "the Christians of America to come to Confucius."[1] Wong knew he was not really inviting Americans to convert to a Chinese religion. His concern was ethical, and he believed that ancient Confucians had taught what became the basic Christian moral and ethical values thousands of years before and that the Chinese people had successfully practiced those precepts ever since.

In many ways Wong was an aberration. Most Chinese did not see their "Confucianism," if they even conceptualized their ethical practices as such, as a functional equivalent of Christianity. Many had in fact converted to Christianity, either in China before immigration or after beginning their lives in America, seeing no discrepancy between their Christian and Confucian loyalties. "Seldom do you find a Chinese Christian who repudiates Confucianism wholesale," says the historian Peter Lee. "Not to speak of repudiation, criticism of Confucianism is uncommon among Chinese Christians."[2] Because many Chinese modernizers had vigorously criticized Confucianism since the May 4th Movement (1919), the congruence that I note here is significant.[3] In fact, it may be that a conversion to Christianity actually strengthened the commitment to Confucianism, since both traditions, in their more conservative forms, had strong antimodernist tendencies and shared moral norms.

The Chinese situation in the United States highlights a difference between Confucianism and the other religious traditions featured in this book. Confucianism should not be considered the functional equivalent of the other American religions. It is not considered a religion either in Taiwan (where it is officially revered as the foundation of Chinese culture) or in the Peoples Republic of China (where it has been alternately vilified or honored, depending on the political climate of the moment). While Confucianism definitely includes religious elements and can perhaps serve as a religion for certain elites,[4] most Chinese regard it as a moral and social philosophy. One could argue that "the essence of traditional Chinese Confucianism was . . . an intense familism that took precedence over all other social relations, including relations with political authorities."[5] Confucianism has for so long been embedded in the very matrix of Chinese life and thought that it is difficult, and perhaps misleading, to try to disentangle it.

In traditional China *family* meant the patriarchal structure of relationships that included, at times, as many as four generations in one large household and included many uncles, aunts, and cousins in the paternal line of descent. In addition to these were the deceased members, who were in many ways more important, because they were more powerful, than the living. And while there was no separate institution for this religion of ancestral worship, there was a strong ritual component, which took the form of a communal meal of offering, remembrance, and celebration. The living worshipped their deceased family members with gifts of food and invited them to share a meal. Upon the dead depended the good fortune of the living. If the living did not perform the worship correctly and regularly, the ancestors might not bless the family.

Today the ancestral religious rites have become more and more attenuated. Some families have abandoned them, while others continue to honor their deceased with more general expressions of respect. Yet I would maintain that the continuing strength of the Chinese family is to a large extent an outcome of these traditional religious practices. If the family meals are now mostly gatherings of the living, they still maintain many elements of past religious practice: formalism, hierarchical arrangement of participants, and the reaffirmation of essential relationships.[6] Julia Ching notes that Confucianism has always been the center of Chinese family life and ethics; it is permeated by religious values and provides a model for social behavior and a strong sense of social solidarity that continues among overseas Chinese today. "If Confucianism remains alive for many generations to come," she adds, "the credit belongs to this sense of human solidarity, based fundamentally on familial sentiments."[7]

The deconstruction of Confucianism as equivalent to a "world religion" has been going on apace since the mid-1980s, perhaps reaching its climax in the

1997 book *Manufacturing Confucianism* by Lionel Jensen. The author asserts that there was no such thing as Confucianism in China until the Jesuits "manufactured" it in the seventeenth century. While his thesis is overstated for rhetorical purposes, Jensen has made some telling points that clearly highlight the differences between Confucianism and the other major "world religions." In the same vein Frank Chin, a contemporary Chinese American playwright, chafing under the stereotype of the "model immigrant," charges that white Americans have created Confucianism for Chinese immigrants to ensure that they remain quiet, unobtrusive, humble, and family-absorbed ethnic presences who will be easy to dominate and control.[8]

My approach to the problem of the noninstitutional character of Confucianism is to regard it as an implicit ethos,[9] an ideology unself-consciously absorbed by most Chinese and legitimated by a variety of means: simple traditional affirmations ("this is the way we have always done it"); proverbs, maxims, and aphorisms; legends, myths, and folktales; and by more rationalized theories formerly propounded by the scholars (*rujia*). The family practices thus created set Chinese Americans apart from their fellow citizens and gave them a unique identity, one that has continued to evolve. "The dominance of Confucian ethical values in the traditional moral order needs no elaboration," a Chinese sociologist said years ago, and his book's first chapter was a discussion of Conficianism's central role in shaping family life.[10] Ever since the Song dynasty (960–1260 C.E.), when Zhuxi, the central neo-Confucian figure, wrote his *Family Rituals*, Confucian norms have been the official ideal of family behavior. Taking the major rites of passage then practiced by Chinese families, he reaffirmed their importance and infused them with Confucian values. And, more recently, Tu Wei-ming has asserted that "Confucianism is still an integral part of the 'psychocultural construct' of the contemporary intellectual as well as the Chinese peasant."[11] Furthermore, much of what I am saying could also be said, with some qualifications, of Japanese, Korean, and Vietnamese traditions, also strongly influenced by Confucianism.[12] All share a strong family ethic, with specific differences rooted in the histories and cultures of their respective pasts. But my remarks focus on the Chinese American community.

Despite its pervasiveness, however, Confucianism thus understood is rarely acknowledged or affirmed by Chinese Americans themselves. When I speak with my ethnically Asian students about these matters, I draw a blank if I ask them about Confucianism's influence, whereas a fascinating conversation always ensues if I ask about family life, the norms that govern it, and to what extent it is changing or not changing in the American environment. Whether they like it or not, they seem to sense that Chinese family life is unique.[13] In the paragraphs that follow I will attempt to define this unique identity and to examine how it may have changed through its dialectical relationship to American culture.

DEFINING THE CHINESE FAMILY CONFUCIANISM

It is well known that the family in traditional China means not the nuclear family characteristic of the twentieth-century West but the extended family, ideally including, according to the famous aphorism, "four generations under one roof" (*si shi tong tang*). While trying to avoid an essentialism that would claim that there exists a normative "Chinese family" that transcends time and place, I am going to understand family "Confucianism" to include convictions, attitudes, and practices expressed in such things as the emphasis on the primacy of the family as a whole over individual members and the dedication of individuals to the welfare of the group. It includes a system of mutuality in which parents and children become engaged in an interlocking system of obligations that has as its goal the preservation and strengthening of the family unit. To put it colloquially, as one of my students did, the system amounts to this: "Parents kill themselves to nurture, support, and educate their children; then children must kill themselves to support and care for their parents in their old age" (in old China this sequence would then have gone on to include the practices of ancestral worship, the continuation of familism after death). While apparently exaggerated, my student's speech reflects a traditional "extremism" in the expression of the central family virtue, filial piety, or its correlative, rigid wifely propriety and chastity. Going to extremes in pursuit of key family virtues points to their religious origins. Chinese literature offers numerous examples of this. Anne Behnke Kinney's studies of the Han dynasty text *Lienu zhuan* (Biographies of Virtuous Women) have made it clear that some Confucians even advocated martyrdom for the sake of female chastity, a virtue important in preserving the purity of the patriarchal line of descent.[14] The *Ershisi xiao* (Twenty-four Stories of Filial Piety) contains accounts of children who are going through various kinds of repellent acts of self-torture to serve their parents.

Other important aspects of Confucian familism include a patriarchal power structure, with the oldest male ruling family affairs, a hierarchic system of relationships (e.g., older siblings hold sway over younger, males over females); arranged marriages (in the United States this is often diluted to strong parental influence in spouse selection); periodic and frequent gatherings focused on the eating ritual; individual hard work and self-discipline (including diligence in the workplace and studying hard at school); working well together (group spirit); postponement of immediate gratification in order to attain family goals, such as education at the best schools (as I will show, Asians have been almost too successful at this), a new home in a better neighborhood, and the like.[15] While some aspects of the old family ethos—such as polygamy, absolute male authority, and rigid hierarchy—have been challenged, other Confucian elements remain: "Age grading; the generational sequence; the dutiful bonding between parents and siblings; the security brought to its members by a complex but

highly effective extended family system; the common core of intensely structured values; an ethical code and a morality widely disseminated and known to
all; a role definition in which everyone had a specified assignment; industri-
ousness, discipline, and the elevated position given to learning."[16] Obviously,
the expression of familism was different in China and the United States, but
for the immigrants it generally meant trying to adjust their social ethics to new
contingencies rather than abandoning the family tradition altogether.

Consequently, if Confucianism is not comparable to other world religions
in respect to its institutions and leadership structure, its strong family emphasis
may be considered an even more powerful social factor than it is in the other
religions, which at some levels are suspicious of and relativize the family. Hinduism, Buddhism, and Christianity have urged the zealous to leave their families and pursue religious life in monasteries, nunneries, or ashrams. Buddhism
and Taoism offered this ideal to the Chinese, sometimes urging them to leave
home and family to seek enlightenment or immortality. In contrast, the Confucian tradition absolutized the family and stood against any weakening of its
influence in Chinese society.

With this understanding of an implicit and extensive Confucianism expressed in the family system, what can be said about its fate in America? Here
we encounter a maze of difficulties, because the Chinese family has faced
entirely different contexts since the first Chinese began arriving in 1840. Variety
also emerges according to location. Does *family* mean isolated Chinatown
ghetto families or those who have moved to the suburbs and had the opportunity
to assimilate? Are we speaking of Chinese who came from Guangzhou in the
nineteenth and early twentieth century, or from Taiwan (with its deliberate
cultivation of Confucian ethics), or, more recently, from the mainland (where
the government repudiated Confucianism)? Are we speaking of illiterate or
educated Chinese; males or females; first, second, or third generations; parents
or children; cultural conservatives; assimilationists; or those seeking an entirely
new Chinese American identity? All these questions simply stress the great
variety of circumstances that the Chinese American family faces and the many
contingencies that challenge it. The following short survey examines these issues through a sketch of the history of the Chinese in America, trying to show
how the family system fared in an often hostile and alien environment, and
against a background of changing historical conditions.

THE CHINESE FAMILY IN THE UNITED STATES

The first Chinese to land on American soil arrived in Baltimore in 1785, on a
Cantonese ship called the *Pallas*,[17] but they did not come in large numbers
until after the discovery of gold in 1848. The next decades saw an unrestricted
and growing number of males come as "coolie" laborers, especially to work on

the railroads and in the mines of the West. They were forbidden to bring their wives, own land, or become citizens. As miscegenation was also proscribed, the Chinese males were in effect condemned to be bachelors, destroying all their hopes for a normal family life. They were the object of racial prejudice, which sometimes included beatings and lynchings, and were legally blocked from education and the higher professions. Deprived of any possibility of forming a family, they were then criticized for being destitute of family values. In 1887–88 legislative supporters of an anti-Chinese bill before Congress claimed that "the Chinese had no regard for the family, did not recognize the relationship of husband and wife, did not observe the tie of parent and child."[18] Deprived of nearly all liberties cherished by American citizens, the Chinese American community nonetheless was approached, apparently with no sense of irony, for donations to support the building of a pedestal for the Bartholdi Statue of Liberty in 1895.[19] Spurred on by constituents who feared the Chinese were taking their jobs, members of Congress passed a number of discriminatory bills restricting Chinese immigration, and these restrictions remained in place for more than fifty years.

Confucianism and family values therefore had little influence during the first period of Chinese immigration. The hostile American environment alone did not cause the problems. The Qing government (the final dynasty, 1644–1911), reflecting earlier dynastic norms, did not allow the educated to leave China, only the illiterate. Until 1893, when emigrants were given the official designation as *huaqiao* (overseas Chinese), they were expected to be "sojourners," temporarily outside the middle kingdom until circumstances allowed them to return.[20] American prejudice and Chinese traditionalism thus created a gender imbalance that continued for many decades. In 1890 the ratio was twenty-seven men to one woman. In the ensuing years the Chinese devised ways around laws and immigration rules, but even as late as 1930 men were still 80 percent of the immigrant population.[21] The Chinese family, with a variety of forces arrayed against it—prejudice, job protectionism, and political pressures—had little chance to maintain and promote its values. It is not surprising that, as recently as the 1930s, many Chinese wanted to leave America and return to their homeland.

The situation changed during the Second World War, when Chinese and Americans were allied in the struggle against the Japanese. New stereotypes arose to replace the old, the Chinese now described in a popular newsmagazine as "placid, kindly, open," in contrast to the Japanese, who were portrayed as "positive, dogmatic, and arrogant."[22] On December 17, 1943, Congress finally repealed the Exclusion Act of 1882, and the United States established an annual quota of 105 immigrants for Chinese. The numbers were so low that they were little help in rectifying the gender imbalance. Yet families used illegal means, such as forged identifications, to bring many "paper sons and daughters" to the United States.[23] The federal antimiscegenation law was repealed in 1946, and in 1947 the War Brides Act allowed the entry of about eight thousand Chinese women. The great majority of these, it should be emphasized, were legitimate spouses who represented long-standing marriage relationships—87 percent had been married for five years or longer.[24] In the same year federal housing restrictions were lifted, allowing Chinese for the first time to buy homes outside Chinatowns. All these changes improved the conditions of Chinese Americans and began to make possible a more normal family-based community.

However, the War Brides Act was not an unmixed blessing, nor did it immediately bring a strengthening of the Confucian family. While correcting the gender imbalance, it also reunited spouses who had grown apart culturally. Generally, this meant that Chinese American men, who had fought in the war and had, over the years, absorbed many American values, were reunited with wives from rural areas, where strongly traditional Chinese attitudes toward marriage and family prevailed. The men now accepted ideals about love, companionship, and intimacy as defining marriage, while the women, formed by strict Confucian norms, were comfortable with a more formal, hierarchical pattern of relationship, with no public expressions of intimacy and affection expected or desired. Most of the evidence for these conflicts comes from a study of the advice columns of Chinese newspapers of the times, along with a few oral histories. The suffering spouses could remain anonymous, vent their dissatisfactions, and get advice from various columnists and editors, both male and female. Neither the writers nor advice givers had to worry about "losing face" in the American community, since the language of the newspapers was Chinese.

Perhaps most revealing was that the advice givers felt obliged to take on the responsibility of moral arbitration, because they were placed in the position of defining moral standards for the community. Generally, they followed a middle ground, urging respect for the Chinese traditions while advising their readers of the need to accept certain American values. In doing so, they placed the needs of the group over those of the individual, a traditional and defining norm in Chinese culture. One husband who complained about his wife's backwardness was given the standard moral admonition not to pursue individual happiness but to make sacrifices for the sake of his family and community. As Zhao notes, "Newspaper editors almost never advised anyone to get a divorce."[25]

The wives, of course, had their own perspective. Their frustrations may be seen in such places as "The Women's Column," written by Wen Ying, a well-educated Chinese American writer for the *Chinese Pacific Weekly*. Her column allowed the war brides and others to vent their grievances and attracted the ire of some male traditionalists who accused her of making the situation worse by publicizing women's complaints. She defended herself by appealing to the American ideal of gender equality. Yet she too, though opposing arranged marriages, urged most of the aggrieved women to compromise and "make their best efforts to repair their marriages."[26] Thus those who were elevated to the position of marriage counselor, both male and female, tended to offer fairly conservative advice and adhered to the Confucian norms.

The later fortunes of the Chinese family continued to follow and reflect changing political attitudes in the United States. During the McCarthy era in the early 1950s many Americans perceived the People's Republic of China as an enemy of the United States, fear of communism and talk of the "yellow peril" were rampant, and Chinese immigrants often lost their recently acquired friendly image in the imaginations of many Americans. But in the 1960s, with the repeal of the prejudicial immigration quotas for Asians, the numbers of Chinese immigrants skyrocketed, first with large numbers coming from Taiwan, and later, after the liberalization and more open policies of the People's Republic of China, even larger numbers came from the mainland. All these changes have improved the chances for the preservation of family values among the immigrant families, and the most recent challenges to familism have come not from legal liabilities and social restrictions but from the usual factor facing all immigrant populations: the confrontation with American values as second- and third-generation Chinese become more assimilated into the mainstream of society. With its emphasis on freedom, individualism, and mobility, American society challenged many Chinese values associated with Confucian social norms, and the traditional family was weakened.

CHALLENGES TO THE FAMILY STRUCTURE

Some scholars have attempted to shift the essence of Confucianism away from familism, locating it in other values. It is not the family system that makes Confucianism relevant to the modern world, asserts one scholar, but three other values: its concern with moral responsibility, which will correct the American overemphasis on freedom and personal rights; its emphasis on the importance of the transmission of values (through education); and its humanistic understanding of life,[27] the last perhaps best summarized in the writings of Tu Wei-ming. Gender issues will certainly change but probably more slowly than ardent Asian feminists hope. Some feminists criticized Maxine Hong Kingston's novel *Woman Warrior* because the heroine does not maintain her independent status but returns to the family fold after her military career ends. Kingston maintains that the last part of the novel is definitely about "how to reintegrate oneself into one's family and community."[28]

Undeniably, the traditional Chinese family has been diminished, yet it also shows evidence of resilience, which is remarkable because the family is backed by no institutional structure, priesthood, authoritative teachers, or religious community. Many values and practices that I listed as "Confucian" earlier find their core of unity in the family system. Even values apparently independent of the family may be explained as either flowing from it or feeding into it. Core virtues supporting family Confucianism would obviously include the primacy of the family group over the individual, mutuality of obligation of parents and children, patriarchal and patrilineal social patterns, hierarchy, marriage control, and eating as a major family maintenance ritual. Peripheral but still important values would be hard work (as mutual obligation incumbent on parents and children), postponement of gratification and frugality to acquire capital for future family projects, achievement by children to honor family and support parents, and, especially, success in education, which Chinese have always seen as the key to future security. Therefore, I would suggest that even such phenomena as the remarkable achievements of Asian Americans in education and the workplace are substantially the result of family values. By 1990, for example, 30 percent of Asians in the United States had gotten a bachelor's degree (compared with 20 percent of the total population), and nearly one-seventh of the doctoral degrees were conferred on Asians and Pacific islanders (members of these groups accounted for one-third of doctorates in engineering and a quarter of those in the physical sciences).[29] This educational success has caused some backlash in admissions policies and resulted in various jokes, such as explaining that MIT stands for "Made in Taiwan" and UCLA is an acronym for "University of Caucasians living among Asians."[30]

There was a time when the forces of assimilation seemed so powerful that it was doubted that authentic Chinese culture could continue in the United States. From a high of more than 100,000 in the late nineteenth century, the Chinese population declined to fewer than 80,000 individuals between 1910 and the 1940s, with the majority born in the United States. Second- and third-generation Chinese Americans, heavily influenced by American values, became the dominant portion of the population group, 70 percent by 1995. There was considerable outmarriage, as high as 75 percent in some areas (in Hawaii, for example, whereas it was 50 percent in Los Angeles and only 30 percent in New York), and this factor too attenuated the influence of Confucianism. But then, beginning in the 1960s with an infusion of new immigrants from Asia, the Chinese population grew exponentially (to 431,583 in 1970, 812,00 in 1980, and approximately two million by the mid-1990s), giving the traditional family system a renewed contact with the cultural values of China and a new opportunity to adjust and maintain itself.[31]

Of course, it was not just a question of maintaining the values of the "old country," for China itself has been in a period of rapid change—people's communes, the Cultural Revolution, and the one-child policy, to mention just the most dramatic shocks to the traditional family. Confucian norms, in fact, have been attacked ever since the May 4th Movement in 1919. But now assimilation no longer seems inevitable or the only option. Instead, there is a new opportunity for self-definition. What the future will bring is difficult to know, but Chinese Americans continue to live by family values that work for them, finding areas where traditional and contemporary values harmonize. Gary Locke, the

Chinese American governor of the state Washington from 1997 to 2005, said in his first inaugural address that his family's success was owed to faith in American ideals and three Chinese values: "Get a good education, work hard, and take care of each other."[32] In other words, traditional family values may not only be defended in modern America but actually provide the very formula for success.

Is the Chinese family alive and well in America? Its health, of course, is a function of how well it has responded to the challenges it faces in a foreign culture, but alive it is, an elephant in the pantry. Psychologists and counselors of Chinese Americans provide clear testimony that the family still looms large, an important reality in both harming and healing those counseled. The most frequent problems noted are mostly those dealing with family matters: conflicts of various kinds, divorce, life choices as perceived by the individual versus the family, educational pressures, and "saving face" issues.[33] Or, as another counselor reports, "If I were to name one particular area of life in which the Chinese Americans I see in psychotherapy have the most problems, it would be the area of family of origin. Most other problems are derivatives."[34] When Vickie Nam was putting together an anthology of the experiences of ethnically Asian girls who grew up in America, she received hundreds of submissions. Although her book was divided into five sections of approximately equal length, one of which was about family issues, the author notes that "submissions I received from girls about their relationships with family members far outnumbered the ones depicting the other general aspects of their day-to-day lives."[35] And Julia Ching, a scholar and teacher who converted to Catholicism in her early life and became a nun, reports that the major conflict she felt in making her commitment was the disapproval of family: "I felt myself a traitor to my family and, in a sense, to my culture. . . . All this created a sense of guilt that has never been resolved, leaving a vacuum in my consciousness that has never been filled."[36]

Another lens through which to study the current relationship of Confucianism and the family is to examine the works of contemporary Chinese American writers. The early group of authors portrays the family as a powerful phenomenon that dominates the lives of its members. C. Y. Lee's *Flower Drum Song*, first published in 1957 (and later made into a Rogers and Hammerstein musical and film), describes a generation gap between the patriarch of the Wang clan and his two sons. The old man, fearing his sons will become too Americanized, turns to his beloved Confucianism. "In order to have you protected in this wild society, I decide to send you to the Chinese school and give you a private lesson of the Four Books of Confucius," he tells them.[37] Old Wang generally uses the teaching of Confucianism as a punishment, making it appear both old-fashioned and futile.

More nuanced is the description of the tensions of family life presented in Jade Snow Wong's *Fifth Chinese Daughter* (1950). Jade Snow had a basically happy childhood in a tight-knit Chinese Christian family in San Francisco, enjoying the support and affection of her parents and siblings. But she chafed under certain aspects of the traditional family system—the preference for boys, stiff interpersonal relationships, and the authoritarianism of her father. When, after four daughters, a son was finally born into the family, Jade Snow noticed the great happiness and celebration that occurred, while her youngest sister's birth occasioned no similar outburst of joy. She complained of this to her father, who explained:

> You are quite familiar by now with the fact that it is the sons who perpetuate our ancestral heritage by permanently bearing the Wong family name and transmitting it through their blood line, and therefore the sons must have priority over the daughters when parental provision for advantages must be limited by economic necessity. Generations of sons, bearing our Wong name, are those who make pilgrimages to ancestral burial grounds and preserve them forever. Our daughters leave home at marriage to give sons to their husbands' families to carry on the heritage for other names.[38]

Her parents paid for her brother's schooling while Jade Snow had to pay her own way in higher education. When she began to work full time for an American family, she saw a very different emotional milieu. Children, she found, were heard as well as seen and their opinions mattered, birthdays were celebrated, natural affections expressed through kissing; they were concerned about having fun together, and the husband turned over his check to his wife to pay bills, "and where, above all, each member, even down to and including the dog, appeared to have the inalienable right to assert his personality—in fact, where that was expected—in an atmosphere of natural affection." When she expressed reluctance to consider marriage, her parents retorted, "You cannot so independently continue to refute the core of our culture."[39] That is, she must marry to have a family of her own, and only in that way will she have any future.

And yet, despite these tensions, the mature Jade Snow continued to prize her heritage and to advocate many of the same Confucian virtues that she was taught as a child. In the introduction to the 1989 edition to her book, written nearly forty years after its first publication, she describes how she and her husband chose to live within walking distance of the same Chinese school she attended as a child so that her own children might be instilled with the Confucian virtues. She offers a resounding affirmation of the tradition. "They know well," she states, "that, in behavior, we emphasize personal modesty, self-reliance, dependability, courtesy, and modulated voices. In values, we esteem love of books and learning, reverence for the natural world, service to fellow man, moderation, living within one's means. Are these values different from those of non-Chinese? Our basic and greatest value is family cohesiveness. From time immemorial, in every culture, for every economic stations, the family is the enduring motivation of human activity. Ours is grateful for our Chinese past."[40]

If the preoccupations of Chinese American novelists and playwrights are any indication, family relationships still seem paramount. Amy Tan is probably the most popular Chinese American novelist today. *The Joy Luck Club, The Bonesetter's Daughter,* and *The Kitchen God's Wife* all deal with family issues as the major theme, dramatizing the strains that pull families apart and the bonds that draw them together. The *Joy Luck Club* documents the tension between the first-generation immigrants (the four mothers, Suyuan Woo, An-mei Hsu, Lindo Jong, and Ying-ying St. Clair), whose lives and outlooks have been thoroughly shaped by Chinese culture, and the second-generation daughters (June Woo, Rose Jordan, Waverly Jong, and Lena St. Clair), who seem thoroughly Americanized. Yet Chinese familism, as mediated through their mothers, is still a powerful factor in their lives. The novel's issues, tensions, climax, and resolution are all rooted in the daughters' response to family.

The same is true of the novels of Timothy Mo (although he is actually a British immigrant), which are dramas of family life. *Monkey King* initially strains under the dysfunctional family of Mr. Poon and alludes to the dark side of traditional familism but then reaffirms the family when Wallace and May Ling create a harmonious household at the end of the novel. In *Sour Sweet* the reader follows the fortunes of the Chen family in London as it slowly disintegrates, the crisis set up when Mr. Chen has to find the money to pay his father's hospital bills back in China. Mrs. Chen (Lily) has been the dominant figure of the novel, while her elder sister, Mui, is pictured as a colorless appendage to the family. But by the end of the novel, as the Chen family disintegrates, Mui surprises everyone by marrying Mr. Lo, and the center of gravity shifts to the newly formed family, with Mui now in control and Lily in her orbit. Family is the basis of strength and stability, the engine of change in the novel.[41] Frank Chin, essayist and playwright, has openly rebelled against the image of Chinese as model immigrants and has criticized Chinese culture and familism. He is the Stokeley Carmichael of Chinese Americans, his language too Chinese for whites (Philip Roth told him it wasn't English!) and too white for Chinatown: "To become white, you shit in your blood, hate yourself and all your kind."[42] The character Tam in *The Chickencoop Chinaman* reduces the meaning of Confucianism thus: "Now there's Confucius in America for you. 'Don't be seen with no blacks, get good grades, lay low, an apple for the teacher, be good, suck up, talk proper and be civilized.'"[43] In another play Chin reveals the dark side of the Chinese family. The Eng family is already spinning into irrational chaos when Pa Eng, without warning, brings "China Mama" into his home. She is his original wife from the old country. Ma Eng, the American-born mother, must try to cope with the new situation. Her children are shocked as well, yet the younger son, Johnny, says to his brother, Fred: "But I believe in the Chinese family." Fred retorts: "What Chinese family? Do you mean China Mama? . . . That Chinese family isn't real, Johnny."[44] The play is gritty realism. There is nothing harmonious or appealing about the group of people thrown together around Pa Eng. Daughter Sissy's husband, Ross, who fatuously admires "Chinese culture," is held up as a figure of ridicule. Yet, as much as he might despise it, Chin continues the image of the patriarchal father, served by his wife and children, in *Year of the Dragon*. The father is still lord of the household, and Chin's characters must deal with the patriarchal family that he represents.

Chinese fiction has an antifamily tradition. If the eighteenth-century *Dream of the Red Chamber* functions as the paradigm of novels focused on the Confucian concerns of the family and its fortunes, then *Journey to the West* would be the antitype. It is a Buddhist/Daoist novel describing the pilgrimage of the monk Xuanzang and his faithful companions—Monkey, Pigsy, and Sandy—to India to bring back the sacred sutras. Despite its comic elements, it is a story of religious quest, leaving home in search of ultimately spiritual goals. Many authors have retold this story. Timothy Mo's novel *Monkey King* references it, and Maxine Hong Kingston's *Tripmaster Monkey: His Fake Book* is a definite reprise set in 1960s San Francisco.

The motivations of Kingston's first two novels are based in family issues or the deprivation of family. As we have seen, her eponymous protagonist of *Woman Warrior* leaves family to take on a Joan-of-Arc role, but in the end, having established her superiority to women who fall into stereotyped gender roles, she returns to the family and reintegrates into the accepted social patterns of her society. *China Men*, a collection of biographical materials about Kingston's male ancestors, describes "the great grandfather" who goes to work on the sugar plantations of Hawaii, and "the grandfather" who works on the railroads. Both must live as bachelors and are deprived of the consolations of family life. Their sense of deprivation is best captured in a description of Ah Goong, the grandfather who wanders around the rural areas of the mountainous West, his lonely status revealed in a number of encounters. "He met miraculous China men who had produced families out of nowhere—a wife and children, both boys and girls. 'Uncle,' the children called him, and he wanted to stay and to be the uncle of the family. . . . On a farm road, he came across an imp child playing in the dirt. 'I wish you were my baby,' he told it. 'My baby.'"[45]

In Kington's recent novel *Tripmaster Monkey*, the hero is the hippy raconteur, Whitman Ah Sing, the family antitype, the picaresque seeker who floats above conventional family relationships. His girlfriend, Tanya, recites the following lines at a party:

> There's a race of men that don't fit in,
> A race that can't sit still.
> So they break the hearts of kith and kin,
> And they roam the world at will.

"That's me," says Whitman. "She knows me and my timber wolf Steppenwolf ways."[46] Whitman does marry Tanya but on the spur of the moment, without consulting family. He meets Gabe, a self-proclaimed minister of the Universal

Life Church (who also ordains Whitman so that he can avoid the draft), who then quickly marries the two. We don't meet Whitman's family until halfway through the novel, when Whitman takes Tanya to meet his mother, who is surrounded in her apartment by a bevy of aged former Chinese dancers and actresses. His father has drifted off, living in a trailer where he gambles with his buddies and promotes gold mining to the gullible. In other words, there is no traditional family for Whitman to rebel against or to hinder his Bohemian quest. Later, as he and Tanya struggle to adjust to life together, he reflects: "Yeah, he ought to be living in Paris, home for his type. . . . Don't get domesticated."[47] As Kingston herself has pointed out, *Tripmaster* reflects the challenge to the traditional family in the American setting: "Whitman is a boyish person and he has just gotten married but there's no commitment or understanding of what marriage is."[48]

I have shown that the question of the continuity of the "Confucian family" in America is complex, because of changing historical circumstances, different geographical and social origins, gender imbalance, and the at best equivocal status of Confucianism as a "world religion." Yet, despite its detractors, it continues to exert a powerful influence on Chinese Americans in the areas of marriage and family morality. Because of the great influx of new immigrants since the 1960s, the fate of the family as an institution, and the Confucian views that undergird it, are still factors to be reckoned with. It may very well be that Confucianism's anomalous character is as much a help as a hindrance in preserving the traditional familial and social forms. Its lack of institutional structure, leadership, and central authority may be seen as a source of weakness and, at the same time, a strength. It allows Chinese Americans, for example, to be Christians, as many are, while reaffirming their Confucian familial principles in areas of converging moral concern.

Generally speaking, Chinese Americans have reacted comfortably to most facets of modernization. If modernization means technical rationality, they have had little trouble in eagerly adopting it. Because the political aspects of Confucianism (i.e., its status as the ideology of the imperial authority) were discredited almost one hundred years ago, and the intelligentsia has generally accepted the value of the "scientific" mentality since the May 4th Movement, Chinese Americans have found it easy to accept that dimension of modernity and, for more recent immigrants with the benefit of higher education, to even lead the way.

Chinese Americans have adjusted to the politics of democracy, forming political action groups, trying to influence legislation, and using the court system to further their aims. The same is true of secularity, if that is taken narrowly to mean the separation of church and state. Areas of difficulty, on the other hand, have been individualism and human rights, especially gender equality, because these values have directly challenged the patriarchalism, clannishness, and group-over-individual viewpoint characteristic of Confucian morality. Changes are already going on in these areas, especially in the area of gender equality, and in the near disappearance of arranged marriages. On the other hand, I would anticipate a continued reluctance to accept easy divorce and an unwillingness to give in to some of the extreme forms of individualism found in American society. It may be that Chinese will consider the preservation of these two values a contribution that they can make to the larger society.

Whether the family is help or hindrance, most Chinese Americans have found it to be a factor that they must contend with. And while it is always risky to predict the future, I will conclude with reference to the words of perhaps the most prominent authority on the status of Chinese people living in other cultures. The last century has shown that "the Chinese outside of China are adaptable and versatile. If it is possible to live among non-Chinese in the modern international economy and still achieve the social autonomy needed to sustain essential parts of their Chinese identities, there should be little doubt that the Chinese will find ways to do just that."[49] The challenges to Confucian familism are very real, and changes will come, yet the family's resources are considerable. Chinese schools in America increased from forty in the 1950s to more than six hundred by the mid 1990s.[50] They have been established specifically to preserve the families' language and culture. It is likely that for the immediate future the family will seek and find new ways to define itself, influenced by American culture but still preserving such traditional values as loyalty, mutuality, hard work, educational and occupational achievement, and strenuous efforts at self-preservation. As Myron Cohen has put it, being Chinese today is "as much a quest as it is a condition."[51]

NOTES

1. K. Scott Wong and Sucheng Chan, *Claiming America: Constructing Chinese American Identities during the Exclusion Era* (Philadelphia: Temple University Press, 1998), 46–47.

2. Quoted in Xinzhong Yao, *An Introduction to Confucianism* (Cambridge: Cambridge University Press, 2000), 242. As one Singapore resident insisted, "I am a Christian and a Presbyterian elder, but I am also a Confucian disciple" (Harmon Ziegler, *Pluralism, Corporatism and Confucianism* [Philadelphia: Temple University Press, 1988], 118).

3. The May 4th Movement is considered a turning point in modern Chinese history. About three thousand students demonstrated on May 4, 1919, at the Gate of Heavenly Peace (Tiananmen) in Beijing against China's treatment in the Versailles peace treaty after World War I. The movement that dated from this event went on to reject many traditional aspects of Chinese language, society, and culture. Scholars see the May 4th Movement as the birth of modern China.

4. See Rodney Taylor, *The Religious Dimensions of Confucianism* (Albany: State

University of New York Press, 1990); Tu Wei-ming, especially his *Confucian Thought: Selfhood as Creative Transformation* (Albany, State University of New York Press, 1985); John Berthrong, *Transformations of the Confucian Way* (Boulder, Colo.: Westview, 1998); and Robert C. Neville, *Boston Confucianism: Portable Tradition in the Late-Modern World* (Albany: State University of New York Press, 2000).

5. Francis Fukuyama, "Confucianism and Democracy," in Larry Diamond and Marc F. Plattner, eds., *The Global Divergence of Democracy* (Baltimore: Johns Hopkins University Press, 2001), 29.

6. Jordan Paper, *The Spirits Are Drunk: Comparative Approaches to Chinese Religion* (Albany: State University of New York Press, 1995), 40–46.

7. Julia Ching, *Confucianism and Christianity: A Comparative Study* (Tokyo: Kodansha International, 1977), 97–98.

8. Frank Chin, *Bulletproof Buddhists and Other Essays* (Honolulu: University of Hawaii Press, 1998), 104.

9. Patricia Ebrey, "The Chinese Family and the Spread of Confucian Values," in Gilbert Rozman, ed., *The East Asian Region: Confucian Heritage and Its Modern Adaptation* (Princeton, N.J.: Princeton University Press, 1991), 45–52. Rozman's own essay, the introduction (3–42), makes a similar point (see p. 13).

10. C. K. Yang, *Religion in Chinese Society* (Berkeley: University of California Press, 1967), 279.

11. Tu Wei-ming, "Confucius and Confucians," in Walter H. Slote and George A. DeVos, eds., *Confucianism and the Family* (Albany: State University of New York Press, 1998), 38.

12. Nazli Kibria, *Becoming Asian American: Second-Generation Chinese and Korean American Identities* (Baltimore: Johns Hopkins University Press, 2002), 120. Also see Rozman, introduction to *East Asian Region*, 3–42.

13. Ien Ang, *On Not Speaking Chinese: Living between Asia and the West* (London: Routledge, 2001), 48.

14. See Anne Behnke Kinney, "Death by Fire: The Story of Boji," *Traditions of Exemplary Women*, http://jefferson.village.virginia.edu/xwomen/boji_essay.html.

15. Tu Wei-ming, "Confucius and Confucians," 33; Harmon Zeigler, *Pluralism, Corporatism and Confucianism* (Philadelphia: Temple University Press, 1988), 122, 188.

16. Walter H. Slote, "Psychocultural Dynamics within the Confucian Family," in Slote and DeVos, *Confucianism and the Family*, 38.

17. Him Mark Lai, "The United States," in Lynn Pan, ed., *The Encyclopedia of the Chinese Overseas* (Cambridge, Mass.: Harvard University Press, 1999), 261. A more personalized and entertaining account of this history of Chinese immigration may be gained from Maxine Hong Kingston's *China Men* (New York: Vintage International, 1989), which traces it through the lives of four generations of her male family members.

18. Shih-shan Henry Tsai, *The Chinese Experiment in America* (Bloomington: University of Indiana Press, 1986), 59.

19. Wong and Chan, *Claiming America*, 65–66.

20. Gungwu Wang, *The Chinese Overseas: From Earthbound China to the Quest for Autonomy* (Cambridge, Mass.: Harvard University Press, 2000), 9.

21. Gloria Heyung Chun, *Of Orphans and Warriors: Inventing Chinese American Culture and Identity* (New Brunswick, N.J.: Rutgers University Press, 2000), 8.

22. Ibid., 50.

23. See accounts given in Tung Pok Chin with Winifred C. Chin, *Paper Son: One Man's Story* (Philadelphia: Temple University Press, 2000), and M. Elaine Mar, *Paper Daughter* (New York: Harper Collins Perennial Library, 2000).

24. Xiaojian Zhao, *Remaking Chinese America: Immigration, Family, and Community, 1940–1965* (New Brunswick, N.J.: Rutgers University Press, 2002), 82.

25. Ibid., 140, 142.

26. Ibid., 147.

27. Yao, *Introduction to Confucianism*, 279–80.

28. Paul Skenazy and Tera Martin, *Conversations with Maxine Hong Kingston* (Jackson: University of Mississippi, 1998), 193.

29. Chun, *Of Orphans and Warriors*, 128–29.

30. Kibria, *Becoming Asian American*, 106.

31. Him Mark Lai, "United States," 269.

32. Kibria, *Becoming Asian American*, 131.

33. Geri Miller and Julia Yang, "Counseling Taiwan Chinese in America: Training Issues for Counselors," *Counselor Education and Supervision* 37, no. 1 (September 1997), 1–8.

34. May Paomay Tung, *Chinese Americans and Their Immigrant Parents: Conflict, Identity, and Values* (New York: Haworth Clinical Practice Press, 2000), 8.

35. Vickie Nam, *YELL-Oh Girls! Emerging Voices Explore Culture, Identity, and Growing Up Asian American* (New York: HarperCollins, 2001), 43.

36. Julia Ching, *The Butterfly Healing: A Life between East and West* (Maryknoll, N.Y.: Orbis, 1998), 25.

37. C. Y. Lee, *The Flower Drum Song* (New York: Penguin, 2002), 74.

38. Jade Snow Wong, *Fifth Chinese Daughter* (Seattle: University of Washington Press, 1989), 108–9.

39. Ibid., 113–14, 228.

40. Ibid., x.

41. Timothy Mo, *The Monkey King* (New York: William Morrow, 1978), and *Sour Sweet* (New York: Vintage, 1985).

42. Frank Chin, *Bulletproof Buddhists*, 69.

43. Frank Chin, *The Chickencoop Chinaman* and *The Year of the Dragon: Two Plays* (Seattle: University of Washington Press, 1981), 26.

44. Frank Chin, *Year of the Dragon*, 124.

45. Kingston, *China Men*, 147.

46. Maxine Hong Kingston, *Tripmaster Monkey: His Fake Book* (New York: Random Vintage Books, 1990), 113.

47. Ibid., 221.

48. Skenazy and Martin, *Conversations with Maxine Hong Kingston*, 194.

49. Wang Gungwu, "Among Non-Chinese," in Tu Wei-ming, ed., *The Living Tree: The Changing Meaning of Being Chinese Today* (Stanford, Calif.: Stanford University Press, 1994), 146.

50. Him Mark Lai, "United States," 273.

51. Myron L. Cohen, "Being Chinese: The Peripheralization of Traditional Identity," in Tu, *Living Tree*, 108.

CHAPTER 11

Family Life and Spiritual Kinship
in American Buddhist Communities

CHARLES S. PREBISH

One of the most quoted summaries of Buddhism's growth in countries beyond its Indian birthplace is Michael Carrithers's remark: "No Buddhism without the *Sangha* and no *Sangha* without the Discipline."[1] For Carrithers Buddhism's growth and survival in countries beyond India required and was predicated upon the establishment of the *sangha* (spiritual community), and its implementation, as the basis for Buddha's spiritual family. Early in Buddhist history the original Buddhist *sangha*, initially conceived as consisting only of monks, was expanded to include nuns and then lay followers of both genders, thus rather quickly including all Buddha's disciples and being identified as "the *sangha* of the four quarters." In a very real way this *sangha* of the four quarters was envisioned as a universal order, transcending both time and space and encompassing all geographical areas.

Within Buddha's spiritual family the most overarching model for familial propriety, and paternity, is that of the *kalyāṇamitra*, or the spiritual friend. In a famous passage from the *Saṃyutta Nikāya*, Buddha is questioned by his disciple Ānanda regarding the status of spiritual friendship, and Ānanda suggests that this state is *half* the holy life. Buddha immediately reprimands him for his faulty understanding, instructing: "Not so Ānanda; not so Ānanda. This association with spiritual friendship, association with virtuous companionship, association with goodness *is the whole of the holy life*."[2] Without delay Buddha goes on to suggest that he himself is the highest *kalyāṇamitra*, and that because of his function in this capacity, beings subject to birth and rebirth are able to free themselves from old age, sickness, and death and, indeed, from suffering (*duḥkha*) itself. With Buddha established as the highest spiritual friend, he necessarily becomes the archetypal model for all subsequent spiritual kinship relationships in his spiritual family. It soon becomes quite clear from Buddha's initial preachings that his spiritual family is modeled on the ideal secular family, and he is quite explicit about both the nature of, and relationships within, that ideal secular family. The remainder of this chapter examines that model, as well as its application to modern America.

THE IDEAL FAMILY LIFE

Although the primary models for the most effective religious lifestyle in Buddhism are the celibate monastic or the committed bodhisattva, members of the laity have always constituted the great majority of Buddhist practitioners. As such, the interpersonal familial social relationships of the laity are especially important and were occasionally the focus of Buddha's most pointed and specific instructions. Hammalawa Saddhatissa, in his classic volume *Buddhist Ethics*, notes that "the duties of children to their parents were stressed in India from a very early date." He goes on to point out that the "Rukkhadhamma Jātaka expressed the value of the solidarity of a family, using the simile of the trees of a forest; these are able to withstand the force of the wind whereas a solitary tree, however large, is not."[3] Perhaps the most famous and important of Buddha's family-oriented sermons is the *Sigālovāda Sutta* of the *Dīgha Nikāya*, in which Buddha provides explicit instructions to the layman Sigāla, who is trying to honor his father's dying wish that Sigāla honor the six directions.[4] Buddha likens worshipping the six directions to proper actions toward six different categories of people. The six directions—east, south, west, north, nadir, and zenith—correspond, respectively, to parents, teachers, spouse and children, friends and companions, servants and other employees, and religious teachers and Brahmins. Before expounding on the specific requirements of proper social and familial relating, Buddha encourages Sigāla to keep the precepts in general and to avoid acting from impulse (*chanda*), hatred (*dosa*), fear (*bhaya*), or delusion (*moha*).

The first relationship that Buddha addresses is that of parents and children. On the relationship between parents and children, Buddha's instructions are straightforward and explicit. As the *Sigālovāda Sutta* proclaims:

> In five ways a child should minister to his parents as the eastern quarter: "once supported by them, I will now be their support; I will perform duties incumbent on them; I will keep up the lineage and tradition of my family; I will make myself worthy of my heritage; I will make alms offerings on their behalf after they are dead." In five ways parents thus ministered to, as the eastern quarter

by their child, show their love for him: they restrain him from vice; they exhort him to virtue; they train him to a profession; they contract a suitable marriage for him; and in due time they hand over his inheritance.[5]

These relational expectations are maintained throughout the Buddhist tradition, especially in East Asia, where filial piety plays an important role as the foundation of ethical life. Kenneth Ch'en even notes that one Chinese rendering of the this text translates one of the child's duties as "not to disobey the commandments of the parents."[6]

The *Sigālovāda Sutta* also offers a similar dyadic pattern of husband-wife relational expectations: "In five ways should a wife as western quarter be ministered to by her husband: by respect, by courtesy, by faithfulness, by handing over authority to her; by providing her with adornment. In these five ways does the wife, ministered to by her husband as the western quarter, love him: her duties are well performed, by hospitality to the kin of both, by faithfulness, by watching over the goods he brings, and by skill and industry in discharging all her business."[7]

Because, as I noted earlier, most marriages in early Buddhism were arranged, Buddha occasionally offered advice to a man's daughters about how to conduct themselves in marriage. Peter Harvey summarizes one of these passages, from the *Aṅguttara Nikāya*, this way: "(1) Regarding her husband 'she gets up before him, retires after him, willingly does what he asks, is lovely in her ways and gentle in speech', not being one to anger him; (2) she honours all whom her husband respects, whether relative, monk or brahmin; (3) she is deft and nimble in her husband's home-crafts, such as weaving; (4) she watches over servants and workpeople with care and kindness; and (5) she looks after the wealth her husband brings home."[8] It should also be noted that divorce, although generally infrequent in early Buddhism, was permitted.

In other words, all familial relationships, like interpersonal relationships throughout Buddhism, are steeped in the ethical values and standards typified by the four "divine abodes" (*brahmavihāras*) of loving kindness (*mettā*), compassion (*karuṇā*), joy (*muditā*), and equanimity (*upekkhā*). These qualities remain a powerful benchmark against which Buddhist family life throughout the world, including modern America, is invariably measured.

COMING TO AMERICA

The first comprehensive book on Buddhism in America, Emma Layman's *Buddhism in America*, written in 1976, devoted an entire chapter to the question "Who are the American Buddhists?" She focused on how Asian American Buddhists compared to American "convert" Buddhists. What she did not consider was just how one determines who is an American Buddhist.[9] Three years later, when I wrote my own book called *American Buddhism*, I suggested that one of the traditional ways of identifying Buddhists in Asian countries—taking refuge and accepting the five vows of the laity—was probably an inadequate and even misleading approach when applied to the American scene.[10]

It shouldn't be surprising that a quarter-century ago, American Buddhists defined themselves in a variety of radically different ways. Asian American Buddhists—who are sometimes called "cradle" Buddhists—brought a complex of identity problems to their involvement in Buddhist practice in America. "Convert" Buddhists found themselves struggling with potential multiple affiliations. Could one be Jewish *and* Buddhist? or Christian *and* Buddhist? If so, how did this so-called ism-crossing translate into an individual's religious life? What seems clear is that the issue of religious identity is complex for both cradle and convert Buddhists, and this has an enormous impact with respect to the interpenetration of family and religious life.

In the search for establishing some sort of "orthodoxy" in determining who is, and is not, a Buddhist in America, the problem is exacerbated because *all* forms of Buddhism, from every Asian Buddhist culture, are present on American soil *at the same time*. This is the first time in more than twenty-five hundred years of Buddhist history that this has occurred. In other words, what works as the defining characteristic for the American convert followers of a Chinese Buddhist sect might not work for the American convert practitioners of a Buddhist tradition imported from Sri Lanka or Thailand, and neither of those sets of characteristics might work for the Asian American followers of those same traditions.

My solution in 1979 was to try to simplify the problem as much as possible. I am convinced that it remains correct and workable today, although some additional problems can now be noted. If a Buddhist is defined as someone who says "I am a Buddhist," when questioned about *her or his most important pursuit*, that definition abandons Buddhists' attachment to ritual formulas that are neither workable nor even uniformly followed, and it provides more than a little freedom for American Buddhist groups—a freedom in which they can develop a procedure that is consistent with their own self-image and mission. What appears initially as an outrageously simplistic definition of Buddhist affiliation serves the double purpose of providing a new standard and a simple method of professing Buddhist commitment while imposing a renewed sense of seriousness on all Buddhist groups.[11]

The yardstick of self-identification does not compromise any specific tradition but rather augments and accommodates the specific requirements of each. What the definition does not provide is some means for determining an "official" membership, which becomes a problem when one tries to actually count the numbers of Buddhists in America. More recently, new interpretations have sought to improve on earlier attempts to establish some sense of Buddhist identification in America. The most persuasive, by Thomas Tweed, simply changes the titles. He calls the cradle Buddhists "adherents" and divides the convert Buddhists into two groups: self-identifiers and "sympathizers" (or sometimes, and more creatively, "night-stand Buddhists," in view of the Buddhist books they often place next to their beds). In the end virtually all the investigators and interpreters of American Buddhism affirm the hybrid nature of all religious commitments and then conclude that Buddhists are those people who simply say they are Buddhists.[12] It is both obvious and true. What is not so obvious is what religious choice the children of convert Buddhists will make in the future and what religious choices the children of third-, fourth-, and fifth-generation Asian American Buddhists will make as the recollection of their original practice dims and is replaced by their immersion in American culture.

In all likelihood no one will ever have a completely accurate total of the current number of Buddhists in America. The 9 January 1970 issue of *Life Magazine*, for example, suggested that 200,000 Americans had joined a sect of American Buddhism known as Nichiren Shōshū. At about the same time another group, called Buddhist Churches of America, estimated that it had 100,000 members. Both figures were almost certainly inflated. The unreliability of membership estimates does not mean that the number of Buddhists in America was not growing, and growing rapidly, at that time. In 1965 Congress made several amendments to the Immigration and Nationality Act of 1952, making it significantly easier for individuals from war-torn Asian countries to find new homes in America. The impact was dramatic. The Chinese population, for example, increased by more than 400,000 by 1985, and by 1990 the Chinese population numbered more than 921,000.[13] Moreover, similar results can be seen in the Vietnamese, Cambodian, Thai, Burmese, Sri Lankan, Laotian, Korean, and Japanese American communities. In addition, the counterculture that swept the American landscape in the 1960s led many people to Buddhism as it sought to create a saner reality based on meditative reflection, social change, and the elimination of personal suffering. Moreover, the American religious panorama was changing because of increasing secularization on the social front. Traditional religious groups within Christianity and Judaism were losing members fast, and many of these disenchanted members turned to alternative religions like Buddhism in their search for human fulfillment.

It wasn't until 1990 that figures based on actual research began to appear. That year Barry Kosmin and Seymour Lachman conducted a general survey on religious affiliation, and their results suggested that American Buddhists constituted about 0.4 percent of the adult population in America. By also factoring in the nonadult population, Kosmin and Lachman proposed a figure of about one million Buddhists in America.[14] In 2001 Barry Kosmin teamed with Egon Mayer to produce a new survey, the American Religious Identity Survey (ARIS). It was based on interviews with 50,281 people (slightly less than half the number who responded to the 1990 survey). *USA Today* reported the preliminary results from ARIS on 24 December 2001, and the overall result suggested

America has fewer than 1.5 million Buddhists. It remains unclear whether these figures are accurate.

Scholars of Buddhism have come to very different conclusions about the number of Buddhists in America. In the mid-1990s Robert Thurman, a Buddhist studies professor at Columbia University and a former Buddhist monk, told *ABC Nightly News with Peter Jennings* that the United States had five to six million Buddhists. Thurman was probably guessing, but by 1997 a German scholar named Martin Baumann postulated three to four million Buddhists in America, based on his own surveys and extensive research. Using the comprehensive current research on immigrant Buddhist communities in the United States, it is quite likely that Baumann's figure was correct for its time, and there now may well be many more Buddhists on America soil.[15] That makes American Buddhism as large as many prominent Protestant denominations.

How did they all get here? Most scholars agree that 75 to 80 percent of the Buddhists in America are of Asian American descent; the remainder are American converts who are primarily of European American ancestry. African American and Hispanic American converts to Buddhism remain a small part of the overall convert community. The easiest way to conveniently identify all these groups is under the two broad headings of Asian immigrant Buddhists and American convert Buddhists. Unfortunately, these two main groups have not always communicated well with one another.

Most recently, it has been suggested that a far more fruitful approach is to focus not on the ethnic/racial divide between the two Buddhist groups but rather on the function that Buddhism plays in their lives.[16] In that respect, in the Asian immigrant community Buddhism serves an important function in maintaining the ethnic group's sense of family life and heritage. On the other hand, in the American convert communities Buddhism provides an alternative religious identity, offering a worldview vastly different from that of the religion of their parents'.

Because these various American Buddhist communities practice different forms of Buddhism, it is important to understand the lines of transmission from Asia, and there seem to be three distinct procedures by which this has happened.[17] In one circumstance Buddhism is imported from one country to another, in this case from Asia. Demand drives this transmission: the host, or new, culture wants this tradition, and thus it is often called "import" Buddhism. Sometimes it is called "elite" Buddhism because its proponents have often discovered Buddhism through travel or education. And they have sufficient leisure, and money, to indulge their interest. Import Buddhism is usually associated with Tibetan Buddhism, Zen, and Vipassanā. A second line of transmission is called "export" Buddhism. It reflects the intent of an Asian Buddhist parent community to share its Buddhist teachings with individuals in other parts of the world. This sort of Buddhism moves throughout the world by means of missionary activities sponsored by the parent Buddhist community. As a result it is often called "evangelical" Buddhism. The best known export Buddhist group is Sōka Gakkai International, but a number of Chinese Buddhist groups also sponsor extensive activities. Finally, there is "ethnic" Buddhism, or that form of Buddhism brought to America by Asian immigrants. One Buddhist scholar has identified this form of Buddhism as "baggage" Buddhism, although the term has proved offensive and insensitive to many Asian American Buddhists.

To summarize, the United States is home to two Buddhisms—Asian immigrant Buddhism and American convert Buddhism—and three lines of transmission from Asia: elite Buddhism, which is imported to America; evangelical Buddhism, which is exported to America, and ethnic Buddhism, which arrives in America with Asian immigrants.

FAMILY LIFE AND PRACTICE IN AMERICAN BUDDHISM

Of the eight leading comprehensive scholarly books on Buddhism in America, only Layman's *Buddhism in America*, Prebish and Tanaka's *The Faces of Buddhism in America*, and James Coleman's *The New Buddhism* even mention American Buddhist family life, and none of these includes more than a half-dozen pages on the topic.[18] To make matters worse, Layman's volume unfortunately misconstrues the role of family life in Buddhism in both its ancient and American expressions when she says, "Buddhism has never placed much emphasis on the concept of family, or the concept of the specific roles of parents and children as determined by their Buddhist identity. . . . Hence, although Sunday Schools were established in some of the Jodo Shinshu churches of America around the turn of the century, most Buddhists of Oriental ancestry did not regard Buddhism as contributing too significantly to a sense of 'family.'"[19] Coleman's volume deals with family issues exclusively in the contexts of gender equality for women in convert communities and the problems encountered by parents in maintaining a rigorous meditation practice schedule for their children.[20] And *The Faces of Buddhism in America* doesn't move beyond a few cursory comments confined to the Pure Land and Zen traditions. So where does one look to find information about Buddhist family practice in American communities?

In 1998 Judith Simmer-Brown, professor of Buddhist studies at Naropa University in Boulder, Colorado, and a long-time student of Chögyam Trungpa Rinpoche, delivered one of the keynote addresses at the second annual Buddhism in America conference in San Diego. An article adapted from her address was eventually posted on the Shambhala International Web site under the title "American Buddhism: The Legacy for Our Children."[21] To be sure, Simmer-Brown's article is an important manifesto for convert practitioners of Buddhism, but practical concerns for children and family life are almost totally absent from the text.

A careful search of the Internet yields precious little in the way of family-oriented Buddhist sites. Ron Epstein has compiled a useful little reference file titled "Buddhism and Respect for Parents" with links to some classic Buddhist sources, but these are general and without specific reference to America.[22] Of the few sites that offered specific information aimed at American Buddhists, one of the very best—if not the best—was a composite picture developed by a woman simply identified as "Vanessa."[23] She assembled a tidy list of materials under the rubric "Family Dharma Connections," including "Dharma Lessons and Daily Practice," "Buddhist Holidays," "Children's Books," "Book Reviews," "Children's Videos," and "Mindful Divorce." The last item on the list is especially useful, not simply because it emphasizes the necessity for placing children first but because it suggests how to use the four noble truths as a primer for understanding and explaining divorce. There is even a Buddhist parents discussion group to which one may subscribe. Unfortunately, the site no longer exists.

Occasionally, some individual convert Buddhist communities establish programs for children, such as Zen Mountain Monastery's Zen Kids' Sunday Program. This program is a monthly, three-hour play practice in which children are exposed to a number of aspects of Buddhist and Zen training, such as the liturgy and meditation practice. "By participating in the Zen Kids Program, children and parents of the sangha create their own personal relationship to the Monastery."[24] John Daido Loori, Rōshi, abbot of Zen Mountain Monastery frequently publishes his teachings, or teishōs, on the Zen Mountain Web site. One of these is called "Caoshan's Love Between Parent and Child," and it provides Daido Rōshi an opportunity to weave together the parent-child and student-teacher relationships in a fashion that evokes Buddha's original teachings. Daido Rōshi says:

> In the beginning, the teacher-student relationship is very similar to a parent-child relationship. The student is in a completely new territory, unsure. There is a need for lot of fundamental instructions from the teacher. After a while that changes and the teacher becomes a guide, fine-tuning the assessment of the student and pointing appropriately. Still the student is dependent on the guide. The next phase is characterized by the teacher being more like a spiritual friend. That evolves into spiritual equality between the teacher and the student. Still, the relationship continues.
>
> At the time of the transmission of the Dharma, the parent becomes the child, the child becomes the parent; the teacher becomes the student, the student becomes the teacher. That fact is concretely expressed in the ceremony of transmission. First, the student circumambulates the teacher sitting on the high seat.

Then the teacher steps down so that the student can sit on the high seat and the teacher circumambulates the student. The differences between the two become blurred.

A student can see the teacher because they are the teacher. A teacher seeing the student is meeting himself. My teacher meeting me is my teacher meeting himself, just as it is me meeting myself. Isn't this the same as the Buddha meeting the Buddha?

We often say that to realize oneself is to be really intimate with oneself.[25]

Teachings such as this are important in advancing rather than trivializing children's knowledge of the Buddhadharma. This problem is evident in articles in popular magazines, such as "Children Talking about 'Buddha'" in the Winter 1993 issue of *Tricycle*. Before 1995 the only book on family life in American Buddhism that I could find was *Dharma Family Treasures: Sharing Mindfulness with Children* (1994, 1997), edited by Sandy Eastoak, a member of a convert Buddhist group. More recently, two very helpful additional volumes have appeared: Myla and Jon Kabat-Zinn's *Everyday Blessings: The Inner Work of Mindful Parenting* (1998), and *Kindness: A Treasury of Buddhist Wisdom for Children and Parents*, written by Sarah Conover and illustrated by Valerie Wahl (2001).

To date, only one empirical study of a mostly convert Buddhist group has been done in the United States: Phillip Hammond and David Machacek's study of Sōka Gakkai International USA (SGI-USA). Nonetheless, their study reveals some interesting data regarding family practice. Initially, membership in this organization was almost exclusively Asian. However, the percentage dropped from 96 percent in 1960 to 30 percent in 1970, and in the survey conducted by Hammond and Machacek in 1997, only 15 percent were Japanese.[26] In addition, according to their 1997 study, "SGI-USA members place significantly less emphasis on marriage and family life than do most Americans," and SGI-USA members scored significantly lower than respondents to the General Social Survey on the importance of being married and having children.[27] It probably wouldn't be going too far to suggest that any survey of other convert Buddhist groups would show similar results, largely precipitated by the convert focus on individualism and meditation practice rather than group- and community-defining activities. In fact, one well-known convert Buddhist teacher only half-jokingly referred to the famous "Three Jewels" of Buddha, *Dharma*, and *sangha* as having been amended in America to "Me, Myself, and I."

In Asian immigrant Buddhist communities the situation is radically different, and in many cases Buddhist family life defines the identity of the entire community. Yet only recently have scholars begun to point out the paucity of studies on Asian American Buddhism (and for reasons that extend beyond the scope of this chapter).[28] Moreover, a unit devoted to the study of Asian American religious communities has been a fairly recent addition to the American Academy of Religion, and attendance at its sessions remains small. However, some fairly current books—such as Tetsuden Kashima's *Buddhism in America: The Social Organization of an Ethnic Religious Institution* (1977), Paul Numrich's *Old Wisdom in the New World: Americanization in Two Immigrant Theravada Buddhist Temples* (1996), and Janet McLellan's *Many Petals of the Lotus: Five Asian Buddhist Communities in Toronto* (1999)—provide ample documentation of how Buddhism functions in these immigrant communities.

More recently, Dr. Kenneth Tanaka, a "scholar-practitioner" who maintains a ministry in the Jōdo Shinshū Buddhist Churches of America organization has written a remarkable tract entitled "Parents Sharing the Nembutsu Teachings with Their Young Children," which addresses all the core issues of Buddhist family life in American ethnic Buddhist communities.[29] Tanaka's paper includes considerations of parenting and sharing in the context of Buddhist values, handling difficult situations and questions, the fundamental outlook on life as stressed in Shin Buddhism, suggested daily activities, the testimonial of a Buddhist mother in San Francisco, and a useful bibliography of suggested books. Perhaps more than any other Buddhist organization in North America, Buddhist Churches of America has emphasized the institution of Sunday school as a means of inculcating the importance of Buddhist family life in America. Nonetheless, despite the organization's efforts, the young adult population of its temples has begun to leave the organization at an alarmingly rapid rate. In an attempt to combat this trend, and to reinforce Buddhist identity in America, the organization has changed the name of its program from Sunday school to Dharma school. Presumably, this was done to "re-focus the goals and to re-establish the propagational, educational aspects of the program away from its Sunday day care image."[30]

To my knowledge, only one popular Buddhist publication addresses the issue of Buddhist family life in America with regularity: *Turning Wheel: Journal of the Buddhist Peace Fellowship*. For many years the journal has run a regular "family practice" column. Between 1995 and 1997 it was written by Patrick McMahon from the Spirit Rock community, and since 1997 it has been (mostly) supervised by Mushim Ikeda-Nash. The column regularly discusses marriage, intimacy, death, and even cooking from a Buddhist perspective. In addition, the journal occasionally devotes an entire issue to family-related matters. The winter 1996 issue, for example, focused on "Family—What Is It?" This compelling issue discussed the full range of Buddhist lifestyle issues in America, from Buddhist marriage to children who are returning home to care for aging and dying parents. One article, "On Retreat for Twenty Years," even identified parenting as essential Buddhist practice. A number of years later—in the fall of 1998—the journal designated an entire issue as the "back-to-school issue," discussing the Buddhist transformation of education . . . in the public schools, monastery, family, university, reform school, and the garden.

One of the most profound developments in the globalization of Buddhism is that the various traditions, once so distinct in their respective Asian homelands, in their new Western settings now find themselves in proximity for the first time in the history of Buddhism. It is not unusual for Theravāda, Mahāyāna, and Vajrayāna groups to find themselves neighbors in the same country, city, and even neighborhood. No doubt one can argue that this represents a great prosperity for the Buddhist tradition, but it also presents serious challenges and even liabilities. Is it possible to make some sense out of the seemingly conflicting emphases of these diverse Buddhist traditions and sects and schools? Is it possible to find some unifying principle or basis by which the huge diversity of global Buddhism might reestablish the sense of spiritual kinship among all Buddhists that prevailed in Buddha's original *sangha* of the four quarters?

NOTES

1. See Michael Carrithers, "'They Will Be Lords upon the Island': Buddhism in Sri Lanka," in Heinz Bechert and Richard Gombrich, eds., *The World of Buddhism: Buddhist Monks and Nuns in Society and Culture* (New York: Facts on File, 1984), 133.

2. Emphasis added. *Saṃyutta Nikāya* 45:2.2ff. See, for example, *Saṃyutta Nikāya*, edited by M. Leon Feer (reprint; London: Luzac, 1960), 5:2–3.

3. See Hammalawa Saddhatissa, *Buddhist Ethics*, 2nd ed. (Boston: Wisdom, 1997), 97. The passage in question reads: "Sādhu sambahulā ñāti api rukkhā arannajā, vāto vahati ekattham brahantam pi vanaspatim."

4. See *The Dīgha Nikāya*, edited by J. Estlin Carpenter (reprint; London: Luzac, 1960), 3:180–93.

5. Ibid., 3:189; see verse 28 of the *Sigālovāda Sutta*. Translations from this text, here and throughout, are adapted from those of T. W. Rhys Davids and C. A. F. Rhys Davids, published as *Dialogues of the Buddha*, pt. 3 (reprint; London: Luzac, 1965).

6. Kenneth Ch'en, *The Chinese Transformation of Buddhism* (Princeton, N.J.: Princeton University Press, 1973), 19.

7. See *Dīgha Nikāya*, 3:190; see verse 30 of the *Sigālovāda Sutta*.

8. Peter Harvey, *An Introduction to Buddhist Ethics* (Cambridge: Cambridge University Press, 2000), 101.

9. Emma McCloy Layman, *Buddhism in America* (Chicago: Nelson-Hall, 1976), 251–63.

10. Charles Prebish, *American Buddhism* (North Scituate, Mass.: Duxbury, 1979), 43–44.

11. Ibid., 188.

12. See Tweed's most recent take on the issue in "Who Is a Buddhist? Night-Stand Buddhists and Other Creatures," in Martin Baumann and Charles Prebish, eds., *Westward Dharma: Buddhism Beyond Asia* (Berkeley: University of California Press, 2002), 17–33.

13. See Stuart Chandler, "Chinese Buddhism in America: Identity and Practice," in Charles Prebish and Kenneth Tanaka, eds., *The Faces of Buddhism in America* (Berkeley: University of California Press, 1998), 17.

14. Barry A. Kosmin and Seymour P. Lachman, *One Nation under God: Religion in Contemporary American Society* (New York: Harmony, 1993), 3.

15. Martin Baumann, "The Dharma Has Come West: A Survey of Recent Studies and Sources," *Journal of Buddhist Ethics* 4 (1997): 198, http://jbe.gold.ac.uk/4/baum2.html.

16. See Richard Hughes Seager, "Making Some Sense of Americanization," in *Buddhism in America* (New York: Columbia, University Press, 1999), 232–48.

17. A review of this topic appears in Charles S. Prebish, *Luminous Passage: The Practice and Study of Buddhism in America* (Berkeley: University of California Press, 1999), 57–63.

18. In addition to the three texts mentioned, I include in this group Rick Fields's *How the Swans Came to the Lake: A Narrative History of Buddhism in America*, 3rd ed. (rev. and updated; Boston: Shambhala, 1992); Charles Prebish's *American Buddhism* and *Luminous Passage*, Duncan Ryūken Williams and Christopher S. Queen's *American Buddhism: Methods and Findings in Recent Scholarship* (Surrey, U.K.: Curzon, 1998), and Richard Seager's *Buddhism in America* (New York: Columbia University Press, 1999).

19. Layman, *Buddhism in America*, 198–99.

20. James Coleman, *The New Buddhism: The Western Transformation of an Ancient Tradition* (New York: Oxford University Press, 2001), 145–49.

21. Judith Simmer-Brown, "American Buddhism: The Legacy for Our Children," 1998, *Shambhala*, www.shambhala.org/member/simmer-brown/americanbuddhism.html.

22. The address for Epstein's Web site is http://online.sfsu.edu/~rone/Buddhism/BuddhismParents/BuddhismParents.html.

23. The site was formerly located at http://ourworld.compuserve.com/homepages/vanessa. The site is no longer active.

24. See "Youth Programs," *Zen Mountain Monastery*, www.mro.org/zmm/youth-programs/index.html.

25. See John Daido Loori, "Caoshan's Love Between Parent and Child," *Mountain Record* 17, no. 3 (Spring 1999), www.mro.org/zmm/dharmateachings/talks/teisho15.htm.

26. See Phillip Hammond and David Machacek, *Soka Gakkai in America* (New York: Oxford University Press, 1999), 43–44.

27. Ibid., 117. The General Social Survey is a personal interview survey conducted almost every year by the National Opinion Research Center. The data cited here are from the surveys of 1993 and 1996. For more information see www.ifdo.org/scosci/general_election.html.

28. See, for example, Irene Lin's "Journey to the Far West: Chinese Buddhism in America," *Amerasia Journal* 22, no. 1 (1996): 107–32.

29. Ken Tanaka, "Parents Sharing the Nembutsu Teachings with Their Young Children," n.d., *Seattle Betsuin*, www.seattlebetsuin.com/parents_kids_nembutsu.htm.

30. See John Iwohara, "The Jodo Shinshu Ritual and Dharma School: A Proposed Rationale," *Hou-u: Dharma Rain* 1, no. 2 (1997), www.vbtemple.org/dharmarain/dr12_rit.htm.

CHAPTER 12

Hindu Family in America

RAYMOND BRADY WILLIAMS

The Hindu couple, in traditional wedding finery of silk and gold, sat with the Brahmin priest before the sacred fire in Houston. He chanted each Sanskrit verse of the marriage ritual and then gave a brief explanation in English. After chanting one verse about the traditional duties of the Hindu wife and husband, he looked up at the young professionals and said, "But you're in America now, so you'll do whatever you want." Observers laughed, some more nervously than others, because he brushed right past tensions in Hindu families between traditional and modern, Indian parents and their American children, religious norms and secular peer pressures, then and there and here and now. Hindu families negotiate these tensions as part of the Asian Indian community created by the new immigration after 1965.

TRANSNATIONAL FAMILIES

Hindu families are part of the new immigration that followed changes in U.S. immigration law proposed by President John F. Kennedy and passed in the aftermath of his assassination. The United States admitted immigrants from Asia and India, selecting the brightest and best through preference categories. The primary preferences are for those with professional qualifications as part of the "brain drain," and family reunification. The Hindu immigrants are not "your tired, your poor, your huddled masses" but physicians, engineers, scientists, computer specialists, and, eventually, their families. The earliest were the single young professionals, predominantly male, who obtained green cards for permanent residence and eventually returned to India to marry and bring wives back to the United States. It was inevitable that some of the early immigrants married non-Asian Indians, and some with temporary visas discovered that marriage to an American citizen expedited permanent resident status. After a few years the family reunification provisions kicked in, and Indians arranged for parents and siblings to join them. The 2000 U.S. Census counted almost 1.7 million Asian Indians, more than double those in the 1990 census. Conservative estimates are that more than a million Hindus live in the United States and that 50,000 arrived in 2001.[1] In 2001 the largest portion of immigrants born in India continued to enter the United States with employment-based preferences (39,010); a smaller group (15,443) arrived under family-sponsored preferences.

The majority of these immigrants possessed language facility in English, professional qualifications, and income levels that enabled them to establish themselves in the American middle class. They become American outposts of transnational families with roots in India and branches that often spread like a banyan tree into East Africa, England, Canada, and, more recently, Australasia. Families provide resources and networks for transnational migration, business, and marriage. The recent Indian government initiative to permit dual citizenship is recognition of the importance of these transnational ties and implies significant changes in the meaning of citizenship. Hindu marriages, whether they are held in India, England, the United States, or elsewhere, are occasions for the gathering of transnational families and the renegotiation of family allegiances and values.

Hindu immigrants, along with other recent immigrant groups, are creating a new model of American family that incorporates transnational networks. *Transnationalism* is a designation for the experience of recent immigrants in maintaining many associations that span several societies and developing identities and in maintaining communications with social networks that connect them with two or more societies simultaneously. Hindu families establish themselves in several countries and along these familial networks travel marriage negotiations, economic transfers, new ideas and customs, implied legal and moral obligations, and viable options for mobility. The networks enable families to protect themselves from threats and disasters in one location through support for relocation in another location. Indeed, emigration often moves along family networks because relatives provide welcome, advice, residence, and financial support for new immigrants. More Americans from the majority population also experience the new transnational model because of new mobility and transnational economic forces that enable family members to live and work abroad for long periods of time. Frequent and instantaneous communication links families. A Hindu immigrant in New York reported talking on the telephone with his sister in London as both were watching live pictures on CNN of earthquake damage in their parents' village in India. Such rapid communication leads to the involvement of families in political, economic, religious, and relief activities in other countries. Analyses of families in America in the future will have to take into account the transnational character of families by tracing the networks that they maintain through frequent travel back and forth and rapid communication as much as through bloodlines.

These networks are different for people in diverse religions; Muslim and Christian Indians create networks that have diverse constellations of population centers in other parts of the world and reach back to locations in India that are different from those cultivated by Hindus. The networks rarely cross or have much interaction, certainly not regarding marriage and family. Mobility travels across these networks, occasionally establishing new beachheads (Australia and New Zealand are becoming more attractive recently). Nevertheless, family connections and relative circumstances around the world create important push-pull factors in migration. The constant arrival of new immigrants and their families from the network in India, East Africa, and the United Kingdom establishes an exponential growth of Hindu relatives who are eligible to apply for permanent resident status in the United States under the family reunification provisions of the immigration laws.

Transnational networks function differently in religions such as Buddhism that developed in several national and cultural settings. As Charles Prebish notes in chapter 11, "One of the most profound developments in the globalization of Buddhism is that the various traditions, once so distinct in their respective Asian homelands, in their new Western settings now find themselves in proximity for the first time in the history of Buddhism." Hinduism and traditional Hindu family structures and ethos developed primarily in India, even though some regional variations exist in India and abroad in East Africa, the United Kingdom, and the Caribbean. All these differences are being negotiated in the United States.

Religious influences travel across these networks and shape immigrants' evaluation of and adaptation to aspects of American religion, family life, and culture. The networks involve a sacred world. Families return to India for visits to temples, sacred shrines, and religious leaders so that some visits back to India take on the character of a pilgrimage. Hindu teachers and gurus tour the United States each summer for visits to temples, homes, and family conferences. Some temples hire priests and teachers from India who emigrate under the administrative policies of the Immigration and Naturalization Service in order to conduct family rituals and teach the children. Influence goes both ways across the religious network, affecting Hinduism in India while it influences the adaptation of Hindus to American society and family life.

Money, in the form of gifts and loans to family members in the transnational network, is a significant part of the global economy. The true wealth of contemporary families depends upon the strength of family ties and the authority of the family leaders, usually brothers and their children. These funds support the education of young people and the business ventures of adults and strengthen the prestige and influence of the family across national boundaries. The brothers send money back to India to support their parents. One area in Bangalore was reserved for the purchase and construction of homes with hard foreign currency. It was called the Dollar Colony and consisted of retirement homes and homes for parents. Transnational funding also helps family members relocate across the transnational network. Some funds also aid transnational religious institutions, and such assistance also contributes to the prestige and honor of the extended family. Lavish gifts at times of weddings and other family rituals, generally reciprocated on appropriate occasions in corresponding measure, provide ways of supporting members of extended families and of strengthening the ties that bind them around the world.

FAMILY VALUES

The first immigrants took great pride in their Hindu family values, which, they often boasted, would be their most valuable contribution to American society. The primacy of the corporate values of the family, rather than individual values and personal rights, undergirds an array of Hindu commitments and practices that are in tension with contemporary American experience. A primary distinction between Hindu and American cultural belief systems lies in the concept of the self. The Hindu self and family are integral, rather than separate, concepts, and individuals of all ages are expected to make sacrifices on behalf of the group. The welfare and integrity of the family always supersedes individual needs and self-identity (Farver, Narang, and Bhadha 2002:340). These recent immigrants raise anew in American society the question of defining *family*: Is the model to be the nuclear family, the extended family, or some new construction?

Great variation regarding marriage and family exists within Hinduism because of regional, sectarian, and social class distinctions, but some beliefs and practices are common among Hindus. These communal rights are preserved in special provisions in Indian marriage, family, and divorce laws (Beri n.d.:12). Surrounding the couple in the Houston temple were representatives of the transnational extended families: the tradition of Hindu weddings is that it is a union of two families, not just the private act of two individuals. Encouraged by her or his parents, the oldest child of immigrants commonly is married according to traditional caste patterns, but younger children follow other patterns (*New York Times*, 25 October 2004, A19). Families gather for rituals—that is one of the major functions of the rituals—so transnational families assemble and are celebrated at Hindu weddings. The roots of the extended family are in the Indian joint family system. The traditional joint family, with sanctions in the sacred Sanskrit texts, are the parents, the father's parents, the married sons and wives with their children, unmarried sons, and unmarried daughters, all living in the same household, with a common kitchen and jointly owning property managed by the father or oldest brother.

Although the joint family pattern is breaking down, especially among urban professionals, the authority of the extended family remains strong. Even though urban professionals and immigrants generally exhibit weaker support for caste identity and prerogatives, ties to the extended family serve some of the functions formerly served by caste as a social institution (Beteille 1992). The detailed structure of relations in the extended family is revealed by the title given to each individual according to that person's relationship to the family, for example, father's mother, husband's older brother, sister's son (Prinja 1998:59). Titles are used within the family rather than personal given names. Learning the appropriate respect, service, and assistance expected from and given to each is a significant part of socialization in the family.

Respect for parents and the responsibility of children, especially the oldest son, to care for them in their old age are important family values. Hindu immigrants regard as a scandal American society's practice of discarding elderly parents to nursing homes or even to live alone in Florida. Early immigrants vowed that would never happen to their parents, but, of course, now retirement centers for American Hindus are being planned.[2] Still, Hindus stress respect for parents and the elderly, and it is not uncommon to see sons and daughters stoop or prostrate themselves to touch the feet of their parents. The authority of parents, particularly fathers, to instruct and correct children and the obedience of children to parents are a source of pride.

The Hindu home is a temple, and the family is the primary center for socialization and for religion. The marriage ritual empowers the wife and husband to be religious specialists at the home shrine, whether simple or elaborate, that is found in most Hindu homes. Home shrines enable Hindu families to be observant while only rarely visiting temples. Many Hindu life-cycle rituals (*samskara*), including marriage, are primarily family rituals. These sixteen prescribed rituals begin before birth and continue after death with the cremation and the death anniversary observances; they are held for impregnation, fetus-protection, pregnancy, childbirth, naming, first outing from home, first solid food, first haircut, piercing of the ears, investing with sacred thread, beginning study of the Vedas, completion of education, marriage, invoking ancestors, taking holy vows, and cremation. Even in India, Hindu families generally observe only the most important of the rituals, such as birth, shaving the child's head, marriage, and cremation. One problem of migration is the difficulty in arranging for the appropriate life-cycle rituals. Some families return to India or other locations so the grandparents can participate with the appropriate religious specialists. Active participation in these rituals by members of the extended family constitutes and reconstitutes the family because certain individuals have distinct roles in the rituals. Marriage, birth, and death change the status and role of every member of an extended family. The process by which these rituals and the accompanying roles are validated and strengthened in the United States is important to adaptation. In some instances fictive relationships are established with friends who fill roles normally occupied by relatives. For example, the pregnancy rituals take on the aura of a baby shower, with friends from work taking a primary role; the naming ceremony has the feel of a baptism, and the sacred thread ceremony is similar to a bar mitzvah. Each family adapts the rituals to its changed circumstances, but the cumulative effect of these rituals in defining Hindu families and family in America should not be underestimated. Hinduism provides the bedrock for much of Indian culture, so the religious socialization in the home undergirds the Hindu or Indian corporate family identity.

Hindu immigrants usually arrived without their parents, and most arrived without their spouses or children, so the older generation was not present in the families as they developed. That is significant because grandparents in India traditionally are powerful figures in embodying and transmitting religious and cultural traditions. One reason that relatively young scientists, physicians, and professionals become more religious and take on leadership roles in religious institutions in the United States more frequently than they did before they emigrated is that their parents were absent until recently.

Religion helps immigrants create and preserve their personal and group identity in their new home. Religion provides a transcendent grounding for closely held beliefs and practices regarding good order, truth, and virtue, enabling individuals and groups to affirm who they are and to resist external societal pressures while they are adjusting to new settings. That is one reason that religion has been such a significant force in this country of immigrants. Just as earlier immigrants both preserved and created patterns that Americans now refer to as "family values," recent immigrants bring their commitments to virtues encouraged by their religious traditions. An increasing percentage of the American population is foreign born. Many immigrants arriving since 1965 are from parts of Asia, Africa, and Latin America that place great value on the extended family, traditional gender roles, corporate decision making, and respect for elders and hold marriage sacred. These values are integral to their religious norms and concepts of virtue. In fact, immigration always involves threats to the plausibility structures of taken-for-granted modes of thought and behavior that support a person's commitment to tradition. Indeed, some models of Americanization stress the power of secularization and individualism to mute religiously supported ethnic and national identities. The result would be the weakening of family ties and values. The alternative is that recent immigrants will reverse the trend of secularization and individualism as they introduce patterns of family life that new immigrants constantly reinforce. Many recent immigrants, including many Hindus, are more conservative and less secularized than elements of American society. The result could be a reconstitution of the American family in new, more conservative forms.

MARRIAGE

The common claim of Asian Indians regarding arranged marriages is that "we come to love the ones we marry; Americans marry the ones they love." Parents arrange traditional Hindu marriage as a union of two families within a caste social structure along established networks. Such arranged marriages seem startlingly different in the United States. Vasudha Narayanan, the immediate past president of the American Academy of Religion, described these arrangements in a recent article:

> I guess my friends [at Harvard] were trying to understand where I was coming from. I particularly remember the time I got engaged. It was soon after the American bicentennial. My parents had matched my horoscope (in some families, these are cast in great detail by the family astrologer soon after birth) with that of a young man studying in Chicago. Our families met in India, and then told us about each other. After several conversations on the phone, he came to Boston to meet me and we got engaged. It was a conventional "arranged" marriage. Obviously if we did not like each other, we could have opted out. Other family members have met and married people of European descent or from other parts of India. We chose to meet the traditional way, although it was in Cambridge. This was something we felt comfortable with, but it was a cultural experience for my friends and they seemed to be quite intrigued with the process!
>
> (Narayanan 2002:10)

Although some Asian Indians, both the first and second generation of immigrant families, enter arranged marriages in America or elsewhere in the transnational network, in both India or the United States fewer are willing to follow the traditional pattern. The traditional age for marriage, near puberty, has been extended by education and professional advancement well into the twenties, and young adults are less pliable than younger children.

The old networks for negotiating arranged marriages are attenuated and are being replaced by other types. "Introduction marriage" involves parents in searching for suitable candidates, contacting their parents, and introducing the young man and woman to see if they consent. Some married couples tell stories of the early days of immigration when fewer suitable candidates were available here. Their parents arranged for interviews back in India with several candidates and their families, so the singles could fly back during short vacations to meet several, select one, have the wedding, and begin the process to obtain the new spouse's green card. Even if parents are responsible for the first contact, few if any marriages are arranged now without the opportunity for the couple to meet, become acquainted, and make an informed decision to consent.

Another type is the "semiarranged marriage"; a couple meets in school, the workplace, or some religious or social gathering and decides that marriage is a pleasant possibility. The man and woman then ask their parents to negotiate the marriage arrangements. Parents often encourage their marriageable children to attend Hindu and other social gatherings that have the latent function of identifying potential marriage partners. The semiarranged marriages also include some of what are called "love marriages," a designation that implies closer contact than is traditionally acceptable and a type of marriage that parents often do not prefer. Several novels and short stories written by Asian Indian women deal with family expectations regarding selection of marriage partners and tensions that result when those expectations are crushed.

Indian parents of American children project preferred marriage partners for their children. The primary characteristics, ranked in descending order, are from family network, *jati* (caste), ethnic/linguistic group, religion, professional status, Asian Indian, and race (fair skin is preferable to dark). These are implicit in family negotiations and explicit in advertisements for marriage partners in Asian Indian newspapers and on Web sites. New cybernetworks are developing on the Internet that list potential marriage partners by region, language, caste, and religion. These enable parents to easily make initial contact with families of several prospective marriage partners. Hindu parents desire a "cultured," or *sanskari*, spouse for their child, which means someone raised to appreciate the Hindu culture, its ways, discipline, and responsibilities. Parental preference patterns reflect the basic values of the group and become lightning rods for crises. Marriages that transgress all these preferences, thereby creating difficult adjustments for the families involved, do occur. Some young men fear that female Asian Indians are tainted by American culture and unwholesome contact with men and prefer brides from India. It is more difficult for young women to adjust to marriage partners from India because the men often expect compliance and traditional patterns of behavior in gender roles. Marriage partners have a market value, and marriage is a test of a family's status. American citizenship or permanent resident status is a valuable characteristic for transnational marriage partners because it makes emigration possible for the spouse's parents and siblings.

Parents feel that they have fulfilled a major social responsibility when they have successfully found spouses for their children, especially their daughters. The father provides the "gift of a virgin" to the groom's family amid the lavish gift giving from the bride's extended family that traditionally constituted her inheritance.[3] India has prohibited the giving of dowry, but the law is often circumvented. Although the wedding ceremony itself is shortened in America, it generally takes several hours. The ultimate moment comes when the bride and groom, joined by a sacred cord, walk around a fire. Then they take seven steps that signify seven vows: the first for prosperity, then strength, wealth, happiness, progeny, the seasons' favors, and companionship (Sahai 1993:55). The seventh step seals the marriage.

The bride's leave-taking at the end of the ceremony is emotionally powerful because it marks her birth into a new family. She goes to her parents and then to each of her natal relatives to touch their feet, receive their blessing, and mark the transition. Much weeping marks the ritual as she leaves for her new home, traditionally with her husband's parents. The new bride comes under the tutelage of her mother-in-law until she is socialized into the ways of the new family. Within the family she occupies an inferior role in relation to males and elders, especially until she bears a son. Traditional preference for a son in some areas of India has led to debates about the use of amniocentesis to mark and abort female fetuses. In some parts of India a deficit of female births exists, but no firm data are available regarding the practice in the United States. Divorce is relatively rare and difficult in Hindu families. It was not until passage of the Hindu Marriage Act of 1955 that Hindu women throughout India were able to divorce their spouses (Gupta 1999a:196). Wives go back to their natal homes for protection by their father and brothers, but the society still does not support divorce. Remarriage by divorcées and widows is generally discouraged. Divorées have reduced value in marriage negotiations.

IMMIGRATION AND CHANGE

Provisions of the immigration law and administrative decisions shape a new form of transnational family. U.S. immigration law makes it possible for citizens to sponsor their parents and siblings, so the attraction of immigration strengthens some types of familial networks. Family members sponsor and support relatives during their adjustment to the different expectations of American culture and economy. As I noted earlier, a right to permanent resident status increases the value of young men and women in marriage negotiations. In last quarter of the twentieth century immigration procedures and processes had become fairly predictable for transnational families, and the marriage networks facilitated the transnational movement of young adults. But since 9/11 these transnational families have faced great uncertainty. The number of refugees admitted to the United States dropped significantly in 2003, and while that does not greatly affect Hindu families, few of whom are refugees, any curtailment of other immigration quotas will significantly affect the development of Hindu families and institutions.

Jeffrey Meyers notes that long-standing immigrant groups like the Chinese have immigrated over time from several different Chinese cultural settings, for example, pre-Communist China, Taiwan, and from Communist China. Confucian family ideals have preserved Chinese identity throughout a long history of immigration. Moreover, they enable modernization under a Chinese umbrella even after some political aspects of Confucianism were discredited. For more recent immigrants from India, Hindu family relations preserve their cultural identity and encourage them to maintain transnational contacts with relatives in several nations.

Migration transforms family relations, threatens plausibility structures, and brings freedom from traditional patterns, which are also changing in India. Attitudinal modernity is the concept used to refer to the Westernization of attitudes in such diverse areas as gender roles, politics, authority, the family, and religious beliefs. Indian immigrant families and those in industrialized parts of India experience forms of attitudinal modernization (Patel-Amin and Power 2002:241). Attitudinal modernity is different from modernization that can be quantified by using data on economic development and industrial output. The attitudes that characterize the modern West have enormous power when transmitted across transnational networks through mobile populations and modern media, even when unaccompanied by wealth or industrialization.

In many societies outside the West a struggle occurs between traditional values and attitudes and those characterized as attitudinal modernization. The wealth and prosperity of the West are often portrayed as the lure for immigrant families, and some religious leaders and social critics describe the West as offering dangerous temptations with its decadent attitudes and behavior. Although education, professional status, and economic advancement are the primary reasons given for moving to the United States, some young people actively seek freedom from social strictures and family dominance. The struggle between tradition and attitudinal modernity now taking place in other parts of the world is also a reality in the lives of individual immigrants and within their families in the United States. Because the negotiation takes place across transnational boundaries and between established and newly arrived immigrants, the issues are always prominent at religious and social gatherings. Another reason that immigrants give for leaving their home country is to seek greater opportunities for their children. Some parents now fear that they made a Mephistophelian bargain, gaining the world and losing their children. Two central family values—gender roles and generational relations—are transformed in America.

The majority of Asian Indian women work outside the home, some providing more income for the family than their spouse, which changes gender relations significantly. Because wages for domestic help are relatively low in India, middle-class Indians can afford a maid, so it is a new experience for many couples to work outside the home in professional positions and have to look after the family chores of cleaning, cooking, yard work, and garbage disposal. The renegotiation of gender roles is delicate and causes a great deal of stress between husband and wife and, in some instances, between the wife and her husband's relatives. The appropriate gender roles for young men and women are topics of intense discussion at Hindu temples and conferences. South Asian women's centers in urban areas deal with these conflicts and with the psychological and physical abuse they occasionally engender.

The tensions are captured in a poem by Chitra Banerjee Divarkaruni, "We the Indian Women in America":

> It is not always easy for us, Indian women in
> America. We came with dreams of instant riches,
> Hollywood or millionaire husbands, not knowing
> how much we'd miss the paint-peeled houses filled
> with grandmothers and aunts, the old *ayahs*
> who loved and scolded us. Weddings and *namskarans*
>   when we made big beds on the floor
> and slept, all us cousins together. Not knowing
> there would be no way back. But slowly we learned
> being alone is not all bad. We learned,
> in this country, to stand straighter,
> speak up for what we want.
>
> And what we want is this: for us and our daughters,
> India *and* America,
> the best of both together.
>
>   (Maira and Srikanth 1996:269f)

Many wish to preserve both the communal aspect of Hindu family life and the values of American individualism and freedom. That may be a pipe dream, or perhaps the communal aspect of Hindu family will be preserved and strengthen American family life.

Although divorce is relatively rare, it is becoming more common. The 2000 census counted 20,899 Asian Indian families with a female head of household (no husband present), and 19,260 with a male head of household and no wife present. A feature of some matrimonial advertisements is a description of a divorcée as "innocent, no issue." It is difficult to estimate the number of Hindus who have divorced because marriage and divorce have very different legal and religious status for different Asian Indian groups, particularly Muslims.

The acronym ABCDs conveys in humorous discourse the confusion of American children of Indian immigrants and some of the tension between the generations. They are called "American-Born Confused *Desis*," using the Hindi word for compatriots from a native area. They jokingly throw a different acronym in the face of recent arrivals, calling them JOBs—Just Off the Boat—and tease them for still wearing Indian dress, not being able to speak colloquial American English, and not being able to fit comfortably in American youth culture. The jokesters may or may not realize that they are making statements about the behavior of their parents a decade or so earlier.

It is simplistic to say that parents value family whereas children value friendship, but it is one way of explaining some of the tensions between the generations. The tradition is that family is the primary unit, and relationships with relatives dominate attention outside work, so that parents in the first generation do not value friendship as the major operative category. A person who becomes close is awarded fictive kinship status as uncle or auntie, or perhaps cousin-brother, even in the United States. Fictive kinship implies privileges and responsibilities not generally associated with friendship. In America new immigrants are separated by distance from family and other Hindus, yet they rarely visit the homes of their children's friends. Hence the immigrant parents have little contact with the wholesomeness of much of American family life. The tendency in cross-cultural exchanges is always to compare "the best of ours with the worst of theirs." Immigrants' attitudes are shaped by what they see in the media, which terrifies them and makes them even more protective of their children. One youth remarked that members of his parents' generation carry in their minds a mistaken view of India from twenty-five years ago and a false view of American society derived from television, so they are doubly removed from reality. An angry exchange results, with the parent telling the child: "You care more about your friends than about your family." Long, agonized, and tearful discussions of these issues take place in Hindu temples and family conferences, among the few contexts in which these issues can be discussed.

Dating is often the flashpoint. Hindu parents view the American practice of casual relationships and long-term dating with alarm. Most Hindu parents prohibit it and nearly all discourage it. Prom nights are nights of terror for Hindu parents because they have heard stories of rampant sex and use of drugs and alcohol. Young people socialized in America see nothing wrong with dating and feel excluded, because of their parents' "old-fashioned ways," from significant contexts for developing and maintaining relationships with young men and young women. Young people commonly acknowledge that they have dated secretly, but the deceit tears at their relationships. Sangeeta Gupta comments that their silence on the subject does not mean that young Asian Indian women are sexually inactive (Gupta 1999b:133). Girls feel that they are more restricted and carefully guarded than their brothers and accuse their parents of sexism, discrimination, and favoritism. Parents view dating as a first inferior step toward marriage and family; their children view dating as a category of friendship. Hindu couples come to love each other deeply, but the statement "my spouse is my best friend" involves a confusion of categories.

Immigrants often comment that they took the risks of migration so their children could benefit from the best of both worlds, and the parents juxtapose corporate Hindu family values with Western individualism and materialism. American Hindu families are engaged in a heated and delicate negotiation regarding gender roles, relations between generations, and transnational family networks. One result may well be the creation of new family relations that preserve the best of both worlds. Perhaps the concession of the Hindu priest at that Houston wedding—"But you're in America now, so you'll do whatever you want"—will lead to a strengthening of American families through the merging and refining of Hindu family values in the crucible of American family life.

REFERENCES

Beri, B. P. n.d. *Law of Marriage and Divorce in India.* Lucknow, India: Eastern Book.

Beteille, Andre. 1992. "Caste and Family: In Representations of Indian Society." *Anthropology Today* 8, no. 1 (February): 13–18.

Farver, J. M., S. K. Narang, and B. R. Bhadha. 2002. "East Meets West: Ethnic Identity, Acculturation, and Conflict in Asian Indian Families." *Journal of Family Psychology* 16 (3): 338–50.

Gupta, Sawgeeta R. 1999a. "Forged by Fire: Indian-American Women Reflect on Their Marriages, Divorces, and on Rebuilding Lives." In *Emerging Voices: South Asian American Women Redefine Self, Family and Community,*, 193–221. Edited by Sawgeeta R. Gupta. Walnut Creek, Calif.: AltaMira.

———. 1999b. "Walking on the Edge: Indian-American Women Speak Out on Dating and Marriage." In *Emerging Voices: South Asian American Women Redefine Self, Family, and Community,* 120–45. Edited by Sangeeta R. Gupta. Walnut Creek, Calif.: AltaMira.

Maira, Sunaina and Rajini Srikanth, eds. 1996. *Contours of the Heart: South Asians Map North America.* New York: Asian American Writers' Workshop.

Narayanan, Vasudha. 2002. "A Presidential View." *Religious Studies News* 17, no. 4:10.

Patel-Amin, Nisha and Thomas G. Power. 2002. "Modernity and Childrearing in Families of Gujarati Indian Adolescents." *International Journal of Psychology* 37, no. 4: 239–45.

Prinja, Nawal K., ed. 1998. *Explaining Hindu Dharma.* 2nd ed. Manchester, U.K.: Vishwa Hindu Parishad.

Sahai, Prem. 1993. *Hindu Marriage Samskara.* Allahabad, India: Wheeler.

NOTES

1. The 2000 census counted 1,678,765 Asian Indians, 893,095 males and 785,670 females. Another 220,000 listed Asian Indian and at least one other racial or ethnic group. More than 70,000 new legal immigrants who were born in India entered the United States in 2001. The latter figure is the basis of the estimate that 50,000 Hindus arrived in the United States in 2001. Data regarding the Asian Indian population in this chapter were generated by customized searches through American FactFinder, an interactive application of the U.S. Census Bureau that is available at http://factfinder.census.gov. This site enables researchers to compile specific information regarding the U.S. population, but the specialized Web page created thereby is not permanently preserved for citation as a URL.

2. The 2000 census counted 4,000 Asian Indians aged sixty-five and older who were living alone and 1,366 Asian Indians older than seventy-five who were also living alone.

3. The classical text is found in the Laws of Manu 3.27–30: "The gift of a daughter, after decking her (with costly garments) and honoring her (with presents of jewels), to a man learned in the Veda and of good conduct, whom the father invites, is called the Brahma rite."

CHAPTER 13

Islam and the Family in North America

JANE I. SMITH

Few topics are higher on the agenda for careful reflection and consideration by American Muslims than the nature and importance of the family. From the time of Prophet Muhammad in the seventh century C.E., family has provided the cornerstone of Muslim society, shaped both in terms of the prescripts of the Qur'an and by the many cultures to which the religion of Islam spread.

Muslims in America look on the family as the bulwark of their existence in this Western (secular) society, the unit through which they filter, accept, or reject various elements of American society that they see as compatible or incompatible with their understanding of what it means to be Muslim. The fifth installment of a major campaign, begun in 2003 to foster better understanding of Islam and counter American Islamophobic rhetoric, is sponsored by the Council of American-Islamic Relations and focuses on family values in the American Muslim community.

There should be no misunderstanding, however, that family necessarily means the same thing to all American Muslims or that there is any kind of uniform acceptance of what might be called "traditional Islamic values" in relation to the family. Muslims in America represent the most heterogeneous Islamic grouping in the history of the world. Not only do they come from virtually every nation, both Islamic and those for which Islam is a minority faith, but they also include a significant portion (perhaps 25 to 30 percent) of African Americans and other American-born citizens who have chosen to adopt Islam as their religion. They are Sunni and Shia, main line and sectarian. Some

American Muslims are religiously observant, while others choose not to be, which may or may not affect the way they construe the nature of the family. Some make concentrated efforts to live their lives as close to Islamic prescriptions as possible (determining which prescriptions are valid in a Western context is an ongoing and flexible process), while others want to appear as Western as possible and eschew any identifying markers that will label them as "different" in American society. In this mix the concept of family—although accepted as of extreme importance by virtually all American Muslims—is interpreted in a great range of ways.

Muslims in general honor the status of the Qur'an as God's word for humanity, and the Sunna, or "way" of the Prophet, as a model for human behavior, whether they themselves are strictly observant or not. The Qur'an portrays nature as operating in pairs, male and female, and thus sets the scene for the partnering structure of human relationships. Males and females are created as mates for each other.[1] The Qur'an speaks specifically about many family concerns, including appropriate partners, marriage, divorce, inheritance, and authority. The Prophet Muhammad spoke often about marriage and family, trying to reform or give some structure to the customs that characterized pre-Islamic life. He is said to have told his followers, "The best of you are those who are best to their families," and in his last sermon to his community he said, "O you people, your wives have a certain right over you and you have certain rights over them. Treat them well and be kind to them for they are your committed partners and helpers."[2]

The Prophet himself had thirteen wives (for political reasons), although the Qur'an technically allows a Muslim man as many as four wives. The Prophet also is often quoted as having said that of all hateful things in the world, divorce is among the worst. In virtually all Muslim societies over the centuries, the family has been such a basic institution that there really have been no alternatives; what Americans used to call bachelors and spinsters have been virtually nonexistent in the Muslim community.

Stipulations and directives from the Qur'an and Sunna have continued to be important ingredients in the development of Islamic law, still applied in many Muslim countries, particularly to matters of marriage (which in Islam is contractual, not sacramental), treatment of women within the family, divorce, and maintenance of children. Muslim family law is one of the main targets for Islamic reform in many countries of the world today.[3] While the details of the law (differing slightly among the four prominent Sunni schools) are too extensive to treat fully here, it should be noted that the process of *fiqh*, or application of the law, is a primary activity among observant American Muslims trying to understand what regulations genuinely apply to people living in non–Muslim-majority countries.

Family law is a key element in this ongoing discussion. Because local custom has been accepted legally as one component, among others (including Qur'an and Sunna), that determine how families should function, the discussion among American Muslims who represent so many different cultures and societies is rich, extensive, and far from unanimous. Traditionally, the primary interpreters of regulations relating to the family have been the four legal schools for Sunnis. Shiites have their own legal codes, along with directives from their imams and ayatollahs. With no school of law predominant in the United States, and with traditional Islamic notions of family relations often at odds with prevailing American ideologies and practices, Muslim leaders are spending considerable time and attention in helping their constituencies understand what is right, appropriate, legal, or not legal in the American context. Among the many kinds of concerns addressed by the Fiqh Council of North America, for example, issues related to marriage and the family, and to divorce, are prominent.[4]

With the growth of the American Muslim community, and the corresponding rise in the number of mosques and Islamic centers (both built for that purpose and adapted from existing structures), has come the development of many different kinds of Islamic organizations. Among those are groups such as the Islamic Society of North America, the Islamic Circle of North America, and the ministry of Warith Deen Muhammad,[5] the latter primarily to African Americans. All have emphasized the importance of maintaining a strong family unit in America, and most regional and national meetings of these kinds of Islamic organizations feature speakers, panels, and discussion groups on the various dimensions of family life and responsibility.

DEFINITION OF FAMILY

In Islamic cultures *family* automatically implies what we would call an "extended" unit, with the husband and wife part of a much wider network of familial relationships. Traditionally, marriage has meant a bonding not just (or even primarily) of individuals but of larger family units. In America the question of what constitutes a family generally has to be seen in a very different way.[6] In some cases a sufficient number of family members have come to this country that some semblance of extended family is possible. More often, however, a husband and wife are the primary and only unit. This focus on the nuclear (neolocal) family obviously has many ramifications, including loneliness (especially for a wife who does not work outside the home), the lack of a larger support group for both parents and children, the difficulty faced by a young mother who is working and has no family to provide child care, and new forms of stress on the husband-wife relationship in isolation from other family members. African Americans, who themselves or whose parents decided to adopt Islam as a way of life, may suffer from a rupture in relationship with their non-Muslim family members, who often do not understand or appreciate the conversion and interpret it as criticism or rejection of themselves and their religion or culture.

American Muslims, therefore, often find themselves turning to other groups or units to substitute for the loss of the natural extended family. Some more recent immigrants choose to find their solidarity in union with others who share the same national or cultural background. This may mean that they avoid contact with non-Muslim Americans or sometimes even other Muslims, preferring to continue to practice their culture and religion with those whose values and definitions align most closely with their own. Others opt to find their "family" in the local mosque or Islamic center, where they share overall Islamic values but may find themselves affiliated with other Muslims whose cultural customs in relation to family and other issues differ. The importance of the mosque as an extended family substitute is underscored at the times of religious holidays, or ʿeids, which traditionally have been occasions for extended family to celebrate and share a meal together. By sharing holidays with coreligionists in the community as well as with immediate relatives, Muslims find new definitions of family that may help to overcome cultural differences.

At a more abstract level some Muslims who are ready to loosen ties with traditional cultures and to work toward the creation of a genuinely "American Islam" might be said to look to the community at the national level as a substitute for traditional family solidarity. This is not to say that they ignore blood ties and personal family relationships but that in the attempt to dissociate Islam from cultural accretions and interpretations, they postulate a national umma, or community in which all Muslims, African American and those of immigrant origins, can function as a kind of great extended family unit. Needless to say, that process is still in the very early stages and faces many obstacles to its realization.

DATING AND MARRIAGE

New definitions and interpretations of family aside, the practical problems of how to begin a family in the American context are very real for American Muslims. A number of ingredients complicate this picture.

According to Islamic law, to which some Muslims try to adhere and others do not, a Muslim man may marry any woman who is a member of what the Qur'an calls "People of the Book," meaning Muslims, Jews, and Christians. A Muslim woman, however, may marry only another Muslim for a variety of reasons, including male authority in the family and determination of the religious affiliation of the ensuing children. For those Muslims who try to follow this injunction, the problems are obvious. In cultures where Muslims are the majority a man has less opportunity to marry outside Islam. In America, where Muslims still make up only a fraction of the population and interaction between Muslims and non-Muslims is virtually unavoidable, the incidence of marriage outside the faith is much higher. This can result, and has resulted, in extreme hardships for young practicing Muslim women who are left with a dwindling pool of available partners. Sometimes parents have arranged to import a husband from the home culture. At other times they capitulate and allow their daughter to marry a non-Muslim, usually with great reluctance. Today, observant Muslims are feeling increased pressures to marry within the faith, despite the legal alternative, not only to solve the problems of marriage partners but to ensure integrity of the family unit.

A Christian woman who marries a Muslim man is not legally obliged to convert, but pressures from the community to provide a home context in which children are not subjected to conflicting faith expectations and practices are high. Non-Muslim men who marry Muslim women are subject to even greater pressures, and sometimes even to ridicule ("sometimes called, half jokingly, half contemptuously, 'cupid's Muslims'").[7] The phenomenon of conversion causes considerable family stress for both the Muslim family into which a new member is to be welcomed and for the blood (often Christian) family of the convert.[8]

For Muslim parents in America who want to ensure that their children (especially, of course, their daughters) meet potential marriage partners whom they consider appropriate, the problems are great. Many need to overcome their initial expectation that a child marry not only another Muslim but someone of their own country or culture and general background. A white male convert to Islam once complained to me that much as he wants to marry a Muslim woman, it seems impossible because families will "release" their daughters only to those of the same ethnic affiliation. In some cases American-born Muslims are serving as dispute mediators to help resolve such cultural conflicts, providing another occasion to further the conversation about what it means to be not just a Muslim living in America but an American Muslim.[9]

Many Muslim families refuse to let their children (especially daughters) socialize with non-Muslims for fear of sexual attraction and do not allow daughters to date even Muslims without appropriate chaperoning. For traditional Muslim families, especially—but not only—those of Middle Eastern origin, the strong commitment to family honor often seems to find its focus in the behavior of its girls and women. Young Muslims in America struggle both to respect the honor of the family and to break free of the kinds of expectations it imposes on them. Muslim girls are becoming more articulate about their own frustrations at the double standards that their parents seem to apply to the girls and their brothers. Both locally and through national organizations such as the Islamic Society of North America and the Islamic Circle of North America efforts are being made to bring young Muslim boys and girls together to socialize and "pursue Islamic purposes" in the context of a highly structured set of activities.

Young people find occasions to meet on university campuses or perhaps at social events provided through the mosque or Islamic center, but if they are religiously observant, they seldom go out with each other in the way that most young American men and women tend to do. "Dating services" are provided by some of the major Islamic organizations, specifically through the matrimonials sections of popular monthly and quarterly journals. Young men and women (or their parents in their stead) can post their credentials and the qualities that they would like to see exhibited in their mates, and Islamically appropriate ways can be set up for potential mates to meet and become acquainted.

In some communities in the United States and Canada, Muslim families still attempt to arrange marriages for their children, a practice more popular with newly arrived immigrants than among longer-established groups. Often the arrangement is modified to make it more appropriate to the Western context, what Murray Hogben calls "semiarranged" marriages in which the parents lay the groundwork but the individuals have the final determination.[10] Some Muslim young people, looking at the high rate of divorce in the West, are willing to concede that there may be wisdom in parental "participation" in decisions about marriage and family life.

HUSBAND-WIFE RELATIONS

It is probably not an overstatement to say that the vast majority of Muslims living in America, those from immigrant backgrounds, African Americans, or other converts to Islam, come from traditions and personal circumstances in which males are the dominant voices within the family circle. Virtually all traditional Muslim cultures support male authority, as do most African American societies. The Qur'an itself has generally been interpreted to give firm support to the dominance of the male in the marriage unit, most directly in chapter 4, verse 34, which usually has been translated to mean that men are in charge of women because they provide for them (financially).

Male authority and control taken at face value, however, tend to run up against the general climate of American understandings of equality and justice between the sexes, and the feminist-initiated but now more generally accepted notion that the family unit is one in which both males and females have an equal share in responsibilities and in decision making. That not all American families (or other units of society) approximate this ideal does not negate its power as a counterimage to the scripture-based and tradition-supported Islamic model of male authority.

Responses from within the Islamic community to this kind of challenge vary hugely. Much of the contemporary discourse, joined by both men and women, portrays the Western model of "equality" between the sexes as unrealistic, unnatural, and leading ultimately to the reality of many Western women: trying to raise children alone while living below the poverty level. The Islamic system, they affirm, will never allow such degradation because it is based on the understanding that male authority over females is always tied to men's responsibility to provide financial support for the women of their families.[11]

Some attempts are now being made to reinterpret the words of Qur'an 4:34 and other texts that seem to support male dominance over women, trying to argue that they need not mean what they appear at first glance to mean. This particular passage is the focus of continuing discussion between male leaders of Islam and Muslim women (and also some men) who find traditional interpretations to be unreasonable and oppressive. If God is just, they argue, and the Qur'an is God's word, then what might appear inequitable and thus apparently unjust in the Qur'an must be reinterpreted in a different way.

One of the first American Muslim women to offer a constructive "feminist" analysis of the Qur'an verses dealing with women was Amina Wadud-Muhsin, who proposed that 4:34 deals not with male control but with resolving disharmony between husband and wife.[12] More recently, Azizah al-Hibri has contended that the Arabic term often translated to suggest male authority over women in fact should be understood to mean that men are the advisers of women, those who provide them with guidance.[13] Al-Hibri and others argue that new circumstances, such as woman's being the primary wage earner in the family, encourage new interpretations of the verse. The recent attempt of Asma Barlas, in an essay entitled "Unreading Patriarchal Interpretations of the Qur'an," reflects a growing movement to see the individual verses of the Qur'an in the context of the whole revelation. Barlas says that the Qur'an describes men as the protectors and maintainers of women, not their guardians or rulers.[14] American women are now privy to interpretations of 4:34 that are coming from women in other cultural contexts, such as Iranian attempts to prove that the verse really calls men the "supporters" of women, giving them aid and encouragement.

The right of both men and women to exercise *ijtihad*, individual interpretation, is being invoked as some Muslim women and men struggle to argue on the basis of their own texts and traditions that Islam does not discriminate between men and women and that, while roles and opportunities may differ between the sexes, they are fair and equitable.[15] The specter of Western feminism in its many permutations looms over these discussions, with the result that most Muslims insist vigorously that whatever new interpretations they try to coax from Islamic tradition are categorically different from the assertions of feminist agitators in the West.[16]

Islamic tradition has long insisted on the right of the woman to formulate her own marriage contract and to receive *mahr* (a marriage gift) from her husband, which is to remain her property even if they were to divorce. Most women in the Islamic world have been poorly or not informed at all that a bride may legally insist on a marriage contract with a number of stipulations. Increasingly, Islamic counselors and advisers in America are talking and writing about the importance of this kind of protection for Muslim women, and more are taking advantage of it. The contract may contain such details as the amount and nature of the *mahr*, prohibiting the husband from taking a second wife, or specifying when and what kinds of divorce may be legally acceptable; it can also include agreements relative to the specific circumstances of the couple in question. In some cases a woman may choose to have a *wali*, or legal guardian (usually a male relative or the husband of a friend), act in her stead; his responsibilities may include everything from helping the woman find an appropriate husband to negotiating the marriage contract and acting as a general intermediary until the wedding.[17]

In reality, of course, legal stipulations do not always ward off family problems. Muslim families are challenged to paint as positive a picture as possible of the advantages of living Islamically, particularly in light of what is obviously a rising tide of anti-Islamic feeling in the West. On the other hand, they are also recognizing that the only way to counter some of the problems Muslim families face, which often are the same as those faced by other Western families, is to acknowledge those problems and move actively toward their solution. Mental health concerns, the reality of AIDS, spousal abuse and abuse of children, homosexuality (unacceptable in Islam)—these and other traditionally "hushed-up" topics are gradually being addressed both through academic research and articles in popular Muslim journals. AIDS in the Muslim community, about which relatively little is as yet known, was the main topic of the Spring 2003 issue of *Azizah* magazine, a journal devoted to Muslim women. Spousal abuse has been the subject of a number of serious studies that examine the persistence of the problem in light of women's fear in reporting abuse by their husbands,[18] stereotypical and discriminatory treatment of Arabs and Muslims by police, and the failure to include Muslims on task forces dealing with violence against women.[19] While many Muslims still want to insist that such things do not occur in the Muslim family, others recognize that the only way to find help is to openly acknowledge reality and seek to provide Islamically guided (and sometimes state-supported) assistance.

Polygyny—the possibility stipulated in the Qur'an for a husband to take as many as four wives under certain stringent conditions—is one of the most difficult concepts for Muslims to explain to their non-Muslim neighbors in America. Deemed permissible by the Qur'an only in unusual cases and when the husband is able to provide equally for all wives, the practice is illegal in the United States and Canada and thus can never be allowed by Muslim jurists or counselors. Nonetheless it does exist in rare cases in America, sometimes when an immigrant turns out on arrival to have more than one wife or when it is encouraged in the ideology of a few African American sectarian groups.

The subtle threat on the part of a husband, that a lack of obedience by his wife might result in her having to share him with another wife, has been real in traditional Muslim cultures and may occasionally have an echo in America. This can be particularly stressful for women who are not educated about the legal reality that multiple marriages are not allowed by U.S. law. For virtually all Muslims in America, however, the idea of multiple wives is both illegal and unappealing.

OTHER CONCERNS WITHIN
THE AMERICAN MUSLIM FAMILY

Many Muslim families in America are second and third generation and have more or less come to terms with the ways in which traditional Islamic concepts of the family must be modified in the Western context. For those who are more recently arrived, or are dedicated to maintaining classical familial structures, the pressures of American society are great. Women are expected to become increasingly independent and to participate in public life rather than "just stay at home." Men must deal with cultural pressures to change their assumptions of patriarchal authority. Social life in America, both by expectation and by necessity, often means finding relationships in nonfamilial structures, a new experience for many immigrants and even for African Americans.

All these challenges pale for most Muslim families in contrast to the concerns they face in raising children in Western society. Parents struggle with such issues as how to keep their children insulated from what are perceived to be dangerous Western secular values even as they acknowledge their children's citizenship in the West and want to prepare them for living their lives in a Western culture; and how to educate children Islamically while providing an academic education that is as sound as possible. A few Muslim families are opting for homeschooling as an alternative to public education. Besieged by concerns about finances and quality education, others work together to establish Islamic schools. Some Muslim homes are the venue for after-school or weekend classes in Islamic subjects, especially when mosques or Islamic centers are not available for such purposes. Islamic parents also struggle with how to keep children aware and appreciative of the values of the "home culture," wherever that may be, while supporting the efforts of young people to work toward an indigenous form of Islam, an American *umma*, or community.[20] While some young Muslims slide almost effortlessly from their public "American Muslim" personas to their familial cultural identities at home, others resent the degree to which their families seem to cling to the old cultural ways. Another dilemma for Islamic parents is how to include young people in the major Islamic movements and organizations as well as in the life of the mosque or Islamic society so that they feel a part of Islam and not chained to what they see as outmoded and irrelevant customs. Such issues are discussed at virtually all local and national meetings of Muslim groups and organizations. Educational materials produced in great quantity and with technical sophistication by groups such as the Islamic Circle of North America tend to reinforce the ideal of a family that protects its children from the temptations of a basically secular Western society.

Closely related to the question of raising children are questions of whether it is appropriate for women to work outside the home, what kinds of work (and what working hours) are advisable, and who makes those decisions. Many Muslims feel that it is simply not right for the wife to have outside employment and they will not permit it. Others may agree with that supposition but are forced for economic reasons to have the wife bring in some outside income. Still others feel that employment for women is acceptable so long as it meets such Islamic restrictions as permitting the woman to wear Islamic dress,[21] not having her in a situation of undue contact with men, or putting her in contact with unacceptable products such as *haram* (forbidden) food.

For other Muslim women such concerns are generally irrelevant—these women are well educated, fully able and eager to participate in the professional workforce, and face no family opposition to doing so. Nonetheless they often do decide to interrupt their careers, or postpone them, to be home while their children are growing up. The price they may pay for such a decision is great difficulty moving back into their profession. It is reasonable to say that for most Muslim women the question of career versus family is not a choice but an attempt to determine whether any kind of employment will interfere with (or somehow even supplement) their responsibilities as full-time parents. Of course, questions of women's employment cannot be divorced from the economic needs of families and are framed differently according to social and economic class, status (including, as in the case of some refugees, limited skill in English), and professional abilities.

In traditional Islamic societies the expectation for a young married woman living under the general authority of her husband and the control of her husband's family has been that her own later years will bring status, respect, and power. For reasons of new family structures, different Western cultural expectations, and more family members employed outside the home, new and serious problems are arising for the older generation of American Muslims. (To some extent, of course, these problems are shared by an American culture in which the proportion of elderly citizens is constantly growing.) Muslim families are facing the reality that the elderly are lonely, isolated, psychologically separated from younger people in the family whose new ideas and ideals they may not understand, and experiencing increasing physical frailties. Other cultures that support the extended family often provide contexts better able to deal with such problems, nurturing an atmosphere in which elders enjoy more respect than they do in American culture.

The nuclear Muslim family in America, often with both husband and wife working full time, can be faced with a painful dilemma. Islamic tradition has no place for isolation of the elderly in special homes separate from the family's. "I would never dream of putting an elderly relative in a nursing home," says an immigrant Muslim, speaking for most in her community.[22] But the choice is sometimes unavoidable, and Muslims face not only the pain of separation but the intense guilt of needing to send their loved ones to a place where they may be even more lonely and isolated. A number of the larger Islamic centers in the United States are developing programs devoted especially to the elderly, and a few are working on plans for constructing special senior housing near the mosque.

FAMILIES IN TRANSITION

The Muslim family in America—or, more accurately, the many different kinds of families that are now representative of the diverse and growing Muslim population—is both the subject of and participant in serious discussion about what it means to be Muslim in the West. Cultural affiliations are being negotiated, and the strength of allegiance to one's original country, language, and particularities inevitably fades with length of time in America. (Somewhat different issues are at stake, of course, for African American Muslims.) Male authority in the family is being challenged and negotiated, and women are increasingly assuming public roles beyond the confines of the home, generally with the support of the community. New patterns of social interaction, including mate selection, are developing for Muslim children and young adults, often leading them away from the close circle of family domination.

At the same time forces within the Islamic community, as well as American society at large, are urging Muslims to deliberate carefully the role of the family and to reappropriate in new forms some of the responsibilities that seem to be slipping from its purview. The family has always been the locus of Islamic ritual identity. Many Muslim homes prominently display calligraphic or other Islamic symbols and art objects.[23] Often shoes are left at the door, a room is specifically designated as appropriate for prayer, and efforts are made to let family members and guests alike know that they have entered "Islamic space."[24] Many religious rituals are still carried out at home, including the celebration of birth and naming ceremonies, study of the Qur'an, and sharing stories from the life of the Prophet. Most religiously observant families pray at home more often than in the mosque, prepare there for the breaking of the fast, and even begin preparation for going on the *hajj*, or pilgrimage to Mecca, at home. Videos, games, and other Islamic products produced by a great range of American Muslim agencies allow the family members to interact in an Islamically oriented atmosphere. Some of the home activities encouraged are specifically for women, such as religious study circles to which neighbors and friends are invited.[25]

However, not only the family is encouraged to foster an Islamic environment. Efforts are increasingly being made by local mosques and Islamic centers to be family centered and as such to function as a kind of larger-context family. "The Muslim sense of community and, even more so, the sense of religious identity, has increasingly been extending beyond the home," says the Muslim family scholar Regula Qureshi.[26] Breaking of the fast at the end of the day during Ramadan, for example, traditionally is done at home with as many members of the extended family participating as possible. In the American context such large family gatherings are generally not possible. Sharing the *iftar* meal at home with only the nuclear family simply doesn't work for many Muslims ("We just can't celebrate with only the four of us in our small family," confided a Muslim friend). As a result Muslims affiliated with mosques or Islamic Associations are going there to break the fast or to hear the Qur'an recited during the evenings of Ramadan. Family thus assumes a broader context, with both the blood relationships of the immediate family and the religious identity of the larger gathering of Muslims—who may or may not share ethnicity—serving the function of the extended family group.

Many aspects of the Muslim family in America, therefore, are now open to negotiation—definitions, role responsibilities, cultural presuppositions, and relationships with the broader Western culture of modernization and secularization. What seems not to be negotiable, however, is the rootedness of American Islam (however it is defined) in the structure of the family and the great importance given to its affirmation by all those who contribute to the discussion of what it means to be Muslim in the American context. Family relationships and responsibilities are on the agenda for interfaith dialogue between members of the Muslim and Christian communities in many areas of the country. Muslims hope that as they are informed by Western norms and inevitably (if reluctantly) are modified by them, they in turn may play some role in helping to redefine and strengthen the institution of marriage in American society.

NOTES

1. See, for example, Qur'an 4:1 ("O mankind! Be careful of your duty to your Lord Who created you from a single soul and from it created its mate and from them both has spread abroad a multitude of men and women") and 30:21 ("And of His signs is this: He created for you mates from your selves that you might find rest in them, and He ordained between you love and mercy").

2. Richard Wormser, *American Islam* (New York: Walker, 1994), 68; Shahid Athar, *Reflections of an American Muslim* (Chicago: Kazi, 1994), 29–30.

3. John L. Esposito with Natana J. DeLong-Bas, *Women in Muslim Family Law*, 2nd ed. (Syracuse, N.Y.: Syracuse University Press, 2001), 156.

4. Yusuf Talal Delorenzo, "The Fiqh Councilor in North America," in Yvonne Haddad and John Esposito, eds., *Muslims on the Americanization Path?* (New York: Oxford University Press, 2000), 73–76.

5. For an excellent treatment of the support of family from Elijah Muhammad's Nation of Islam to the now "orthodox" Sunni organization of his son Warith Deen, see Na'im Akbar, "Family Stability among African-American Muslims," in Earle Waugh, Sharon Abu-Laban, and Regula Qureshi, eds., *Muslim Families in North America* (Edmonton: University of Alberta Press, 1991), 213–31.

6. Sharon McIrvin Abu-Laban offers a comprehensive (though now somewhat dated) "typology of Muslim immigrant families" in "Family and Religion among Muslim Immigrants and Their Descendants," in Waugh, Abu-Laban, and Qureshi, *Muslim Families in North America*, 6–31.

7. Wormser, *American Islam*, 7.

8. See, for example, the study of women converts to Islam by Carol Anway, detailed in her *Daughters of Another Path* (Lee's Summit, Mo.: Yawna, 1996).

9. See Ron Kelley, "Muslim in Los Angeles," in Yvonne Haddad and Jane Smith,

eds., *Muslim Communities in North America* (Albany: State University of New York Press, 1994), 141.

10. W. Murray Hogben, "Marriage and Divorce among Muslims in Canada," in Waugh, Abu-Laban, and Qureshi, *Muslim Families in North America*, 158.

11. Another persistent Islamic interpretation, not generally called forth by contemporary interpreters of Islam, is the assumption "that the paternalistic protection of male relatives is necessary because women are more vulnerable to poverty, harm and exploitation than men" (Ingrid Mattson, "Women, Gender and Family Law," in *The Encyclopedia of Women and Islamic Cultures* [Boston: Brill, 2003–5]), 2:452.

12. Amina Wadud-Muhsin, *Qur'an and Woman* (Kuala Lumpur: Fajar Bakti, 1992), 74.

13. Azizah al-Hibri, "Islam, Law, and Custom: Redefining Muslim Women's Rights," *American Journal of International Law and Policy* 5, no. 12 (1997): 27.

14. Asma Barlas, *Believing Women in Islam* (Austin: University of Texas Press, 2002), 185.

15. See the work of female Muslim interpreters of the Qur'an such as Amina Wadud-Muhsin and Asma Barlas.

16. Many commentators have observed that Western feminists seem to focus on the individual, while Muslims who may choose to call themselves feminists operate within the broader context of the family and society. See, for example, Elizabeth Fernea, ed., *Women and the Family in the Middle East: New Voices of Change* (Austin: University of Texas Press, 1985), 2.

17. Aminah Beverly McCloud, *African American Islam* (New York: Routledge, 1995), 99.

18. "Muslim women are much less likely to report abuse and to whom will they report? To the male Imam? Do we have a social support agency or should they call non-Muslim law enforcement agencies and have their bread earners imprisoned?" asks Shahid Athar (*Reflections of an American Muslim*, 32).

19. See, for example, Nawal H. Ammar, "Simplistic Stereotyping and Complex Reality of Arab-American Immigrant Identity: Consequences and Future Strategies in Policing Wife Battery," *Islam and Christian-Muslim Relations* 11, no. 1 (2000): 51–68; Shaheen Hussain Azmi, "Perceptions of the Welfare Response to Wife Abuse in the Muslim Community of Metropolitan Toronto," Ph.D. diss., Faculty of Social Work, University of Toronto, 1996.

20. "The kids . . . come into the house wearing Levi 501s. They take off their makeup and jackets. They put on their Indian clothes . . . and eat Pakistani curry and their parents think everything's OK. They don't know that when their kids walk out of the house, they're totally American" (Kelley, "Muslim in Los Angeles," 140–41).

21. The many issues relating to the definition of Islamic dress, its necessity (or not) as understood in the Qur'an and Sunna, and how and where it is worn are extremely complex and outside the immediate concerns of this chapter.

22. Yvonne Yazbeck Haddad and Adair Lummis, *Islamic Values in the United States: A Comparative Study* (New York: Oxford University Press, 1987), 87.

23. McCloud, *African American Islam*, 106.

24. See, for example, Juan Campo, *The Other Side of Paradise: Explorations into the Religious Meanings of Domestic Space in Islam* (Columbia: University of South Carolina Press, 1991).

25. Marilyn Giorgio-Poole details women's religious activities inside and outside the home in "The Religious Lives and Ritual Practices of Arab Muslim Women in the United States," Ph.D. diss., University of Pittsburgh, 2000.

26. Regula Qureshi, "Transcending Space: Recitation and Community among South Asian Muslims in Canada," in Barbara Daly Metcalf, ed., *Making Muslim Space in North America and Europe* (Berkeley: University of California Press, 1996), 59.

PART III

*Public Frontiers for
American Religions and the Family*

CHAPTER 14

Religion and Modernity in American Family Law

LEE E. TEITELBAUM

The religious interest in families and the law governing them is pervasive, touching on virtually every aspect of the constitution of the family, the terms of family relationships, and the distribution of authority and responsibility within the family. My intention in this chapter is to review, from the perspective of someone who is not closely tied to a faith community, the relationship of religion and modernity in American family law. In fact, that role cannot be discharged within a brief essay. Accordingly, I will address only a few major points of connection between faith-based norms and practices and legal norms and practices; then I will explore only one or two challenges presented by modern approaches to the constitution and conduct of family life.

THE POSTURES OF RELIGIOUS CLAIMS AND PUBLIC AUTHORITY

Steven Carter, among others, asserts that the preferred posture of faith communities and believers is "oppositional."[1] While there is a sense in which that is correct, it is also clear that the claims made by faith communities under the banner of opposition differ substantially. That "resistance" might take at least two different forms, as Carol Weisbrod, among others, has shown.[2] In both modes the faith community seeks respect from the state for the religion's beliefs and views of proper conduct. For minority communities of faith respect takes the form of an exception from generally applicable rules, and instances of such claims—say, Mormons' unsuccessful claim to a religious obligation to plural marriage—can be found throughout the domains of family law Similar concerns can be found in legislation favoring religious matching in adoption, a claim made successfully by immigrant and minority religious groups seeking to avoid placement of their children in the homes and religious lives of members of the dominant religious group in the community. Claims to respect by minority communities can often be seen in relation to the functioning as well as the constitution of the family. They appear in custody cases, where one parent seeks, on religious grounds, to teach his children that their mother is damned to hell,[3] or where a parent will refuse medical treatment, either in all cases or in particular cases, such as blood transfusions.[4] In all these instances, opposition is to control by majoritarian values and views of the good life.

In the other mode faith communities or groups of communities, usually in the majority, seek to have their views of the good life and right behavior respected through *adoption* by public entities at all levels—school boards, public health agencies, legislatures, and courts. Here, religion sees itself as oppositional to any competing set of values, whether expressed as secular humanism or as liberalism understood as an insistence on value neutrality. It is on this claim to respect, rather less often examined, that this discussion focuses.

MAJORITY RELIGION DOCTRINE AND MARRIAGE LAW

For a considerable part of American history, the posture of public authority was consistent with positions taken by the dominant religious culture. As Carl Schneider and Margaret Brinig quite rightly say in their fine casebook on family law: "Perhaps the most familiar, influential, succinct, and eloquent description of marriage as a social (and moral) institution is the Book of Common Prayer's marriage service. . . . In addition, it reminds us of religion's large part in building the Western view of marriage."[5] The elements of marriage celebrated in the Book of Common Prayer include "this Man and this Woman," who must "take" each other as husband and wife. They will forsake all others; their union will last until "death them [do] part," and they will care for and support each other, "in sickness and in health." The oaths are not quite identical, of course. The bride is to obey and serve her husband; the husband is not so charged. This ritual provides a clear summary of traditional Western religious and legal marriage principles.

The relationship between religious tradition and legal doctrine was clear in the nineteenth century, when judicial discourse more comfortably invoked moral language. In the British case of *Hyde v. Hyde and Woodmansee*, Lord Penzance famously observed that marriage "as understood in Christendom may

. . . be defined as the voluntary union for life of one man and one woman to the exclusion of all others," neatly capturing the position of both church and state.[6] And since Christendom had turned its face on plural marriage, a union between Mormons was not entitled to recognition because it contemplated the possibility of polygamy. The U.S. Supreme Court was not quite as explicit as Lord Penzance when faced with its own polygamy case, but it sustained the conviction of a Mormon for the crime of plural marriage with the observation that "polygamy has always been odious among the Northern and Western nations of Europe and, until the establishment of the Mormon Church, was almost exclusively a feature of the life of Asiatic and African people."[7] Substitution of the words *Christian* for "Northern and Western" and *non-Christian* for "Asiatic and African" would leave the sense unchanged.

The Book of Common Prayer's expectation of permanence has likewise found expression, supported by religious values and communities, in domestic relations law. Judicial divorce was unavailable in England until the middle of the nineteenth century and only variously available in this country. The Archbishop of Canterbury may be considered the primary opponent of no-fault divorce in England, and it is claimed that his opposition in the 1960s to a bill permitting divorce after seven years' separation accounted for withdrawal of that proposed legislation.[8] In this country religious opposition to judicial divorce, and then to no-fault divorce, has been long and well established. To take only one example, opposition by the Roman Catholic Church largely accounted for the limitation of divorce in New York to cases of adultery until 1967, although many efforts to liberalize the law had arisen during the preceding three decades.[9]

In addition to the questions of how many partners one may have and how often one may marry, religion has something to say about who may marry. The Book of Common Prayer speaks of "this Man and this Woman." No major religion formally recognizes same-sex marriage,[10] and some militantly oppose proposals for civil recognition. The Church of Jesus Christ of Latter-day Saints undertook a substantial public role against same-sex marriage in Hawaii when it seemed that, by judicial or legislative action, such marriages might be recognized,[11] and the Roman Catholic Diocese of Burlington, Vermont, filed an amicus curiae brief in *Baker v. Vermont*, also supporting prohibition of same-sex marriage.[12]

MODERNITY IN MARRIAGE AND RELIGIOUS COMMUNITIES

For most of American history, then, the law of marriage was consistent with and supported—if not created—by the views of dominant religious communities. To the extent that the majority faith communities were oppositional, it was to value sets that argued for change in the formation of families. Sometimes, those whom the majority faiths opposed were minority religions, as in the case of Mormon polygamy. Most recently, the opposition has been directed to secular humanism and, most particularly, a strong version of liberal theory that highly values individual choice and places in question the ability of the state to choose among competing visions of the good life and of proper conduct.

Since the 1950s this close association of dominant religious views and marriage law has weakened dramatically. The doctrinal changes are familiar to everyone. Until the 1950s or 1960s, for example, the connection between marital stability and social welfare was taken for granted. The interests of society were understood to require that spouses remain together except in cases of proven serious physical or mental injury. Legislatures and courts understood, of course, that married people could be frustrated or even deeply unhappy in less drastic cases of marital failure. But the importance of maintaining the family "as an institution" made it necessary for individual spouses to bear that cost. As one New York court observed in a 1968 case in which the plaintiff failed to establish severe injury, "The innocent spouse may continue indefinitely to suffer misery and unhappiness, but that is the risk he assumed when the marriage took place."[13]

Current policy regarding marital dissolution is fundamentally different. All states now allow divorce on grounds that do not suppose fault—that is, objectively defined injury—by either spouse.[14] It is typically enough for one spouse to satisfy the court that, from his or her point of view, the marital relationship is irretrievably ended. The Uniform Marriage and Divorce Act provides that "the [court] shall enter a decree of dissolution if: . . . the marriage is irretrievably broken, if the finding is supported by evidence that (i) the parties have lived separate and apart for a period of more than 180 days . . . or (ii) there is serious marital discord adversely affecting the attitude of one or both of the parties toward the marriage."[15] A New Hampshire case could stand for many decisions that interpret no-fault divorce statutes in holding that, where one spouse wishes a divorce and the other does not, the divorce should be granted on the unilateral demand of the plaintiff when "it is clear that . . . there is no reasonable possibility of a change of heart."[16]

The effect of this recent approach is to transfer authority for deciding on the duration of marriage from legal institutions, supported by religious authority, to individual spouses. From a critical perspective the result is to replace a view of marriage as an enduring entity with a relationship that resembles contract at will.

In March 2003, when the papers that became chapters in this book were originally prepared, the limitation of marriage to one man and one woman had not changed. But even then the Book of Common Prayer was already at some risk. The Vermont Supreme Court had come close to holding the limitation of marriage to heterosexual couples unconstitutional, and it clearly did hold that the state constitution prohibited any differentiation in the legal treatment of married couples and same-sex couples in substantial relationships. To avoid recognizing same-sex marriage the Vermont legislature enacted a "civil unions" statute extending to same-sex partners all the benefits associated with marriage.[17] Earlier the Hawaii legislature, also faced with the likelihood that the state supreme court would find the prohibition of same-sex marriage violative of the state constitution, adopted a similar (although not quite as extensive) set of provisions for same-sex couples.[18]

In *Goodridge et al. v. Commonwealth of Massachusetts*, however, the state Supreme Judicial Court held that denying same-sex couples the right to marry violated state constitutional guarantees of equal protection and due process of the law.[19] In doing so, the court rejected several legislative justifications for prohibiting same-sex couples from marrying, including "providing a favorable setting for procreation; ensuring the optimal setting for child rearing which the department defined as a two-parent family with one parent of each sex," and preservation of scarce state and private financial resources. The majority of the Massachusetts court concluded that "we construe civil marriage to mean the voluntary union of two persons as spouses, to the exclusion of all others. This reformulation redresses the plaintiffs' constitutional injury and furthers the aim of marriage to promote stable, exclusive relationships. It advances the two legitimate State interests the department has identified: providing a stable setting for child rearing and conserving State resources. It leaves intact the Legislature's broad discretion to regulate marriage."[20]

The legislature promptly requested an advisory opinion from the Massachusetts Supreme Judicial Court concerning whether a law permitting civil unions, like that adopted in Vermont, would satisfy the court's constitutional concerns. In an opinion issued in January 2004, the Supreme Judicial Court categorically held

> that civil unions were not equivalent to marriage. The court held that differentiating same-sex unions from opposite-sex unions "cannot possibly be held rationally to advance or 'preserve' . . . the Commonwealth's legitimate interest in procreation, child-rearing, and the conservation of resources. Because the proposed law by its express terms forbids same-sex couples entry into civil marriage, it continues to relegate same-sex couples to a different status. The holding in *Goodridge* is that group classifications based on unsupportable distinctions, such as that embodied in the proposed bill, are invalid under the Massachusetts Constitution."[21]

This pair of decisions provides the most dramatic instance of continued litigation, lobbying, and political action with respect to same-sex marriage. However, they did not stand without context or example. Shortly before the *Goodridge* decision the U.S. Supreme Court had categorically repudiated its 1986 decision in *Bowers v. Hardwick,* which had upheld state criminal laws punishing intimate sexual relations between people of the same sex.[22] In *Lawrence v. Texas* Justice Anthony Kennedy, writing for a majority of five, reviewed the historical and theoretical premises of the *Bowers* majority and rejected them.[23] To the extent that the opinion was based on historical grounds, the majority in *Lawrence* found those grounds "not without doubt and, at the very least . . . overstated." To the extent that the opinion rested on a long tradition regarding homosexual conduct as immoral, that "history and tradition are a starting point but not the ending point of the substantive due process inquiry."[24] The Supreme Court's opinion reflected both changes in its own jurisprudence and in international developments, including interpretation of the European Convention on Human Rights.

As the Court noted, issues of same-sex marriage have been the subject of wide attention internationally as well as domestically. Two decisions in Canada have resulted in decisions holding that exclusion of same-sex couples from the common law definition of marriage violates the Canadian Charter of Rights and Freedoms and is invalid.[25]

Two European nations have also recently adopted laws allowing same-sex couples to marry. The Netherlands was the first country to recognize same-sex marriage. The Dutch Civil Code was amended in 2000, effective April 1, 2001, to recognize same-sex marriages. Title 5, Article 30(1) provides that "a marriage may be entered into by two persons of a different or of the same sex."[26]

While these developments are significant, the range of their implications remains to be determined. In Massachusetts an effort is underway through the state constitutional revision process to restore the traditional understanding of marriage. A first step has been attempted in Congress to amend the U.S. Constitution with the same general goal. While the state constitutional amendment process is lengthy and the initial congressional action was unsuccessful, the issue is hardly off the table. The Massachusetts decisions have generated activity of every kind. Litigation in both directions is abundant. On the one hand, no state other than Massachusetts has held that same-sex marriage is required under state constitutional law. On the other hand, litigation seeking that result has been brought in a number of jurisdictions. And state legislatures are widely considering, or have even adopted, constitutional amendments to make judicial interpretation leading to same-sex marriage difficult or impossible.

Apart from judicial stimulus and state and federal activity, a number of cities and municipalities have considered, and some have enacted, ordinances granting to same-sex couples some benefits previously associated solely with marriage. And the American Law Institute's *Principles of the Law of Family Dissolution* recommends provisions for both same-sex and opposite sex domestic partners, expressly taking the view that "normatively . . . family law should be concerned about relationships that may be indistinguishable from marriage except for the legal formality of marriage."[27] The issue thus seems to be on every table in one form or another, and often several.

These doctrinal changes and near-changes can be understood in a general way as a shift in the actual form of discourse about family law. Two related developments in the discussions of courts and commentators are apparent. One is a decline in a certain kind of moral discourse that was familiar in cases like *Woodmansee* and *Reynolds*. The associated change is in the relocation of responsibility from the law itself to the individuals whom law once regulated.[28]

Another way to think about the revolution in family law is to compare two theories of the family. One, long traditional in American law, regards the family as a unit or entity. The "family unit" is characterized by publicly held expectations for its composition and conduct, captured in the notion of marriage as a "status." A more recent interpretation of the family has emerged, however: that of the family as a contract or partnership, in which the parties are free to define their relationships. In my own view neither theoretical model is satisfactory, but the discussion suggests how American law has moved, in quite a short time, from one approach to the other.[29]

The meaning of these changes for faith communities, especially those representing majority views, is difficult to gauge. It surely raises the possibility, however, of a substantial shift not only in thinking about domestic relations law but in the role and authority of faith communities in forming that body of law. The previously close association between the law of marriage and the beliefs of religious groups can be seen as an endorsement of the religious role in setting policy for the family. From the perspective of religion this association is entirely warranted generally and especially in the field of family relations, which was once generally committed to the authority of religion. Moreover, religion, in its various forms, has traditionally and powerfully influenced both individual and collective understandings of human nature and of what is right and wrong for humans to do. From this perspective it seems only right that those understandings be embraced by public authority, either because they are right in themselves or because a civil government that ignores those views risks illegitimacy. Whether we are a Christian nation or, at least, a nation devoted to a "civil religion" whose duty it is to carry out God's will,[30] religious precept is rightly related to civil authority.

The perspective to which religion in the dominant mode is opposed, and which may be thought in the ascendancy, seeks to remove religion from a position of authority in civil government. This perspective may also seek to remove religious discourse from decision making in civil government. From this view public authority may not rest on any claim that legislators, judges, or public servants, or those who influence them, can know and follow divine direction in reaching policy decisions.[31] It may also follow, in stronger versions, that reliance on comprehensive systems of thought (such as religion) is illegitimate in the public arena, at least for public officials and perhaps for others as well.[32] Liberals may consider it inappropriate in debates about same-sex marriage to take into account that the religions to which most citizens belong regard such alliances "unnatural" or "sinful." Or they may think it inappropriate in the judicial arena to permit religious organizations a seat at the bench, through intervention or as amicus curiae, where the civil regulation of marriage will be decided. Put another way, there must be a "wall of separation" between religion and the acts of public agencies, and that wall must be high.

Certainly, some commentators do associate what is generally called divorce reform with a change in the role of religious belief in civil government. Richard John Neuhaus's much-cited *The Naked Public Square* suggests that "the operative values" of the American people, values "overwhelmingly grounded in religious belief," have been "systematically excluded from policy consideration."[33] The "covenant marriage" movement is an effort to restore, now on a voluntary basis, the commitment to marital stability that religion and civil society had previously embraced. However, covenant marriage also represents an effort to restore the role of religious communities as well as marital stability. The principal drafter of the Louisiana statute, Katherine Shaw Spaht, observes that one purpose of this legislation, reflected in its provision that only religious authorities can perform the required premarital counseling, is to invite "religion back 'into the public square'" for the purpose of performing a function "for which religion is uniquely qualified—preserving marriages."[34] In this enterprise Spaht, prompted by a divine "calling" to promote divorce reform, enlisted an evangelical Protestant state legislator in her cause, and he in turn consulted a group of pastors in his district to draft a bill expressing the biblical ideal for marriage.[35]

It is worth a few moments to consider whether faith communities have been excluded from the public square when family law and policy are considered and, if so, in what sense. The strongest separationist view may seem to require that faith communities avoid, and perhaps be denied, participation even as amicus curiae in cases where they have no direct stake. If, one can imagine the argument going, public policy may not appropriately be influenced by religious doctrine or comprehensive systems of thought, including religious thought, civil authorities should not receive arguments grounded in these ways in the course of decision making.

That argument—as opposed to the argument that decision makers should not rely on religiously founded arguments—has never been adopted and has rarely been made. Faith communities participate regularly in legislative and judicial matters related to morality generally and to moral issues touching on family relations in particular. I have already noted their participation in cases involving same-sex marriage. Faith communities and their representatives have filed briefs as well in cases dealing with "atypical" sexual relations, abortion, educational choice, and school prayer. The American Jewish Congress, Council on Religious Freedom, Hadassah, Interfaith Alliance, Jewish Council for Public Affairs, and Unitarian Universalist Association filed amicus briefs opposing school prayer in *Santa Fe Independent School District v. Doe*.[36] The

Liberty Counsel and Liberty Alliance, Northstar Legal Center, and Christian Legal Society filed briefs supporting the school district. In *Mitchell v. Helms* addressing public aid to parochial schools, briefs favoring aid were filed by, among others, the Catholic League for Religious and Civil Rights, American Center for Law and Justice, Christian Legal Society, National Association of Evangelicals, Knights of Columbus, National Jewish Commission on Law and Public Affairs, and Avi Chai Foundation. Briefs in opposition were submitted by the American Jewish Committee, American Jewish Congress, Hadassah, Interfaith Religious Liberty Foundation, and Baptist Joint Committee on Public Affairs.[37]

Faith communities have also successfully supported legislation for covenant marriage in two states, and similar bills are under discussion in other states as well. And communities of faith are actively involved in debates about other matters within the realm of family relations, such as school prayer and parental choice in education.

These seem significant forms of participation in public life, and there is no strong impetus to limit them. Even if the state should seek value neutrality—which I do not argue here—organizations need not do the same. Many groups that believe that they can shed light on matters of public importance are invited to submit their arguments, and religious groups have light to shed as well. Moreover, there is no such thing as the "religious voice" in these matters. Faith communities and groups representing them often have appeared on both sides of issues having to do with either religious activity or public morality. This is obviously true of issues such as school prayer, which is typically supported by organizations such as the Christian Legal Foundation and Northstar Legal Alliance but opposed by religious groups representing minority religious traditions, such as the American Jewish Congress and Unitarian Universalist Society. It is also true, however, of issues of general morality. A number of religious groups filed briefs on both sides of the controversy regarding same-sex marriage in *Baker v. Vermont*.[38] And, finally, the content of the arguments on behalf of religious communities and believers typically is founded in sociology and history rather than theology. It may be that theology lies at the base of acceptance of those arguments, but the arguments themselves do not usually seem different from those presented by other communities.

This last observation may capture the heart of the concern about religion's place in public discourse. Only occasionally do the arguments of religious communities or organizations invoke frankly religious sources in legal or other civic settings. The brief filed by the Roman Catholic Diocese of Burlington, Vermont, and Burlington Stake of the Church of Jesus Christ of Latter-day Saints in *Baker v. Vermont* illustrates the form that frankly religious argument might take. It quotes from Corinthians—"Neither is the man without the woman, neither the woman without the man, in the Lord"—and asserts that marriage has a "covenantal and sacramental meaning" that is "emblematic of Christ's love for his Church."[39] Another form, more commonly taken, is to associate "the law of nature and nature's God."[40] However, the former kind of argument is exceptional, and even the latter, which is entirely familiar in earlier judicial decisions, is unusual (at least in its most direct form).

Most frequently, the arguments advanced by religious organizations are like those made by any other group interested in public policy. They draw on social statistics, demography, medicine, psychology, and sociology. The importance of limiting marriage to heterosexual couples may be explained in terms of child rearing, because children need both male and female role models to learn the importance and value of the opposite sex.[41] Arguments regarding the status of a fetus are more likely to be supported by biology and gynecology texts and by reference to constitutional doctrine than by religious or moral authority. The amicus curiae brief filed by the National Right to Life Committee, Christian Legal Society, Concerned Women for America, and Southern Center for Law and Ethics (among others) in *Stenberg v. Carhart*, dealing with "partial birth" abortions, focuses primarily on Supreme Court case law and medical testimony. The same is true of the brief filed by the U.S. Catholic Conference, Ethics and Religious Liberty Commission, Greek Orthodox Archdiocese of America, Church of Jesus Christ of Latter-day Saints, Lutheran Church—Missouri Synod, and National Association of Evangelicals in the same case.[42] A similar observation has been made of discourse in nonjudicial settings. Public figures with strong religious commitments report that they feel obliged to rely on arguments that traditional forms of marriage and family relations produce good results in the world—stronger domestic relationships, better child rearing, and the like—rather than on frankly religious argument, in their discussions of marriage and family policy.[43]

SOME THOUGHTS ON
TRANSFORMATION OF DISCOURSE

As I noted earlier, Carl Schneider observed the shift in discourse of the kind discussed here many years ago in his important article "Moral Discourse and the Transformation of American Family Law." In commenting on that article I suggested that the shift is, in part, from an Aristotelian teleological framework to a utilitarian and empirical approach. In the Aristotelian framework, each "thing," or relationship, has a goal or purpose and the goal of each thing is to be or act consistently with the distinctive characteristics of its kind. Both discourses are teleological. In the Aristotelian form, however, the purpose to be served is intrinsic to the thing or relationship, while in a utilitarian approach the purpose is to accomplish external social goods such as human happiness.

Acceptance of the classic teleological view requires, of course, the acceptance that some qualities are intrinsic to each thing or relationship, against which the goodness of any instance of that theory or kind is to be measured. Everyone must agree that the fundamental character of a watch is to keep time in order to say that a good watch is one that keeps good time or that the fundamental character of friendship is the sharing of life together in a comprehensive way in order to say that a good friend is one who sympathizes sincerely with the joys and pains of others.[44] That agreement is, in turn, classically derived from reason or right thinking, to which religion and natural law had much to contribute. The specific relationship of natural law and religious discourse to a "classic" teleological approach is that it supplies a set of views about the intrinsic character of social phenomena. Thus, for example, Bishop's midnineteenth-century treatise on marriage and divorce declared that the source of marriage, understood as "one man and one woman legally united for life," lies in "the law of nature, whence it flowed into the municipal laws of every civilized country."[45] And thus the U.S. Supreme Court observed of Mormon plural marriage that "the organization of a community for the spread and practice of polygamy . . . is contrary to the spirit of Christianity and of the civilization which Christianity has produced in the Western world."[46] And again, with relation to roles within the family, the opinion of Justice Joseph P. Bradley in an 1872 case upholding an Illinois decision denying women the right to practice law, observed that "the civil law, as well as nature herself, has always recognized a wide difference in the respective spheres and destinies of man and woman. . . . The constitution of the family organization, which is founded in the divine ordinance, as well as in the nature of things, indicates the domestic sphere as that which properly belongs to the domain and functions of womanhood."[47]

Agreement that the family has certain essential characteristics and functions, universal at least within American culture, has diminished substantially. Schneider rightly attributes that decline to a number of forces, including the rise of moral relativism, an ideological commitment to liberal individualism, and the immanent appearance of "psychologic man" for whom the question is not, "Is it right," but, rather, "Does it make me feel good?"[48] I have suggested other forces as well, including the principles of a republican political and social theory that required equality rather than hierarchy in family relationships, social and economic conditions associated with the industrial revolution, and the widening assumption by courts of authority over family matters, particularly child custody, with a mandate to achieve "good results" for children and parents.[49]

None of these circumstances entails exclusion of religious organizations or even religiously grounded discourse from the public square. They do suggest, however, that arguments based on the essential nature of the family, whether drawn from religious authority, natural law, or historical experience, will not enjoy the easy acceptance that they once did, at least in the form they once took.

That is not to say that family policy should not seek to determine essentials of family relationships or that arguments related to what society expects of the "good family" are inapposite. It is also not to say that family policy should be approached in utilitarian terms. In fact, policy regarding families is especially difficult to study empirically.[50] And, I have argued elsewhere, traditional liberal rights discourse, with its emphasis on individual claims, applies poorly to the behaviors and agreements that arise, and are redefined routinely and often tacitly, within an intact family.[51]

At the same time, it is clear that discussion of the essentials of family relationships will not be convincing if it is unrelated to modern conditions. As I have also suggested before, the romantic images of the colonial family seem romantic only to a society safely removed from indenture and the stocks. It is not possible to revert to a prerepublican world in which the commandment to "honor thy father and thy mother" provided sufficient justification for the authority of kings at the national level and the authority of husbands in the home. It is not sensible to think about financial relationships as if the family remained a principal engine for the production of wealth.[52]

I would suggest that what is needed is a reexamination of the essentials of the constitution and conduct of family life. In that reexamination I would further suggest that Americans abandon the metaphors and images that have influenced discussion of the family. The metaphor that has long dominated Americans' thinking, and in many quarters still has considerable authority, is that of the family as a "unit" or "entity." For reasons that I have set forth in other places, this mode of thinking about the family is, in important ways, a fiction. While the "entity" notion has value in capturing some of the sense of solidarity and mutual support that people expect from families, it obscures both the identities of family members and the operation of power within the family.[53] This image of the "family unit" also implies an independence from other social institutions that is not convincing under modern conditions. Families now can better be imagined as hubs connected to a wide range of such institutions—schools, businesses, markets, health care agencies, and many others—with which they share responsibilities for many of what once were considered "family functions."[54]

Because the "family unit" notion seems ambiguous and perhaps misleading, an alternate theory and metaphor has emerged. Talk about the family now often seems to regard that group not as a unit but as an association of individuals who define for themselves the relationship into which they enter. For a variety of reasons that image also seems to me to be misleading and inadequate, both descriptively and normatively. It is descriptively inadequate insofar as it supposes an anonymity of parties and an emphasis on formally calculable decisions that misses the sense of trust, other-directedness, and complexity of family life.[55] It is normatively inadequate in that society does not wish family members to behave as if this relationship is primarily self-directed and subject to modification whenever self-interest suggests that is useful.

In place of either metaphor it might be useful to think of the family as a special set of relationships—perhaps as a system, in the sense that a system is a network that "integrate[s] parts into a whole."[56] The family is a more intimate and dynamic association than most understandings of contract can provide. However, families include individuals whose identities are not entirely submerged in the domestic enterprise or entity and whose aspirations, needs, and values change over time and with the particular experiences that they, individually and as spouses and parents, encounter. The notion of a system, or perhaps "interactive community," can capture both the sense of individual membership in the family and the identifiable and special relationship into which the members have entered.

While this is not the place for an extended discussion of the "family system," I would suggest that it would permit Americans to avoid assigning a fictional agreement to a "unit," effectively ignoring choice by family members, and to avoid the equally unrealistic contractarian notion that decisions are made as if each was a formal agreement. Americans can rather suppose that choices are made, not formally but as a matter of everyday life and often without specific awareness of consequences. They can also suppose that choices are not simply expressions of individual wills but occur within a system or community that does not expect formal election or negotiation and in which, indeed, family members cease to think of their wills as radically independent of those of others.[57]

The concept of a system or a community can also be understood as referring not only to the internal behavior of family members but their interaction with and response to the environment in which it is situated—a reference that cannot be avoided in a time and in a society where schools have much to say about the education a child receives and employment markets have much to say about how family members spend time and the economic resources on which they can draw. Rather than imagine the family as independent of these intermediate social institutions, it would be better to recognizes that choices made by families are affected profoundly by them and to encourage educational institutions, employers, health care institutions, and even those who create tax laws to expressly take account of the effects of their policies on the choices available to families.[58]

Faith and faith communities have always had something to say about the internal ordering of families and have always been part of the environment with which families interact. The challenge for faith communities is in recognizing and addressing what is essential in a system or community that is neither static nor simple and that is complexly and variously related to a vast array of social institutions that, like faith communities themselves, have much to do with the life course of the family.

NOTES

I wish to thank my colleagues Steven Shiffrin and Gary Simson for their helpful comments on this chapter and, even more, for discussions about the issues it presents. An unknown amount of anything good in the essay is due to their kindness.

1. See, for example, Stephen L. Carter, "Liberal Hegemony and Religious Resistance: An Essay on Legal Theory," in Michael W. McConnell, Robert F. Cochran Jr., and Angela C. Carmella, eds., *Christian Perspectives on Legal Thought* (New Haven, Conn.: Yale University Press, 2001), 25.

2. Carol Weisbrod, "Family, Church and State: An Essay on Constitutionalism and Religious Authority," *Journal of Family Law* 26 (1987–88): 741–70.

3. *See Kendall v. Kendall*, 687 N.E.2d 1228 (Mass. 1997).

4. A parent who is a devout Christian Scientist believes that physical illness can be cured by spiritual means alone. See *Baumgartner v. First Church of Christ, Scientist*, 490 N.E.2d 1319, 1321 (Ill. App. Ct. 1986). One who is an adherent of the Jehovah's Witness faith community will believe that blood transfusions, even if medically indicated, are proscribed by biblical authority.

5. Carl E. Schneider and Margaret F. Brinig, *An Invitation to Family Law: Principles, Process, and Perspectives* (St. Paul, Minn.: West, 1996), 3–4.

6. *Hyde v. Hyde and Woodmansee*, 1 L.R.—P. & D. 130 (1866).

7. *Reynolds v. United States*, 98 U.S. 145, 164 (1878).

8. *See* Olive M. Stone, "The Matrimonial Causes Act and Reconciliation Bill 1963," *Journal of Family Law* 3 (1963): 87–102; J. Herbie DiFonzo, "No-Fault Marital Dissolution: The Bitter Triumph of Naked Divorce," *San Diego Law Review* 31 (1994): 519–54.

9. See Herbert Jacob, *The Silent Revolution: The Transformation of Divorce Law in the United States* (Chicago: University of Chicago Press, 1988), 30–37.

10. That is not to say that all religious subgroups oppose same-sex marriage. In *Baker v. Vermont* a coalition of religious groups, including the Vermont Organization for Weddings of the Same Gender (V.O.W.S.), Session of Christ Church Presbyterian, Unitarian Universalist Society, Putney Monthly Meeting of the Society of Friends, Congregation Beth El of Putney, and United Church of Putney filed an amicus curiae brief supporting same-sex marriage under the umbrella title of Amicus Curiae Vermont Organization for Weddings of the Same Gender et al. in *Baker*, 744 A.2d 864 (Vt. 1999).

The Reconstructionist Commission on Homosexuality of the Jewish Reconstructionist Federation and the Reconstructionist Rabbinical Association recommends consideration by its members of a principle that accepts the validity of Jewish ceremonies conducted to celebrate the loving commitment between members of same-gender couples and to enjoy the same rights accorded to all member families in the life of the congregation, independent of legal recognition. See Jewish Reconstructionist Federation and Reconstructionist Rabbinical Association, *Homosexuality and Judaism: The Reconstructionist Position: The Report on the Reconstructionist Commission on Homosexuality*, rev. ed. (Elkins Park, Pa.: Jewish Reconstructionist Federation, 1993).

11. The Church of Jesus Christ of Latter-day Saints sought to intervene in *Baehr v. Miike*, after the Hawaii Supreme Court held that the Hawaii Constitution required strict scrutiny of the statute prohibiting same-sex marriage and remanded it for a lower-court hearing on the existence of a compelling state interest to justify that prohibition. Intervention was denied. See *Baehr*, 910 P.2d 112 (Haw. 1996). The church was also active in the legislative activity following the decision that resulted in adoption of a constitutional amendment prohibiting same-sex marriage and a statute granting many of the rights of married couples to same-sex partners.

12. The diocese was represented by Kirton and McConkie, a law firm in Salt Lake City, Utah, that regularly represents the Church of Jesus Christ of Latter-day Saints.

13. *Pierone v. Pierone*, 293 N.Y.S.2d 256, 258 (N.Y. Sup. Ct. 1968).

14. "1985 Survey of American Family Law," *Family Law Reporter* 11 (1985): 3015–28.

15. Uniform Marriage and Divorce Act § 302(a). See also sec. 305(b). Although not all states have adopted UMDA, "by 1987, all fifty states had adopted no-fault divorce laws, exclusively or as an option to traditional fault-grounded divorce" ("Family Law: Divorce/Separation/Annulment," *Families.com*, http://law.families.com/family-law-divorce-separation-annulment).

16. *Desrochers v. Desrochers*, 347 A.2d 150 (N.H. 1975). The same result was reached in *McCoy v. McCoy*, 225 S.E.2d 682 (Ga. 1976), 539 U.S. 558, 123 S. Ct. 2472 (2003).

17. Vt. Stat. Ann. tit. 15, §§1201–7 (Supp. 2000).

18. Haw. Rev. Stat. Ann. §§572 C-1–C-7 (Michie Supp. 1998).

19. *Goodridge et al. v. Commonwealth of Massachusetts*, 798 N.E.2nd 941 (Mass. 2003).

20. Ibid., §IV. In the result the court stayed entry of judgment for 180 days to give the legislature time to act. According "Same-Sex Marriage: Developments in the Law," at www.nolo.com, "In February 2004, the court ruled that offering civil unions instead of civil marriage would not meet the requirements set forth in *Goodridge*. As a result, same-sex couples in Massachusetts can enter into civil marriages, and a few thousand of them have done so already. The Massachusetts legislature is currently considering an amendment to the state constitution to forbid marriage between same-sex couples, but the soonest such an amendment could take effect is 2006."

21. Opinions of the Justices to the Senate, 802 N.E.2d 565 (Mass. 2004). As in the other cases reviewed, a variety of organizations participated as amicus curiae, among them, the Massachusetts Family Institute; National Association for Research and Therapy of Homosexuality; Common Good Foundation; Nebraska, Utah, and a number of other states; Catholic Action League of Massachusetts; National Legal Foundation; Marriage Law Project; Religious Coalition for the Freedom to Marry; Ethics and Religious Liberty Commission; Coalition gaie et lesbienne du Quebec; Free Market Foundation; Boston Bar Association; Massachusetts Psychiatric Society; and Agudath Israel of America.

22. *Bowers v. Hardwick*, 478 U.S. 186 (1986).

23. *Lawrence v. Texas*, 123 S. Ct. 2472 (2003).

24. Ibid., 2480.

25. In *Halpern et al. v. Attorney General of Canada et al.* (www.ontariocourts.on.ca/decisions/2003/june/halpernC39172.htm), the Court of Appeal for Ontario relied on principles of human dignity, embodied in the Charter (and the Ontario Human Rights Code), in its decision. See also *Egale Canada Inc. v. Canada (Attorney General)*, 2003 B.C.J. No. 994.

26. Katharina Boele-Woelki, "Registered Partnership and Same-Sex Marriage in the Netherlands," in Katharina Boele-Woelki and Angelika Fuchs, eds., *Legal Recognition of Same-Sex Couples in Europe* (New York: Intersentia, 2003), 231; statute translated by Ian Sumner. Belgium followed suit in 2001. See Belgium Bill, Belgische Kamer van Volksvertegernwoodigers. 52 Session de la 502 legislature, Doc. 59 216555/001, 20 January 2003.

27. American Law Institute, *Principles of the Law of Family Dissolution* (Philadelphia: American Law Institute, 2002), 33.

28. Carl E. Schneider has documented this compellingly. See "Moral Discourse and the Transformation of American Family Law," *Michigan Law Review* 83 (1985): 1803–1979; and "Marriage, Morals, and the Law: No-Fault Divorce and Moral Discourse," *Utah Law Review* (1994): 503–85.

29. See Lee E. Teitelbaum, "The Family as a System: A Preliminary Sketch," *Utah Law Review* (1996): 537, 540–48.

30. See, generally, Robert Bellah, "Civil Religion in America," in William McLoughlin and Robert Bellah, eds., *Religion in America* (Boston: Houghton Mifflin, 1968).

31. See, for example, Isaac Kramnick and R. Laurence Moore, *The Godless Constitution: The Case against Religious Correctness* (New York: W. W. Norton, 1997), 12.

32. See, for example, Kent Greenawalt, *Private Consciences and Public Reasons* (New York: Oxford University Press, 1995); Kent Greenawalt, "Some Problems with Public Reason in John Rawls' *Political Liberalism*," *Loyola of Los Angeles Law Review* 28 (1995): 1303–18. My colleague Steven Shiffrin argues in "Religion and Democracy," *Notre Dame Law Review* 74 (1999): 1631–56, that judges and legislators should not use religious arguments in their official acts but that participants in political debate may appropriately use religious arguments. Another colleague, Gary Simson, seems to go further in taking the position that if it can be demonstrated that a law was adopted because it served a religious purpose, the law should be invalidated even if it also serves some secular purpose. See Gary J. Simson, "The Establishment Clause in the Supreme Court: Rethinking the Court's Approach," *Cornell Law Review* 72 (1987): 905, 910.

33. Richard John Neuhaus, *The Naked Public Square: Religion and Democracy in America* (Grand Rapids, Mich.: W. B. Eerdmans, 1984), 37.

34. See Katherine Shaw Spaht, "Louisiana's Covenant Marriage: Social Analysis and Legal Implications," *Louisiana Law Review* 59 (1998): 63, 75. Not all religious communities seem equally ready to accept this invitation. Spaht reports that the Catholic bishops of Louisiana support the emphasis on permanence of marriage but not the instruction on divorce; the Episcopal bishop-elect opposed the return to a fault-based system with its risks of cynicism and collusion; and Jewish community leaders indicated little support for covenant marriage. Also see her notes 49 and 50 on page 76.

35. W. Bradford Wilcox, "Sacred Vows, Public Purposes: Religion, the Marriage Movement and Marriage Policy," report for the Institute for the Advanced Study of Religion, Yale University, May 2002, 8–9.

36. *Santa Fe Independent School District v. Doe*, 530 U.S. 290 (2000).

37. *Mitchell v. Helms*, 530 U.S. 793 (2000).

38. Ibid.; see text at note 10 and note 10 itself.

39. Brief of Amici Curiae Roman Catholic Diocese of Burlington, Vermont et al., *Baker*, para. 14.

40. This position is articulated by the National Legal Foundation's amicus curiae brief in *Baehr*, www.nlf.net/About/briefs/hawbrf.html.

41. See, for example, Brief of Amici Curiae Roman Catholic Diocese of Burlington, Vermont, et al., *Baker*, para. 31–32, 34.

42. *Stenberg v. Carhart*, 530 U.S. 914 (2000).

43. See Wilcox, "Sacred Vows, Public Purposes," 12–16, reporting on interviews with Wade Horn (former president of the National Fatherhood Initiative, now assistant secretary for children and families of the U.S. Department of Health and Human Services) and Arkansas governor Mike Huckabee, among others.

44. See Lee E. Teitelbaum, "Moral Discourse and Family Law," *Michigan Law Review* 84 (1985): 430, 431–32.

45. Joel Prentiss Bishop, *Commentaries on the Law of Marriage and Divorce* (Boston: Little, Brown, 1852), § 29.

46. *Mormon Church v. United States*, 136 U.S. 1, 49 (1890).

47. *Bradwell v. Illinois*, 83 U.S. 130, 141 (1872) (Bradley, J., concurring).

48. Schneider, "Moral Discourse and the Transformation."

49. Teitelbaum, "Moral Discourse and Family Law," 434–36.

50. For a brief summary of the difficulties, see Teitelbaum, "Moral Discourse and Family Law," 437.

51. Ibid., 439–41.

52. Ibid., 441.

53. See Teitelbaum, "Family as a System," 537, 541–44; Lee E. Teitelbaum, "Family History and Family Law," *Wisconsin Law Review* (1985): 1135–81.

54. Teitelbaum, "Family as a System," 544.

55. Ibid., 540–47.

56. Ibid., 549, quoting Niklas Luhmann, *The Differentiation of Society*, translated by Stephen Holmes and Charles Larmore (New York: Columbia University Press, 1982), 37.

57. Ibid., 554–55.

58. Ibid., 555–59.

CHAPTER 15

Comparative Religion, Ethics, and American Family Life: Concluding Questions and Future Directions

DAVID A. CLAIRMONT

The interactions between families in their diverse forms and the inherited religious texts and rituals used to guide them through the challenges of modernity present a fruitful and timely subject for scholarship in religion. The complexities of modern family life complement and challenge the received wisdom about the American religions. The essays in this book offer portrayals of intricate family realities that are deeply affected by the normative influence of religious traditions. They also describe the internal tensions and adaptive strategies that these traditions have preserved and imparted during their histories.

How diverse religions, families, and the wider society address this topic will become clearer with the emergence of future studies. Changing economic circumstances, developments in law and public policy, and continuing demographic shifts will pressure all parties involved to seek a more grounded understanding of the contours of religious discourse and motivations. One striking feature of American religious communities that is central to these investigations is their extraordinary internal diversity of life and rhetoric. These ideological differences within the religions influence how individuals, families, local congregations, and national collectives understand and react to the forces of modernization.

As various American religions grow in strength and visibility, so does the potential for conflict. This conflict may occur among the different religions or among various strands of interpretation within the traditions themselves. While the potential for productive dialogue is evident from the essays gathered in this collection, a tension remains between the optimistic desire for analogy and the realistic necessity to foreground a nuanced account of difference. The successes and setbacks of family life signify one of many practical domains in which this equilibrium will be tested.

The current situation requires not only that the family stories of religions be told but also that we should soon take an additional step, toward a more careful and systematic academic comparison and criticism of family traditions influenced by religious discourse. Such a task necessitates the introduction of an emerging discipline: the field of comparative religious ethics. This is required to promote deeper self-understanding within each religious tradition, better public understanding of their teachings on family, and a more informed critical knowledge to assist public debate, public policy, and law.

In this concluding chapter I build a case for the relevance of comparative religious ethics to the study of American religions and their family traditions. I begin by clarifying why a more systematic approach to comparison is important by reviewing different reasons for undertaking a comparative study. Next, I define what comparative religious ethics is as a field of study, discuss some of its more prominent models, and suggest which combination of approaches might be productive for the study of families. Finally, I consider how the study of families poses significant original questions to the comparative study of religion, calling upon scholars of religion to respond by bringing the insights of their work to bear on the discussion of families.

I contend that, in the end, the value of comparative religious ethics to the study of American religions and the family lies in its ability to balance approaches to and motivations for studying the family issue. A comparative consideration of family can soften each religion's drive to impose its own family models on the public debate by reminding each tradition of its own historical contingency and record of underachieved ideals. The same model for considering families can also reduce the resistance of the disciplines of law and public policy to religious voices by helping them to acknowledge the shortcomings of their often oversimplified understandings of religious traditions. This creates a space in public dialogues because it dares to see families not only as formal social structures about which we must settle normative debates but also as works-in-progress subject to multidimensional evaluations.

WHY COMPARE THE AMERICAN RELIGIONS' REPONSES TO FAMILY AND MODERNITY?

The chapters in this book are, for the most part, not comparative. The process of thinking through the implications of each tradition's strategies for integrating religious resources into plans for family life is a comparative project left largely to the reader. This means that questions linger about why such comparative investigations are important and how they might be carried out fairly and responsibly. There seem to be various motivations for undertaking comparisons and different kinds of comparison that are helpful on a variety of levels in different social situations.[1]

If the diversity of American religious life gives comparative investigations an initial credibility, the ongoing value of such comparisons and the shape of future studies will depend on whether the scholars undertaking them can demonstrate the value of these studies to a wider public audience. This challenge is deeply related to the problems of modernity discussed throughout this book. Comparative investigations must strike a delicate balance between studying traditions in order to understand how they have adapted to the ambiguous legacy of modernity, finding elements held in common with other traditions to address shared moral problems, and preserving the traditions in their varied historical expressions.

When people compare material goods, cultures, personalities, or expressions of belief, they are tempted to look for similarities and differences in various areas of life for the purpose of understanding themselves and others in the service of their own agendas. This kind of comparison is often instrumental to the extreme. It facilitates communication, tolerance, and economic and social development and may therefore be called the facilitative motivation for comparison.[2]

Sometimes people compare one set of judgments *with* another in an effort to convert one set of judgments *to* another. That is, they compare in order to find weaknesses in physical and mental defenses; they compare in order to influence other people to accept their way of thinking. They compare in order to draw people into their cosmological portrayal of the world and its corresponding evaluations. I call this second rationale the persuasive motivation for comparison. The existence of these first two motivations suggests that comparison is itself a phenomenon as old as the first encounters among individual people and their social and religious groups.

In addition, people try to appreciate differences as well as similarities and, admittedly, this kind of activity is probably a more recent historical development, at least when it is undertaken in an explicitly self-conscious way. People study similarities and differences, but in doing so they also seek new understandings about their own prejudices and presuppositions in the hope of putting some of these to rest. These conversations have the capacity to produce a new unity out of two dissimilar positions. People compare allegiances, affiliations, and lifestyles. These kinds of comparisons sometimes foster what Lee Yearley has called "the virtue of spiritual regret," that is, the ability to look with longing and admiration at what is different, even if in the end we judge that the bounty and beauty of these traditions or forms of life are both out of our reach and not ultimately desirable for ourselves or for those closest to us.[3] But within such evaluations these comparisons can also produce new horizons for shared human life. I call this third rationale the dialectical motivation for comparison.

People may also compare the dilemmas of life, its trials and tragic outcomes, and the ways people have developed for coping with setbacks and working through them. In this way people compare, not so much to see themselves in a new way but rather to see problems they did not see previously and to consider solutions they did not previously envision as possibilities. The experience of immigrant families' enduring discrimination and suspicion might be an object of such comparison, as might the struggles of families to honor their commitments and obligations after divorce. This kind of comparison is instrumental only in the very broadest sense, insofar as it illuminates areas of common human concern that demand the attention of all people. Let us call it the reconstructive motivation for comparison.

The last element of this typology is a bit more tentative, because it concerns how the object of a comparison strengthens and transforms the agent who compares. This comparative motivation implies that whoever works to analyze a tradition should also work to preserve it, in all its various expressions. This is important precisely because we do not yet know how these traditions will affect the future of our life together. People do not know, for instance, when or how the resources that have maintained kinship networks in Native American families might be called upon to provide answers to questions that the wider culture has not yet asked. People do not know, for example, how the patterns of ritual that help to preserve transnational Hindu families might provide a model to replace the exhausted resources of the dominant culture. This motivation for comparison demands attention to real diversity while shunning the ultimate incommensurability of visions about what is good for and proper to human beings. I refer to this as the transformative motivation for comparison.

Because the discussion of families in the United States is just beginning to reach beyond the strands of Christian theology and secular response that first characterized it as a "debate," the motivations for comparative examinations of family are still unclear. I submit that the facilitative and persuasive motivations for comparison have been and are likely to remain the dominant public rationales for comparative investigations of religious behaviors. Both motivations are instrumental in expressing a desire to control uncertainty and threats, especially in times of personal and institutional crisis. Yet the discussions of family life across cultures will persist after the crises have waned. At that point, the dialectical motivation might be embraced, and the reconstructive and transformative motivations are likely to follow thereafter. However, trust and risk are required to imagine that the family traditions to which people cling might be expanded, or that people's attempts to live these expanded family visions might lack the strength that any one religious or familial community can gather.

STRATEGIES FOR COMPARATIVE ETHICS AND
THE QUESTIONS OF RELIGIONS AND FAMILIES

The increasing proximity of diverse religious communities to each other in the
United States necessitates careful comparative thinking. The motivations for
undertaking comparisons will change with precedent and opportunity. Moreover, comparing religious traditions is no easy matter, and determining suitable
approaches to comparisons around practical moral problems is difficult. Even
so, comparison remains a call for all thoughtful people and not only scholars
of religion.

At the beginning of this chapter I suggested that the systematic comparison
of religious ethics provides an important second step for the project initiated
by this book. Because family life involves judgments about behavioral norms,
personal and group values, and critical responses to wider cultural trends, the
study of family life and the issues confronting families constitutes a distinct
mode of religious ethical thinking. Scholars have developed several strategies
for examining the plurality of ethical visions across cultures, some of which
highlight the "prospects for a common morality,"[4] whereas others emphasize
differences and allege that rival moral visions are incommensurable. Questions
also arise about whether comparative religious ethics is fundamentally a descriptive or a normative endeavor and to what extent scholars in this area have
a responsibility to engage in wider public deliberations about the pressing moral
issues of the day.[5] In each case these approaches are often used not in isolation
but rather in conjunction with one another and should, I believe, be viewed as
flexible when employed with reference to the study of religion and American
family life.

While the six comparative strategies that I will outline here can rightly be
used together, the relative emphasis of one approach over another will depend
substantially on the expertise of the person performing the comparison, which
religions or religious thinkers are being compared, and, most important, the
precise issue within the practical domain of family life that a comparison is
developed to engage.

One comparative strategy follows an approach known as patterns of moral
reasoning.[6] Advocated by David Little and Sumner Twiss, among others, this
method suggests that the best way to compare the teachings of diverse religious
traditions is to analyze the structures of their moral reasoning. Moral statements
are those "expressing the acceptance of an action-guide that claims superiority,
and that is considered legitimate, in that it is justifiable and other-regarding."[7]
Within the context of any religious belief system, one distinguishes genuinely
ethical concerns by looking for patterns of "practical justification," by which
Little and Twiss mean a procedure for "giving of authorizing reasons for the
performance of an action."[8] Therefore, if a religious community, family, or state
organization enunciates a particular norm for its members, one possible object

of comparison is the advice for action that a group promulgates and how this advice is generated. In the context of families this means analyzing how norms for family life are commended and defended in a religious tradition from one generation to the next or how, for example, decisions about the care of children or grandparents are justified.

A second comparative strategy follows an approach that describes the logic of religion, and it examines how the religious dimension of human life is required to resolve certain fundamental conflicts among desires, social conventions, and understandings of just punishment and reward. Ronald Green offers a version of this approach that begins with an investigation of human rationality, offering a distinction between the prudential and moral modes of rationality. Each type of reasoning contains, Green suggests, a performative contradiction. In prudential reason the desire of each person to seek her or his own happiness conflicts with the rules imposed by communities that make all individual pursuits possible. In moral reason one is faced with the reality that, although just people alone would seem worthy of happiness, the world does not always apportion reward and punishment in accordance with this principle. Both these contradictions necessitate resolution into a religious dimension of existence and mode of thinking that can be called distinctly religious.[9] The logic-of-religion approach differs from the patterns-of-moral-reasoning approach because it focuses on the necessity of religion for resolving conflicts inherent in the moral life rather than on the structure of moral decision making as such. This approach reminds us that the difficulties faced by native and immigrant families in the United States, particularly the incongruity between their hard work and care for their extended families and their treatment by local communities and government, can often strengthen the immigrants' reliance on traditional religious interpretations of life. Such an approach might give first consideration to the contemporary challenges of family life, such as the education of children and the career achievements of parents. It is easy to interpret such changes as a series of sacrifices and conflicts among competing goods that offer no easy resolutions. In this context the basis of comparison is how the various religions resolve these contradictions.

A third comparative strategy follows an approach of cultural coherence. Robin Lovin and Frank Reynolds presented an example of this approach in exploring the meaning of "ethical naturalism."[10] Broadly speaking, this approach suggests that "a [comparative] method that begins with the particulars of a moral system and tries to understand them in relation to other elements in the culture is congenial to a naturalistic understanding of ethics. It presumes a close connection between moral ideas and other ideas about what persons find good and what they think their world is like."[11] This approach also addresses the interesting problem of intratraditional comparisons, recognizing that part of the comparative study of religious ethics should be an exploration of how a single "tradition" often carries within it multiple strands of ethical thought based

on assumptions about the right way to balance various sources of ethical thinking. When analyzing any particular tradition, Reynolds suggests that "the choice
of a particular line of action . . . is justified less by direct reference to the goal
that is sought than by how that action is understood in the context of a worldview
shaped by one or more of the canonical cosmogonies."[12] If one were to take
this model as the starting point for a comparative study of family teachings, the
focus would be on understanding how particular moral norms governing family
life are coherent with other cultural influences in this practical domain. It also
means that the coherence of family life could override particular goals that the
family judges to be valuable and worth pursuing under ideal conditions. This
approach, in its sensitivity to diversity within a tradition, is particularly important
for those who engage in political debates about families. Because political discourse tends to situate and atrophy positions in an attempt to gain or deny
support, diversity of opinion within a given trajectory of thought tends to become obscured. The relative lack of balanced religious interpretations in discussions about family demonstrates the need for the cultural coherence approach to comparison.

A fourth comparative strategy follows a goods-and-virtues approach. With
respect to families this approach can inform both the ways families reconcile
individual pursuits with the well-being of the whole and the strategies used to
respond to wider cultural forces that threaten deeply held religious values. Lee
Yearley has developed a refined version of this approach in his cross-cultural
work on the topic of virtue.[13] Seeking a balance between the critical and comparative study of religion and its need to be relevant to the complex concerns
of modern societies, he notes that "we can help to bridge this gap, I think, by
focusing on virtues, because virtues connect intimately with both injunctions
and ways of life. They connect with injunctions through their conceptual form
and claims to universality and with ways of life through their embeddedness in
particular cultural contexts."[14] The comparative process, as Yearley envisions it,
is one of charting "similarities within differences and differences within similarities," with respect to what he calls "practical theories" that aim to "guide
people toward full actualization and therefore [use] concepts like virtue, obligation, and disposition."[15] This approach too may be instructive for the comparative study of families because it taps into a fundamental motivation of family
life: that families wish success or excellence for themselves as groups and for
their individual members, proportionately according to the cultural heritage
from which they draw. However, as the forces of modernization affect the ability
of families to address these concerns, looking to visions of excellence in other
models of family life may become more urgent while being mindful that not
all particular strategies will resonate across traditions.

A fifth comparative strategy follows an approach that I call narrative exemplarity. This approach is suggestive for one of the basic problems of marriage
and family life noted earlier, namely, how does one adjudicate conflicts among

goods and what role do community leaders (religious and civic) play in this kind of decision making? Darrell Fasching and Dell deChant formulate the problem of exemplarity in terms of a process of comparative storytelling that is based on the assumption that people recognize exemplary lives, particularly those of individuals who do not share their cultural presuppositions, more easily than they recognize the complexities of theory and argumentation about how people ought to live.[16] This approach also recognizes that disagreement is often the strongest between people within a single tradition rather than between people from different cultures. The stories of the family traditions presented in this book seem to use one version of this approach. Moral exemplars affect people at different levels of social specificity, thereby making possible complicated models for family life. On some occasions exemplars strengthen commitments to parents, siblings, and other relatives. On other occasions exemplars challenge commitments to family in the service of wider social goals.

A final comparative strategy follows a critical interpretations approach. One reading of this approach regards acts of critical assessment, particularly those that challenge long-standing interpretations of religious traditions, as necessary for preserving a space in which people can discuss shared moral problems and potential solutions and in which they can appreciate their shared obligations to each other.[17] Another reading of this approach regards acts of interpretation as fostering a deeper understanding of other traditions, mindful of the power dynamics at work in modes of religious discourse.[18] While this approach considers the necessary conditions for the possibility of mutual understanding (particularly as individuals come to see themselves as responding to shared moral worlds), it implies that any comparative consideration of families in American religious life must consider how mutual responsibilities are formed and to what extent religious discourse is a necessary part of the creation and maintenance of mutual public and private obligations. It also addresses the perennial public concern that religious discourse about families often runs the risk of reducing the complex moral lives of parents and children into a single, inflexible model disguised as a religious ideal.

Using these comparative strategies to think about families can proceed in one of two directions, although both must eventually be considered. On the one hand, it is possible to examine the role that families play in religious communities. On the other hand, it is possible to examine the place of religious practices and beliefs in the creation and maintenance of family life. If one begins with the role of families in religious communities, the critical interpretations approach and the cultural coherence approach would likely display certain advantages. These approaches recognize that families and religious communities are social entities engaging each other on multiple levels within shared cultural frameworks. These approaches also demonstrate that families, no less than individuals, have the power to critique the broad ideals and specific directives of religious communities. If one begins with the place of religious practices and beliefs in family life, both the patterns-of-moral reasoning approach, as well as the logic-of-religion approach, would display certain advantages in considering how families integrate religious teachings into their common life. Similarly, the goods-and-virtues approach would offer a set of categories that are at least recognizable across traditions and even between religious traditions and public groups charged with the formation and implementation of family policies. The narrative exemplarity approach, it seems to me, would befit both ways of analyzing families and religion, because it considers a genuine and underaddressed issue in the comparative study of religious ethics and in family studies: the ability of people to live by the ideals they promote.

COMPARING AMERICAN FAMILIES: WHAT APPROACHES DO THEIR SITUATIONS DEMAND?

I began this chapter by considering the various motivations for undertaking a comparative investigation of religion and family life. I then reviewed the strategies for comparative religious ethics, noting how each of these might be used to investigate families as a practical domain. It is important to ask one further question, however, that addresses the distinctive situation of families in the United States today: Does the critical recovery of religious heritage among the American religions, in conjunction with the changing constitution of American immigrant communities, require a new form and level of comparative engagement to meet the challenges facing contemporary families?

Debate about American family life since the mid-1980s has seen a number of important developments. The increasing importance of the social sciences in describing demographic trends has contributed to our knowledge of how family structures have changed, the effects of marriage and divorce on couples and their children, and the effects of economic trends (particularly employment opportunities) on the ability and willingness of couples and single people to support themselves, their children, and their extended relations. Pressure from certain religious groups, advocating a return to "family values" and a focus on the role of the conjugal couple, were moderated by other voices who ascertained oppressive tendencies within traditional marriage structures that required reforming. It is fair to say that the voices of the former group have had a more lasting effect on the public's perception of the ability of religious traditions to approach a complex issue such as family life with the requisite nuance and sensitivity.

However, several issues still interfere with the possibility of sustained public conversation about the place of religious discourse in discussions about family life. One issue is the lack of appropriate channels to discuss, much less demarcate, what a religious tradition is. Contemporary scholarship in religious studies can at least establish a range of topics that might be classified as religious beyond the strict boundaries of confessional statements. Religious symbols, including their use in religious stories and texts and the relationship between symbols and beliefs, coexist with structures of ritual activity and the reciprocal effects of such activity on the behaviors of individual participants and collectives.

A second issue is that, when we speak of "religions," we must specify exactly which level of abstraction we intend to discuss. While it is true, as many have argued, that there is no universal, recognizable datum available to the scholar by which religion can be finally and exhaustively determined, there are many ways in which a community's practices and beliefs can be said to constitute a religious tradition. Among these are its reason for discourse, the scope of its practices, the way of constituting its community, and its techniques for maintaining and reforming its institutions.[19] This way of speaking about religion affects possible interpretations of family life in several ways.

Religious practices might be used to bend individual aspirations to conform to the goals of the family collective, or individual interests might challenge the primacy of family goals when the interests of its members are neglected. Religious discourse might have more than one intended effect on family life, in one sense affirming its importance while also relativizing it in favor of other goals. Religious beliefs might contribute to the maintenance of social arrangements and foster group unity but, depending on how those beliefs are interpreted, might also have the potential to fracture a group and turn its segments against each other. Religious authority might be used to influence public policy and to critique existing social arrangements, but it also could be called upon to serve existing political agendas.

A third issue addresses how one sorts out responsible interpretations of a tradition from those that are problematic. The relevance of comparative ethics in this regard should now be clear. In comparing the teachings of religious traditions, we are confronted time and again with conflicting interpretations. Comparison illuminates the blind spots in interpretive strategies that can remain concealed if one works exclusively within a single tradition. While we may not be able to sort out definitively the relative merits of these interpretations, initial efforts in this regard should at the very least be strong warnings against simple dismissals or simple appropriations.

These issues imply that future projects on American religions and the family can proceed in multiple directions. One possible direction is to map the moral concerns that occupy a central place in the family life of the American religions. The concerns of long-standing families of social and religious privilege may not prove to be the same issues that challenge immigrant and native families that do not yet have the political resources to assert the feasibility of their religiously motivated forms of life in the public space.

Another direction for future studies might be to concentrate on the multiple interpretations of family life within the American religions. Many essays in this book have taken an important step in that direction. Further studies should include investigations into how religious resources function to support the multiple visions of family life that are inspired and sometimes demanded by new historical contexts.

Another way of approaching the study of American religions and families would be to make a comparative analysis of how individuals navigate conflicts among personal and social goods. The American religions, as this book has demonstrated, represent complexities within trajectories, particularly in the practical domain of family life. They preserve numerous ways of navigating conflicting goods in bewildering cultural contexts. These goods take many forms, including personal and family wealth, unity of the extended family, personal freedom, adherence to family and religious customs, and many others. Which goods are chosen and why illuminates what religious traditions consider feasible and desirable resolutions to these conflicts. In other words, to the extent one can isolate distinct visions of family life in the American religions, one is simultaneously considering how religious traditions debate and prescribe ways of choosing among conflicting goods.

The wisdom of immigrant and native communities, as they attempt to bridge cultural, economic, and ideological divides in their experience before and after immigration, provides a powerful picture of the coherence of values and forms of organization for family life. However, these same communities also illustrate how particular traditions make critical appropriations of their own internal resources (often preserving ongoing disagreements) to meet the challenges of unfamiliar situations. Careful attention to the variety of religious ideals, interpretive strategies, and justifications for actions in family life can strengthen the ability of religious traditions to defend, refine, and transmit their models of family in a pluralistic society.

It is possible to view families as goal-oriented interpreters of inherited traditions, responding to changing contexts. They often reveal what larger collectives tend to obscure: that commitments to interpreting long-standing traditions can be worthy of public consideration without the fear that unexamined private commitments will unduly influence public dialogue. Interpretive acts that risk challenging public stereotypes about religions are firmly rooted in debates about the place of religion and families in public life, and about the place of religion and public life in families. Such interpretive acts are necessary not only to bring the voices of multiple traditions into public dialogue about the meaning and importance of families in modern democratic polities, but these same acts also ensure that those who often speak for religious communities are not uniformly assuming their traditions to be settled systems with easily articulated messages.

The public discussion about religious influences on the American family would do well to recognize that religious disagreement is an instance of interpretive emphases worked out in the minds and hands of frail moral agents interacting in multiple areas of social and private life. These interpretive emphases both address the problem of conflicting goods, which all communities face, and require resolutions that, at the very least, acknowledge the depth and breadth of religious traditions. The success of the contribution of comparative religious ethics to the public discussion about families could then be evaluated based on its success in communicating religious traditions as coherent patterns of debate. These traditions are constantly moving between moments of critical self-assessment and moments in which they issue strong challenges to prevailing cultural norms.

At their best, sensitive interpretations of religion preserve rather than erase disagreements. Families in the United States acknowledge this as they resist oversimplifications used to interpret their religious and social lives. This may become more evident as the vitality of immigrant religions inspires new directions in public dialogue. It may also be that the personal and social complexities of religious life have found a home in one of the defining issues of our time.

NOTES

1. Projects on comparative religion have gained popularity recently. For further reading in this area I point the reader to the volumes of four separate projects that are only a sampling of what has been undertaken recently. From 1980 to 1985 the Berkeley-Harvard Program in Comparative Religion: Values in Comparative Perspective produced a number of conferences and books that spanned scholarly concerns in both research and teaching. On the research side it produced Robin W. Lovin and Frank E. Reynolds, eds., *Cosmogony and Ethical Order: New Studies in Comparative Ethics* (Chicago: University of Chicago Press, 1985); John Stratton Hawley, ed., *Saints and Virtues* (Berkeley: University of California Press, 1987); and Russell F. Sizemore and Donald K. Swearer, eds., *Ethics, Wealth, and Salvation: A Study in Buddhist Social Ethics* (Columbia: University of South Carolina Press, 1990). On the pedagogical side it sponsored Frank E. Reynolds and Sheryl L. Burkhalter, eds., *Beyond the Classics? Essays in Religious Studies and Liberal Education* (Atlanta: Scholars Press, 1990); Mark Juergensmeyer, ed., *Teaching the Introductory Course in Religious Studies: A Sourcebook* (Atlanta: Scholars Press, 1991); and John B. Carman and Steven P. Hopkins, eds., *Tracing Common Themes: Comparative Courses in the Study of Religion* (Atlanta: Scholars Press, 1991). In the early 1990s this program segued into another series of conferences at the University of Chicago Divinity School, Toward a Comparative Philosophy of Religions, resulting in volumes edited by Frank E. Reynolds and David Tracy and published by the State University of New York Press in Albany: *Myth and Philosophy* (1990), *Discourse and Practice* (1992), and *Religion and Practical Reason* (1994). Most recently, the Comparative Religious Ideas Project, convened and directed by Robert Cummings Neville at Boston University, produced three separate volumes, all released in 2001 by the State University of New York Press in Albany: *The Human Condition, Ultimate Realities,* and *Religious Truth*. All these projects are focused on more theoretical issues. Even those that address teaching comparative religion are not dealing with the many practical ethical issues that arise in the lives of religious practitioners but rather the practical aspects of teaching religion. The new Ethikon Series

in Comparative Ethics, published by Princeton University Press, has begun to address several important practical issues (immigration, the global economy, war, and cultural pluralism, to name a few), gathering in a single volume essays written from both religious and secular perspectives. See, among other volumes in this series, Terry Nardin, ed., *The Ethics of War and Peace: Religious and Secular Perspectives* (1996); and Richard Madsen and Terry B. Strong, eds., *The Many and the One: Religious and Secular Perspectives on Ethical Pluralism in the Modern World* (2003). On a related topic see Brian Barry and Robert E. Goodin, eds., *Free Movement: Ethical Issues in the Transnational Migration of People and Money* (University Park: Pennsylvania State University Press, 1992).

2. M. Christian Green helped me to develop labels for the five motivations for comparison that I examine here.

3. Lee Yearley, "New Religious Virtues and the Study of Religion," Fifteenth Annual University Lecture in Religion, Department of Religious Studies, Arizona State University, Tempe, 10 February 1994, 12–16.

4. This phrase is taken from the title of a collection of essays that cover positions advancing as well as critiquing the possibility of a common morality. See Gene Outka and John P. Reeder, eds., *Prospects for a Common Morality* (Princeton, N.J.: Princeton University Press, 1993).

5. The collection of essays edited by Sumner B. Twiss and Bruce Grelle under the title *Explorations in Global Ethics: Comparative Religious Ethics and Interreligious Dialogue* (Boulder, Colo.: Westview, 2000) engages these former issues and, in some places, takes up the practical domains of politics, international business, and the environment. Bruce Grelle's "Politics, Hegemony, and the Comparative Study of Ethics," Ph.D. diss., University of Chicago, 1993, takes up the implications of the comparative study of ethics for analyzing such questions as "What roles do religio-moral ideas and discourses play in the constitution and transformation of systems of social relations? What role do they play in struggles between social groups for power and influence over such systems of social relation?" (4). These questions seem to display immediate resonance with current discussions about family structure, gender roles, and the involvement of government in family life.

6. The labels one uses to map the strategies of comparative ethics are not as important as understanding the basic features of each approach. For instance, in labeling the first strategy, I adopt Bruce Grelle's "moral reasoning approach," which he provides in "Politics, Hegemony," opposing it to what he calls the "holistic approach" and the "critical-contextual approach" (2–3), but I limit the category more drastically than Grelle does, including only those who actually use patterns of moral reasoning as the primary object of study for comparative ethics. In practical domains as layered and situated as families, it seems to me better to be more specific rather than more general about defining approaches, as this will help to limit the specific dynamics and issues of one's investigation and thereby produce more focused results.

7. David Little and Sumner B. Twiss, *Comparative Religious Ethics: A New Method* (New York: Harper and Row, 1978), 28–29.

8. Ibid., 96.

9. Ronald M. Green, *Religious Reason: The Rational and Moral Basis of Religious Belief* (New York: Oxford University Press, 1978), 108–21.

10. Lovin and Reynolds, *Cosmogony and Ethical Order*.

11. Ibid., 4.

12. Ibid., 13. The term *cosmogony* denotes the origins of religious worldviews, including formative oral traditions and eventually texts as well as rituals that exhibit a normative, internal coherence with other aspects of the religious tradition. *Cosmology* denotes the structure and logic of systems of belief and practices, of religious construals of the universe, which are often connected with the traditions' cosmogonies.

13. Lee H. Yearley, *Mencius and Aquinas: Theories of Virtue and Conceptions of Courage* (Albany: State University of New York Press, 1990). Yearley is helpful in situating ideas about comparative ethics within the wider context of the comparative study of religion as the following passage shows: "Most work in comparative religious ethics has focused on either injunctions or ways of life. (Indeed, much work in comparative religion echoes this distinction; one group deals with the logic of theoretical statements, another with the complexities of cultural practices.) Ways of life have been the province of anthropologists and historians of religion who, assuming cultural holism, emphasize the importance of fine-grained analysis. They also argue culture determines the actual form ethical life takes; it provides the concrete guidelines that constrain both specific activities and abstract pictures of human flourishing. Philosophical or religious ethicists, in contrast, usually work with universal injunctions. The bolder of them argue that enough similarity exists among human beings to enable us to find universals in the structure, arguments for, and even content of injunctions. Other ethicists are more hesitant. They attempt only to formulate general definitions and supposedly universal procedures of ethical reasoning, although they may also speculate about normative conclusions. Finally, some ethicists are even more hesitant. They argue that ethical universals can be found only if basic presuppositions are shared, such as that humans are rational agents and nature operates by morally neutral laws" (10–11).

14. Ibid., 11.

15. Ibid., 1, 7. Yearley positions practical theories between what he calls primary theories and secondary theories: "*Primary* theories, concerning subjects like water's effect on the growth of plants, provide explanations that allow people to predict, plan, and cope with the normal problems the world presents. Such theories appear evidently true to most in a culture and often have a universal character. *Secondary* theories, which differ from culture to culture, usually are built from primary theories to explain peculiar or distressing occurrences, such as why water suddenly kills not nurtures plants. They utilize ideas about a class of beings (such as malevolent spirits) that differ from visible phenomena and therefore appear even to those in the culture to mix the familiar and the strange. Practical theories often work on the ideas primary theory produces and can link with the notions in secondary theory. But practical theory presents a more theoretical account than primary theory and stays closer to normal phenomena than secondary theory" (7). It seems to me that the various methods of investigation that fall under the "social" or "human" sciences, in their execution rather than in their ideal approximation, fall somewhere between what Yearley calls primary and practical theories and that whether or not this assessment is correct could significantly influence how one understands the project of comparing religious traditions' responses to modernity around the issue of family structures and activities.

16. Darrell J. Fasching and Dell deChant, *Comparative Religious Ethics: A Narrative Approach* (Malden, Mass.: Blackwell, 2001), 5–7.

17. For an example of this approach see William Schweiker's essay "Responsibility and Comparative Ethics" in his *Power, Value and Conviction: Theological Ethics in the Postmodern Age* (Cleveland: Pilgrim Press, 1998), esp. 131–34.

18. A comparison of religious traditions' moral visions in the service of mutual understanding, mindful of the power dynamics and class struggles implied in moral discourse, characterizes Bruce Grelle's approach to comparative religious ethics, as detailed in his "Politics, Hegemony."

19. This division is an adaptation from the definition of religion that Bruce Lincoln gives in his essay "Culture" in Willi Braun and Russell T. McCutcheon, eds., *Guide to the Study of Religion*, 409–22 (New York: Cassell, 2000). Specifically, Lincoln says, "I take religion to include four different components, which can relate to one another in various ways, including disjuncture and contradiction. These components are: (1) A discourse that claims its concerns transcend the human, temporal and contingent, while claiming for itself a similarly transcendent status. (2) A set of practices informed and structured by that discourse. (3) A community, whose members construct their identity with reference to the discourse and its attendant practices. (4) An institution that regulates discourse, practices and community, reproducing and modifying them over time, while asserting their eternal validity and transcendent value." In this same essay Lincoln goes on to say that "what religion does—and this, I submit, is its defining characteristic—is to invest specific human preferences with transcendent status by misrepresenting them as revealed truths, primordial traditions, divine commandments and so forth. In this way, it insulates them against most forms of debate and critique, assisting their transmission from one generation to another as part of a sacred canon" (416). Here the usefulness of Lincoln's explanation for my purposes breaks down on two levels. On the one hand, it postulates an internal ideological unity of tradition that the evidence does not bear out. Traditions carry on vigorous internal debates about the meaning of beliefs and the justification of practices. The difference lies in the standard by which one commends and limits criticism. On the other hand, religious traditions are often quite "concerned" with matters of this world, not just with communicating "the great perhaps" to subsequent generations. The fractious quality of religious dialogue on families, as well as the many examples of complex family ethics presented in this book, address these points. The other essays in this book offer many useful examples on both points.

CONTRIBUTORS

Margaret Bendroth is the librarian/executive director of the American Congregational Association and former professor of history at Calvin College, Grand Rapids, Michigan. Her research focuses on modern American religious history, especially women and American Protestantism denominations. She is the author of *Growing Up Protestant* (2002) and *Fundamentalism and Gender, 1875 to the Present* (1993) and coeditor of *Women and Twentieth-Century Protestantism* (2002) and *Faith Traditions and the Family* (1996).

Don S. Browning is the Alexander Campbell Professor Emeritus of Religious Ethics and the Social Sciences at the University of Chicago Divinity School and director of the Religion, Culture and Family Project. Among his many books are *Marriage and Modernization* (2003) and *A Fundamental Practical Theology* (1996), and he is coauthor of *From Culture Wars to Common Ground: Religion and the American Family Debate* ([1997] 2000).

Raymond A. Bucko is professor of anthropology in the department of sociology and anthropology at Creighton University in Omaha, Nebraska. His primary research interests include contemporary Native American peoples and religion and identity, and he conducted his fieldwork among the Lakotas of Pine Ridge. He is the author of *The Lakota Ritual of the Sweat Lodge* (1999) and several articles on Lakota religious ritual, Lakota humor, the anthropological study of Native American religion, the Buechel Memorial Lakota Museum, and the martyrdom of Peter the Aleut.

David A. Clairmont is assistant professor in the department of theology at the University of Notre Dame. He specializes in the comparative study of religious ethics, particularly the moral thought of Roman Catholicism and Theravada Buddhism. He is interested in questions of moral formation, moral weakness, and the importance of interreligious dialogue for the future of Catholic moral theology. He is revising a manuscript for publication entitled "Moral Motivation and Comparative Ethics: Bonaventure, Buddhaghosa and the Problem of Material Simplicity."

David C. Dollahite is professor and associate director in the School of Family Life at Brigham Young University, where he has been an Eliza R. Snow University Fellow. He has been a visiting scholar at the University of Massachusetts—Amherst, Dominican University of California, and the Maharaja Sayajirao University of Baroda in India. His scholarship focuses on religion and family life, Latter-day Saint family life, and faith and fathering. He and his wife, Mary, have seven children.

Robert Franklin is Presidential Distinguished Professor of Social Ethics at the Candler School of Theology at Emory University. He is the former president of the Interdenominational Theological Center and was visiting professor at the Harvard Divinity School before joining Emory. He also has served as dean of black church studies at Colgate Rochester Divinity School, director of black church studies at Emory, and as a program officer in human rights and social justice at the Ford Foundation. He is the author of two books, *Liberating Visions: Human Fulfillment and Social Justice in African American Thought* (1990) and *Another Day's Journey: Black Churches Confronting the American Crisis* (1997), and with Don S. Browning and others wrote *From Culture Wars to Common Ground: Religion and the American Family Debate* (1997).

Jeffrey F. Meyer is professor of religious studies at the University of North Carolina at Charlotte. His research interests include sacred cities, pilgrimage, and gardens in Chinese Buddhism, Confucianism, and Taoism. He is the author of *Myths in Stone: Religious Dimensions of Washington, D.C.* (2001) and *Dragons of Tiananmen: Beijing as a Sacred City* (1991).

Paul D. Numrich is chair of the Program in World Religions and Inter-Religious Dialogue at the Theological Consortium of Greater Columbus and is affiliate research associate professor in the sociology department at Loyola University Chicago. He co-directed the Religion, Immigration and Civil Society in Chicago Project. He has contributed to *Buddhists, Hindus, and Sikhs in America* (2001). He is the author of *Old Wisdom in the New World: Americanization in Two Immigrant Theravada Buddhist Temples* (1996). He has also worked with the Religion in Urban America Program at the University of Illinois at Chicago since 1994, contributing chapters on religious diversity and congregations to that project's first book, *Public Religion and Urban Transformation* (2000).

Charles S. Prebish is professor of religious studies at Pennsylvania State University. His research interests focus on Indian Buddhism, particularly Buddhist monasticism and Vinaya literature, and Buddhism in America. He is cofounder of the online *Journal of Buddhist Ethics* and is the author of seventeen books, including *Buddhism— The eBook*, and *Buddhism—The American Experience* (2004) and *Luminous Passage: The Practice and Study of Buddhism in America* (1999). He has also edited (with Kenneth Tanaka) *The Faces of Buddhism in America* (1998).

Julie Hanlon Rubio is associate professor of Christian ethics in the Department of Theological Studies at Saint Louis University. Her research interests include marriage and family in American Christian communities and social ethics in the Roman Catholic tradition. She is the author of *A Christian Theology of Marriage and Family* (2003) as well as articles on divorce, parenting, and sexuality.

Jane I. Smith is professor of Islamic studies and codirector of the Duncan Black Macdonald Center for the Study of Islam and Christian-Muslim Relations at Hartford Seminary in Connecticut. She is the author of *Islam in America* (1999), coeditor of *Muslim Women in America: The Challenge of Islamic Identity Today* (2006) and *Muslim Minorities in the West: Visible and Invisible* (2002), and coauthor of *Mission to America: Five Islamic Sectarian Communities in North America* (1993).

Lee E. Teitelbaum was the Hugh B. Brown Professor of Law at the University of Utah, College of Law and formerly the Allan R. Tessler Dean and Professor of Law at Cornell Law School. His scholarship included studies of family law, juvenile law, and the legal treatment of children and parents. He wrote and coauthored many books, including *Children, Parents and the Law* (2002) and *Family Law* (2000) and coedited *Family Law in Action: A Reader* (1999).

Jack Wertheimer is provost and the Joseph and Martha Mendelson Professor of American Jewish History and the director of the Joseph and Miriam Ratner Center for the Study of Conservative Judaism at the Jewish Theological Seminary of America. He is the author of *Unwelcome Strangers: East European Jews in Imperial Germany* (1987) and *A People Divided: Judaism in Contemporary America* (1997) and edited *The American Synagogue: A Sanctuary Transformed* (1987).

W. Bradford Wilcox is assistant professor of sociology at the University of Virginia. His research includes the bearing of religious practice on marriage and child rearing. He has written several articles on parenting among conservative Protestants and on the role of religious belief in paternal involvement. Most recently, he has published *Soft Patriarchs, New Men: How Christianity Shapes Fathers and Husbands* (2004).

Raymond Brady Williams is the Charles D. and Elizabeth S. LaFollette Distinguished Professor in the Humanities Emeritus at Wabash College. He is the author of many books, including *Christian Pluralism in the United States: The Indian Immigrant Experience* (1996), *Religions of Immigrants from India and Pakistan: New Threads in the American Tapestry* (1988), and *An Introduction to Swaminarayan Hinduism* (2001).

Elizabeth Williamson is a graduate student in the Department of Sociology at Rutgers University.